For the eventual edification of
Elizabeth and Edward

THE
PENGUIN BOOK OF

CARD GAMES

BY DAVID PARLETT

JENNINGS

CRESCENT BOOKS
New York

First published in Great Britain in 1979 by
Allen Lane

This 1987 edition published by Crescent Books,
distributed by Crown Publishers, Inc.,
225 Park Avenue South, New York, New York 10003

Reprinted 1988

By arrangement with Octopus Books Limited

Printed in Czechoslovakia

ISBN 0 517 64731 1

Contents

Only major game headings are shown, with a note (in brackets) of the number of players required. Nearly all games have relatives and variants suitable for the same or other numbers of players. For a complete list of games see the index.

Introduction

'I have made a heap of all I have found.'

(Nennius, *Historia Brittonum*)

Card playing has brought pleasure to millions of people for some six centuries and is popular the world over, so it is not surprising to discover that enough games have been invented to keep Sheherazade's sultan occupied for well over a thousand and one nights. This book seeks to present as many of them as possible to as many people as possible, and in a manner as acceptable to the buff as it is intelligible to the beginner. Having discovered the delights of card play comparatively late myself (and then only with the aid of a Sheherazade) I am bothered by the realization that many people go through life without discovering them at all. (As Talleyrand is supposed to have said – and I translate very freely – 'You can't play cards, young man? What a boring old age you're laying up for yourself!') Worse, I suspect that not a few have been positively put off anything to do with cards by the enthusiastic but misguided attempts of unqualified Bridge tutors to teach them to run before they could walk. Too many people play Bridge and nothing else, which is rather like a supposed music lover listening to nothing but Beethoven's Ninth all the time. It is my hope to show that Bridge is only one of many good card games and that some of the others may turn out to be more to any given reader's particular taste.

To make this guided tour easier to follow I have grouped the games together in related families. Most books today go by number of players, starting with Patience, then games for two, and so on. It is true that what you play is mainly governed by how many you are; but in my experience people tend to start with the sort of game they want to play and then find the nearest thing to it that matches the number available. By putting like games together, with a clear indication of how many each is designed for, I have succeeded in saving space that would otherwise be wasted on repetitious description. The space saved has been used to increase the games covered.

Some 300 games are described in sufficient detail to enable anyone to play them. Where several games are based upon similar principles, one of them has been selected as the main entry for detailed description and the others appended as relatives or variants with some such note as 'play as described above but with the following differences'. About a quarter of the total qualify for detailed treatment, including suggestions for good play, and, where necessary, a sample hand to show how the game goes.

Each chapter is devoted to a group of kindred games, and is introduced by a sort of family portrait enabling you to pick out the one most likely to appeal. Since any form of classification must to some extent be arbitrary, it might be useful to outline the system followed here.

Ten families of trick-taking games come first, as tricks are the most natural and exciting way in which cards can be used. (The meaning of tricks is explained on p. 20. These start with the family comprising Whist and its modern descendant Contract Bridge, in which the object is simply to win the majority of tricks, or as many as bid at the start of play. Next, Solo Whist introduces a large family of Solo games, in which it is generally one player who has to take a certain number of tricks against the combined efforts of all the other players. Third, the Five-card family, including Nap and Euchre, in which the object is to win at least three out of five tricks played. Games of this type are older than, and probably ancestral to, the Whist and Solo families. Fourth, the Hearts family, in which the object is to avoid winning tricks. Fifth, the All Fours family, in which an additional object is to capture the Jack of trumps and certain other cards. Sixth, a couple of Italian games in which tricks only count if they contain high cards. These two families lead naturally on to Skat and other games of Germanic origin in which tricks have no value in themselves, the object being to capture point-counting cards contained in them. Eighth, the

Jass games, including Klabberjass, which have a similar card-counting system and also give credit for holding or acquiring certain combinations of cards. Ninth, the family including Bézique and Pinochle, which generally follow the same card-point system but attach more importance to combinations or 'melds' of matching cards. Tenth, Piquet, in which combinations are almost more important than tricks.

Of the next eight more variegated families the Rummy–Canasta group of meld-making games follows naturally on from games listed above that give credit for card combinations. In this family the whole object is to collect cards that go together. The twelfth and thirteenth groups, respectively Cribbage and the Cassino family, also involve card combinations but have a distinctly arithmetical flavour too. Fourteenth, Poker and Brag are based on combinations, but these are gambling games in which the object is to bluff your opponents into thinking you hold the best combination whether you do or not, and then charge them for seeing it. Fifteenth, Pontoon/Blackjack and other gambling games of the banking variety. Sixteenth, the Stops family, including Newmarket/Michigan, which can be played for money or buttons and are equally suitable for children and grannies. Seventeenth, a small selection of Patience games serving as an introduction to a larger volume which I have yet to write.

Finally, the inevitable odds-and-end-games which do not fit any of the categories above but are too good, or too much fun, to leave out. Don't forget these games just because they come last, but save them for a rainy day, when you will enjoy them even more. They include some of my favourites.

Now to explain what has been left out, and why. Card games, it has been said, 'assert the mastery of mind over the chaos of chance'. This is an impressive way of pointing out that, in a typical game, the cards you are dealt or otherwise acquire come from a shuffled pack and are therefore random and unpredictable – the chance element – whereas how you then make use of them to thwart your opponents and achieve your own ends is a matter of personal skill. Some games allow skill to influence the outcome more than others, but the whole essence of a true card game is that both elements exist – even that there is a conflict between them. So, as there is not enough space for everything, I have cut out those few games which are virtually pure skill, and a great number which are more or less pure chance. The former, I feel, appeal to Chess players rather than true card lovers, while the latter amount to little more than betting on which cards will turn up and are more in the nature of lotteries than games.

For much the same reason, if with more regret, games played only by children have had to be excluded. It may, in fact, be questioned whether there is any call for traditional Snap or Beggar-my-Neighbour now that all are commercially available in presentations specially designed for children. When children are ready for real cards they will be ready for real games, the chief requirement being that the rules be simple and the objectives clear. At time of writing my three-year-old son and six-year-old daughter (the dedicatees) enjoy Switch or Swedish Rummy. With children, incidentally, use Patience cards: they are smaller than standard cards and easier for little fingers.

More defensibly, though with equal regret, I have omitted games playable only with special packs, such as the Tarot cards and the Japanese Flower Game (Hanafuda).

*

There is a widespread belief that all card games have 'official' rules and that none is genuine that has not first been strained through a man called Hoyle. Hoyle is a red herring. He only wrote about some half-dozen card games and died in 1769, before most of the games covered here had evolved. Anyone can now compile a collection of games and include Hoyle in the title: his name is a pretence and not a guarantee. In any case, Hoyle never did lay down official rules. His speciality was guidelines to good strategy, and it is that which players used to evoke by the phrase 'according to Hoyle'.*

* 'Hoyle,' wrote one correspondent to the *Gentlemen's Magazine* for February 1755, 'tutored me in the several games at cards, and under the name of guarding me from being cheated, insensibly gave me a taste for sharping.'

As to the officialness of rules, the situation is complex and best ignored. Widely played games with basically simple mechanics, such as Bridge, tend to be played everywhere in much the same way. National or regional games such as German Skat may have official rules published by an organization devoted to the game, but these are happily ignored in local and family play. Of course, it is essential to establish a set of rules for club or tournament play, but these should be regarded as the rules of the club, not the rules of the game. In homes and pubs people play cards for enjoyment, and will naturally introduce, modify and drop rules to suit their tastes. It is because tastes vary from place to place and generation to generation that card games evolve. One that no longer evolves is extinct. (Some games in this book are extinct, but included because of intrinsic merits that appeal to catholic tastes.) No textbook can do more than describe how games are played, or are said by other books to be played; nor should it expect to. The only important thing is that everybody playing around the same table at the same time should be following the same rules. If it helps to have them written down, then the most authoritative reference book is the one nearest to hand.

Not wishing to appoint myself an arbiter of proper play – a task that may be left to more arrogant members of the compilers' species – I should explain the principles upon which I have decided between alternative rules where the choice existed. After careful testing, I have generally preferred, in this order, the skill-rewarding to the uncontrollable, the simple to the complex, the traditional to the possibly transient, and the natural to the artificial. I have also preferred the form of a game played in its country of origin, unless (as in the case of Five Hundred) it has flourished more successfully elsewhere.

*

Information on current pub games rests heavily on researches carried out by Arthur Taylor (see Select Bibliography), and I am grateful to many correspondents for communicating historical and field notes to me, especially to Robin Good-fellow, Jeremy Secker and John McLeod. Mr Goodfellow kindly but critically read through the manuscript and drew my attention to numerous opportunities for improvement and correction, all of which I have been glad to act upon. I must also render grateful acknowledgement to my wife Barbara and those many friends and relations with whom, over the years, I have explored all the main-entry games in this collection and a high percentage of the stragglers. Any errors that remain are all my own work, and suggestions for improvement will be gratefully received.

How to Play Cards

THE PACK A complete set of cards is called a *pack*, though the old-fashioned term *deck* is still used in America. The pack in commonest use contains 52 cards, divided into four groups of 13 each. The four groups are called *suits*; and their 13 members *ranks*.

SUITS Each suit is distinguished by a symbol. The two black suits are spades (♠) and clubs (♣), the red ones hearts (♥) and diamonds (♦). The four suits are basically of equal status, none being higher or better than another, except as the rules of a particular game may specify.

RANKS Each suit contains 13 ranks as follows: Ace, 2, 3, 4, 5, 6, 7, 8, 9, 10, Jack, Queen, King. Theoretically, the Ace or 'one' is the lowest card and the King the highest, but in the vast majority of games the Ace is promoted to top position, beating the King and all the others down to the lowest numeral, which is Two.

Note: in this book the numeral Ten is represented by the initial T, although it appears as 10 on the actual card. In many games the Ten is also promoted to a higher place than the King, being beaten only by the Ace. (The terms *deuce* and *trey*, for the Two and Three of a suit, are more commonly used in America than in Britain and are largely avoided in this book.)

ALTERNATIVE PACKS The suit symbols described above are French in origin. There are also German, Swiss, Italian and Spanish suit systems, but they need not detain us here. More important is the fact that many games, other than those of English origin, are played with shorter packs, which can be reproduced by rejecting certain ranks from the 52-card pack. Games of Italian and Spanish origin are played with a

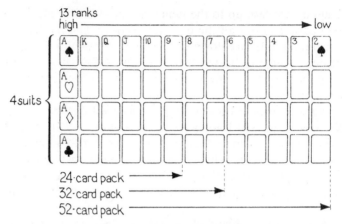

1. FULL PACK contains four suits and thirteen ranks. Shorter packs, required by various games, are made by rejecting lower ranks. Ranks normally beat one another in the order shown, but suits are usually of equal status except as a particular game requires. In this diagram they happen to be arranged in Bridge 'bidding order', with spades high and clubs low.

40-card pack lacking all Eights, Nines and Tens, the highest numeral being Seven. Older German and modern Swiss games are played with a 36-card pack lacking Twos, Threes, Fours and Fives. Most games of French origin are played with the so-called Piquet pack of 32 cards, nothing lower than Seven. Few games call for just 28 or 20 cards; but the 24-card pack, with nothing lower than Nine, is not uncommon.

Some games are played with more than one pack shuffled together. For example, Calypso is played with four 52-card packs (making 208 cards), Six-pack Bézique with six 32-card packs (192), Pinochle with two 24-card packs (48).

THE JOKER Most modern packs contain one or more odd cards called Jokers. Not all games require them, and in those that do they are used in different ways.

TRICKS The commonest way in which cards are played is in the form of *tricks*. A trick occurs when everybody in turn plays a card face up to the table and the one who plays the best card captures all the others, which he then places in a squared-up pile face down on the table before him. In some games the object is to win tricks, in others it is to avoid winning them, and in some it is to capture certain scoring cards contained in them.

Normal rules of trick playing are as follows. One player, the *leader*, starts by leading any card he likes. Everybody else must then follow suit if they can, i.e., play a card of the same suit as the one led. Whoever plays the highest-ranking card of that suit wins the trick. He thereby earns the privilege of leading to the next trick, and thus deciding which suit to play next.

A player who is *void* of the suit led (has no cards of it) cannot win the trick, and will have to play a card of some other suit instead. This is generally called *discarding*, though

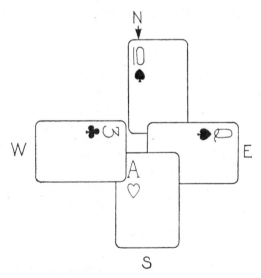

2. HOW TRICKS WORK North leads spades with the Ten; others must follow suit if possible. East overtakes with the Queen. South has no spades, discards an Ace, which cannot win. West also cannot follow, discards a Three. East wins unless hearts are trumps, in which case South wins, or clubs are, in which case West takes the trick. Whoever wins leads to the next trick.

the correct term is *renouncing*, as the player who cannot follow renounces all hope of winning the trick. A player who can follow suit but fails to do so is said to *revoke*, an action which usually incurs some sort of penalty.

TRUMPS At the start of play it may, in some games, be agreed that a particular suit should become the *trump* suit. The word is a corruption of 'triumph', and denotes that the agreed suit is superior to the other three, which are called *plain* or *side* suits. If the leader to a trick starts with a plain suit anyone who is unable to follow suit may win the trick by playing a trump, which beats all cards of the suit led regardless of rank. This is called *trumping* or *ruffing*. If several players cannot follow and decide to ruff instead of renouncing, then the trick is won by the highest trump played. It will be noted that the Two of trumps beats the Ace of any other suit, while the Ace of trumps is the highest card in the pack. If a trump is led, by definition nobody can ruff, and anyone unable to follow suit can only renounce.

SPECIAL RULES The trick rules outlined above are widespread enough to be described as 'normal'. Be prepared, however, to encounter games which have other rules. In some games there are comparatively 'relaxed' rules whereby a player is not obliged to follow suit but may follow, trump or renounce as he pleases. Others apply 'strict' rules – for example, a player must not only follow suit if he can but must also *head* the trick if possible, i.e., play from that suit a card higher in rank than any so far played to it. If unable to head he must still follow, and if unable to do either he may be obliged to trump if he can, a renounce being illegal unless there is no alternative.

MELDS A meld is a combination of two or more cards which match one another according to the particular rules of the game. Examples of melds include the *marriage*, denoting a King and Queen of the same suit; the *flush*, denoting three or more cards of the same suit; the *sequence*, denoting three or more cards in ranking order, such as 9–T–J; the *pair*, denoting two cards of the same rank; and many others. Some games consist entirely of melds instead of playing tricks. In Rummy games, for example, the object of play is to collect matched cards and meld them together, while in Poker and Brag the object is to bluff opponents into believing the cards you were dealt form a better meld than anyone else's. Some games, such as Piquet and the Bézique/Pinochle family, involve both tricks and melds. (The word is basically a Rummy term and is not yet universally applied to other games, so melds in this book are often referred to merely as 'combinations'.)

CARD-TABLE PROCEDURE

Card play takes place against a backdrop of long-established ritual, of traditional procedures, which should be observed for two main reasons. First, they are all rooted in the practical necessity of preventing any player from gaining over his opponents an unfair advantage due to anything other than the lie of the cards and the extent of his skill. Second, their observance is a sign of civility, a gesture to the effect that the player agrees to subordinate his personal interests to those of the group in which he is playing.

LOVE OR MONEY? Whether or not to play for money depends partly on the game but chiefly on the players. There are those who will not take any card game seriously unless it is played for money, and those who, on principle, will never play for money at all. Extremists of both sorts (and I speak as one of them) can do no more than respect the views of the other, and avoid meeting at the same table. Probably the happy medium is represented by those who do not mind whether or not they play for money, so long as the stakes are not so great as to interfere with proper concentration on the game itself.

As to the games, there are some, such as Poker, which have no scoring system and are essentially games of money management – to play them otherwise defeats the whole object. At the other extreme, games that call for a high degree of skill at card play and have a refined scoring system which fairly measures the extent of that skill, such as Bridge, can be played for the satisfaction of a good score.

PLAYERS, PARTNERS AND POSITIONS Many card games are played by four players in two partnerships of two each, partners sitting opposite each other so as to play alternately instead of consecutively. If partnerships are to be determined at random, it is customary to spread the pack face down across the table and for each to draw one card. Those drawing the two highest ranks become partners against the other two, the one with the highest having choice of seats and the privilege of dealing first. Tied players draw again. When there are not partnerships, the same system is used to determine seats and first deal. The importance of seating may be regarded as a hangover from more superstitious times, in which hard-bitten gamblers still tend to live.

ORDER The order in which cards are dealt around the table, in which the participants take turns to play, and in which the deal passes from person to person, is normally clockwise (to the left). In games of Spanish, Italian and south Germanic origin it is normally anti-clockwise. The person who comes next after the dealer (i.e., who sits at his left in clockwise games, his right otherwise) is called *eldest* (*hand*) or *forehand*. In nearly all games it is eldest who leads to the first trick, or otherwise makes the first move, or has priority of some sort over everybody else, and the dealer himself who comes last or has least priority.

GAME It is important to establish at the outset what constitutes 'game' – that is, at what point play ceases and the group breaks up. In many games this is a part of the rules, which may specify that each deal is a separate event, or that the game ends when one player reaches a target score or the pool is empty. If the game is not so defined, then agree to play up to a target score or for a fixed length of time or number of deals. If not playing to a target score it is desirable for all players to have dealt the same number of times in order to equalize the advantages of position.

THE SHUFFLE The purpose of shuffling is to ensure that cards are randomized before being dealt, as the act of playing tends to put them in order. Perfect random is impossible to achieve in a short time, but that is not the point: the object is merely to prevent anyone from memorizing the location of any particular card. In any game involving melds or other combinations, especially Rummy and Poker, more thorough shuffling is required than in others. Shuffling cannot be taught in words; it can only be copied from watching others. The rules of shuffling are that any one or more players may shuffle if they wish, but the dealer is entitled to shuffle last.

THE CUT After shuffling, but before dealing, dealer should offer the pack to the player on his other side from eldest, by placing it face down on the table before him. This player may then (but is not obliged to) cut the pack by lifting off the top half of the pack and placing it beside the bottom. Dealer then completes the cut by placing the bottom half on top of the former top half. The purpose of this ritual is to ensure the burial of the former bottom card of the pack, which may have inadvertently become visible during the shuffle. How many cards should each 'half' contain? Different games specify different minima, but it is frankly silly to lift off or to leave below less than one-tenth the total number of cards in the pack.

THE DEAL Cards are dealt from the top of the pack downwards, face down to each player unless otherwise stated, the first to eldest, the second to the player after him, and so on, dealer himself normally receiving the last card of each round. In some games cards are dealt not one at a time but in batches of two or more at a time to each player. Each game has developed its own traditional method, the purpose of which is to enliven the play by ensuring that cards are not completely random but comparatively ordered in each hand.

(This does not invalidate the need to shuffle, whose chief point, as we have seen, is to prevent the locatability of cards. On the contrary, it takes deliberate advantage of the inevitable imperfection of the shuffle.) It is bad manners to start picking one's cards up before the deal is complete.

IRREGULARITIES IN THE DEAL Any irregularity in the deal, such as cards dealt in the wrong order or the wrong number, or being exposed or even dropped on the floor, must, if demanded by at least one player who has not yet picked up his cards, be rectified by gathering the cards in, re-shuffling and re-dealing by the same dealer. This is a recommendation. A very few games have been equipped with club laws (which is what most people mean by 'official rules') to cover such irregularities, and these may be preferred if known.

PLAY Habits during the play which mark a player as ignorant and uncivilized include saying anything which is not necessary and to the point of the game; saying anything that *is* necessary in a manner or tone of voice, or with a gesture, which conveys more than it should, especially to a partner; handling or playing cards to the same effect; playing too fast or too slow, especially with signs of anguish or excessive deliberation; criticizing or questioning another person's play, especially a partner's; foretelling the next cards to be played; and, at the end, explaining how one's success was due to brilliance or failure to bad luck.

IRREGULARITIES IN THE PLAY An irregularity is a move counter to the rules of the game, such as playing out of turn or revoking. Many games now (or once) played in clubs have been equipped with laws specifying corrections and penalties for all conceivable irregularities, as well as some tortuously inconceivable, but space prohibits their being detailed in this book. In a partnership game the exposure of a wrong card (the usual result of an irregularity) gives useful information to one's partner and ought, strictly, to be penalized by forfeiture of the game by the side committing it. If, however, it is agreed to correct the mistake, with or without a point or cash penalty, the false card should be laid face up on the table and played at the earliest legal opportunity. Once a trick has been quitted, i.e., taken and turned down, it is too late for correction. Where the player at fault has no partner and benefits no one else by his mistake, he need not be penalized if there is time to correct it. The basic principle is that nobody should derive unfair advantage from an irregularity, especially when money is at stake. Ways of dealing with such irregularities must be left to consensus and common sense.

CHEATING This interesting subject can only be mentioned in passing. To be effective, cheating must be carried out by a dedicated expert, who will normally either have doctored the pack in some way or be working with the aid of a secret partner – not necessarily one participating in the game. When playing with strangers for money, assume all men guilty, until proved innocent, but make no accusations in case you are wrong. If in doubt just make an excuse and leave.

THE PAY-OFF Some games are played with 'hard' currency, i.e., coins or objects such as chips or counters which represent coins and are redeemed at the end of play. Technically these are 'zero sum' games, meaning that one person's loss balances another's gain and the end result is a redistribution of the wealth put into the game by all its players at the start. By strictly applying the rule 'if you can't pay you can't play', no one need lose more than he can afford. Others are played for the 'soft currency' of point scores and players may conclude the game by settling up on the basis of the resultant score differences at some previously agreed conversion rate, such as a pound a point or a penny a hundred. Care must be exercised here because the mind contains an endless supply of points which the pocket may later be unable to match. Such games as it were create wealth out of nowhere, as everybody may finish in the black yet some have still to pay. It is therefore essential to agree in advance upon the rate of exchange involved and to permit a player to withdraw when his account reaches the maximum he can afford to lose.

KIBITZERS Deriving from the German word for 'peewits', possibly because of their twittering, kibitzers are onlookers who tend to offer unwanted advice (dictionary definition). Kibitzers by law should sit down, keep quiet, not fidget, and refrain from distracting or encouraging the players.

The Good Game Guide

All card games are worth playing – provided that the right number take part, for it does not follow that a good game for two players will be as good for three, even if playable by that number. All games in this book are accompanied by an indication of how many *can* take part and what the best number is. The best number is also indicated by the appropriate symbol, shown below, in the case of all major games, while some of the minor games and variants are similarly picked out if particularly recommended for that number. The easily recognized symbols are also useful if you have a particular number of players and are browsing through the book for something suitable.

8   A good game for two players

8   A good game for three players

88   A good partnership game for four players

8   Not everybody likes playing in partnerships so this sign denotes a good game for four individualists

88   A good game for five players

888   A good game for six players

◎   Any number of players, which, in practice, usually means from three to seven

Whist/Bridge Family

In the simplest of all card games 52 cards are divided equally among four players, a trump suit is determined at random, and the winner is the player who takes most of the 13 tricks. To avoid ties, players sitting opposite each other play as partners, helping each other to win tricks and counting all their won tricks together. Now one partnership is bound to take a majority of tricks (seven or more), and that side wins. In essence this game is Whist and is the point at which all beginners should begin.

Contract Bridge comes first in this collection because it is the most prestigious card game in the world. Yet, in both complexity and historicity, it follows on from Whist, being a direct descendant of it and only now occupying the high status that Whist had previously occupied for centuries. The steps by which Whist became Bridge may be traced from Biritch or Russian Whist in about 1883, through Bridge Whist, Auction Bridge and Plafond to the formulation of modern Contract in 1925–6. Since then, millions of devotees all over the world play nothing else.

Also included in this section are Ninety-Nine and Oh Hell. The former, invented by the present writer, is a modern member of the family which seeks to adapt basic Whist/Bridge principles for three players instead of four. The game usually called Oh Hell represents comic relief, being a light-hearted exercise for any number from three to seven players.

Contract Bridge ⚋⚋

4 players
1 pack (52)

Chico:	He bids one.
M. Dumont:	One what?
Chico:	Never mind. You'll find out. Now I bid two.
M. Dumont:	But two what?
Chico:	Er – two the same as what he bid.

(Animal Crackers, 1930)

Contract Bridge is an advanced form of Whist in which the interest and skill are increased by the introduction of the following features. First, instead of turning a random card to establish trumps, players bid for the right to choose the trump that suits them best. Then their object is to win not just a majority of tricks but at least the number of tricks they contracted to win in return for the privilege of nominating trumps. In the actual play one member of the contracting side lays his hands face up on the table and leaves his partner to do all their playing from both hands. The scoring system is also refined in that the only points which contribute towards winning the game are those made for tricks contracted and won. Any extra tricks taken, together with various bonuses, are kept in a separate account and not added in until the game is won. What gives the game its real point is the method by which the contract is arrived at – the auction itself. For, although two partners are bidding on what they can see in their own hands, they are also conveying information about their hands to each other in the way they bid, and listening in on their opponents' conversation at the same time. The complexity of Bridge lies less in the play than in the use of bidding systems to convey information.

Modern Contract Bridge, which may be called Bridge for short as nobody plays original Bridge any more, was developed and refined by American millionaire Harold S. Vanderbilt on a winter cruise in 1925–6. The first comprehensive bidding system was developed by Ely Culbertson, who was also responsible for launching the publicity campaign which put Bridge at the top of the social status ladder, a position from which it has not yet been toppled.

CARDS A standard 52-card pack. It is customary to use two packs alternately, one being shuffled while the other is dealt.

PRELIMINARIES Scores are kept on a sheet divided into two columns, one for each partnership, and it is customary for both sides to keep a record, as a check on accuracy, each in columns headed WE and THEY. The sheet is divided into a top and bottom half by a horizontal line cutting across both columns. Points which score towards the winning of a game are entered below the line, and premiums (bonuses) above it. (Printed pads of sheets are obtainable from stationers.) After determining partners and seats (see p. 24), and shuffling and cutting, all play and the turn to deal pass to the left, i.e., clockwise around the table.

GAME For home as distinct from tournament play a *rubber* is won by the first side to win two games, each game requiring one or more deals. A side that has won one game is said to be *vulnerable*, and is subject to increased scores or penalties as the case may be.

DEAL Thirteen each, one at a time, face down.

RANK Cards rank in their normal order, from high to low AKQJT98765432. Spades and hearts are major suits, diamonds and clubs minor.

OBJECT In the first part of the game, the auction, each side's object is to discover as much as possible about how the cards lie and to arrive at a contract that best suits their combined hands. In the second part the declarers, having nominated trumps, must win at least as many tricks as they bid, while the defenders try to stop them. There is an increased score for winning a contract to take 12 or all 13 tricks, known as a little and a grand slam respectively. In any contract the only points which count towards game – below the line – are those made for tricks contracted and won. Any extra or over-tricks made by the declarers are scored separately as bonuses, above the line, as are scores made by the defenders for defeating a contract.

THE AUCTION Dealer first, each player in turn may pass, call, double or redouble. If all pass immediately there is no play, the cards are gathered in, and the deal passes to the left. A player passes by saying 'No bid', but this does not prevent him from bidding on his next turn. A call consists of a num-ber of tricks more than six and a proposed trump suit (or none), and represents the number of tricks which the caller is offering to take in conjunction with his partner. (Example: 'one club' is a bid to take seven tricks with clubs as trumps, 'seven no trump' an offer to win all 13 without a trump suit.) Each bid must be higher than any previous one, i.e., it must be either for a greater number of tricks or for the same num-ber of tricks as the previous bid but in a higher suit. For this purpose suits rank from low to high: clubs, diamonds, hearts, spades, no trump. Thus the lowest bid of all is 'one club', which may be overcalled by one anything else. A bid at 'no trump' can only be overcalled by a higher number, and the highest possible bid is 'seven no trump'. Instead of bidding or passing, a player may announce 'double' if the previous bid was made by an opponent, or 'redouble' if the previous announcement was a 'double' from an opponent. The effect of doubling or redoubling is to double or quad-ruple whatever score may be made if the bid concerned is established and played as the contract. But if a double/redouble is followed by another bid it is automatically can-celled. When three players have passed in succession, the last-named bid becomes the contract, whether or not doubled or redoubled. This ends the auction.

PLAY That member of the contracting side who, in the

course of the auction, first named the trump now prevailing is known as the *declarer* and it is for him to play both hands. The opening lead is made by the opponent sitting immediately to declarer's left. When the first card has been led declarer's partner lays his hand of cards face up on the table, each suit in an overlapping column of cards in order of rank. This hand is the dummy. The second card to the trick is played by declarer from dummy, the third by the leader's partner, and the fourth by declarer from his own hand. Normal rules of trick-taking apply. Follow suit to the card led if possible; if not, trump or renounce *ad lib*. The trick is captured by the highest card of the suit led or by the highest trump if any are played, and the winner of one trick leads to the next. It is the declarer's responsibility to play both hands, and his partner may not advise him or interfere in any way except to draw attention to any breach of rules he may be about to commit (such as revoking or leading out of turn). The tricks won by one partnership are kept in one place face down but overlapping so that the number taken is clear to all. If declarer wins a trick with a card from the dummy he leads to the next from dummy; if from his own hand he leads from his own.

SCORE For details, see Table 1. If declarer succeeds in the contract his side scores below the line the appropriate amount for the number bid and the trump concerned, and doubled or redoubled if appropriate. Any overtricks – those taken in excess of the number bid – are scored above the line, together with the appropriate bonus, if applicable, for the very fact of having successfully bid a small or grand slam.

If declarer is beaten ('goes down'), his opponents score above the line a certain amount for every trick by which declarer fell short of his contract ('undertricks'). This amount depends on whether or not the contract was doubled and whether or not declarer's side was vulnerable.

Regardless of success or failure in the contract itself, any player who had held the top five trumps in his own hand, or all four Aces if the contract was no trump, scores 150 'for honours'. A player who held all but one of the top five

WE	THEY
500 G	
200 G	
150 F	*60* E
500 F	*150* C
100 A	*30* C
20 A	*100* B
80 A	*130* C
120 F	*20* D
	60 E
140 G	
1810	*550*
550	
1260	

3. SCORING AT CONTRACT BRIDGE (a) We bid 4♣, made 5♣, scoring 80 below for the two bid and 40 above for the overtrick. One of us held AKJT of trumps, counting 100 for honours above. (b) We bid 3♥, were doubled, and made only two. They score 100 above for the first (and only) undertrick, doubled. (c) They bid 4NT and made five, scoring 40 for the first and 30 for the other three below the line, plus one overtrick for 30 above. One of them held four Aces, gaining 150 for honours. We had a part-score of 80, which we keep, but they win the first game. A line is drawn to mark the game and they are now vulnerable. (d) They bid and make 1♣, scoring 20 below the line. (e) They bid 2♠ and make four, for 2 × 30 below and 2 × 30 (overtricks) above, increasing their part score to 80. (f) We bid and make a small slam – 6♦, for 120 below the line, giving us the second game and making ourselves vulnerable also. We also count a bonus of 500 above for the slam, plus 150 for honours as one of us held the top five trumps. (g) We bid 2NT, are doubled, and make three. This gives us 2 × (40 + 30) below the line, plus 200 above for the (doubled) overtrick made when vulnerable. Our 140 below gives us the game, and we therefore win the rubber with a bonus of 500 for two out of three games. The results are then totalled.

trumps scores 100 for honours. Scoring for honours is an archaic feature that depends entirely upon chance and is ignored in serious play.

TABLE 1: CONTRACT BRIDGE SCORING

Contract succeeds

Declarer scores below the line for each trick bid and won	With minor suit trump, ♣ ♦ : 20			× 2 if doubled × 4 if redoubled
	With major suit trump, ♥ ♠ : 30			
	At NT	for the first trick : 40		
		for each subsequent : 30		

Declarer scores above the line if applicable	Per overtrick:	basic trick value
	Per overtrick if doubled:	100
	Ditto if also vulnerable:	200
	Bonus if contract (re)doubled:	50
	For making a little slam	500 not vulnerable
		750 if vulnerable
	For making a grand slam	1000 not vulnerable
		1500 if vulnerable

Contract fails

Defenders score above the line for each undertrick	If undoubled:	50 not vulnerable
		100 if vulnerable
	If doubled, for 1st undertrick	100 not vulnerable
		200 if vulnerable
	Ditto, per subsequent undertrick	200 not vulnerable
		300 if vulnerable

Scores independent of individual contract

For five honours in one hand (AKQJT trumps):	150
For four honours in one hand (trumps, any four):	100
For four Aces in one hand in a no-trump contract:	150
For winning rubber in two games:	700
For winning rubber in three games:	500
Unfinished rubber: for one game won:	300
Unfinished rubber: for part-score in unfinished game:	50

When a side's score below the line reaches or exceeds 100, which may take one or more deals, they win the game and become vulnerable. Another line is drawn below across the sheet and the next game begins at zero, all previously recorded scores remaining unaffected until the end of the rubber. When one side wins its second game it also wins the rubber and adds a bonus of 500 above the line, or 700 if the other side failed to win one game. All above and below line scores made by both sides are then totalled and the difference is the margin of victory.

NOTES ON PLAY

Bidding at Bridge is the subject of numerous systems and conventions. A system is a whole process of bidding in accordance with agreed principles so that a partnership who employs it will reach the best contract for their particular combination of hands. A convention is a single bid used to convey a particular message, such as opening 'two clubs' to indicate a strong hand without necessarily indicating strength in clubs. A given convention may be used in more than one system and a given system may employ alternative conventions for the same purpose.

Most English tournament players use the Acol system while home and social players use the Two Club system. The two are similar and have tended to grow together, and may be regarded respectively as the detailed and the simplified end of the same system. American players use the Goren system also known as Standard American. There are other internationally recognized English and American systems besides several Italian systems and one, Precision Club, of Chinese (Taiwan) origin.

At international tournament level partnerships must register the systems and conventions they propose to use, and unregistered ones are not permitted, as it is a rule of play that both sides should be able to interpret messages conveyed in bidding code between their opponents. Even in less august circles strangers partnering each other for the first time must find a common ground of system and conventions that both can follow if they are to get any-where.

Beginners are advised to start with the Two Club system as introduced below. It may be regarded as Basic Bridge, as its alternative name 'Utility' suggests. For further details and accounts of other systems see Fox's *Modern Bidding Systems in Bridge* (Allen Lane/Penguin), from which some of the following illustrations are taken.

ASSESSING THE HAND Tricks are won with high cards, long cards and trumps. Significant high cards, or honours, are Ace, King, Queen and Jack; lower ranks are generally referred to as *X*, and appear as such in sample hands unless their rank has any particular significance.

High cards are the first things to look for and the easiest to assess, as there is a simple device for evaluating a hand's high-card strength, called the Milton Work count. By this method you count 4 points for each Ace held, 3 per King, 2 per Queen, 1 per Jack. The total strength points in the pack is 40, so the average hand counts 10 and the average combined cards of a partnership 20. Experience shows that a partnership holding 37 can expect to win a grand slam, with 33 a small slam, and with 25 a game. A hand generally needs to be worth at least 13 (one King better than average) to be strong enough to open but can be below average – worth as little as 7 – to support a partner's opening bid.

Example: ♠AQJXX ♥KQJ ♦AK ♣AQJ. This hand counts 27. If your partner has an 'average' 10 points you can bid towards a grand slam, since he must hold the other Ace and Kings. If he has at least 6 (two Kings), the small slam can be made. Few hands look like that. Most look like this: ♠KXX ♥XX ♦QXXX ♣AJXX, worth 10. A hand without a single honour is called a Yarborough but is rarely dealt.

Long cards are those in excess of the average number dealt. As there are 13 in a suit each player expects to receive 3¼ of each suit. A suit of four or more is therefore long and the excess cards – even the lowly 'X's – can be set up to win tricks when they are led and no one else can follow. Of course, long cards in plain suits can be trumped when led, but long cards in trumps are eventually invulnerable, so long cards and trumps are considered together. This aspect of a hand, of equal importance with high-card strength, is called *distribution* and denotes the relative numbers of cards you have in the four suits.

A hand with suits distributed 4–3–3–3, 4–4–3–2 or 5–3–3–2 is balanced, and suggestive of a no-trump contract if it also has adequate high-card strength. Any other distribution is unbalanced and suggestive of a trump contract in its longest suit – again, assuming adequate supporting strength. It is possible to add distributional points to high-card strength as an aid to quantitive evaluation of the hand, though distributional points do not apply to prospective no-trumpers and their counting is not officially recognized in the Two Club system anyway. Since short plain suits offer the prospect of winning tricks by ruffing when they are led, the simplest method is to count 1 for a doubleton (holding no more than two of a given suit), 2 for a singleton and 3 for a void. A more accurate method, and rather to be trusted if it produces a different result from the short-suit count, is the long-suit count, whereby you reckon 1 distributional point for each card in excess of four in the prospective trump suit and 1 per card over three in each plain suit. By this reckoning a hand such as ♠KXXXXX ♥KX ♦A ♣XXXX, though worth only 10 for high-card strength, counts 13 including points for long-suit distribution and so reaches the opening requirement.

Also relevant to the assessment of a hand are various methods of counting probable trick winners. Simplest is the count of 'quick tricks', which is useful in the assessment of borderline hands for trump contracts. Count 2 quick tricks for a suit holding headed by A–K, $1\frac{1}{2}$ for A–Q, 1 for A or K–Q, and $\frac{1}{2}$ for K–X. A hand should contain at least two quick tricks to open, or more if worth under 13 points.

Relevant to the assessment of balanced hands with a no-trump bid in view is the counting of *stoppers*. A stopper is a high card which will stop the opponents from running

through a solid suit from the top down and put you in the
lead. An Ace is obviously a stopper; so is K–X and Q–X–X
and, to stretch a point, J–X–X–X. An opening bid at no
trump normally requires a hand with stoppers in at least
three suits.

By way of summary, consider these hands:

(a) ♠KXX ♥AQX ♦KXXX ♣AJX
(b) ♠AQXX ♥XX ♦KQXX ♣QXX
(c) ♠AKJXX ♥KXXX ♦XX ♣XX
(d) ♠K ♥KXXXX ♦QXXXX ♣QJ

Hand (a) is balanced 4–3–3–3, counts 17 strength points and
is stopped in all suits, therefore suitable for a bid at no
trump. (b) is also balanced, 4–4–3–2, but is only stopped in
three suits, and two suits are weak. But it counts 13 for
strength (14 with distribution) and offers 2½ quick tricks, and
is therefore suitable for a bid in spades or diamonds. (c) is
unbalanced in favour of spades and hearts. Though counting
only 11 for cards it offers distributional strength and 2½
quick tricks, and is worth a bid. (d) also counts 11 for high
cards but, even with another 3 for distribution, only offers
half a quick trick. It would be prudent to pass.

OPENING BIDS The opening bid is the first one of the
auction and also the most important to the side that makes
it (usually the dealer's) as it seizes the initiative and enables
the opener's side to pursue communications at a lower level
than their opponents. The first bid made by the opener's
partner is by definition a responsive bid and he may expect
the opener to reply in his turn with a re-bid. The first bid
made by the opponents, unless they both pass, interrupts the
communication established between the opener and his
partner and is by definition a defensive bid. Hands must be
assessed in different ways depending on whether they are
opening, responsive or defensive bids. On average a contract
should be reached after two bids by the opener and two by
his partner.

We consider, first, opening bids of one in suit, no trumps,
two in suit, then three or more in suit, together with usual

responses and possible re-bids. Where points are referred to they do *not* include distribution unless otherwise stated.

ONE IN SUIT A hand should be opened with a bid of one in suit if it has

(a) 13–20 points
(b) at least two quick tricks
(c) a biddable suit.
(d) a satisfactory re-bid

A biddable suit is any of at least five cards, or four including A or K or Q–J. A satisfactory re-bid, whether or not in the same suit, is necessary in case partner responds with a bid in another suit, the purpose of which is merely to give information and not necessarily to suggest a contract. The fact of opening one in suit must imply a promise to re-bid in this event. A hand worth 11–12 may be opened with a fair five-card suit and/or more than two quick tricks; one worth 10 may be opened with a fair six-card or two five-card suits. (For a seven-card holding see opening bids of three in suit.) A hand worth 14 may justify a pass with less than two quick tricks or other obvious weaknesses.

Of two biddable suits open with the longer or, if they are of equal length, with the higher suit. But of two four-card suits which are not *touching* (i.e., adjacent in bidding power, such as ♥ and ♦) prefer 1♣ to 1♠ if both are black, otherwise bid the suit ranking immediately below the doubleton holding (spades if the doubleton is clubs). The purpose of these perhaps arbitrary-sounding rules will become obvious in practice: it is to leave enough bidding space in which to explore other possibilities without pushing the level too high.

A convention known as the Prepared Club is sometimes employed on a balanced hand that does not qualify for a (strong) no-trump opening bid, and has no biddable suit, but seems too strong to pass – for example, ♠XXXX ♥AQJ ♦KXX ♣AXX. The hand is worth 14 but a bid of 1♠ would be as dangerous as it is misleading. By previous agreement such a hand may be opened with 1♣, in order to show preparedness to enter into a contract exploration, and partner can equally conventionally reply 1♦ to show that he has nothing to offer. But there are obvious drawbacks to this convention, not least of which is the danger of being unable to communicate a serious club holding.

Assuming that no defensive bid has intervened partner's response to a 1-suit opening is based on the possibility that, for all he knows, opener's hand is worth anything up to 20 points. He may therefore respond on as little as 6 provided he has something relevant to add to the opening announcement. The possibilities open to him are to (a) pass, (b) bid 1NT, (c) raise the bid in the same suit, (d) bid a suit *take-out* (i.e., offer another suit).

With less than 6 in high-card strength, pass. Example: pass to 1♥ on ♠QXX ♥XXX ♦QJXX ♣XXX.

With 6–9 points reply 1NT if unable to support partner's suit (for which you need four or more) and unable to offer one of your own at the 1-level. This response is a sign of weakness. But a balanced hand with no marked weakness in the suit quoted may justify a response of 2NT to show 11–12 points, or 3NT to show 13–15.

Make a higher bid in the same suit if able to support it with four trumps, or three and a probable ruff, e.g., ♠QXX ♥X ♦KXXXX ♣XXXX stands a raise from 1♠ to 2♠ by virtue of three trumps and a ruff in hearts. Double raise from 1 to 3 with four good trumps and additional support, amounting to 10–12 points including distribution, e.g., to 1♠ reply 3♠ on ♠KXXX ♥XX ♦AJXX ♣KXX. A particularly unbalanced hand with over 13 including distribution justifies a treble raise, e.g., to 4♠ on ♠QJXXX ♥X ♦AXXXX ♣XX. Generally, prefer to raise when the suit is major, as a minor suit bid with sufficient strength may be convertible into a more profitable no-trump contract at a lower level. If counting points for distribution, value a void at 5 and a singleton at 3 in response to an opening bid.

Any response in a different suit at the lowest possible level is forcing for one round – it commands the opener to make a re-bid in case your response does not suit his hand. Complication is introduced if your suit is lower in rank than the one he opened, as you must then make a response of two-over-one (e.g., 2♦ over 1♥) instead of the less risky one-over-one (e.g., 1♥ over 1♦). A one-over-one response may be made on 6–15 points or a good five-card suit; for example, raise 1♣ to 1♥ holding ♠KXXX ♥KXXX ♦XXX ♣XX or ♠QXX ♥QJ987 ♦XX ♣XXX. A two-over-one response requires at least 8 or 9 points (opinions differ). After 1♠ reply 2♣ on ♠KXX ♥XX ♦KQXX ♣AQXX.

A suit take-out at a higher level than necessary is forcing to game – it tells opener to keep the bidding open until a contract is reached that will win game,* indicating strength in your own hand. This can be done on less than 15 in high-card strength, but 16 is safer. Given a choice, prefer a suit with top cards even if not the longest. For example, after 1♠, bid 3♦ on ♠AQXX ♥KX ♦AKX ♣JXXX, rather than 3♣.

Opener is not obliged to re-bid if the response is no trump, though a bid of 2 or 3 NT implies strength rather than weakness and may suggest other possibilities. Otherwise, a response does call for a re-bid. If partner replies with a suit take-out at a higher level than necessary, forcing you to keep the bidding open, prefer to examine suit contracts rather than rush into no trumps. For example, you open 1♠ on ♠AQJXX ♥AKQXX ♦KX ♣X and are offered 3♥ in return; re-bid 4♥ rather than 3NT.

NO TRUMP OPENINGS A balanced hand of 4–3–3–3 or 4–4–3–2 invites a no-trump opening bid. So does 5–3–3–2, unless the five-card suit is major (♠♥), when a trump contract may prove more profitable to pursue.

On a balanced hand worth 16–18 bid 1NT. (This is the 'strong' no-trump opening, as opposed to the 'weak' opening on 12–14 points. Some players prefer to open strong when vulnerable, weak when not vulnerable; some always open 'weak'. The point must be agreed beforehand. Officially, the Two Club system opens 'strong' only.) Bid 2NT with 20–22. With 19 it is proper to open with a bid of one

---

* Since 'game' is 100 points, the requirement from a zero score is at least 3NT, or 4 in a major suit, or 5 in a minor suit.

in suit, while a count of 23 is a borderline case for the conventional 2♣ opening. A 3NT opening has a special use to be explained later.

In response to 1NT, pass with less than 7 points and no long suit. With 8, or a good 7 including a five-card suit open to development, raise to 2NT. This gives the opener useful information to consider for his re-bid. With 9 or more reply 3NT; with 15 or more, bid towards a slam.

To respond to 1NT with a bid of 2 in suit denies no-trump support (under 7 points), but promises at least a five-card suit with the possibility of a perhaps more profitable contract. Under the so-called Stayman convention the response of 2♣ to 1NT asks opener if he hold a four-card major, to which the latter replies 2♦ if not or 2 in the major suit if so. Responder should not use this convention unless he has a hand worth at least 8, a four-card major himself, and good reasons for preferring the trump contract. Having opened 1NT opener should normally pass following a response of 3NT, 6NT or 2 in suit (especially minor, unless Stayman).

In response to an opening 2NT, raise to 3NT with preferably not less than 5 points as it is not desirable to play the contract with strength concentrated in one hand. Raise to 4NT with 11, 6NT with 12+, 7NT with 16+. Alternatively, bid 3 in a *major* suit if at least five are held or if the hand is so strong that further bidding may lead to a slam contract in it. Example: raise 2NT to 3♠ on ♠QJXXX ♥XX ♦QXX ♣XXX. A response of 4 in a major suit, however, merely suggests a contract at exactly that level, using opener's strong hand for support, rather than a probe towards a slam. Example: to 2NT reply 4♥ on ♠XX ♥KJXXXX ♦AXX ♣XX. A response of 3♣ is a conventional call for the re-bid of opener's next higher four-card suit, but this can lead to complications.

To open 3NT is sometimes used to denote a balanced hand worth 26 points, but in the Two Club system it has given way to a more tactical use borrowed from Acol. Since a really strong hand is opened with the conventional 2♣, as explained below, and this is several bids below 3NT, the latter can be more usefully employed for other purposes. It has, in fact, come to denote a solid minor suit with some support such as ♠AX ♥QX ♦AKQJXXX ♣JX, and has a good pre-emptive value in cutting communications between the others. In response to this rather sophisticated opening, pass, unless anything positive can be offered.

TWO IN SUIT The Two Club system is so called because it is characterized by a conventional opening bid of 2♣ on a hand that promises strength enough for game in a suit contract, even though clubs may not have anything to do with it. It is proper to open 2♣ on (a) a balanced hand of 24+ points, or possibly a good 23, and (b) an unbalanced hand that looks capable of yielding nine tricks on its own account. Examples:

(a) ♠AQX ♥AKX ♦KQJX ♣AQX (25, balanced)
(b) ♠KQX ♥AKQXXX ♦AK ♣XX (9+ tricks)

The bid is forcing to game – i.e., it instructs partner to keep bidding until game level is reached.

The negative response to 2♣ is an equally conventional bid of 2♦ to indicate overall weakness. If then opener rebids a major suit, partner can still deny support by (equally conventionally) replying 2NT, leaving room for further exploration in minor suits until the best fit is found between the two hands.

A positive response should be made with a hand containing not less than A, K or K, K, K or K, K–Q, the best suit being offered in return. With 8–9 points and two Aces reply 2NT, or 3NT if stronger.

Bids of 2 in a suit other than clubs (following Acol rather than the original Two Club principle) are made on unbalanced hands too strong for an opening 1 in suit, too flexible for 3 in suit, but not quite strong enough for 2♣. Such bids are forcing for one round only and imply something like 17–20 points and a probable eight tricks in hand. Example: open 2♥ on ♠X ♥AKQJXX ♦KQX ♣AXX.

The negative response is 2NT, after which opener's re-bid in the same or another suit is not forcing and should normally be passed. For this reason it is worth offering another suit if at all feasible, a fair suit with 1 quick trick being required for a response at 2-level, or 1½ quick tricks if the suit is lower ranking and so needs a comeback at 3-level. Naturally, trump support would justify a raise in the same suit.

THREE OR MORE IN SUIT (PRE-EMPTIVE) An opening bid of three or more in a suit is described as pre-emptive, as it generally prevents the opponents from opening up communications. It does not imply a particularly strong hand, except in respect of one suit, of which at least seven should be held (regardless of point count). Its general effect is to communicate that the hand is useless for anything except a contract in that suit. Such a hand as ♠KQJXXXX ♥XX ♦XX ♣XX justifies an opening bid of 3♠. But if one of the plain-suit holdings were improved to A–X the hand would offer itself some support, making it too strong for a 3♠ opening – a better approach would then be by means of 1♠.

Since the shape of the hand is communicated fairly precisely opener's partner will normally pass and hope that the contract will be made. With good support raise to 4 in the suit, and with overall strength on a balanced hand raise to 3NT. But remember that the original bid denotes weakness not strength. In response to 3♠ pass with a hand such as ♠JX ♥AQXX ♦KQX ♣JXXX.

An opening bid of four indicates the same thing, but with at least eight trumps, and similar considerations apply. Higher opening bids are pointless, except on hands containing consecutive top cards in all suits represented, and they tend to be rarely dealt in honest games.

SLAM BIDDING Because slams earn hefty bonuses on their own account the whole course of the bidding becomes shaped towards the establishment of a correct slam contract should it become clear that one is in sight. By the time bidding has reached the levels of three and four, and a suit is agreed, it becomes imperative to identify precise top card holdings – certainly all the Aces for a small slam and the Kings as well for a grand slam.

The most popular convention for this purpose is Blackwood. With a slam in view, and a suit agreed, one player initiates the convention by making an artificial bid of 4NT. This requests partner to show how many Aces he holds by replying as follows: 5♣ = none or all four, 5♦ = one, 5♥ = two, 5♠ = three. If it then becomes clear that all four are held by the partnership, a further bid of 5NT calls for partner's number of Kings according to the same code, except that all four is represented by the reply 6NT so that the response 6♣ is an unambiguous 'none'. A void suit can also be indicated by means of a jump in level – e.g., to 4NT, the response 6♦ (instead of 5♦) shows one Ace and a void.

Blackwood is not without drawbacks, and other conventions are capable of greater precision. The important thing to note is that a bid of 4NT is not necessarily a Blackwood call for Aces. If no suit has been agreed it is a natural 4NT bid as, for example, in the following sequences: (a) 1NT–4NT, (b) 1♠–1NT, 4NT–?, (c) 2NT–4NT. But it would be conventional in (d) 1♥–3♦, 3NT–4NT, where, although no trump has been agreed, the jump-raise from 1 to 3 is forcing enough for the whiff of a slam.

Here is an example of Blackwood in practice, with a twist in the plot.

South: ♠2 ♥KQT ♦AKQ62 ♣KJT6
North: ♠AKQJ4 ♥J6 ♦QJ ♣Q985
S: 1♦ 18 pts, diamonds longest
N: 2♠ jump bid forces to game
S: 3♣ shows a second suit
N: 4♣ shows support for it
S: 4NT asks for Aces (Blackwood)
N: 5♦ shows one

This is an embarrassment to South as they are short of two Aces and cannot therefore bid beyond 5-level. The best contract is 5NT but if he called it North would regard it as the Blackwood call for Kings and reply 6♦ with disastrous results. He therefore employs a 'transfer' bid of the already rejected heart suit so that his partner can name the contract:

S: 5♥ space-filling transfer bid

N: 5NT, which South passes, leaving them in the right contract.

DEFENSIVE BIDDING A defensive bid is the first one made by an opponent of the opening bidder. Typically, South as dealer opens, and West 'butts in' with a defensive bid before North can respond. The normal requirement for butting in is length rather than strength, as without a solid suit there is the danger of being immediately doubled and going down expensively. Thus a hand such as ♠KQJT9X ♥XX ♦KXX ♣XX would justify butting in with 1♠ though it counts only 11 including distribution and would be useless as an opening bid. But a hand like ♠AXX ♥XXX ♦AXX ♣AJXX, though worth 13 and strong enough to open, would be fool-hardy as a defence attempt. A two-over-one butt-in, of course, needs strength in addition to length. Generally, a defensive bidder must expect to be able to play the contract in the suit he names, as there may not be enough bidding space for niceties of communication.

His partner, similarly, should respond in the same suit if he has at least three prospective trumps; otherwise, and with under 10 points, he should pass.

With a long suit and additional strength, defender can jump-bid one level higher than necessary to overcall, suggesting at least a solid six-card suit, or two of five, with self-support. The sort of hand on which he might have opened 3 in suit may justify a pre-emptive double-jump to three-over-one.

Other options are: bidding at NT, raising the opener's suit (*cue-bidding*). and doubling (informatorily).

Bid 1NT with normal opening requirements for that purpose, but not if unguarded in the opener's suit. A stronger hand, such as ♠AJX ♥AQX ♦AKXX ♣KJX, following an opening bid of 1♥, would justify a defensive 2NT but it is tactically better to double and await partner's response.

Cue-bidding, which denotes butting in with a raise of opener's own suit, is a purely conventional device (it could hardly be a serious bid) to show sufficient strength to open up an exploration of game possibilities. Example: 1♠ is opened by your right opponent and you hold ♠X ♥AKQXXX ♦AKQXX ♣A. Jump in with 2♠. A slam could be on the cards.

Assuming a pass from opener's partner, respond to a minimum overbid only with considerable support from your hand, as weakness is implied; but a jump overbid implies strength, so raise if you can support the suit. Respond to 1NT as if partner had opened.

If lying fourth to an opening bid, followed by two passes, any bid you make is a protective reopening. From this position you know that opener may have anything from 12 points up but that his partner is weak. It follows that your own partner passed, not necessarily out of weakness, for you must now credit him with some points, but for lack of information: he may have avoided butting in for fear of being doubled and finding you with a hopeless hand. In such a situation it would be wasteful to pass on a hand good enough to open.

INFORMATORY DOUBLES A useful option open to a defender is to double. This is described as an *informatory, take-out* or *negative* double and is forcing for one round (partner must make an offer). Such a move requires 12–13 points and support in unbid suits, or a little less with a well-distributed hand such as 4–4–4–1. An opening bid of 1♦ can be doubled on ♠AJXX ♥KXXX ♦XX ♣AQX. (Sometimes a better way of showing strength is to make a suit take-out. Example: with ♠X ♥AQJXX ♦AQXX ♣QJX it would be better to call 2♥ than to double an opening 1♠, otherwise a call of 2♠ from your left could shut you out of the bidding.)

In response to a double followed by a pass, you must not pass except with an extraordinarily long holding in the suit opened, sufficient to invite a trump lead. With a weak hand, bid as cheaply as you can but prefer a major suit if possible.

It is important to recognize an informatory double when you hear one. A double has this conventional use only when (a) doubler's partner has not yet spoken; or, if he has, has only passed; (b) doubler has doubled at his first opportunity to do so; (c) the doubled bid was in suit and not above 3-level (unless pre-emptive). Otherwise the double is a genuine business or penalty double.

PENALTY DOUBLES Contrary to beginners' expectations low contracts are generally safer to double than high ones. Much depends on how the contract was reached. If opponents have been bidding without competition it is on principle unwise to double without at least one trick in trumps and the expectation of two undertricks. An uncontested slam bid is even riskier because of the potential loss/gain balance: if they make it, they get a hefty bonus as well as the doubled values; if not, you just get the doubled values. When the bidding has been competitive be on the look-out for doubling possibilities. A shortage in your partner's suit, four trumps including an honour and two defensive tricks in plain suits make for a promising double. But do not double where it could be more profitable to pursue your own contract, and take more care at higher levels.

REDOUBLING It is often wiser to redouble on the risk of going down by one trick than on a cast-iron contract, as the redouble of a sure thing is only likely to provoke the opposition into bidding further.

CARD PLAY – GENERAL Basic principles of trick-play are much the same as at any other Whist-like game, knowledge of which can be carried over successfully into Bridge and thereafter improved with practice. The chief difference is that, in Bridge, much more information about the lie of cards is known from the outset – partly through the bidding and particularly through sight of the dummy. This requires the declarer, especially, to play in a far more calculating and Chess-like way than is possible in any other conventional card game. To appreciate this point fully, and be able to take advantage of it, it is really desirable for complete beginners to gain experience at Whist before embarking upon Bridge.

DECLARER'S PLAY As soon as dummy goes down declarer must evaluate all 26 cards and determine his line of play.

Few contracts, if properly made, play themselves, and advance planning is essential to bring them to a successful conclusion. In particular, he will be constantly planning the entries to each hand to ensure that the lead comes from the right side of the table at the right time.

In a no-trump contract it is a comparatively straightforward question of counting high-card and possibly long-card tricks and ensuring that all suits are kept under control so that the defenders may not jump in with their best suit and take too many tricks. Always count the number they need to beat the contract, and identify their possible sources of defensive tricks. Normal practice for the declarer is to establish his side's longest suit first, though, with top controls in three suits, it may be advantageous to tackle the problem suit first.

At no trump do not always win a trick just because you can. Some cards are sure losers and are better lost early than late by means of the *hold-up*. (Example: King is led from your left against X–X in dummy and A–X–X in hand. The 'X's are losers anyway; by throwing them to the first two leads of that suit and holding up the Ace until the third round you retain command of the suit and reduce the number of leads in it that can be subsequently made against you.)

Basic procedure in a trump contract is to draw trumps first then play the rest of the hand as at no trump. But this is not the commonest procedure, as it depends upon having unbeatable trumps and no plain suit weakness, which is not usually the case. At the opposite end there are hands on which trumps should not be drawn at all, notably those in which the contract can only be made by constant cross-ruffing – i.e., so planning the play as to permit each hand to win tricks by ruffing leads in its eventually void suit. In between are the commonest trump situations requiring the delayed or gradual drawing of trumps, some being reserved for strategic ruffing.

The use of the *finesse* (see Whist) to gain a needed trick is often over-used by beginners. In some situations it is the only way of succeeding, but as success is a 50/50 chance experienced players will generally look around for (and usually find) an alternative means to the same end.

DEFENDERS' PLAY From the defenders' point of view the opening lead is critical, as it is made before dummy goes down and is therefore the most blindly played card of the pack. Yet the right lead can sometimes break a contract against which a wrong lead would have no chance. For this reason a number of standard openings have been developed which experience shows to be the best available in the long run.

Against a no-trump contract, lead your partner's suit or, if he made no bid, your own longest suit. Of partner's suit lead (a) the lowest from a three-card holding of A–X–X, K–X–X, Q–X–X or J–X–X; (b) your fourth highest from J–X–X–X or from five or more 'X's (see section on Whist for significance of fourth highest); (c) your highest from two or more consecutive honours, or from a sequence of three or more headed by an honour. But with A–K etc., lead the King. Your general object thereby is to attack the contract in your partner's longest suit, allowing yourselves the best chance of taking the first trick, and at the same time communicating something about your holding in it.

The lead against no trumps from your own hand if partner has not named a suit must be from your own longest suit, with the aim of establishing it and eventually running through it. Lead the fourth highest, or the highest from a sequence of three or more headed by an honour. Of course, if this suit has been mentioned in the bidding against you, its lead would play right into your opponents' hands. In this event try another long suit, or lead the lowest from A–X–X or K–X–X. Avoid leading a singleton or from a doubleton.

Against a trump contract the object is not to establish a long suit but to make the most of high cards before they can be trumped. From partner's suit (assuming he has bid and you have nothing outstanding to offer) lead the lowest from K–X–X, Q–X–X or X–X–X–X, otherwise the highest. From your own best suit lead the highest of a sequence, or the Ace if held, or the King from A–K and at least one other. The lead of a singleton or from a doubleton, with a view to early ruffing, is not bad and may be the only way, given contract, but it can have the disadvantage of enabling declarer to place key cards. Trumps may be led if nothing better offers itself and you feel it more advantageous to have your plain suits led into.

For the rule of eleven and the device of petering, see Whist.

Bridge Variants

AUCTION BRIDGE Forerunner of Contract, Auction Bridge was introduced in 1904 and is characterized by competitive bidding to determine trumps and by above/below-line scoring; it has simpler but less refined than scoring than Contract (it is possible to win a game by taking enough over-tricks, which tends to favour underbidding). Play as Contract except that each odd trick taken above 6, whether or not bid, scores 6 in ♣, 7 in ♦, 8 in ♥, 9 in ♠, 10 at NT, increased by doubling/redoubling as the case may be. These count below the line towards game, which is 30 points. First to win two wins the rubber for 250 above-the-line bonus. Above-the-line bonuses are also awarded for winning doubled contract 50, redoubled 100, plus 50 per overtrick doubled or 100 doubled; for winning small slam 50, grand slam 100; for defeating contract 50 per undertrick, or 100 doubled, 200 redoubled. There are elaborate scores for honours (AKQJT of trumps, or Aces only at NT), also above the line: at NT, 100 for four Aces in one hand, 40 for four divided, 30 for three whether or not divided; in suit, value of trump suit multiplied by 10 for five honours in one hand, 9 if split four-one, 8 for four only but in one hand, 5 for five split three-two, 4 for four divided, 2 for three whether divided or not.

BIRITCH (BRIDGE) First published in Britain as Russian Whist in 1883, though introduced some six years earlier, the original game from which all Bridge developments sprang was a cross between Whist and the native Russian game of Vint. Its distinguishing feature, besides the scoring, was that the trump suit was nominated by the dealer.

BRIDGE-WHIST 1896 development of the above. Dealer could nominate trumps or 'bridge' this privilege to his partner. It was this form of the game that started the craze which virtually wiped Whist off the social map. Supplanted by Auction Bridge.

BRINT Version of Contract with Vint scoring (*q.v.*), which has much to commend it. (Devised by J. B. Chambers.)

DUPLICATE BRIDGE Arrangement used in tournaments whereby the same hands are dealt at different tables.

FOUR-DEAL BRIDGE (CHICAGO) Contract with souped-up scoring. A rubber is four deals, with neither side vulnerable in the first, both vulnerable in the fourth, dealer's side only vulnerable in the others. Bonus of 300 for 'game' (100 below) or of 500 if vulnerable. Bonus of 100 for a part score on fourth deal.

FIVE-SUIT BRIDGE See Quintract.

LILY BRIDGE Alternative name for Bridge-Whist. Spades as trumps normally ranked low (2 per trick), but could be raised above hearts (8) for a value of 9 by bidding 'royal spades', also known colloquially as 'lilies'.

NULLOS A contract to *lose* the stated number of odd tricks, playing at no trump, ranks between spades and no trump. Thus a bid of 'two nullos' is an offer to win no more than five tricks in all, and 'seven nullos' is a complete misère. Admirable in principle, but over-complicated in practice as it nullifies existing bidding systems.

PIRATE BRIDGE Version of Auction which cuts across pre-fixed partnerships by enabling any player to accept another's bid and so become his partner for one deal.

PIVOT BRIDGE A 'change-your-partners' method of playing Bridge in large gatherings so that partnerships are equalized.

PLAFOND Transitional between Auction and Contract, this French development (*c.* 1918) introduced the feature whereby only *contracted* odd-tricks counted to game, overtricks being relegated to above-line status. It was from this that Vanderbilt developed modern Contract, adding the element of vulnerability (amongst other scoring changes).

PROGRESSIVE BRIDGE Arrangement whereby players progress from table to table.

QUINTRACT Silly name for five-suited Bridge, briefly popular in the 1930s, including a suit of (green) crowns called Royals in Britain, or of (blue) Eagles in America, and ranking between spades and no trump.

ROYAL SPADE BRIDGE See Lily Bridge.

ROYALTON Scoring-variant of Auction Bridge.

RUBBER BRIDGE Standard home-and-club form of Contract in which two won games win the rubber, as distinct from tournament Bridge in which rubbers are not counted.

SUPER CONTRACT The inevitable 'add a Joker for super fun' variant. The 53rd card is dealt face up and declarer may take it in exchange for any card in his hand, which is discarded face up. The Joker may be used by its holder as the highest card of any suit he chooses but not one that he has already renounced. It counts as an honour, both in suit and at no trump, and a player holding all honours scores 300.

Three-hand Bridge

3 players
1 pack (52)

BOOBY Deal 17 each and one face down to dummy. Each player selects four cards from his hand and throws them face down to dummy. Bid in the usual way but with the addition of misère bids of nullo ranking between hearts and spades. (See *Nullos* above for explanation.) Declarer plays dummy as at four-hand Bridge. Nullos are valued at 30 points. (Game devised by Hubert Phillips.)

CUT-THROAT BRIDGE Deal four hands, including a face-down dummy. Bid as at Contract. Declarer plays dummy as at Contract. If declarer is defeated each opponent scores above the line. Players are individually vulnerable or not vulnerable. First to win two games scores 500 rubber bonus, or 700 if neither opponent has won a game (or 250 if Auction Bridge scoring is used). There are several variations on this theme.

TOWIE Deal four hands and turn six of the dummy cards face up. The highest bidder becomes the declarer, turning up and playing the whole of the dummy hand as at contract. If all players pass, or if the proposed contract is insufficient for game (i.e., worth less than 100), the same dealer redeals a 'goulash' hand as follows. Each player sorts his hand into suits so that cards of one suit are together, though not necessarily in ranking order. Dealer sorts all dummy cards in the same way, permitting the others to see how they are arranged. Then dealer lays his own hand face down on the table, upon which are placed, face down and in this order, those of his left opponent, dummy, and fourth player. After a cut, dealer redeals in batches a 5–5–3. Finally, he shuffles the dummy cards and turns six face up. The same procedure follows until a sufficient contract is reached. Odd tricks contracted and won score as at Contract except that NT tricks count 35 throughout. Overtricks score 50 each unless doubled or redoubled (100 and 200 respectively), and (re)-doubled overtricks are doubled again if declarer was vulnerable. Bonus of 50 for making a doubled contract, or 100 redoubled, in either case doubled again if vulnerable. Honours and slams as at Contract. Undertrick penalties are 50 each, or 100 doubled or 200 redoubled, but are greater if declarer was vulnerable: 100 for the first undertrick, 300 for the second, 500 for the third and so on in 200 increments, these penalties being twice or four times as great if doubled or redoubled. Bonus of 500 for game, 1000 for the rubber. (Game devised by J. Leonard Replogle.)

Two-hand Bridge

DOUBLE DUMMY Deal four hands, two of them face down. Players bid on what they can see in their own hands. After the auction the dummy opposite each player is turned face up and each plays alternately from his own hand and from his dummy's. Alternatively (and more realistically) the dummies are not open to both players. Instead, after the bidding, each places his own dummy in such a position that the other cannot see exactly how the opposing cards are split. (An easily home-made card-holder for this purpose consists of a shoe box, with lid, placed upside down on the table. The dummy cards are slipped down between the lid and the side of the box. If only one box is available, the players play at opposite sides of it.)

DRAW AND DISCARD Shuffle the cards thoroughly and place them face down to form a stock. Starting with non-dealer each in turn draws the top card of stock, looks at it, and either (a) keeps it, ending his turn, or (b) discards it face down and draws the next, which he must then keep. As soon as a player has 13 cards he stops drawing. When both have 13 they bid and play in Contract Bridge fashion. The rejected cards have no part to play in the game.

DRAW BRIDGE. See Honeymoon Bridge.

HONEYMOON BRIDGE Deal 13 cards each and place the rest face down as a stock. Non-dealer leads and tricks are played at no trump. It is theoretically obligatory to follow suit if possible but, as the rule is unenforceable, it may be dispensed with. The winner of a trick throws it face down to one side, as it has no part to play in the rest of the game or the scoring, and draws the top card of the stock to add to his hand before leading. His opponent then draws the next before replying. As soon as the last card has been drawn players bid on and play their last 13 cards as at Contract Bridge and score accordingly. Variant: before leading to each trick, leader exposes the top card of stock so that each player may gauge whether or not he wishes to win the trick. The loser of a trick draws an unknown card, of course. This version considerably improves the strategy of the game.

MEMORY BRIDGE Deal 13 each and place the rest face down to form a stock. The first 13 are played as tricks at no trump. Non-dealer leads and it is obligatory to follow suit. There is no drawing from stock. The player who takes more scores in Contract Bridge fashion, as for a bid of 1NT, and adds a premium of 100 above the line. The remaining cards are then dealt, bid on, played and scored as at Contract Bridge.

SINGLE DUMMY Deal four hands of 13 cards including two dummies. After the deal one dummy is turned face up. Players bid as at Contract. Bidding over, the declarer announces whether he will play with the exposed dummy or take his chance with the concealed one. Then the concealed dummy is turned up and play proceeds as at Double Dummy.

Whist ⚇

4 players
1 pack (52)

I was delighted to see him again, and suggested we should have a game of Whist with a dummy, and by way of merriment said, '*You* can be the dummy.' Cummings (I thought rather ill naturedly) . . . said he couldn't stop, he only called to leave me the *Bicycle News*, as he had done with it.

(G. and W. Grossmith, *The Diary of a Nobody*, 1892)

Whist derives from a sixteenth-century English game called Trump, or Ruff and Honours, which may or may not have had some connection with the French game of Triomphe, the ancestor of Ecarté. During the seventeenth century it became known as Whisk and then Whist. In one of the earliest books on card games, the *Compleat Gamester* of 1674, Charles Cotton did not bother to detail how the game was played since 'Every Child almost of Eight years old hath a competent knowledg in that recreation'. For another fifty years it remained a pastime of the lower orders, probably because of its uncommon simplicity. But in 1728 Lord Folkestone and friends, who hob-nobbed at the Crown Coffeehouse in Bedford Row, suddenly discovered logic and precision in its very simplicity and discovered ways of playing the game systematically. Hoyle's *Short Treatise* on the game appeared in 1742, and from then until the appearance of Bridge at the very end of the nineteenth century, Whist was universally regarded as the greatest card game in the world. Since its eclipse by Bridge, Whist has reverted to its original status, remaining a popular family game and still widely pursued in communal Whist drives. Whist is now unjustly neglected by serious players. Nobody should learn Bridge without playing Whist first and many Bridge players would improve their game immensely by going on a crash diet of Whist only. Of the variants listed after the main description Contract Whist may be recommended as a transition between the two games.

CARDS Standard 52-card pack, ranking AKQJT98765432.

DEAL Thirteen each, one at a time and face down. The last (52nd) card is turned face up to determine a trump suit before being taken up into dealer's hand.

OBJECT Players sitting opposite each other are partners. A rubber is won by the first side to win two games. A game is won by the first side to win 5 points, which may take one or several deals. The object of play is to win a majority of the 13 tricks, i.e., seven or more. A partnership scores 1 point for every trick it takes in excess of six. (Six tricks constitute a *book*; those in excess are called *odd tricks*.) Points are also scored for *honours*, these being the AKQ and J of trumps. A side scores 4 points for holding four honours or 2 for holding any three, but these are not credited until the hands have been played out, and must therefore be remembered.

PLAY The player at dealer's left leads to the first trick. Others in turn must follow suit if possible, otherwise may trump or renounce *ad lib*. The trick is won by the highest card of the suit led, or by the highest trump if any are played. The winner of one trick leads to the next.

SCORE Whichever side took more tricks scores 1 point per odd trick. Whichever side held three or four honours, whether in one hand or between the two, scores 2 or 4 respectively – unless, however, they already have a score of 4 points towards game, in which case the honours are not counted. If both sides have two honours, no honours are scored.

PENALTY SCORE The penalty for a revoke (a player failing to follow suit though able to do so) is 3 points, which the opponents may either add to their own score or subtract from that of the revoking side. In counting towards game the score for a revoke takes priority over the score for tricks.

GAME SCORE The side first to reach or exceed 5 points wins the game (and, if applicable, thereby prevents the other from scoring for honours). The winning side counts a single game point if the other made 3 or 4 points, a double if the other made only 1 or 2 points, a treble if the other made no score. The side that first wins two games adds two game points for the rubber. The margin of victory is the difference between the two sides' total of game points (as distinct from trick and honour points). Thus the highest possible game score is 8–0, the winning side having won two trebles plus 2 for the rubber.

VARIANTS

These affect the scoring only. The game described above is the classic form of English Short Whist. Also to be noted are:

AMERICAN WHIST The first side to reach or exceed 7 points for tricks wins the game, its value being the difference between the two sides' scores. Honours are not counted.

LONG WHIST Until about 1800 the game was played up to 10 (sometimes 9) points, and was subsequently known as Long Whist to distinguish it from the faster and more exciting 5-point game. Serious players continued to maintain that Long Whist was the more 'scientific' game.

NOTES ON PLAY

Normal strategy is for each side to win tricks in their longest suit – the one in which they hold most cards between them. First, each partner seeks to indicate his best (usually longest) suit by leading it at the earliest opportunity or by discarding a low card from it when unable to follow suit to the card led. Next, they seek to establish their suit by forcing out any high cards the opponents hold in it so that they cannot win when that suit is constantly led. Having established it, however, they must first try to clear the trumps out of play so that the opponents cannot beat the established suit by ruffing and so get into the lead with their own best suit or suits.

It is usually right for the person lying second to the trick to play low unless he is certain of winning the trick or has only two of the suit led (as explained below). The third should normally play high in an attempt to win unless he is sure that his partner's lead is unbeatable. The fourth, of course, is in the most favourable position and will play as he sees fit.

The player who leads to the first trick has the advantage, besides that of setting the pace, of being best able to communicate information to his partner about the state of his hand, as his choice of card is completely free. He must therefore lead from his longest suit to show his partner which one he thinks they have a good chance of establishing, and his partner, in turn, will normally be expected to lead the same suit back as soon as he gets the chance – unless he feels he has a better suit. It is possible, by carefully selecting the rank of the first card played, to convey to the partner what sort of holding the lead is made from, whether strong or weak. For this purpose some highly elaborate signals or 'conventional leads' were worked out when the game was most in vogue, many of which have subsequently been carried over into the game of Bridge. They may be condensed and simplified as follows.

Lead from your longest plain (non-trump) suit, a suit of which you hold four or more cards. From two of equal length, play the one that has the highest cards.

If the top cards of the opening suit form one of the following patterns, lead to the first and second tricks as indicated below:

AKQJ: lead K then J
AKQ–: lead K then Q
AK–J: lead K then A
A–QJ: lead A then Q
–KQJ: lead J

With any other Ace holding, lead the King if you have it; if not, lead first the Ace and then the fourth best card of that suit (as it was before the Ace was led). Holding neither Ace nor King, lead your fourth best of the suit. Example: from Q9873, lead the Seven.

Trumps may be led if you hold five or more, the appropriate signals being:

AKQJ: lead J then Q
AKQ: lead Q then K
AK: lead K then A if holding seven trumps at least. Otherwise, and lacking all these patterns, lead your fourth best trump.

The lead of the fourth best is not a meaningless convention but enables a partner to get a good idea of the lie of the cards against him by means of a calculation called the 'rule of eleven'. If your partner leads his fourth best you subtract the value of that card from eleven and the result tells you how many higher cards are lacking from his hand. By subtracting from that total any you hold yourself, you learn how many lie with the other side. For example: your partner leads the Seven and you hold the King and Jack of the suit. Seven from eleven means four cards against him, of which you hold two. If he were leading from Ace and others he would have led the Ace, so that must be held by an opponent. So his original holding must have been any four cards out of QT987 (regardless of anything lower), and the opponents hold between them the Ace and any one of QT98.

If you are third hand and your right opponent plays higher than your partner's lead in a suit of which you hold the Ace and Queen, it is proper to attempt to win the trick by playing the Queen, in the hope that your left opponent does not hold the King. (The chances are equal that he or your partner holds it.) This attempt to win a trick with a card that is not the highest in its suit is called a *finesse*. If the Queen wins, the finesse succeeds against the King and your Ace/Queen combination wins two tricks instead of one. The same principle can be extended to other combinations of cards and other playing situations. By its nature the finesse is a risk and should therefore not be employed if its failure is likely to lose more than its success would gain. It is applicable to all trick-taking card games.

Except when trying to win a trick, always play the lowest you can of the suit led. But if you have only two left in the suit it is proper to play the higher first and the lower to a subsequent trick. This conventional device is a way of indicating to your partner – if he is awake – that you are thereafter void in the suit and so able to trump it if led. By extension, any play of an unnecessarily high card before a lower one in the same suit is a signal (known as the Blue Peter, from which has derived *petering* in Bridge) that you wish him to lead trumps at his earliest opportunity.

Advantage may be gained from a suit in which you are void (have none left). If the suit is led you may either seek to win the trick by ruffing or renounce by playing a card of some other suit. A renounce may be used for one of two purposes. Early in the game, if you have a strong suit but have not yet taken a trick, you may discard low from that suit in order to draw your partner's attention to your best suit. Or, since you nearly always have one or more cards that are certain losers, you take advantage of the opportunity to throw a losing card on it, possibly for the purpose of voiding yet another plain suit. When both partners are void in different suits they may be able to set up an annihilation of the opposition by a process of *cross-ruffing*: one player leads into his partner's void suit, his partner wins the trick by ruffing, and then follows by leading into the first partner's void suit . . . and so on.

In connection with voids, avoid the beginner's habit of leading from a suit in which he holds only one card (a singleton) or exactly two (doubleton). The idea is to create an early void in order to start trumping. But the effort is pointless. For one thing it prevents one from making an informative opening lead, which is to waste a strong advantage. For another, the short suit will be led eventually with precisely the same effect, so nothing will be gained.

ILLUSTRATIVE DEAL West deals, turns up ♠J for trumps. The hands are:

North: ♠A983 ♥93 ♣AQJT2 ♦Q6
East: ♠KT6 ♥AK ♣965 ♦KT842
South: ♠Q72 ♥J852 ♣84 ♦A753
West: ♠J54 ♥QT764 ♣K73 ♦J9

North leads; the winning card of each trick is underlined.

N	E	S	W	
♣A	♣5	♣8	♣3	Leads from longest suit
♣Q	♣6	♣K		Second conventional lead
♥3	♥K	♥2	♥6	West leads 4th best of longest
♥9	♥A	♥5	♥4	East pursues partner's suit . . . .

N	E	S	W	
♦Q	♦4	♦3	♦J	. . . and leads 4th best of his own
♠3	♠6	♠Q	♠4	North starts to clear trumps
♠A	♠T	♠7	♠5	South helps by leading them
♠8	♠K	♠2	♠J	Now North has the only trump left
♦6	♦K	♦A	♦9	East tries his partner's suit
♠9	♦2	♦5	♥7	But South noted North's peter
♣J	♣9	♦7	♣7	North can now bring clubs home . . .
♣T	♦8	♥8	♥T	. . . and, with the suit established
♣2	♦T	♥J	♥Q	. . . even the lowest wins a trick

North/South win by nine tricks to four, scoring 3 for odd tricks. Honours divided.

Whist Variants

BID WHIST Instead of turning a trump card, each in turn may bid how many tricks he would propose to take in conjunction with his partner if allowed to nominate trumps. But no suit is stated in the bidding – just the number of odd tricks, and each bid must be numerically higher than the preceding. When a bid is followed by three passes, the bidder announces trumps and play begins. If the contract succeeds bidder's side scores 1 point per odd trick taken; if it is beaten opponents score 1 point per odd trick they took and bidder's side is set back by the number bid – i.e., a bid of 2 odd tricks reduces their score by 2 if lost. There are variations on this theme, but by far the best game of its type is Contract Whist.

BRIDGE WHIST See Bridge variants.

CAYENNE At each deal a suit is established as the cayenne suit by cutting either the playing pack or, preferably, a second pack and noting the suit of the top card of the bottom packet. The purpose of the cayenne suit is to establish, for that deal only, an order of preference in the suits as follows:

If cayenne is	♥	♦	♣	♠	× 4 if trumps
Second colour is	♦	♥	♠	♣	× 3 if trumps
Third colour is	♣	♣	♥	♥	× 2 if trumps
Fourth colour is	♠	♠	♦	♦	× 1 if trumps

Each player receives 13 cards in batches of 4–4–5. Dealer may select the trump suit, or, if his hand is indeterminate, he may call upon his partner to do so, who must then name the game. Whoever decides has six options and announces one of the following: cayenne, second colour, third colour, fourth colour, grand, nullo. If the bid is grand or nullo there is no trump suit. The object at grand is to win the majority of tricks and at nullo to lose the majority (i.e., to take fewer than seven). If one of the suits is named the object is to win the majority. At the end of play whichever side took the majority of tricks counts a basic 1 point per odd trick, and whichever side held the majority of honours (AKQJT of trumps) scores a basic 2 if they held three, 4 if they held four, or 6 if they held five. In either case the basic score (for tricks and/or honours) is then multiplied by the value of the suit selected as trumps in accordance with the above table. For example, if the cayenne suit was clubs and the trump suit spades (second colour), the basic score is multiplied by 3. At grand the multiplier is 8 but there are no honours. At nullo the winning side scores the number of odd tricks taken by their opponents × 8 and also without honours. Eldest hand leads and normal rules of trick-taking apply except that, at nullo, the Ace of each suit ranks below the deuce *unless* the player of one declares it to be higher than the King before the next card (if any) is played to the trick. The first side to make 10 points wins a game and the first to win four games wins the rubber for a bonus of 8 points.

CONTRACT WHIST A cross between Whist and Contract Bridge invented by Hubert Phillips and combining the best of both worlds, i.e., the trick-play of Whist with the bidding of Bridge. It forms a good introduction to Bridge for those who already know Whist, or acts as an advanced form of Whist for those who dislike the dummy feature and excessively complex scoring of Bridge. The preliminaries, deal and auction proceed as at Contract Bridge. Bidding systems and conventions employed in Bridge are applicable to Contract Whist but may be modified by the fact that there is no scoring distinction between major and minor suits and no bonus for slams. Scores are made above and below the line as at Bridge and only tricks contracted and won count towards game, which is 10 points below the line. The opening lead is made by the player sitting at the left of that member of the declaring side who first named the suit of the final contract, and play proceeds as at Bridge except that declarer's partner does not reveal his cards but plays from his own hand concealed. If the contract succeeds the declarers score (below the line) 3 points per contracted odd trick in a trump suit or 4 at no trump, or twice that amount if doubled or four times if redoubled. Any overtricks, whether in suit or at no trump, score (above the line) 2 each, or 5 if doubled, or 10 if redoubled. In addition there is a flat bonus of 5 for succeeding in a doubled contract or 10 if redoubled. If the contract is beaten the defenders score (above the line) 10 points for each undertrick, or 20 if doubled, 40 if redoubled. The first side to reach or exceed 10 below the line wins a game, and the first to win two games wins the rubber and a bonus of 50.

CHINESE WHIST A non-partnership variant, also playable by three or two players. Deal six each face down, which each player lines up (without looking at them) on the table before him. On top of these deal six more cards face up in one-to-one correspondence. Finally, deal the last single cards which each player takes into hand. Dealer nominates trumps and the first lead is made by the player at his left. Normal rules of trick-taking apply. A player may play any of his face-up cards or the one in his hand, but not a face-down card. When a faced card is played the card it covers is immediately exposed and becomes available for play.

DUPLICATE WHIST System of team play whereby the same hands are dealt at different tables.

DUTCH WHIST A partnership game with different rules on each of four deals. Deal 1: play as standard partnership

Whist. Deal 2: ditto, but with no trump. Deal 3: ditto, but no card is turned for trump, which instead is announced at his pleasure by eldest hand as he leads to the first trick. Deal 4s standard Whist again except that a trump is cut before play instead of being turned as last, and everyone is confronted with the onerous task of remembering what it is. There is a three-player equivalent called Bismarck.

FAVOURITE WHIST Whichever suit is turned for the first deal remains the 'favourite' for the rest of the rubber, and in the first deal and whenever it comes up again the scores for tricks and honours are automatically doubled.

NORWEGIAN WHIST No card is turned and there are no trumps (ever). The game is played either grand, in which case each side's object is to take a majority of tricks, or nullo, in which case it is to lose the majority. Eldest hand has first option to proclaim grand or nullo and if he passes (having middling cards) the privilege passes to the left until someone makes a decision. If all pass the game is played nullo. If the bid is grand the player at bidder's left makes the opening lead; if nullo the player at his right (or dealer's if all pass) leads first, though in either case all play still rotates to the left. At grand, bidder's side scores 4 per odd trick, or, if they fail, opponents score 8 per odd trick. At nullo, either side scores 2 for each odd trick taken by the opponents. Game is 50 up.

PRUSSIAN WHIST Superfluous name given to ordinary Whist when a trump suit is established by cutting a second pack.

REJOUÉ Alternative name for Duplicate Whist.

RUSSIAN WHIST See Vint.

SUIT-VALUE WHIST Odd tricks score 1 point each with spades as trump, 2 with clubs, 3 with diamonds, 4 with hearts. Game is 10 up; honours not counted.

VINT A Russian Whist-like game ancestral to Bridge. Play as Whist except that a trump suit is established by bidding. Bid as at Bridge except that suits rank from low to high ♠ ♣ ♦ ♥ NT. Contract is established after *eight* consecutive passes. The chief point of interest is the scoring. Regardless of the trump situation each contracted odd trick scores (below the line) 10 times the value of the contract – i.e., 10 if the bid was 'one', 20 if 'two', and so on. Game is won by the first side to make 500 below the line. Above-line bonuses as follows: for winning a game, 1000; for winning the rubber (two games), 2000 extra; for taking 12 tricks 1000 + 5000 if 'six' was bid; for taking 13 tricks 2000 + 5000 if 'six' or 10,000 if 'seven' was bid; for defeating a contract 100 × trick value per undertrick. (Complicated scores for honours also apply.)

Three-hand Whist

3 players
1 pack (52)

BISMARCK Each player deals four times in succession, so that a game lasts twelve deals. Dealer receives 20 cards, from which he rejects any four face down, the others receive 16 cards each. As at Dutch Whist there is a different procedure at each deal. Deal 1: no trump. Dealer scores 1 point for each trick he takes above eight, each opponent 1 point per trick taken above four. Deal 2: a trump suit is established by cutting or turning the last card and the scoring is as before. Deal 3: dealer chooses the trump suit, and the play and score are as before. Deal 4: there is no trump and the object is to avoid winning tricks. Dealer scores 1 point for every trick he took less than four, each opponent for every trick he took less than six. Eldest hand always leads and normal rules of trick-taking apply throughout.

CHINESE WHIST As for four players (see p. 67), but deal eight each face down, eight face up, one in hand, and leave the 52nd card face down out of play.

DUMMY (DUMBY) Deal three hands and a dummy hand, the latter face up on the opposite side of the table from the person playing it. Each takes the dummy for the duration of a rubber, which is five points up, and a game is three rubbers. Lowest cut at the start of the game takes dummy in the first rubber, highest in the third.

SERGEANT MAJOR A similar sort of exercise to Bismarck (above), with the dealer discarding four from a 20-card hand after turning the last for trumps. Each deals in turn and the object in each deal is for the dealer to win at least eight tricks, the player on his left five, and the other three. Each scores 1 point per trick taken in excess of his quota.

Two-hand Whist

DOUBLE DUMMY Players sit at connected sides of the table (not opposite each other), the one cutting the lower card choosing whether to sit to the right or left of his opponent (right is advantageous). Deal four hands including two dummies, one opposite each player, the first card of the pack going to dealer's dummy. Turn the dummies face up. Non-dealer leads and play proceeds to the left, each playing alternately from his own hand and from dummy.

GERMAN WHIST Deal six each and place the rest face down to form a stock. Face the top card to establish trumps. Non-dealer leads to the first trick, normal rules of trick-taking apply (it is obligatory to follow suit if possible) and the winner of a trick draws the top card of the stock and adds it to his hand. The loser draws the next card unseen and the previous trick-winner, before leading to the next, faces the top card of stock. Play continues normally when the stock is exhausted until neither has any left, and the player who has taken the majority of the 13 tricks scores the difference between the two totals.

HUMBUG Players sit opposite each other. Deal four hands, two of them dummies. Each player announces whether he will play with the cards dealt him or exchange. In the latter event he exchanges his hand for the dummy on his right, which he takes as his new hand and must then play. Thirteen tricks are then played each consisting of two cards only. Scoring and trump-establishment as at Whist.

Ninety-nine   ⚇

3 players
1 short pack (36)

Ninety-nine is a modern descendant of the Whist family and, unlike most, is specifically designed for three players. A further unusual feature is that all three players make a contract and it is even possible for all three to succeed. Other circumstances arise in which two are playing more or less co-operatively against one and to this extent the 'solo' element is noticeable. The game was first published in *Games & Puzzles* in February 1974. It is covered in length in the author's book of *Original Card Games* (1977).

CARDS 37, consisting of a Joker plus AKQJT9876 in each suit, ranking from high to low in that order.

GAME consists of nine deals, the deal passing to the left so that each player deals three times in all.

DEAL Twelve cards each, one at a time. Turn up the last (37th) card and place it to one side to establish trumps for the deal. If the turn-up is the Joker or any Nine, the deal is played with no trump.

JOKER The Joker has no independent value but assumes the identity and power of the turned-up card. Its holder uses it exactly as if it were the turn-up.

OBJECT Each player rejects three cards face down and plays out the remainder to nine tricks. Each player's object is to win exactly the number of tricks (no more, no fewer) indicated by his three rejects *(bid-cards)* in accordance with the following code:

Any ♣ discarded counts 3 tricks
Any ♥ discarded counts 2 tricks
Any ♠ discarded counts 1 trick
Any ♦ discarded counts 0 tricks

Example: a player may bid to win three tricks by discarding any three spades $(1 - 1 + 1 = 3)$ or any club and two diamonds $(3 + 0 + 0 = 3)$ or ♥♠♦ $(2 + 1 + 0)$. The rank of bid-cards has no effect on the bid; only the suits count. It will be noted that not all bids can be expressed by three alternative suit combinations (for example, a bid of zero can only be represented by three diamonds, nine by three clubs).

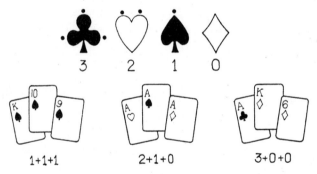

4. NINETY-NINE (a) Easy way of remembering value of suits for bidding. A club has three blobs, a heart two cheeks, a spade one point. A diamond is essentially the same shape as a zero. (b) Three different ways of bidding three tricks.

DECLARING Normally, bid-cards remain face down until the end of the round and are only shown to prove that a bid has been fulfilled. One player, however, may offer to play with his bid-cards face up so that the others know his objective: this is called 'declaring' and carries a bonus score. Only one player may declare. If more wish to do so, priority goes to eldest hand and least priority to dealer.

REVEALING An offer to declare may be overcalled by an offer to reveal, which means playing with one's hand of cards face up on the table as well as with bid-cards revealed. If more than one wish to reveal, priority goes to eldest, least priority to dealer. This carries a yet higher bonus and the player who reveals has the advantage of nominating a leader to the first trick.

PLAY If no one declares or reveals, eldest hand immediately leads to the first trick. If a game is declared the declarer turns his bid-cards face up before eldest leads. If the game is revealed the revealer first turns his bid-cards face up, then announces which player he wishes to lead. As soon as the first card has been led, but before the second is played, the revealer places his hand of cards face up on the table. Normal rules of trick-taking apply: follow suit if possible; if not, trump or renounce *ad lib*. The trick is captured by the highest card of the suit led or by the highest trump if any are played. The winner of one trick leads to the next.

SCORE At the end of play any player who has succeeded in his bid must turn up his bid-cards to prove it (but need not show them otherwise). Each player's score is made up of two or three parts:

    1. *Tricks.* 1 point per trick actually taken, regardless of bid.

    2. *Success.* A bonus for taking exactly the number of tricks bid, the bonus depending on how many players succeeded:

If all three succeed, score	10 each
If only two succeed, they score	20 each
If only one succeeds, he scores	30 alone

    3. *Premium.* The bonus for a declared bid is 30 points, for a revealed bid 60 points. This goes to the soloist if he is successful (in addition to his normal success bonus), or to *each*

opponent otherwise (whether or not they also count a success bonus). It may be noted that the highest possible score in one deal is 99, counting nine for tricks, 30 for being the only player to succeed, and 60 for having revealed (or beaten an opponent's revealed bid).

GAME The winner is the player with the highest score after nine deals. Nine games may be held to constitute a match. An optional scoring adjustment may be made in order to accentuate differences between the final results, as may be required when games are played over long series or for money. The adjustment is effected by multiplying each player's final score by the number of hundreds it contains. Thus a score of 100 to 199 is unchanged (× 1), 200 to 299 doubled, 300 to 399 trebled and so on. It follows that a player failing to exceed a score of 99 multiplies by nought, resulting in a final score of zero.

Ninety-nine Variants

ADVANCED NINETY-NINE In this game the Joker is not used and no card is turned for trump. Starting with eldest, each in turn may offer to declare or reveal on the understanding that he will then have the right to nominate trumps (or no trump). As before, an offer to reveal overcalls an offer to declare, and priority goes first to eldest, last to dealer. A soloist having been established, he announces the trump suit and players then bid and play in the usual way. If no one is prepared to make a premium bid the trump suit is automatically the same as it was in the previous deal (or, on the first deal of a game, automatically no trump).

NINE-TRUMP VERSION This may be applied to the standard or advanced game. Instead of a no-trump deal, the opposite of a suit-trump deal is one in which the four Nines do not belong to the suits marked on their faces but form a short, four-card trump suit in their own right, ♣9 being highest, followed by ♥9, ♠9 and ♦9. A player unable to follow suit may trump by playing a Nine. If a Nine is led Nines must be played to it if possible and the highest Nine wins. Because Nines do not belong to the suits marked on their faces they may not be used as bid-cards. The Joker, if used, plays its usual role. This version (borrowed from the game of Skat) considerably reduces the advantage of position that otherwise accrues to eldest hand in an ordinary no-trump deal.

TWO-HAND NINETY-NINE Use 37 cards and deal three hands and a turn-up in the usual way. Take the top three cards of the dummy hand and lay them face down to one side, where they remain untouched until the end of the game. The two live players bid, declare and reveal in the usual way, and non-dealer leads to the first trick. Before doing so, however, he turns up the dummy hand and arranges the nine cards in suits so that all are clearly visible. At the first trick eldest leads, dealer plays next, then eldest plays any card he wishes from dummy. Throughout the game if a live player wins the trick he places it face down before himself, leads to the next from his own hand, waits for his opponent to play second, then himself plays third from dummy. If dummy wins a trick the person who played dummy places the trick face down by the dummy hand, leads to the next trick from dummy, waits for his opponent to play second, then plays third from his own hand. It follows that neither player 'owns' the dummy, but may use it to play to his advantage each time he wins a trick from his own or dummy's hand. At the end of the deal all bid-cards are turned up, including dummy's, and all three hands make a score in the usual way. A player who fails to beat the dummy – it can happen, as the dummy scores a bonus if its bid happens to coincide with the number of tricks it takes and also for any failed declaration or revelation on a live player's part – may be penalized by some mutually agreed arrangement.

FOUR-HAND NINETY-NINE Use a standard 52-card pack plus Joker. Each plays for himself. Deal 13 each and turn up the 53rd card for trump (no trump if Nine or Joker, unless Nine-trump or Advanced Version played). Each player discards three bid-cards face down and plays the remaining ten to tricks. A bid of ten is represented in the same way as a bid of nought, i.e., by discarding any three diamonds. If such a bidder declares or reveals he must state which it is before any card is led. Scoring is exactly the same as in the three-hand game with the addition that no success bonus is scored if all four succeed (or fail) in their bids. A game is eight or twelve deals as preferred. The maximum score possible on a single deal is 100.

NOTES ON PLAY (THREE-HAND)

The strategic skill of the game lies in selecting three bid-cards whose absence from the hand leaves exactly the right number of tricks to be made from the remaining nine. Sometimes more than one reasonable bid is possible, in which case prefer the bid that involves throwing out cards whose absence from play will most confuse the opponents. For instance, with diamonds trump:

♦AKQ ♣AT86 ♥76 ♠T86

it is possible to discard all three diamonds for a bid of zero (the ♣A being easily thrown to a trump lead or the third round of hearts) or all three spades for a bid of three which will be made with the top trumps. The better of these is zero, as the holders of lower trumps will almost certainly take too many tricks. Position is also important. The bid of three would be acceptable with the lead, as trumps can be led immediately and the rest of the hand made after an escape via ♥7. Without the lead there is the danger that hearts will be drawn before you have a chance to trump in. The later the tricks are made the more difficult it will be to lose the lead.

In selecting bid-cards it is desirable primarily to throw out cards of middling rank, especially Nine, Ten, Jack, as they cannot be relied upon as either winners or losers. Because the object is to take an exact number of tricks it is important to be left with a playing hand that contains Aces and Kings for proposed trick-winners and Sixes and Sevens for proposed losers. In this respect Ninety-Nine differs markedly from other trick games in which only high cards are really significant. Here, Sixes are as important as Aces, and Sevens as Kings. If it is not possible or not necessary to discard middling ranks it is useful (if possible) to discard Aces or trumps, as their absence from play is not normally expected. Example (hearts trump):

♥J86 ♠AQ9 ♦AQ976 ♣A

Given the lead, and even without it, the most sensible bid is of two, by discarding ♠Q ♠9 ♦A. This gets rid of two middling ranks with the expectation of taking a trick with both black Aces. The spade Ace might be lost, in which case the trump Jack can almost certainly be used to ruff a club lead; otherwise, if all goes well, the Jack should not be difficult to throw to a higher trump. A psychic bid, designed to confuse the others, would be to discard ♣A and two diamonds for a bid of three, hoping to make two spades and the trump Jack, or else to bid two by throwing the Jack with two diamonds. In either case the problem will be to safely lose the two middling spades. They could be lost to club leads, but early spade leads – which may be expected from the holder(s) of Six and Seven – would mean defeat.

The most remarkable feature of Ninety-Nine is that the four suits have distinctive strength characteristics in play. Because the average bid is three, diamonds and spades (representing low numbers) are more frequently discarded in bids than hearts and clubs. It follows that, in play, clubs and hearts tend to be held long and spades and diamonds short. Therefore, clubs is a more 'reliable' suit than diamonds. For example, a holding of Ace, King, Seven, Six in clubs can be expected to win two tricks with the lead more often than not, whereas the same holding in diamonds may be trumped on the first lead and almost certainly will be on the second. Conversely, if the first trick is to be lost, the lead of the Seven from a holding of AQ987 in clubs will almost certainly succeed in being overtaken, whereas from the same holding in diamonds it is likely to be followed by the Six and a renounce.

Similar remarks apply to the suits in their capacity as trumps. As the first hand quoted above shows, it is not infrequent for the top three diamonds to be out of play for a bid of nought when diamonds are trumps, but when hearts or clubs are trumps it is practically certain that all nine of the suit will be in play. Experienced players find that, as trumps, clubs are usually reliable to the point of boring inevitability, diamonds so unreliable as to unbalance the play in the direction of luck rather than skill, hearts not quite as reliable as they may appear and therefore somewhat treacherous, spades usually the most interesting and skill-demanding. No-trump games tend to favour the player who leads.

Declarations should be made only on hands containing cards whose trick destinations are fairly predictable. Bids of one to four are usually envisaged. Revelations should be undertaken only on exceptional hands containing consecutive high trumps, or Sixes and low cards in all represented suits. Non-trump Aces can only be counted in short holdings. Revelations are best played defensively, for which reason they are best undertaken on a bid of nought without the lead, or perhaps up to three tricks with the lead, provided they can be made immediately and safely. The opponents of a declared or revealed bid must play cooperatively in order to beat it, as at any 'solo' game, for they will score more by defeating the contract at the cost of losing their own bids than by making their own bids but failing to defeat the soloist.

Final tips: a long non-trump suit containing the Six is best regarded as a run of positive losers. For example, AK876 counts better as no tricks than as one or two with the top cards, which are liable to be trumped. From a sequence always play the card least useful to your opponents' bank of information. For example, from the above holding lead the Eight to lose rather than the Six, as the latter gives too much away. Above all – if in doubt, bid three.

Oh Hell ◎

3–7 players, 4–5 best
1 pack (52)

This game, said to have been devised by Geoffrey Mott-Smith in 1937, is more fun than serious, though it does appeal to Bridge players. It is also known as Jungle Bridge or Blackout and sometimes either bowdlerized into 'Oh Well' or strengthened for effect.

CARDS Standard 52-card pack.

OBJECT A game consists of several deals, the turn to deal passing to the left. In the first deal each player receives one card; in the second, two; in the third, three; and so on, the cards being gathered in and shuffled at the end of each deal. This continues until there are not enough cards to go around for the next deal, so the number of deals in a game depends on the number of players. At each deal each player's object is to take exactly as many tricks as he bid – neither more nor fewer.

PLAY Deal the appropriate number of cards and turn up the next to establish a trump suit. If no cards are left over, play at no trump. Starting at dealer's left, each player announces how many of the tricks he proposes to win – i.e., none or one in the first deal; none, one or two in the second, and so on. Dealer notes his bid for future reference and, after bidding himself, announces whether the total of bids equals, exceeds or undercuts the number of tricks to be played. Eldest hand leads and normal rules of trick-taking apply: follow suit if possible; if not, trump or renounce *ad lib*. The winner of one trick leads to the next.

SCORE A player who takes exactly the number of tricks he bid scores that number plus 10; any other result scores nothing. (Some players vary the score for bidding and taking no tricks – e.g., 5 plus the number of tricks in the deal.)

VARIANTS Most variants are concerned only with the scoring. There is, however, a version called Up the River, Down the River in which, when the maximum card deal has been played, the whole sequence is gone through again in reverse so that the last deal is again of one card and one trick. In this version, too, players bid by simultaneously raising their hands with the appropriate number of fingers extended. This prevents one from being influenced by another's bid.

Solo Games

The following are fairly straightforward trick games in which one player – let us call him the soloist – states his objective and the others gang up on him in an attempt to beat it. In contrast to fixed-partnership games like Whist and Bridge, players find themselves working in temporary *ad hoc* partnerships when they combine against the soloist, or, in some games, are called upon by the soloist to assist him in return for a cut of the rewards.

The game best known to English speakers is Solo Whist, or its advanced form, Auction Solo. How 'Whist' got into the title is unclear. It is neither a direct derivative of partnership Whist, nor even particularly English. Solo is virtually the national card game of Belgium and was formerly known as Whist de Gand, or Ghent Whist. Before Solo surged in popularity at the end of the last century the equivalent game was Boston Whist, which was played in various forms. Boston games are briefly described in this chapter and are worth looking into for a change of scenery.

Similar if not related to this family is the once great, now almost defunct, Spanish game of Ombre, which was Europe's most fashionable trick game until Whist took over in the eighteenth century. Despite its superficial complexities it is a splendid game for three and exhibits some interesting features of play that well reward the effort of discovery. Appended to it is the somewhat simpler derivative called German Solo.

Also described in this section are Brandle, a German game of commendable simplicity, and Preference, a possibly Russian game, designed for three players.

Solo Whist

4 players
1 pack (52)

As no one seems to know where Solo comes from we may suppose it to be in some way related to German Solo, which in turn derives from Ombre, in which there is a bid called 'solo'. Somewhere along the route it seems to have become involved with Boston which would explain its French terminology – for Boston, despite its name, appears to be French rather than American in origin. The original meaning of solo was that of a bid in which the lone player took on the others with the hand as dealt to him, without the advantage of exchanging cards from a stock with a view to improving it. The secondary meaning of 'lone player' has taken over in games such as this where all the cards are dealt out.

In England Solo has long been a great family and commuters' game and many schools have devised their own variations to add to the excitement. We will start with the comparatively 'straight' game first then list the variants separately.

PRELIMINARIES Solo is a game for four, each playing for himself. Each deal is a separate event and settled as such in chips or coin. Shuffle to start, but not between deals.

CARDS A standard 52-card pack, cards ranking AKQJT 98765432.

DEAL 13 each in batches of 3–3–3–3–1. The last card which belongs to dealer, is turned face up on the table before him to propose a suit as trump.

OBJECT The highest bidder plays solo against the other three in an attempt to take the number of tricks he bid. A partnership bid is possible if no one wishes to play alone.

BIDDING Eldest hand speaks first and the turn to bid passes to the left. Each in turn may pass or make a higher bid than any previously made, or (as explained below) accept a 'proposal'. A player who has passed once may not bid again, and as soon as a bid has been followed by three consecutive passes the last bidder becomes the soloist and play begins. From lowest to highest, the possible bids are:

1. *Proposal (and acceptance)*. A player proposes if he thinks he and a partner can take at least eight tricks between them using the turned suit as trump. He does so by saying 'I propose', or, popularly, just 'Prop'. Provided that no other bid has intervened a subsequent player at his turn to bid may ally himself with the proposer by saying 'I accept', or, popularly, 'Cop'. If his acceptance is not then overcalled by a later player the bid stands and the two partners play against the other two in an attempt to win eight tricks. But any of the following higher bids automatically annuls a 'prop and cop' attempt.

2. *Solo*. A bid to win at least five tricks using the turned suit as trump.

3. *Misère*. A bid to lose every single trick playing at no trumps.

4. *Abundance* (properly, *abondance*). A bid to win at least nine tricks using a trump suit other than the one turned.

5. *Royal abundance* (properly, *abondance royale*). A bid to win at least nine tricks using the suit of the turned card as trump.

6. *Misère ouverte* (or spread misère). A bid to lose every trick, playing at no trump, but with one's hand of cards face up on the table after the first trick has been played.

7. *Abundance declared* (properly, *abondance déclarée*). A bid to win all 13 tricks without a trump suit but with the advantage of leading to the first trick. This cannot be overcalled as it is the highest possible bid.

ELDEST PRIVILEGES Eldest hand has certain privileges relating to the bid of prop and cop. First, if eldest proposes and the others all pass he is then permitted to raise his call to a solo. Alternatively, if eldest starts by passing, a subsequent player proposes and no higher call is made, eldest is then permitted to accept the proposal. No other player has these privileges.

ALL PASS If all four pass, the book-rule is that the hands are thrown in without play and the deal passes to the left. As there are several alternatives to the book-rule they are given later under Variants.

LEAD A contract having been established, dealer takes the turned-up card into his hand and the first card is led by the player on his left – except in the case of abundance declared, when it is led by the soloist himself regardless of position. If the contract is for misère ouverte, the soloist lays his hand of cards face up on the table after the first trick has been taken but before the second is led to.

TRICKS Normal rules of trick-taking apply. Players must follow suit if possible; if not, they may trump or renounce *ad lib*. The trick is captured by the highest card of the suit led or by the highest trump if any are played and the winner of one trick leads to the next.

SETTLEMENT If the soloist succeeds in his contract he receives the appropriate amount from each opponent; if not, he pays it to each opponent. The amounts are:

Proposal/acceptance	2 units
Solo	2 units
Misère	3 units
Abundance (or royal)	4 units
Misère ouverte	6 units
Abundance declared	8 units

In the case of proposal/acceptance each partner pays to or receives from each opponent. (Thus although prop/cop and solo have the same nominal values, a single partner gains or loses 4 units but a solo player gains or loses 6 units in all.)

REVOKE A simple method of dealing with revokes is as follows. If any player revokes he may correct it before the next trick is led: subsequent players may withdraw their cards and play differently but the revoker lays his misplayed card face up on the table and must play it at the earliest legal opportunity. Once the next trick has been led it is too late and the soloist is deemed to have won or lost his game (depending on who revoked) regardless of the actual outcome. For 'soloist' read 'partners' where appropriate.

VARIANTS

Many aspects of this long popular game have been subject to local variations of which the following are but a selection.

SELECTING TRUMPS Some dislike exposing one of dealer's cards. Method 1: use two packs (playing them alternately) and turn up the top card of the second pack for trump proposal. Method 2: rotate suits for trumps in a predetermined order (e.g., 1st deal spades, 2nd hearts etc.), or associate each dealer with a fixed and predetermined suit. Method 3: incorporate a Joker in the pack. Turn the 53rd card face up for trump. The holder of the Joker counts it exactly as if it were the faced card, which itself remains untouched.

ABUNDANCE In some schools, the first trick of an abundance (not royal) is played with the turned suit as trump, the announced suit not taking effect until the second trick. In others, the trump is not announced until the first card has been led to the first trick.

IF ALL PASS Some dislike throwing cards in without play and prefer to follow one of the following automatic procedures with the cards as dealt. Method 1 (Grand): play at no trump. Whoever takes the last trick loses at the same rate as a solo. Rare, but recommended. Method 2 (Competitive Misère): play at no trump. Whoever takes the most tricks loses as for a solo. Method 3 (Royal Misère): play with the turned suit as trump. Solo value is lost by the first player to take five tricks, or four if no one takes five. Method 4 (Kimberley, or Flying

Colours): the bidding is reopened and taken by the first player offering to play a solo in a suit of his own choice.

ALTERNATIVE BIDS Some players abolish proposal/ acceptance. This is not recommended. Some introduce a bid of abundance declared (13 tricks) in a trump suit of one's choice as an alternative to the normal abundance declared at no trump, or as an overcall to it. As an alternative it is not desirable, because any safe bid playable in suit is equally playable at NT, but not vice versa, so the effect is to make the bid even rarer than it is already. As an overcall it is for all practical purposes redundant. An overcall of the mythical 'royal abundance declared' is nonsensical. Players seeking a wider range of bids will prefer to play Auction Solo or possibly Boston.

ALTERNATIVE STAKES Systems alternative to the 2–2–3–4– 6–8 here presented as standard include 1–2–4–6–8–12 and 1–1–2–3–4–6. Some pay bonuses for overtricks or exact penalties for undertricks at some agreed fraction (e.g., $\frac{1}{4}$ or $\frac{1}{5}$) of the unit employed.

NOTES ON PLAY

Substantial volumes were written about strategy and tactics at Solo in the good old days before Bridge monopolized the card-game business. The following notes can therefore only scratch the surface of a much under-estimated game that can be as deep as you wish to play – if not deeper.

First, a word about position. Eldest hand is in a good position to make a positive (i.e., non-misère) bid because he has the lead and can therefore choose his point of attack. With a possible but not certain game he should at least propose, for if all then pass he has the opportunity to convert his bid to a solo against the appearance of weakness in the others' hands. Dealer is well placed for any sort of bid, for by the time his turn to speak has come he will know what sort of opposition there may be against him. Three passes, for example, enable him to bid solo on somewhat weaker cards

than might be appropriate for second or third hand. Second
hand – the player opposite dealer – is worst off for a positive
bid, partly because he will be playing second to the first trick
(always a weakness) and partly because he does not know
what third hand or dealer has against him. For a misère bid,
whether or not open, eldest is less well placed, as most good
misère hands require to be led up to, not from. From this
point of view dealer is in the best position and third hand
not badly off.

But 'good position' is also often determined by the shape
of the hand, some solos (for example) demanding the lead,
and being therefore most biddable by eldest, and others
requiring to be led into, a shape more suitable for dealer.
Two examples, with spades trump:

♠AKQT2 ♥J8 ♣JT9 ♦J43
♠AQ2 ♥AQ2 ♣AQ2 ♦A964

The first of these is good for eldest, as he can lead out his top
trumps and probably take five tricks straight off, dropping
the Jack. For dealer, however, it would be more than risky.
It is axiomatic not to lead trumps against a solo. By the time
he is in a position to trump plain suits he runs the danger of
either ruffing low and being overtaken by the Jack, or else
ruffing high and so strengthening the Jack in whichever hand
it may be.

The second, in contrast, is a solo by dealer but not by
eldest. A fifth trick must be squeezed from one of the
Queens, for which purpose the holder must be in a position
to play last to a trick led in whichever Queen suit it may be.
It is certainly not a hand to lead from (nor would be unless
diamonds were trumps).

In general, a bid of solo should be founded on trump
strength (or length, more accurately) rather than on high
cards in plain suits, and trumps should, unless held exceptionally long and high as in the first example above, be
exploited by ruffing rather than by playing the suit.

The next bid most comparable to solo is that of abundance
(royal or not), to which similar remarks apply as to position,
shape of hand and use of trumps. There is a temptation to

raise one's bid of solo to one of abundance on the strength of eight tricks and a stroke of luck. Not only is this no substitute for nine tricks but also, quite frequently, the actual result is eight tricks and a stroke of bad luck, resulting in seven. It is often helpful to consider such a hand the other way round and count the probable losers instead of probable winners. With more than four probable losers the bid is no abundance. Abundances are called on hands of various shapes, such as exceptionally long trumps (the suit is spades in each case):

♠QJT87642 ♥A2 ♣7 ♦AK

or overall strength:

♠AQJ73 ♥AK ♣AKQ ♦AK6

or two-suited hands:

♠AJT953 ♥AKQJ63 ♣8

Abundance declared – 13 at no trump – requires only to be recognized when seen. Cast-iron hands obviously contain consecutive top cards in every suit held, be it four lots of AKQ and a Jack to boot, or a holding of all thirteen of a suit. Whether or not to gamble on such a hand as, say, AKQ in every suit plus the deuce in one of them depends on what you can afford to lose in the event that one player can hold back the right suit for the last trick.

Proposal/acceptance is an interesting bid and those who abolish it forgo as much fun as opportunity for skilful play. What must be avoided when the bid is undertaken is the danger that both partners will have bid on trump strength alone, in which case the opponents may take their six tricks on the side; or both may bid on side-suit support alone, in which case they will find themselves out-trumped. Tests prove that it is best for eldest to propose on overall strength and to be accepted on the basis of strong trump support, but for other hands to propose on trump strength and be accepted on overall support.

The rationale behind prop and cop is that if no one has a hand strong enough for a solo (five tricks), any two players with hands strong enough for four each may get together in a bid of eight. Even so, it is advisable to prefer a proposal on a hand containing many possibilities, such as

♠Q985 ♥KQJ53 ♣KQ92

to one containing only four certainties, such as

♠AK85 ♥A53 ♣AJ2 ♦984.

The play of proposal/acceptance when partners happen to sit opposite each other is much the same as at partnership Whist; but when they are next to each other more thought is needed. They are clearly best placed when playing first and fourth to a trick, worst when playing first and second. If eldest was accepted by the player on his left he should lead top trumps if he has them, or try to put his partner in with weak plain suits if not; if accepted by dealer he should lead his best trumps regardless.

The difference between misère and misère ouverte is that the latter is called on a hand that should lose tricks regardless of the distribution of cards in opposing hands, whereas a non-open misère is called in order to conceal some feature of the hand that may prove a weakness against an unfavourable distribution. (It does not follow that a non-open misère is necessarily beatable if only the opponents can discover its weak point in time to exploit it.)

An unbeatable, and therefore ouverte, misère is one which, preferably not having the lead, enables the soloist to get under any card that may be led at any trick in the game, such as:

♠432 ♥642 ♣AKQT8642

Here spades are safe because no one has anything lower. Hearts are safe because, whatever is led, the soloist can get under and still be left with the lowest cards of the suit. In other words, an alternating low sequence is just as good as a solid one. Clubs show an extension of the alternating low sequence. The suit is safe not because the AKQ can be thrown to leads in diamonds but because it would still be safe against as many leads in clubs as can be made against it. Even if one player held the outstanding cards (J9753) and led them consecutively he would find every lead undercut by the soloist, and, by the time the latter has only AKQ left, there are no more to lead. But the alternate holdings in hearts and clubs are not good for leading from. Eldest, on this hand, must start with the unbeatable spades.

An alteration to one card would make this hand unbiddable as an ouverte:

♠732 ♥642 ♣AQT8642

The ♠7 sticks out of this hand like a sore thumb. The only sure way of losing that Seven is to throw it to a diamond lead, which would be unlikely if played ouverte (even bearing in mind that the hand is not exposed until after the first trick). Seeing this hand the club holders would lead clubs until the high spade holders were out of high spades, and three spade leads may then force the Seven to take a trick.

Whatever the bid the opponents must play together as a team, noting one another's strengths and weaknesses in different suits and playing accordingly. It is always advantageous to place the trick with the player on the soloist's right, so that he may lead through the soloist and force him to play against probabilities rather than visible cards.

Three-hand Solo

Several three-hand versions have been devised but none is really a satisfactory substitute. Alternative three-hand games of comparable type include Preference and Ninety-Nine. Proceeding from most to least recommended:

40-CARD SOLO Remove all Twos, Threes and Fours from the pack. Deal 13 each and turn up the 40th card for trump proposal. The turned card remains unused. There is no proposal/acceptance but if all pass the turn-up is turned down and players may bid a six-trick abundance.

OPEN DUMMY SOLO Deal four hands, including a dummy hand face up, the last card of which proposes trumps. The lowest bid is proposal: if not overcalled, proposer plays the dummy hand as if it were his partner at Contract Bridge (playing alternately, not consecutively). Higher bids are played one-against-two, the dummy remaining unused but face up to show which cards are out of play.

SEVENTEENS Deal 17 each and turn up the last for trumps. Each player then discards four cards face down, and play proceeds as before but without proposal/acceptance.

CLOSED DUMMY SOLO Deal four hands face down. Turn the top card of dummy to propose trumps but leave the rest face down and out of play.

THREE-SUIT SOLO Remove one suit and play with 39 cards.

For two players 'Double Dummy Solo' is pointless and 'solo' a contradiction in terms. The nearest substitute is German Whist.

Auction Solo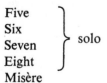
4 players
1 pack (52)

In this extension of Solo, proposal/acceptance is dropped but higher bids increased for greater variety. Bids of solo and abundance may be made in a trump suit of one's own choice but can be overcalled by bids of the same number made in the suit of the turned card. When bidding, therefore, do not state the intended trump unless it is the one turned. The bids are:

Five ⎫
Six ⎪
Seven ⎬ solo
Eight ⎪
Misère ⎭

Nine ⎫
Ten ⎬ abundance
Eleven ⎬
Twelve ⎭
Misère ouverte
Abundance declared (NT, with lead)
Abundance declared (in turned suit)

Misère ouverte is played as at ordinary Solo.

Abundance declared with no trump is played, with the lead, as at ordinary Solo, but can be overcalled by abundance declared in the suit of the turn-up (but not in any other suit). In this case the lead is still made by eldest hand, not automatically by the soloist.

The values of the various contracts, paid by each opponent to the soloist if he succeeds, and by him to each opponent if he fails, are:

Solo	2 + 1 per over/undertrick
Misère	4
Abundance	6 + 1 per over/undertrick
Misère ouverte	8
Abundance declared	12 + 1 per undertrick if lost

Boston ⚇

4 players
1 pack (52)

At the turn of the century several varieties of a game called Boston were much played in America. All of them may be derived from a game still played in Europe. Boston itself, with one or two more bids possible than in Auction Solo, was chiefly characterized by an extraordinarily complicated system of payments for bids and over/undertricks. Boston de Fontainebleau exhibited a richer variety of bids but was blessed with a comparatively intelligible rate of exchange. Russian Boston was the same but with the addition of *carte blanche* (explained below). French Boston – a name sometimes wrongly applied to Fontainebleau – was apparently little played but often detailed in card books of the period.

Those who turn to this branch of the family will be looking for something more varied and rococo than Auction Solo, in which case Russian Boston may be recommended and the others relegated to the position of footnotes. This, then, is the form described below.

PRELIMINARIES Each player should be equipped with counters or poker chips in three denominations equivalent to 1:2:5 or 1:5:10, the highest possible payment needed on any one deal lying between 40 and 50.

CARDS Standard 52-card pack, cards ranking normally (Ace high).

DEAL 13 each in batches of 4–4–5.

BIDDING Each player in turn passes or makes a higher bid than any previous one. Except where it is no trump by definition, a bid consists of a number of tricks and a proposed trump suit. A given bid in a lower suit can be overcalled by the same bid in a higher suit, for which purpose suits rank from low to high: spades ♠, clubs ♣, hearts ♥, diamonds ♦. Thus the lowest possible bid is of 'Boston in spades'. The various bids are, from lowest to highest:

Boston (five tricks)
Six tricks
Little misère (lose 12 after discarding any card)
Seven tricks
Piccolissimo (NT, win exactly one trick after discarding any
    card)
Eight tricks
Grand misère (lose all 13 tricks)
Nine tricks
Little spread (as little misère, but ouverte)
Ten tricks
Grand spread (misère ouverte)

Eleven tricks
Twelve tricks
Slam (13 tricks)
Spread slam (13 tricks, ouverte)

Once a player has passed he may not re-enter the bidding (even to re-bid a misère, which is permitted in Boston). When three consecutive passes have been made the last-named bid becomes the contract and establishes the soloist, who may not change his bid – except to call for a partner.

PARTNER In a bid of six, seven or eight tricks, the soloist may call for a partner. If anyone accepts, the two play as partners and are obliged to take at least four more tricks than the quantity bid (thus raising its value).

CARTE BLANCHE If the contract is in a trump suit any player whose hand contains not a single trump may, before play begins, declare it and receive 2 chips from each other player. (He need not show it.)

HONOURS If there is a trump suit the Ace, King, Queen and Jack of it are honours. If three or four honours were dealt to the soloist, or to the bidder and his partner (if any) between them, they count for a bonus equivalent to overtricks provided the bid is successful. Three honours count as two overtricks, four as four. Honours may be scored only by the bidding side and only if the bidding side wins.

PLAY No matter what the bid, eldest hand always leads to the first trick. In bids of little misère, piccolissimo and little spread, the soloist discards any card face down before the first trick is led, and only 12 tricks are played. In any game played spread (ouverte) the soloist's hand must be laid face up on the table before any card is led. Normal rules of trick-taking apply.

SETTLEMENT If the soloist wins he receives the appropriate amount from each opponent; if not, he pays it to each opponent. When there are partners each one of them receives it from or pays it to the player on his right, if he is an opponent, or on his left otherwise. The appropriate amount is shown in the following table. 'Extra trick' means overtrick or undertrick as the case may be. (In the original schedule all figures are multiples of five. In the following table all original figures have been divided by five.)

Game	None	Trump: ♣ or ♠	♥	♦	Per extra trick
Boston (five)		2	4	6	1
Six tricks		6	8	10	1
Little misère	15				
Seven tricks		10	12	14	1
Piccolissimo	20				
Eight tricks		14	16	18	1
Grand misère	30				
Nine tricks		18	20	22	1
Little spread	40				
Ten tricks		22	24	26	1
Grand spread	50				
Eleven tricks		26	28	30	1
Twelve tricks		30	32	34	1
Slam (thirteen)		80	90	100	—
Spread slam		120	140	160	—

It would appear from this curious table that the loss for a failed slam was fixed and not affected by undertricks. One account of the game indicates that any bid in suit can be overcalled by the same bid at 'grand' (no trump) but fails to give credit for it in the schedule. It will be noted that no-trump bids can be overcalled by trump bids that are paid off at a lesser rate.

OPTIONAL EMBELLISHMENTS included (a) a pool to which each dealer contributes in turn and to which payments are made for revokes and other crimes, and which can be won in certain conditions; and (b) a *misère partout* played in the unlikely event of all four passing.

VARIANTS

BOSTON The bids at Boston were: Boston (five), six, seven, little misère, eight, nine, grand misère, ten, eleven, little spread, twelve, grand spread, grand slam. Before play a second pack was cut and the top card of the bottom half turned. This established a suit called *first preference*, and the other suit of the same colour became automatically the *colour*, or second preference. A bid in any suit of the other colour could be overcalled by the same bid 'in colour', and that in turn by the same suit in first preference. The scoring schedule was unbelievably complicated.

BOSTON DE FONTAINEBLEAU is basically Russian Boston as described above but without *carte blanche* and with the requirement that the acquisition of a partner calls for three extra tricks instead of four.

FRENCH BOSTON A game consisted of 40 deals, the last eight paid double. The suit turned on the first deal was called *belle* for the rest of the game, and in each subsequent deal the suit turned was *petite* for that deal only (unless *belle* was turned again in which case there was no *petite*). A bid in *belle* overcalled a bid in *petite* (if any); no other trump could be proposed. Cards ranked normally except that ♦J was always the top trump, or ♥J if diamonds were trumps.

Brandle ♣

4 players
1 short pack (28)

In complete contrast to Bostonian luxuriance, Brandle, one of the oldest German card games known, is a neat and simple member of the Solo family. It is therefore a fast game, eminently suitable for beginners and those who prefer the classical to the rococo.

CARDS 28, ranking AKQJT97 in each suit. (This is traditional; but the Sevens may be replaced by Eights if preferred.)

DEAL Seven each, in batches 2-3-2.

OBJECT The highest bidder plays a solo game against the other three, who seek to prevent him from making what he bid.

BIDDING The bids and their values are as follows. The highest bidder will nominate the trump suit, if any, but no suit is named until the bidding is over.

Brandle (three tricks)	1
Four tricks	2
Five tricks	3
Six tricks	4
Bettel (no tricks, NT)	5
The kill (seven)	6
Overkill (seven at NT)	7

The player on the left of any bidder must either pass or make a higher bid. If he passes, however, the next in turn need not bid higher but may say '(I) hold,' and if all then pass the holder becomes the soloist at the bid he held. He may, however, be overbid by a subsequent player, in which case the same procedure applies again. Three consecutive passes establish the last bidder as the soloist, who then announces the trump suit (if any).

TRICKS The soloist always leads to the first trick. Unusual rules of trick-taking apply, in that each player must not only follow suit to the card led, if possible, but also play a higher card of it than any already showing. If unable to head the trick he must still follow suit if he can (but need not play his highest). A player unable to follow suit at all may either trump or renounce as he pleases. The trick is captured by the highest card of the suit led or by the highest trump if any are played. The winner of one trick leads to the next.

SETTLEMENT If the soloist succ~~e~~eds he receives the value of the game from each opponent; if not, he pays that amount to each opponent.

Note: the German title is *Brandeln*. *Bettel* is a common German word for misère. A bid of seven is *Mord*, meaning 'murder' or 'death'; seven no trump is *Herrenmord*, which appears to be the same only more so. Translations are therefore approximate.

Preference ⚇

3 players
1 short pack (32)

Worth noting for its three-handedness and some unusual features of play, Preference is a curiously misunderstood game which is said to be of Russian origin and yet only seems to be described in German books – in a form which may well have borrowed much from Germany's national card game, Skat. The description offered by most Anglo-American authors leaves much to be desired. None is given in the *Guide Marabout*, a French Hoyle-equivalent. The one which follows was published by the German playing card company, A.S.S., in 1975, based on an account in Anton's *Encyclopaedie der Spiele* of 1884.

CARDS 32, ranking AKQJT987 in each suit.

DEAL Ten each in batches of 3–4–3, with a widow of two cards laid face down to the table before the first batch of four is dealt.

OBJECT The player who makes the highest bid plays solo against the other two, usually with the object of taking at least six tricks. Each opponent is obliged to take at least two tricks if he plays, but may instead drop out.

BIDDING The suits have a bidding value as follows: ♣1, ♠2, ♦3, ♥4. A simple bid is an offer to win at least six tricks after naming the trump suit and improving one's hand by taking up the widow and discarding any two cards in its place. Eldest, unless he passes immediately, starts by bidding 'one', regardless of his intended suit. Second hand may then pass (in which case dealer takes over) or make a higher bid, for example, 'two', thus undertaking to play in any suit higher than clubs. Eldest may then pass, or 'hold', which means that he will play a game worth at least two himself and second hand will have to bid higher if he wants to take over. This continues until one of them passes – either second hand because he cannot raise his bid, or eldest because he cannot accept the last raise. At that point dealer may step in and continue to raise against the first survivor in the same manner until one of them drops out. The final survivor becomes the soloist.

It is possible to bid higher than four, the full range of bids being as follows:

One ♣
Two ♠
Three ♦
Four ♥
Misère (no tricks, no trump)
One hand ♣ ⎫
Two hand ♠ ⎪ without
Three hand ♦ ⎬ exchanging
Four hand ♥ ⎭
Misère hand (no tricks, no trump, without exchange)
No trump (six tricks in succession)
Misère ouverte (without exchange, hand played open)

In a simple misère the soloist takes the widow and discards any two face down before play. In any hand game he plays without the widow, which remains face down and out of play for the rest of the deal. For the no trump bid, which need not be played from the hand, the soloist must take at least six tricks and he must take them in succession; but he does not have the lead and is permitted to lose from one to four tricks before taking his run of six. For misère ouverte he lays his hand of cards face up on the table after the first card has been led to the first trick but before the second is played.

CONCEDING If the bid is for six at least, each opponent in turn states whether he will 'go along', in which case he obligates himself to win at least two tricks, or 'keep out', in which case he lays his hand face down on the table and leaves his partner to battle it out. In this event, however, the partner may insist that they both play together, in which case it does not matter how the tricks fall so long as they beat the soloist. Yet again, both players may concede the game and the soloist wins without further play.

TRICKS The soloist leads to the first trick except on a bid of 'no trump', when the lead is made by the player on his right. Rules of trick-play are somewhat unusual. Except in a misère each succeeding player must follow suit if he can and must head the trick if he can (that is, play a higher card of the led suit than any so far played to it). If unable to follow suit he must trump if possible. Only otherwise may he renounce.

When the soloist leads a low card it is a rule of the game that the second player must not seek to take the trick if there is any chance that his partner can do so, and to this end he need not head the trick (though he must still follow suit). He must give the third player an opportunity to win, even if the third has made his two tricks and eldest has not.

In a misère it is necessary to follow suit but not obligatory to head the trick. The opponents may discuss with each other how best to defeat the contract.

SETTLEMENT The game is designed for play with immediate settlement in chips or counters but the equivalent can be recorded notionally in writing. At the start of each deal each player chips to the pool an agreed amount (the ante), which must be divisible by ten and remains unchanged throughout the game.

If the soloist wins a bid of six he draws one-tenth of the contents for each trick he won. In two circumstances he is also paid an additional amount out of each opponent's own pocket. For a successful bid of 'four, hand' (hearts) this amount is half the ante; for 'no trump' it is the full ante.

For a successful misère the soloist draws nothing from the pool but is paid the following proportion of the ante by each opponent separately: misère $\frac{6}{10}$, misère hand $\frac{8}{10}$, misère ouverte $\frac{12}{10}$. For losing a misère he pays exactly the same proportion to each opponent – six, eight or twelve tenths as the case may be. This is additional to what he pays to the pool.

For any failed bid – whether misère or six tricks – the soloist pays into the pool an amount equivalent to twice the ante, less $\frac{1}{10}$ for each trick he succeeded in winning. (For taking three tricks, for example, he would pay $\frac{20}{10}$ less $\frac{10-3}{10} = \frac{13}{10}$.)

Either opponent who 'went along' but failed to take the necessary two tricks pays to the pool an amount equivalent to the ante. This does not apply if he wished to concede but was 'summoned' to do so by his partner.

VARIANT

In the version of the game usually described in American books, the suits rank spades, clubs, diamonds, hearts. There is a round of bidding to play from the hand, each in turn passing or naming a higher suit than one that has been previously mentioned. If no one bids to play from the hand there is a second round at which each player passes or chips a certain number to the pool. The player who chips the greatest number becomes the soloist, takes the widow, announces trumps, discards and leads in the usual way. No further details are given beyond noting that 'hearts, hand' sweeps the whole pool, and there is no mention of misère bids.

Ombre ⚇

3 players
1 short pack (40)

Card playing is greatly out of mode; very likely there are not six
ladies of fashion in London who know the difference between
Spadille and Manille.

(W. M. Thackeray, *The Virginians*, 1858)

Ombre, that venerable but exceedingly complicated game of
matadors and sundry hispanicisms, was described in 1727
as 'a game at cards that the better sort of people play three
together at', and in 1975 as 'a game played now only by card
gourmets and snobs'. Such potted history speaks for itself.
Suffice to say that it swept Europe during the late seventeenth
century, was particularly favoured by ladies (the gentlemen
preferring Piquet and Whist), gave rise to all sorts of deriva-
tives of which the best known was Quadrille, heavily
influenced such central European games as German Solo,
Skat and Jass, and was finally driven out of business some
hundred years ago by the dominance of Whist and later
Bridge.

The complexities of the game lie mainly in the peculiar
ranking or pecking-order of the cards. Once this is mastered
the mechanics of play are fairly straightforward and will be
found to present interesting features of marked originality –
such as the bid of *voltereta* or *tourné*, and the objective of
winning more tricks than either opponent individually.
Details of play varied from country to country. Those following are as played in England before the game died out.

CARDS Use a 40-card pack containing AKQJ765432 in each
suit, either by rejecting all Eights, Nines and Tens from a 52
card pack or by using a traditional Spanish pack. (In the
latter case, equivalences are: *oros* (coins) = diamonds, *copas*
(cups) = hearts, *espadas* (swords) = spades, *bastos* = clubs,
caballero = Queen, *sota* = Jack.)

COUNTERS Each deal is a separate event and settled immediately in chips, counters or coins, though it is feasible to keep a written tally if counters are not available.

ORDER By tradition, all play proceeds to the right, i.e., anticlockwise around the table. The player to the dealer's right is called eldest hand, to his left the pone. Each deals in turn, the turn also passing to the right.

DEAL If the players are of different sexes the one that is outnumbered deals first; otherwise, cards are dealt around face up and the first to receive a King deals first. After shuffling and offering for cut to the pone, place five chips in the pool and deal nine cards to each player in three batches of three. Place the remaining thirteen face down and slightly spread at the centre of the table. These form the stock or *talon*.

OBJECT The highest bidder becomes the soloist or *ombre* and seeks to win more tricks than each opponent individually. With five tricks he is bound to win but with four he only wins if the others fall three to two in his opponents' hands. He may or may not exchange cards before play, depending on his bid (as explained below). Before bidding, however, it is necessary to understand the order in which cards rank.

RANK OF CARDS Cards rank for trick-taking purposes in different orders according first to their colour, red or black, and second to whether or not they are trumps. It is therefore necessary to assess one's hand for bidding purposes on the assumption that one will be permitted to choose the trump suit.

Table 2 summarizes the ranking of cards. The top trump is always ♠A, called Spadille. The second trump, called Manille, is the Two of trumps if black or the Seven if red – in other words, the card that would be normally *lowest* in its suit if the suit were not entrumped. The third highest trump is always ♣A, called Basto. These three cards are called *matadors* and have special privileges in play as explained later.

The next highest card is the Ace if a red suit is trump, this being called Punto. If a black suit is trump there is no Punto.

In each suit the King, Queen and Jack are the highest (or, in trumps, the next highest) cards and these are followed by the numerals. In black suits the order is normal: 76543 and 2 lowest, except when promoted to Manille. In red suits the numerical order is reversed, Ace ranking below Jack (except when promoted to Punto), and followed by 23456 and 7 lowest, except when promoted to Manille.

TABLE 2: HOW CARDS RANK AT OMBRE

in trumps only —	♠ A	= Spadille	
	tr 2 or 7	= Manille	= matadors
	♣ A	= Basto	
	(**tr** A	= Punto, if red)	

in all suits —	King
	Queen
	Jack

in red suits — ♦ ♥	(A)	7	— in black suits ♠ ♣
	2	6	
	3	5	
	4	4	
	5	3	
	6	(2)	
	(7)		

Note: () denotes a card which is promoted and therefore absent from that position when it belongs to the trump suit.

BIDDING From lowest to highest the basic games that can be bid (but see also Variants) are as follows:

1. *Simple.* A bid to win after announcing trumps, discarding unwanted cards from the hand, and drawing a like number from the stock in an attempt to improve the hand.

2. *Voltereta.* A bid to win after turning the top card of the stock and accepting its suit as the trump, whatever that may be, and then exchanging as before.

3. *Solo.* A bid to win after announcing the trump suit and playing without exchanging any cards.

Eldest bids or passes first, dealer last. Anyone who passes may not bid again and if all three pass without bidding the cards are thrown in and the next player deals, so increasing the pool (but see Variants). No suits are mentioned in the bidding. If the first to speak bids a simple game the next must name a higher game or pass. But if a player is over-called he may assert his priority by bidding the same game as the one that overcalled him. (Example: Eldest says 'Play', meaning a simple game; the pone can only overcall and bids 'Voltereta'; so can dealer who bids 'Solo'. If now Eldest really insists on playing against such opposition, which is unlikely, he could assert his priority by bidding 'Solo'; or he could pass and the pone could equally bid 'Solo'. Had dealer passed, Eldest could have relieved the pone of his 'voltereta', and the latter would have to pass or raise to 'Solo'.) When two players have passed the third becomes *ombre* and must play a game equal to or higher than the one he bid.

EXCHANGE If the bid is a simple game, *ombre* first announces the trump suit and then discards face down as many cards from his hand as he wishes, drawing a like number from the top of the stock in order to restore his hand to nine. Theoretically, the player on his right can then discard and draw in the same manner, and the third player do likewise, up to as many cards as there may be left in the stock. In practice, however, *ombre*'s two opponents may decide between themselves which of them shall have first draw from the stock. (The reason for this is that their hope is for one of them to take at least as many tricks as *ombre*, for which purpose at least one of them must have a strong hand. Therefore an opponent with a weak hand should not spoil their chances by drawing many cards in second position and leaving few, if any, for his partner.) Rules differ as to whether anyone may see or reveal any cards left undrawn from the stock. This must be agreed in advance.

If the bid is voltereta, *ombre* faces the top card of the

stock and declares whatever suit it may be to be trumps. He then discards and draws in the usual way, and his opponents do likewise as described above.

If *ombre* is playing solo he announces the trump suit and leaves the stock to his opponents. The first to exchange may not discard more than eight.

TRICKS Eldest hand always leads to the first trick. Normal rules of trick-taking apply except in respect of matadors (see below). Each player must follow suit to the card led if possible; if not, he may trump or renounce *ad lib*. The trick is captured by the highest card of the suit led or by the highest trump if any are played, and the winner of one trick leads to the next. Each player keeps his own tricks separately.

MATADORS The three top trumps are matadors and have special privileges in play, in that they cannot be forced out by the lead of lower trumps. Thus if a non-matador trump is led to a trick, each other player must follow suit if possible, but if he has only matadors in that suit, he need not play one but may instead 'renege' by discarding another suit. Similarly, the lead of a lower matador cannot force the play of a higher one. But the lead of a high matador can force out a lower one. Thus if Manille (the second trump) is led, a player holding only Spadille need not play it but a player holding Basto must play it if he has no lower trump – he may not renege.

THE VOLE If *ombre* wins the first five tricks in succession he may cease play and claim the pool immediately. If he leads to the sixth trick, however, he thereby automatically undertakes to win all nine tricks (the vole), earning a bonus if he succeeds or a penalty if he fails.

SURRENDER If *ombre* feels he cannot win he may surrender at any time before playing his card to the fourth trick. If both opponents accept the surrender, which they are obliged to do if *ombre* played voltereta, *ombre* loses the game and pays *puesta*, as explained later. Either opponent, however, may say 'I defend,' and so force a continuation of the game with the object of taking the majority of tricks himself. *Ombre* is not permitted to surrender if playing a solo game.

OUTCOME If *ombre* takes more tricks than either opponent he wins *sacado*; if he fails to win and there is a tie (e.g., 4–4–1 or 3–3–3) he loses *puesta* (is 'bested'). If an opponent wins a majority of tricks he wins, and *ombre* loses, *codille*.

For winning *sacado, ombre* takes the contents of the pool plus a certain number of units from each opponent on the side. These personal 'extras' are as follows:

Game. 5 for winning, plus
Vole. 25 for taking all nine tricks, plus either
Voltereta. 2 for having played voltereta, or
Solo. 10 (formerly 8) for having played solo

Certain other gains may made in addition, as follows:

Primeras. 1 for having won the first five tricks in succession, unless the vole was also made.
Estuches (honours). 1 unit for each consecutive top trump which he played with or without in his hand. For example, if he held Spadille but not Manille, or lacked Spadille but held Manille, he would take 1 unit from each player. If he had held the top two trumps but lacked the third, or lacked the top two but held the third, he would take 2 units; and so on. Further honours, of course, are more likely to have been held than not held.

If *ombre* is bested (a tie), he loses *puesta*. For this he doubles the pool and adds to it a further 5 units for each player in the game. (Though three-handed, the game was often played by four, the dealer receiving no cards and taking no part in the play, but being involved in all transactions here described.) In addition, he pays the appropriate extras to *each* opponent, as detailed above, for simple, voltereta, solo, and *estuches*. He also pays *primeras* if he lost the first five tricks.

If *ombre* loses *codille* he pays exactly the same amount as he would do for *puesta*, but what, in the latter case, he would have paid to the pool he pays instead to the player who took most tricks.

If *ombre* won the first five tricks, went on for the vole, but failed to win all nine, he pays 30 to each opponent, less any extras due to him for voltereta (2), solo (10), and estuches (as many as applicable).

If *ombre* surrendered and a defender took over, the latter wins if he succeeds in taking an individual majority of tricks, and *ombre* pays as for *codille* in the usual way. If the defender is bested he pays *puesta* as described above; if beaten, he pays *codille* to the player who beats him. In either case *ombre* also pays to all concerned as if he had played the game through and had been bested.

RESERVED PUESTAS It may be agreed that when the pool reaches a certain size, say 100 units, any subsequent payments for *puesta* are kept separately. When the pool is taken it is immediately refilled with the largest *puesta* – not necessarily the one most recently paid.

VARIANTS

FAVOR This denotes a previously agreed preferred suit, usually diamonds. A bid of *favor* – to win a simple game with diamonds as trumps – overcalls an ordinary simple game, and solo favor overcalls an ordinary solo. Whether won or lost, all payments for favor are double what they would be for the same game and extras in any other suit. (It is not clear whether voltereta pays double if diamonds are turned for trump or whether favor only counts double if specifically bid. The point should be settled beforehand.)

IF ALL PASS One or more of the following games were playable if all three players passed immediately. (a) Gascarille: a bid to win after discarding and drawing eight cards and naming the trump after drawing (instead of before the discard). The game value is three units. (b) Countervole (*contrabola*): a bid to lose every trick. For this purpose no player may discard, and *ombre* must hold at least one card of the suit he declares to be trump. If he takes no trick he wins *sacado*; he takes any, he loses *puesta*. (c) Forced Spadille: the player dealt ♠A is forced to play if all pass. One method requires him to play a voltereta, which is paid as for a solo whether won or lost.

NOTES ON PLAY

The undertaking of a simple game requires usually at least five trumps including two matadors; with only one matador the others should include at least the King and Queen. Voltereta may be regarded as the bidding equivalent of a no-trump game, as it requires high cards in all four suits but not necessarily any great length. Suitable holdings include both black Aces; Spadille, three potential Manilles and a King; Spadille and three Kings; Basto and four Kings. A solo should never be undertaken without at least two matadors, a majority of trumps and a good forcing suit, though in red suits Punto may for this purpose be assessed as a matador.

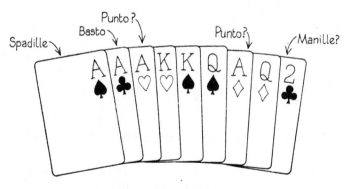

5. OMBRE A good hand for a bid of voltereta. Spadille and Manille are always first and third highest trumps. If hearts or diamonds are turned, the hand also contains Punto, the fourth highest; if clubs, it has Manille, the second highest; if spades, King and Queen are fourth and fifth highest.

The exchange of more than four cards is frequently self-defeating: a hand requiring it is hardly biddable. Exchange with a view to getting rid of weaknesses, such as low, short holdings or unguarded Queens, not in the hope of drawing high cards.

The partners should remember that their object is primarily to prevent *ombre* from succeeding and only secondarily to take tricks themselves. The partner with stronger cards should exchange first. A partner with weak cards, having taken one trick, should try to avoid taking a second, otherwise there is a real danger that *ombre* will win with a 'dominant four' – four tricks to three and two. When a partner has taken four, however, it is better to take tricks oneself in order to encourage a *puesta* rather than *codille*. *Ombre*, for his part, should seek as far as possible to distribute tricks evenly between his opponents. In playing for the vole remember that any matador held by an opponent may well have been held back with a view to the defeat of such an attempt.

German Solo ⚬⚬⚬

4 players
1 short pack (32)

This descendant of Ombre serves as a good introduction to it. Four players, 32 cards, deal eight each in batches of 3–2–3. The dealer antes four units to a pool. Cards rank from high to low AKQJT987 except in trumps. The highest trump is always ♣Q, called Spadille, followed as second highest by the Seven of the current trump suit, called Manille; followed as third highest always by ♠Q, called Basta; followed by the rest of the trumps down – AKQ (except in black suits) JT98. The object is for one player to win at least five tricks, either alone or with the aid of a partner.

If one player holds both black Queens he is obliged to play *grand (Grossfrage)*. He calls for a partner to assist him by naming any Ace he does not hold himself. Whoever has that Ace declares himself and chooses a trump suit, which may not be that of the Ace called. If the player with both Queens also has all four Aces he is obliged to bid Solo, as explained below. Grand may also be bid by anyone who does not have both Queens.

Otherwise, the lowest bid is *request (Frage)*. In this case the bidder becomes the soloist and calls for a partner by naming an Ace which is not in his own hand and not that of the trump suit, which he also announces. The partner may not declare himself verbally, only by the way in which he plays.

The highest bid is *solo*, in which the bidder, as soloist, announces trumps and plays to win five tricks without the aid of a partner.

If nobody makes a bid the holder of ♣Q must play an *obligation (Mussfrage)*, which is the same as *grand* (above) but costs (and wins) less.

The lowest bid is request, overcalled by grand, overcalled by solo. Starting with eldest hand (left of dealer) each in turn may pass or bid higher than the previous bid. If one player bids, and the next overcalls, the first may raise his bid to that of the overcaller and so claim priority. The highest bidder becomes the soloist and is permitted to raise his bid before announcing trumps or calling for a partner. He may also declare that he (if solo) or his partnership undertakes to win all eight tricks.

The soloist leads and strict rules apply: players must follow suit and head the trick if possible; if unable to follow they must trump; and only if unable to do either may they renounce. As soon as the soloist or his side has taken five tricks the game is won and the cards thrown in unless all eight tricks were bid. But if he (or his side) wins the first five tricks in succession, then leading to the sixth trick automatically becomes an undertaking to win all eight.

The pay-off is as follows. Request and obligation are worth 2 units, paid by each opponent to the soloist's side and shared with the partner; but, if the bid is lost, the soloist pays each opponent 2 units and his partner neither gains nor loses. Grand is worth 4 units, received by each partner from one opponent if successful, or paid by each to one opponent if not. Solo receives 4 from or pays 4 to each opponent. In all cases the soloist, or the initiator of a partnership, wins the pool if successful.

Settlement for winning or failing to win all eight tricks is made independently of that for the main game. The value is 8 units if not announced at the start of play, 16 if announced.

Whichever suit is entrumped in the first deal becomes the 'colour' or 'favourite' suit for the rest of the game. Any bid in colour overcalls the same bid in a different suit, and all payments in colour are doubled.

Five-card Family

Five cards are dealt to each player, and the object is to win at least three tricks, preferably all five, and certainly to avoid taking none at all.

This simple format underlies all the following games, although in one case only three cards are dealt, and in another ten. It may be traced back to an archetypal fifteenth-century French game called Triomphe, known in England as Trump or French Ruff (as distinct from English Ruff, the ancestor of Whist). The family of games is large and diffuse, some of its members having apparently interbred with other game types such as All Fours.

Described here are the following major representatives: Ecarté, for two; Euchre, for any number but particularly good as a four-hand partnership game; Five Hundred, a derivative of Euchre best for three; Nap, a popular English round game; Loo, a family gambling game somewhat old hat but simpler than it looks (the word is short for *lanterloo*, a cooing refrain once used in French lullabyes, but don't ask why); Rams, a Germanic relative of Loo; and Spoil Five, which was once Ireland's national card game and now lives on across the Atlantic in the form of Auction Forty-Fives.

Ecarté ⚇

2 players
1 short pack (32)

Ecarté ousted its centuries-old parent Triomphe (French Ruff) from the casinos of Paris early last century and reached England about 1820. An English code of play was drawn up in 1878 and published with an exhaustive treatise on the game by Cavendish, who has been accused of killing it by over-analysis. Although Ecarté is for two players, one of whom is the dealer put up by the house, its continued popularity in some French casinos lies in its suitability for side-bets on the two players from bystanders. European casinos are increasingly dominated by American card games and in this country Ecarté is practically defunct. This is a pity as it is a fast-moving game of simple mechanics but pleasing depth and variety, and works perfectly well without the monetary interest. The name means 'discarded' in allusion to its most characteristic feature of play.

CARDS 32, ranking KQJAT987 in each suit. Note the position of the Ace. It is convenient to use two packs so that one may be shuffled while the other is dealt.

GAME The first to win 5 points wins the game. The best way of recording the score is by means of counters: each player starts with five on his left and transfers one to his right for each point he scores.

GENERAL IDEA A trump suit is established at random and five tricks are played with 'strict' rules of following. A player scores 1 point for taking three or four tricks, 2 points for winning the vole (all five). The distinctive feature of the game is that there may be several rounds of changing cards before the play begins and good judgement is called for in deciding when to stop exchanging and start playing.

DEAL The deal alternates. Shuffle thoroughly, offer to cut, and deal five cards to each player in batches of two then three (or vice versa, but whichever method you start with you must stick to during the game). Place the remainder face down to form a stock. Turn up the top card and place it to one side. The suit of the turn-up is the trump suit for the deal. If the turn-up is a King, dealer scores 1 point for it. (If this gives him 5 points he wins without further play.)

DISCARDING Non-dealer may start the play by leading to the first trick, in which case he will be penalized if he does not win, or he may call for cards ('Propose'). If he proposes, dealer may either refuse, insisting that the hands be played out as they stand (in which case *he* will be penalized if he does not win), or accept. If dealer accepts, both players must change at least one card.

Cards are exchanged as follows. Non-dealer discards from one to five cards face down and is dealt a like number from the top of the stock. Then dealer does likewise. The trump turn-up remains untouched.

Again, non-dealer may lead or propose and dealer may accept or refuse. This continues until non-dealer decides to lead, or dealer refuses a proposal, or the stock is exhausted. Neither player may call for more cards than remain in the stock, and when no more cards remain non-dealer is obliged to start play.

MARKING THE KING After the exchange, but before the play, if either player holds the King of trumps he may declare it and score 1 point. This privilege ceases if and as soon as its holder plays some other card to the first trick.

TRICKS Unusual rules of trick-taking apply. Non-dealer leads to the first trick (announcing, as he does so, what suit he is leading – a matter of convention which some modern players ignore). The second player to each trick must not only follow suit but also win the trick if he can. If unable to follow he must trump if he can, and only if unable to do so may he renounce. The trick is captured by the higher card of the suit led, or the higher trump if any are played, and the winner of one trick leads to the next.

SCORE If any cards were exchanged the winning of three or four tricks scores 1 for the 'point', the winning of five 2 for the 'vole'. But if non-dealer loses after failing to propose, or dealer loses after refusing the first proposal, then the winner scores 2 points regardless of the number of tricks he took.

The game is won with 5 points. By agreement, the game is won singly if the loser has 3 or 4, doubly if 1 or 2, trebly if he has marked no points.

IRREGULARITIES If the dealer faces one of his own cards in the deal the deal stands; but if he faces one of his opponent's the latter may call for a new deal. A proposal accepted may not be retracted. A card once played cannot be retracted except to correct a revoke or a lead out of turn, and the latter only if the opponent has not yet played to it. A player who abandons his hand is held to cede the remaining tricks to the other, who scores accordingly. If a player is found to have revoked, or to have underplayed when able to win a trick, his opponent may (even if he abandoned his hand) call for the hands to be restored and played again; in this case the offending player, if he wins, scores 0 for the point, or 1 for the vole or any other circumstance in which he would normally mark 2 points.

VARIANTS More than two players may take part in a game of Ecarté but only two are active in each deal. Three or more are therefore better off playing some form of Euchre.

NOTES ON PLAY

At first sight the 'strict' rules of following that require a player to win the trick if possible may appear to restrict the exercise of skill. A little experience will soon show that there is more subtlety to the game than first appears, perhaps even enough to justify an assertion of the French that good Ecarté players are born, not made. Good judgement is called for in knowing when to exchange and when to play.

As non-dealer you should realize that you have two advantages over your opponent: first, the lead; second, that the odds are against his holding more trumps than yourself. If you hold three or more power cards (trumps and Kings) you should play without proposing; conversely, if you propose and are accepted, you should throw out all cards which are not trumps or Kings and thereby exchange at least three. Certain hands are known to be at least twice as likely to win as to be beaten, and should therefore be played without proposing. Such hands are called *jeux de règle* ('obligatory hands'). The full gamut of *jeux de règle* has been worked out to a considerable degree of refinement, but may be broadly summarized as follows:

ECARTÉ: HANDS PLAYABLE WITHOUT PROPOSING
(jeux de règle)

trumps held:	non-trumps include:
3+	any
2	King and a void suit
	Queen and one of same suit
	Any three of a suit
1	KQJ of one suit
	Queen and two of same suit
	Queen and another in two suits
0	Any four court cards better than four Jacks

The normal strategy of such hands is to lead the top card of the longest suit and to press it until trumped. Experience will show which hands are susceptible to other strategies and particularly how to bluff by leading the dealer into believing you are playing orthodoxly when not, and so miscalculating his game.

There are some sound exceptions to the above hands. If you hold the King of trumps (or the Queen, if the King was turned) it is safe to propose as often as you feel uncertain about the strength of your hand and are permitted to do so, as dealer cannot then win the vole to score 2 against you, and you can keep building up power cards until you are in a position to win the vole yourself. But remember that you must exchange at least one card if your proposal is accepted, so do not fall into the beginner's trap of 'bluffing' on a cast-iron hand more likely to be weakened than strengthened by any exchange.

Whether or not to propose may also be affected by the state of the score. If dealer is in the lead with 3 points it is dangerous to play without proposing, for if you lose the deal he will score 2 for the game. You therefore need a stronger than average *jeu de règle*. But if he stands at four you should prefer to hold to a weak hand unless you hold the King of trumps (or it is turned), for if you invite an exchange of cards he need only draw the King and mark it to win without further play.

As dealer you may usually assume that a proposal is made on the basis of a weak holding (exceptions being provided by your own knowledge of the non-dealer's strategy and perhaps of your opponent's style of play) and accordingly refuse on any holding that would be a *jeu de règle* in the other position, or marginally weaker. In effect you should certainly refuse on a holding of three or more trumps, and nearly always on a two-trump holding backed by two or more cards in another suit. Even so unprepossessing a holding as Seven, Eight in trumps, Nine and Ten of another and Ten of a third suit gives odds of nearly two to one in your favour if the proposal is put. Holding the King of trumps, however (or the Queen if the King is turned), it may be worth accepting proposals with a view to the vole.

ILLUSTRATIVE DEALS

1. Baker deals as follows, turning up a small spade for trumps:

Abel   ♠J ♥Q ♣K7 ♦Q   (proposes)
Baker   ♠7 ♥97 ♣J ♦K   (accepts)

Abel's hand is not quite a *jeu de règle* and he stands to lose double if he plays. He discards both Queens and the Seven.

Baker also discards the three of his cards that are not trumps or Kings, and the new hands are:

Abel   ♠JT ♥K ♣KT   (plays)
Baker   ♠Q7 ♣Q9 ♦K

Unless Baker has the King of trumps Abel, to lead, has a chance of the vole. He therefore starts with ♥K, the card least likely to be trumped, in order to see whether or not Baker has the King to announce. In this case the King of the longer suit should not be led as Abel has altogether seen three clubs (counting his discard) to only two hearts, and hearts are therefore more likely to be followed. Here is the play with winning cards underlined:

	1st	2nd	3rd	4th	5th
Abel –	♥K	♠T –	♣K –	♣T	♠J
Baker	♠7 –	♦K	♣9	♣Q –	♠Q	(scores 1)

His lead trumped, Abel could only play for the point. At trick two Baker refrained from showing strength in trumps in order to mislead his opponent. At trick three Abel refrained from playing the trump (♠J) for fear that Baker might hold the Queen and more diamonds. In the event he would have won by leading clubs, in which suit Baker was unfortunate enough to hold a minor tenace (second and fourth highest).

2. Abel deals as follows and turns ♥J:

Baker   ♥QT ♣T8 ♦8   (plays)
Abel   ♥8 ♣J ♦AJT

Being forward in the score, Baker chances his arm on two trumps and a doubleton – not quite a *jeu de règle* but worth playing.

Baker leads from his longer non-trump suit:

	1st	2nd	3rd	4th	5th
Baker –	♣T	♦8	♥T –	♥Q –	♣8	(scores 1)
Abel	♣J –	♦A –	♦J	♥8	♦T

He would have lost the point by following the beginner's gambit of leading trumps.

3. Baker deals as follows and turns ♣Q:

| Abel | ♣7 ♥7 ♦KT7 | (proposes) |
| Baker | ♣9 ♠KQ ♥KQ | (refuses) |

	1st	2nd	3rd	4th	5th	
Abel	– ♦K	♥7	♣7 –	♦T –	♦7	(scores 2)
Baker	♣9 –	♥K –	♥Q	♠Q	♠K	

Abel's hand was theoretically not strong enough to play without proposing and Baker's was theoretically strong enough to play without accepting – but what happens in practice may be a different matter altogether. Abel scores 2 for winning the point after a refusal.

Euchre 🂠 ◎

2–7 players, 4 best
1 short pack (32)

'Those who are familiar with life in the United States must be aware of the enormous popularity that the game of Euchre enjoys,' wrote R. F. Foster in 1909, shortly before it was ousted from its prime position by the ubiquitously over-whelming Bridge. It is, indeed, an essentially American game, variously attributed to the French of Louisiana and the 'Dutch' (Germans) of Pennsylvania. It remains popular in the north-eastern states of the US, and in Canada, and boasts an historically unexplained following in the west country of Britain. Euchre, not Poker, is apparently the game for which the Joker was invented, under its original name of 'Best Bower'. One explanation of the word Euchre itself describes it as a sort of Germanic mispronunciation of Joker. Others range from the implausible to the improbable.

Euchre is generally held to be at its best as a partnership game for four but is playable by virtually any number. Having presented the basic principles we shall take the various formats in numerical order.

CARDS 32. The normal ranking in each suit is AKQ(J)T987. But . . .

TRUMPS In the suit selected as trump the highest card is the Jack, known as the Right Bower, and the second highest is the Jack of the other suit of the same colour as trumps, known as the Left Bower. ('Bower' comes from the German *Bauer*, which basically means 'farmer', but also is one of several words for 'Jack'.) It follows that there will be nine cards in the trump suit, but only seven in the other suit of that colour, and eight in each of the others. It must always be remembered in play that the Left Bower belongs to the trump suit and not to the suit marked on its face. The Ace is then the third highest trump, followed by KQT987.

DEALER'S PRIVILEGE In most versions of the game a card is turned up for the purpose of proposing a trump suit. This suit may be accepted or rejected as trump, but if it is accepted then the dealer has the privilege of discarding one of the cards he was dealt and counting the turn-up as part of his hand. This is called 'taking it up'.

DEAL Five cards each are dealt in batches of two and three, and the next is turned up to propose a trump suit.

OBJECT The object of each player or partnership is to win a majority of the five tricks, i.e., three or more ('the point'), and preferably all five, which is known as 'the march'. A player or partnership that fails to win after accepting the proposed suit as trump is 'euchred', and penalized accordingly.

TRICKS Usual rules of trick-taking apply. Suit must be followed if possible; if not, a player may trump or renounce *ad lib*. The trick is captured by the highest card of the suit led, or the highest trump if any are played, and the winner of one trick leads to the next.

Euchre Variants

2–6 players
1 short pack (32)

EUCHRE FOR TWO

MAKING TRUMPS Non-dealer may accept the proposed suit as trump, which he will do if he thinks he can win three tricks thereby, by announcing '(I) order it up,' meaning that he orders the turned card up into the dealer's hand. If not he passes this option to the dealer, who may himself either 'Take it up' or pass. If the dealer also passes he turns the trump card face down. Now non-dealer may announce another suit as trump, thereby obligating himself to win three tricks. If he passes, dealer may nominate a trump suit to the same effect. If he also passes, the cards are thrown in and non-dealer becomes the new dealer.

PLAY Non-dealer leads to the first trick and usual rules apply (see above). If the turned suit was accepted as trump by either player, dealer discards a card before playing to the first trick and counts the turn-up as part of his hand.

SCORE The trump-maker scores 1 for the point (three or four tricks) or 2 for the march (all five). If he fails to take three he is euchred and his opponent scores 2 points. The winner is the first player to reach 5 points (or 7 or 10 or any other agreed number).

VARIANT The game may be played with a 24-card pack, lacking Sevens and Eights.

EUCHRE FOR THREE (CUT-THROAT EUCHRE)

This would more accurately be described as Solo Euchre, as there is only one trump-maker and the other two therefore play in temporary partnership to defeat him even though each plays to his own score in the long run. Preliminaries and trick-play as above. Player left of dealer may order it up or pass; if he passes, the player on dealer's right may order it up or pass; if he passes, dealer may take it up or pass. If all pass, the turn-up is turned down and each in turn has one opportunity to make another suit trump (thereby obligating himself to win at least three tricks) or pass. If all pass, the hands are thrown in. If not, the lead is made by eldest hand after dealer has discarded if appropriate.

SCORE The trump-maker scores 1 for the point or 2 for the march. If euchred he loses 2 points, which may give him a negative score. Game is 5, 7 or 10 up. Some credit a score of 3 for the march, a practice which may be recommended.

EUCHRE FOR FOUR (PARTNERSHIP)

Partners sit opposite each other. Starting with dealer's left opponent, each in turn may order it up or pass. (The phrase used by dealer's partner is '(I) assist,' since an acceptance of the trump suit by one player obligates his partnership to win at least three tricks.)

If all pass, the turn-up is turned down, and the privilege of nominating another trump suit starts with dealer's left opponent and passes around the table until a suit is named. If all pass again the cards are thrown in and the next to deal does so.

If trumps are made, the opening lead is made by eldest hand.

GOING IT ALONE The maker of trumps has the option of announcing 'I play alone,' in which case his partner lays his hand of cards face down on the table. The lone player must then win three or more tricks out of his own hand against both opponents, for the advantage of a higher score if he wins the march. In this event the opening lead is made by the lone player's left-hand opponent.

SCORE The making side scores 1 for the point, 2 for the march, or 4 for the march if won by a lone player. If it is euchred the opponents score 2.

VARIANT If the maker elects to play alone, either opponent may similarly elect to defend alone. If the lone defender wins he scores 2 for the point or 4 for the march.

REVOKE A revoke may be corrected before the trick is gathered. If not, the opponents may either score 2 points or deduct from the offender's side 2 points, or 4 if he is playing alone.

NOTES ON PLAY (PARTNERSHIP)

In the first or 'ordering up' round each player should remember that dealer has a double advantage: one certain trump (the turn-up), and another probable by the 'law of averages', and the certain ability to void a side-suit by his discard in order to win a trick by ruffing. This knowledge will affect other players' considerations according to their positions in relation to him.

Eldest hand, the first to speak, should not normally order it up unless he himself holds three probable tricks. Even with two bowers he would be well advised to pass, for if the dealer takes it up he will probably be euchred, and, if he does not, eldest will then have first choice of another trump suit and can 'make it next' – i.e., nominate the other suit of the same colour. (Nominating a suit of the opposite colour is called 'crossing it'.) An exception to this rule is when his own side is 'at the bridge', i.e., needs only one point to game, the opponents lying two or three points behind. In this circumstance there is the danger that dealer or his partner may play alone, win the march and so the game. By ordering it up he restricts his opponents to at most 2 for the march. Similarly, if both sides are level and need one for game, it may be worth chancing an order-up on cards that give an outside chance of winning.

Dealer's partner usually 'assists' on the strength of side suits, such as two non-trump Aces, bearing in mind that his partner can probably be relied upon for strength in trumps. If his side is in the lead and at the bridge, he may need to assist on weaker than average cards in order to prevent his left opponent from playing alone and possibly winning the march and the game.

Dealer's right opponent must have a good three tricks in hand if he is to order up, for his partner's pass will have shown weakness. An exception arises when he is at the bridge (needing one to game), for if his partner had *no* safe trick he would have ordered it up in order to prevent an opponent from stealing a march and winning the game: his failure to do so suggests that he can probably beat an attempt to win all five tricks, which in turn means he has one himself. In this case another two tricks will win.

Dealer is in the best position to take it up. With three or more trumps he should always do so, and with two he should do so if he has only one plain suit in hand, no matter how small the trumps are.

A lone hand may be undertaken by any player with three certain tricks (obviously), such as the three top trumps, or five cards which are Aces or strong trumps. Apart from that, only eldest hand and dealer are in a good position for this feat: dealer because he has the advantage of an extra trump against implicit weakness in opponents' hands (since they passed); eldest because he has the lead – though this applies only to the first round of trump-making.

If the first trump is rejected then, on the second round, eldest and partner should generally prefer to make it next (i.e., nominate the suit of the same colour as the turned down card), dealer and partner to cross it. The reason for this is that, since dealer and his partner turned it down, they presumably had no bower in the colour of the turn-up and may therefore be strong in suits of the opposite colour. Dealer's right opponent, however, should not normally make a trump unless he is strong enough to play alone, for two passes from the opposite side of the table show decided weakness.

With so few tricks to play there is no time to 'establish' suits and it is better to lead (say) a guarded King than hold it back in expectation of the Ace. It is generally best to lead high cards of plain suits, and especially so against a lone hand. Eldest, however, may lead trumps in many cases, though not when dealer has taken it up of his own accord. Only trump your partner's winning card if you really need the lead. The second player to a trick should normally play the best he can, trumping if necessary. Discard singletons (except Aces), especially of suits being trumped by opponents.

RAILROAD EUCHRE (4-PARTNERSHIP)

This denotes any form of the partnership game (above) spiced up with one or more of the following variants, devised, as the name implies, by railway commuters to enliven and speed up the game as played in the train on their comparatively short way to work.

JOKER added as the top trump or 'best bower'. If turned, the suit below it determines trump (or else it is a fixed suit, by previous agreement). Thus there are ten cards in the trump suit.

CALL FOR BEST If the maker plays alone, he may discard one card and call upon his partner to give him his best card, the partner deciding which one that is. A lone defender may do the same.

PAT HAND If a lone player plays without exchanging a single card he scores 5 for the march; but his opponents (who may not defend alone) score 1 if he fails the march, or 3 if he is euchred.

JAMBONE The lone maker plays an unbeatable hand open on the table and the opponents may not defend alone. When the maker leads, his left opponent tells him what to play; when he has to follow, his right opponent does so (such plays must, of course, be legal). The opponents may not consult with each other.

JAMBOREE If the maker has the five top trumps he shows them and scores 16 without further play. This is combined with . . .

LAPS Any excess score at the end of one deal is carried over to the next.

SLAMS A game is won doubly if the losers scored zero.

EUCHRE FOR 4–6 PLAYERS

CALL-ACE EUCHRE Four use 24, five 28, six 32 cards and five each are dealt, or else four or five use 32 and six each are dealt. As in the basic game the trump turned may be ordered, taken or made. The maker then names any suit, and the holder of the highest card of that suit in play becomes his partner – without revealing that fact by any means other than the way he plays. The maker may unwittingly prove to be his own partner; or, as in the basic game, he may elect to play alone. Each member of a side scores the points due to his side as a whole.

BLIND EUCHRE Vary the number of cards in play as required. Each plays for himself. Method 1: deal five each and a blind or widow of two cards face down. The maker, before play, takes up the blind and discards any two cards from his hand. Method 2: deal five each and a blind of five. The maker, before play, may look at the blind and swap his whole hand for it but not exchange individual cards with it. Method 3: deal five each and a blind of five. Each in turn may look at the blind and swap his whole hand for it, his discarded hand becoming the new blind for the next player. When all have had one opportunity to exercise this option the round of trump-making begins.

JACKPOT EUCHRE Four use 24, five 28, six 32 cards, and a Joker is added as Best Bower. Each plays for himself, chips one to the pool and receives five cards; the topmost of the undealt cards is turned for trump. The maker is not obliged to win three tricks. Instead, each player draws a chip from the pool for each trick he wins, or pays another chip to it if he fails to win any. The pool is swept by the first player to win a march or make a score of 12.

AUCTION EUCHRE Best for five players. Use 28 cards, deal five each and leave a blind or widow of three face down (or use 32, make a blind of five and leave two cards out of play). Each in turn has one opportunity to bid at least three tricks using a named trump, or to overcall a previous bid. A bid of 5 may be overcalled by a bid of 8, which is an undertaking to play a lone hand after exchanging cards, and that by a bid of 15, which is to play alone with the hand as dealt. The maker, before play, first takes the widow and discards any three cards from his hand (unless he bid 15); then calls for a part-partner (unless playing alone) by naming any specific card not in his own hand. The holder of that card becomes his partner but may not reveal that fact except by his play. Method 1: the maker may lead instead of eldest hand. Method 2: if he bid 4 or 5 tricks the maker may call for two partners by the same method as for one. This is not recommended.

HASENPFEFFER For four in partnerships, this word is German for 'peppered hare' or 'rabbit stew', an unexplained but savoury alternative to the more prosaic 'Bid Euchre'. It seems also to have been somewhat flavoured by Pitch.

Use 24 cards (nothing lower than Nine) plus Joker as top trump or Best Bower. Deal six each in threes and leave the last card face down. Each in turn bids or overbids a number of tricks, without as yet mentioning a trump suit, which he intends his partnership to win. Bids range from one to six. If all pass, the holder of the Joker is obliged to bid three. The highest bidder takes the odd card, names the trump suit, discards any card face down, and leads to the first trick. If the bidding side fails to make as many as it bid, it is set back by the amount of the bid, possibly resulting in a minus score; but if successful it scores 1 point per trick taken. In either case the non-bidding side scores 1 point per trick taken. Game is 10 points. Variant: Jacks are not bowers but rank as normal in all suits.

DOUBLE HASENPFEFFER For four or six players in two partnerships, this uses a Pinochle pack (2 × 24 = 48 cards, nothing lower than Nine). There is no Joker. Deal all the cards around. Each player has one chance to bid or overbid, the minimum being for three tricks, with no trump as yet mentioned. If three pass, dealer is obliged to bid at least three. The high bidder may play alone, in which case he discards any two cards face down and receives from his partner any two cards the latter wishes to give him. If the making side takes at least as many as it bid it scores 1 point per trick taken; if not, it loses the amount of the bid, except that the dealer, if forced to bid, is set back by only half the amount he bid. A lone player wins or loses double for his side.

Five Hundred

2–6 players, 3 best
1 pack (53)

Five Hundred was devised in the early 1900s as an extension of Euchre and copyrighted by the American Playing Card Company in 1904. Its avowed intention was to improve Euchre by putting all cards into play and introducing a refined bidding system comparable to that of the then novel game of Bridge – which, as card historians will note, explains the bidding order of suits for trumps. For about a decade it remained America's major social card game but then fell before the onslaught of Auction Bridge and was later administered the *coup de grâce* by Contract. Fortunately, it managed to survive in other far-flung corners of the civilized world and has subsequently become the national card game of Australia. Australian '500' cards incorporate Elevens, Twelves and two red-Thirteens to make a 62-card pack (plus Joker or Best Bower) for play by up to six, though it is nearly always played there as a four-hand partnership game. A major reason for its perpetuation in Anglo-American game anthologies, however, is its particular suitability for three-hand play. As this is a more desirable (because rarer) quality than four-handedness, Five Hundred is here presented in its classical form as an excellent game for three.

CARDS 32 plus Joker. Normal ranking from high to low is
AKQ(J)T987.

TRUMPS In the trump suit, established by bidding, the cards
rank as follows:

1. Best Bower – the Joker
2. Right Bower – Jack of trumps
3. Left Bower – other Jack of the same colour as trumps
4. Ace of trumps, followed by KQT987.

Hence there are ten cards in the trump suit, seven in the other
suit of the same colour, and eight each in suits of the opposite colour. Note that the Left Bower belongs to the trump
suit, not to the suit marked on its face.

In a 'no trump' game there is no trump suit and all the
Jacks rank in their normal position between Queen and Ten.
The Joker, however, retains its position as Best Bower and is
the only trump in the pack.

DEAL Each player receives ten cards dealt as follows: a batch
of three to each player, then three face down to the table,
then four each, and finally three each. The face-down cards
form the 'kitty' (or 'widow' in Anglo-American play).

OBJECT The ultimate objective is to score 500 points before
anyone else, whence the name of the game. This generally
takes several deals. In each deal the highest bidder names the
trump, exchanges through the kitty, and aims to take at least
as many tricks as he bid. The opponents play cooperatively
in an attempt to beat him, but each one also scores for any
tricks taken by himself.

BIDDING Starting with eldest hand, each in turn may pass or
make a higher bid than any that has gone before, announcing either the number of tricks he proposes to win and the
intended trump suit, or the value of the contract in accordance with the contract valuation table. Once a player has
passed he may not re-enter, and once two players have passed
the third has no opportunity to increase his bid.

FIVE HUNDRED: CONTRACT VALUATION TABLE

Tricks contracted:		6	7	8	9	10
in spades	♠	40	140	240	340	440
in clubs	♣	60	160	260	360	460
in diamonds	♦	80	180	280	380	480
in hearts	♥	100	200	300	400	500
at no trump	N	120	220	320	420	520

Misère (250) overcalls any bid of 240 or less
Open misère (520) overcalls every other bid

Misère is a bid to lose every single trick; open misère to do so with one's hand of cards exposed on the table. Both are played at no trumps, except for the Best Bower.

ALL PASS If all pass, the game plays as follows. The kitty remains untouched; eldest hand leads; and tricks are played at No Trump. Each player scores 10 points per trick won by himself.

THE KITTY When two players have passed, the third becomes the solo player and must take at least as many tricks as he bid in order to win. He is not permitted to increase his bid and gets no credit for taking more tricks than necessary. He first takes up the kitty and adds it to his hand, then discards any three cards face down to the table, where they remain out of play. Having already announced trumps or no trumps ('no-ies') he leads to the first trick. If he is playing an open misère he waits until the first trick has been captured and then immediately lays the rest of his hand face up on the table.

TRICKS Normal rules of trick-taking apply. Players must follow suit if possible; if not, they may trump or renounce *ad lib*. The trick is captured by the highest card of the suit led, or the highest trump if any are played, and the winner of one trick leads to the next. Remember that the Left Bower is the third highest card of the trump suit, not the fourth highest card of the suit marked on it, and the Best Bower (Joker) is the highest trump. In a no-trump game the Best Bower may only be used to ruff a trick if its holder is void in the suit led. If the holder leads it to a trick he must specify a suit to be played to it, which the others must follow if possible; but he may not specify a suit in which he has already shown himself to be void (by discarding to it when led).

SCORE If the soloist makes his contract he scores the value of that contract. He gets no credit for taking more tricks than contracted, but if he succeeds in taking all ten in a contract worth less than 250, he scores 250 instead of the lower contract value. If he fails to make his contract his current score is reduced by the value of the failed contract, which makes it possible for players to be 'in the hole' with negative scores during the course of the game. Whether or not he makes his contract each opponent scores 10 points per trick captured by himself, except in a won misère. In a lost misère the soloist is set back by 250 (520) and each opponent scores 10 per trick taken by the soloist.

GAME Game is either 500 up or 500 down, i.e., the winner is the first player to reach or exceed a score of 500, or the player with the greatest score if and when one player is reduced to *minus* 500 or more. If two or more stand to reach 500 in the same deal the soloist scores first and wins if he thereby reaches the target; or, if both opponents reach 500 but not the soloist, then the winner is the one who took the trick that gave him 500 first.

REVOKE A revoke may be corrected before the trick is turned down but the card wrongly played remains face up on the table and must be played at the earliest legal opportunity. (If made by the second player the third may retract the card he played and play another.) If an opponent's uncorrected revoke is discovered the soloist scores as if he had won the contract, whether in fact he did or not, and the revoking player may score nothing for tricks. If a soloist's uncorrected revoke is discovered he loses the contract value whether he made it or not.

VARIANTS

VARIANTS IN PLAY The scoring schedule followed here is known as the Avondale; others, such as the Original and the Inverted, are no longer used. The misère bid, which has long been popular, is ignored by many writers, especially Bridge experts, who seem to regard it as not quite nice. Though valued at 250, published Australian rules imply that misère cannot overcall 8♠ (240). Some appear to play without the Joker but this negates the essence of the game.

FOR TWO PLAYERS Method 1: use 33 cards and deal as if for three players but leave one hand face down and out of play. Method 2: use 24 cards (nothing lower than Nine) and no Joker. Deal 10 each and a kitty of four; bid and play as in the three-player game.

FOR FOUR PLAYERS Use 42 cards plus Joker, rejecting from a full pack all Twos, Threes and black Fours. Play in partnerships. Follow the rules of the three-hand game.

FOR FIVE PLAYERS Use the full pack of 52 cards plus Joker. Each plays for himself but the highest bidder may either play alone or call for a partner by nominating a specific card. The holder of that card becomes his partner and immediately identifies himself. The card called may not be a trump but may be the Joker if the bid is at no trump. The called partner wins or loses half the appropriate score and each opponent scores 10 per trick in the usual way.

FOR SIX PLAYERS Use the special 62-card pack with Elevens, Twelves and red Thirteens, plus Joker; deal ten each and leave a kitty of three in the usual way. Method 1: play in three partnerships of two players each, each pair of partners sitting opposite each other with two opponents intervening on either side, and play as in the three-hand game. Method 2: play in two partnerships of three players each, such that each player sits between two opponents, and play as in the four-hand game.

NOTES ON (THREE-HAND) PLAY

Five Hundred should present no problems to players of simple trick games like Whist and family, or comparable three-handers like Skat, as the management of trumps and long plain suits, *mutatis mutandis*, is much the same. Whist and Bridge players, however, must from the outset be aware of the facts that (a) in a suit contract one-third of the cards in play are trumps (10 out of 30, as distinct from one quarter in other games), and (b) in a no-trump game there is in fact *one* trump – the Joker or Best Bower. This can make all the difference.

Before bidding assess your maximum safe bid and make it immediately, as you will have no chance to increase it if both opponents pass. If you lack the Joker do not think in terms of a no-trump bid unless you have Aces or at least guarded Kings in all four suits. For a suit bid you should normally hold at least five trumps, including a bower, though four with two bowers may be playable with good side-suit support. Unless you have exceptionally long trumps – seven or more – you must also have side-suit support in the shape of Aces and guarded Kings, or a long suit. A void after the exchange is good for ruffing, if you can afford to use trumps for that purpose rather than for clearing the trump suit, but is less useful before the exchange because of the likelihood of finding cards of that suit in the kitty. A hand containing only average trumps and one other good suit is dangerous, as you may be forced to spend all your trumps before getting an opportunity to play the long suit. But with two possible trump suits and adequate support it is usually better to entrump the weaker – diamonds, for example, on the following hand, rather than hearts:

♦J ♥J ♦K98 ♥AKQ ♣AQ

The hand is good for seven tricks in diamonds before the exchange, and is unlikely to be improved.

If you hold the Joker look first to any possibility of playing a no trumper. The fact of having the lead enables you to run through a long suit unbroken from the Ace, and the Best Bower will give you one opportunity of defending against one attack in a weak suit (but not more: you cannot afford two bad suits). Some hands that look like trump contracts at first sight prove to be 'no-ies' on closer inspection and should be so played for the sake of a higher score. This, for example:

Jo ♠KQT987 ♥A ♣Q8

The hand should yield seven in spades as it stands, for a value of 140; yet it can equally well hold as 7 NT for 220. By leading spades until the Ace falls, then trumping in and leading the by-now unbeatable spades again, no more will be lost than the two clubs and a spade.

6. FIVE HUNDRED This hand is good for a bid of six in hearts in the three-player game, as it contains the top three trumps (*bowers*, the Joker and both red Jacks), a good forcing suit (clubs) and a void (diamonds) upon which to make a low trump. The bid can be raised to seven in the expectation that, even if the outstanding hearts are not evenly divided (3 + 2), some benefit may be afforded by the widow. If an opponent takes the game in spades, this hand gains strength from its ♣J as left bower in addition to the Joker as best.

The kitty should not be looked upon as a device for increasing your trump holding, as the chances are (obviously) against drawing more cards in the suit you hold longest, and much in favour of drawing cards in a suit you expect to void, or have void already. At most, hope that the kitty will improve six tricks to seven or perhaps eight, or seven to eight; but if you are bidding eight to start with do not expect it to yield a ninth. The kitty should be regarded not as a source of strength but as an opportunity to eliminate weakness. For example, having been dealt an unguarded King or Queen, you may either draw cards of that suit to guard or cover it from the kitty, or else draw none of the suit and so be able to void it by means of the discard.

Use the discard as a means of voiding a weak suit if you have good enough trumps to keep ruffing it when led, but beware of voiding a suit that one opponent may have been bidding against you, as he will then use it to force your trumps out and throw up weaknesses elsewhere. It is better to keep such suits stopped. Keep a long side suit but retain a guarded King in preference to a long weak suit.

The lead is a great advantage and must be fully exploited. In a trump contract, usual procedure is to play the trump suit and keep leading it at every opportunity, in order to draw two for one and so increase the power of those remaining. Having weakened opponents' trumps, and especially forced out any high ones, proceed to your longest suit and press that at every opportunity. If possible, however, refrain from leading from a suit headed by a tenace (A–Q or K–J(T)) as it may be made to yield two tricks if you can afford to wait until it is led up to. In a no-trump contract lead and press your longest suit of five or more; or, if you have overall strength but no long suit, work upon the forcing out of adverse Aces and Kings in preference to leading your certain tricks. Use the Joker to trump in very circumspectly, as you have only one opportunity to do so. Sometimes it is better to forgo the ruff in order to throw out a weak card in some other suit, such as the Queen from a holding of Ace–Queen only.

The opponents should play as partners and concentrate on beating the contract rather than on seizing miserly trick points individually. As an opponent, therefore, refrain from trumping or overtaking tricks won certainly or probably by your partner, unless you have a good reason for taking the lead. Remember, if he made any bid, what his proposed suit was. Lead that suit to him, even if only to force out the soloist's trumps, and avoid blocking it, especially in a no-trumper. In a suit contract, the partners should weaken the soloist's trumps by leading into his void suit when possible, and particularly so when the soloist is lying second to a trick, which is the worst possible position for him. At no trumps they should force him to use up his lone trump as early as possible.

Misères play as at any other comparable game (see, particularly, Hearts and related games). Open misères should not be undertaken lightly, and especially not in the hope of voiding a short suit with high cards. For example:

♠J97 ♥KT87 ♣7 ♦AQ

As it stands the spades cannot be beaten (unless led from), the hearts are equally safe, the ♣7 is a good lead, and the hope is to discard both diamonds after taking the kitty. Now suppose the kitty produces the Joker, ♣J and ♦9. The Joker must be discarded, as it is a trump and must take a trick. If the two original (high) diamonds are thrown, the holding of ♣J7 ♦9 is impossible to play open; no better would be the ♣7 ♦Q9 by another discard.

ILLUSTRATIVE DEAL

Abel   ♥KQJ97 ♣AJ87 ♦7
Baker   Jo♠AKQ ♣K9 ♦AJ98
Charlie ♠JT98 ♥AT8 ♦KQT

Abel, first to speak, has a pretty strong misère and open it straight away. Baker was thinking in terms of 7♦, for which purpose he already has five trumps including the best and right bowers, and a good side suit in spades. In raising the bid to 8♦ he takes a chance, trusting that, even with no improvement through the exchange, he may lose no more than one trump and the guard to the ♣K. Charlie passes. Abel declines to open his misère and passes.

Baker draws from the kitty ♣Q ♣T ♠T and throws the

last two back together with ♣9. This slightly strengthens his club holding, as he would be able if necessary to lead it in order to drive the Ace out.

Baker leads his Best Bower in the attack on trumps and draws two low ones in return. This leaves ♥J ♦K ♦Q in play. If he next led ♦J the chance of drawing the other bower and so winning the suit would be one in three, and if it failed he would be left without command of trumps. So he leads ♦8 instead, drawing ♦Q and the left bower.

At the third trick Abel leads ♣A and Baker throws ♣K as if threatening to trump another club lead. Now Baker's Queen is high and the suit is safe – unless Charlie holds a void in clubs *and* the outstanding trump. As it happens he does. At trick four, therefore, the lead of another club will beat the contract, the lead of a heart save it. Play it through and see.

Nap ◎
2–7 players, good for 5
1 pack (52)

We played penny Nap after supper. We played for about an hour and a half, after which time George had won fourpence and Harris and I had lost exactly twopence each. We thought we would give up gambling then. As Harris said, it breeds an unhealthy excitement when carried too far.

(J. K. Jerome, *Three Men in a Boat*, 1889)

This popular English game, which only purists refer to as 'Napoleon' in full (it bearing no explained relation to that worthy), is clearly a five-card game in line of descent from Triomphe, possibly through Ecarté. It was described by one writer in 1881 as 'comparatively new' and, as mentioned in *Three Men in a Boat* which first appeared in 1889, we may suppose that it was then, like George's banjo, 'all the rage this season'. It is almost pointless if not played for pennies.

CARDS 52, ranking normally (Ace high, Two low in each suit).

DEAL Five each, either singly or in batches of two and three as agreed.

OBJECT The player who bids to take the highest number of tricks chooses the trump suit and has to make that number to win.

BIDDING Each player has one opportunity only to pass or make a higher bid than any previous bidder. No suit is yet named. The minimum bid is theoretically 'one' but may be set higher by agreement. The payments from each opponent if successful, or to each if lost, are:

One	1
Two	2
Three	3
Mis	3 (no tricks, no trump)
Four	4
Nap	10 won or 5 lost
Wellington	10 won or 10 lost (optional)
Blucher	10 won or 20 lost (optional)

If all pass, the hands are thrown in and the next player deals.

Wellington and Blucher are also bids to win five, but Wellington may only be called against a player who has already bid Nap, and Blucher against one who has already bid Wellington. They are both optional and can easily be spared if fewer than five play. Blucher is only worth introducing with seven players.

PLAY The highest bidder makes the opening lead, and whatever he plays is automatically trump, except in a misère bid, at which there is no trump. Normal rules of trick-taking apply.

SETTLEMENT The caller wins from, or loses to, each opponent the value of his bid, with no credit for any excess tricks.

Note that he pays each player singly for a failed five-bid but wins doubly from each player if successful.

REVOKE If the caller revokes he loses his bid and pays accordingly; if an opponent does so the caller is deemed to have made his bid and the amount due to him is paid fully by the player who revoked, the others paying nothing.

VARIANTS

Numerous variants and aberrations may be encountered in different localities, and others may easily be invented for fun. The following are frequently encountered in textbooks, if nowhere else. Nap is distinctly a folk-game, offering great scope for field research.

MODERN NAP Modern players have increased the skill factor by stripping the pack, from the lowest rank upwards, until it consists of approximately one more hand than the number of players. For example, five would play with a 32-card pack containing no rank lower than Seven. There is no bid of Wellington or Blucher, but 'Nap' can be overcalled by Napoleon, in which the caller must lead his lowest trump. Tricks are not gathered but all played cards are left face up in a pile.

PEEP NAP Method 1: the caller, before leading, may peep at the top card of the stock and exchange it for a card in his hand if he so wishes. Method 2: an extra card is dealt face down. Each player is entitled to a private peep at it for a penny or other fixed sum. The time to do so is just before making a bid, but players lying behind the caller may also exercise that option. When everyone has had a chance to do so, caller may exchange it for a card in his hand as in Method 1. Method 3: as above, but each player in turn may peep *and* exchange before making a bid, so that the odd card – the 'floater' – keeps changing.

Payments in methods 2 and 3 go to a pool which is taken by the next player to win a bid of five.

POOL A separate pool or kitty may be kept to be taken by the winner of a bid of five. It may be fed in various ways but particularly by requiring a caller who fails his bid to pay to the kitty as if it were an extra player.

SIR GARNET OR WIDOW NAP An extra hand of five cards is dealt face down. A player who bids nap (or Wellington, etc.) may take up these cards, add them to his hand, reject any five face down and then lead in the usual way. It is a device for making bids of nap more frequent.

PURCHASE (OR ECARTÉ) NAP This more skilful or more artificial variant, depending upon your point of view, is practically a different game – in fact, it is virtually Ecarté for more than two players. After the initial deal, but before any bids are made, the dealer addresses himself to each player in turn and sells him, at a penny each (or other agreed figure), as many more cards as he wishes to buy. The purchaser must reject that number from his hand before receiving their replacements and may not subsequently change or refer to his rejects. The purchase price so paid goes to a pool to be won by the first to win a bid of five. Dealer may sell cards to himself in like manner. The books say that only one round of sales may be made, but . . .

NOTES ON PLAY (BASIC GAME)

Nap is a game of judgement, probabilities and wrinkles and if the oldest player does not consistently win he should be put out to grass.

Whether and what to bid depends not only on the number of people playing but also on the position from which you are to call. In a three-player game, for example, the odds that one opponent holds the Ace above your King are 2:1 against; with five playing, only 9:7 against. That your Queen is the highest of its suit in play is worth counting on if three play, but not amongst five. As to position, take a hand like:

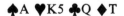

♠A ♥K5 ♣Q ♦T

This makes a worse than dubious bid of three if you are first to call, but may be bid from fourth or fifth position if those before you all passed. Its outcome depends largely on whether or not your lead of ♥K wins.

Since you should always reckon on at least one opponent's holding two of your trump suit, a prudent minimum-three bid requires you to hold at least three trumps, including an honour, and Queens at the very least in side suits. As we have seen above, however, the requirement relaxes as more players pass before the bid is made. Except when three play, nap should rarely be bid without the Ace of trumps, but one loser is permissible in side suits as the opponents will not know which suit to keep back.

In the play get rid of probable losers early rather than late, except on a bid of nap, of course. In the hand quoted above it would be correct to lead the Queen rather than the Ace at trick two (assuming the King won), leaving yourself with a probable winner if either black suit is led back. If that goes the Ace can be led hopefully for the third trick.

As an opponent of the caller you should win what tricks you can from him rather than underplay and leave it to someone else. At the same time, however, it is desirable to lead through the caller rather than up to him. Thus to a non-trump lead from caller the player to his immediate left may underplay, or discard rather than trump, partly to avoid putting himself in the lead and so allowing caller to play last to the trick (his best position), and partly in the complementary hope that the player at caller's immediate right may win the trick, so putting caller in the second and worst position to play to the next.

Trumps should be led when the caller needs but one trick, and held back when he needs two or more.

Loo ⊙

3–8 players
1 pack (52)

A venerable old gambling game, more complicated in the description than in the play, Loo is perhaps now best played as a party game with chips or counters, as 'Unlimited Loo' with real money can prove expensive. First described is Three-card Loo. Variants include Five-card Loo, and Irish Loo, which is Five-card Loo played with three cards.

CARD 52, ranking normally (Ace high, Two low).

ANTE Dealer antes three counters to the pool. A pool of only three counters is a 'single'; if it contains more, left over from the previous deal, it is a 'double'.

DEAL Three cards each, one at a time, and an extra hand of three face-down cards called 'miss'. Upturn the next card to establish trumps.

OBJECT To win at least one of the three tricks and so avoid being looed, as the player who takes none must increase the pool.

PRELIMINARIES From the left around the table, each in turn announces whether he will play or throw his hand in. One who offers to play may exchange his hand for miss, sight unseen, but may then neither drop nor change it back. The first to exchange prevents any subsequent player from doing so. If all pass, dealer wins the pool. If one exchanges and the others all pass, the exchanger wins the pool. If just one player before the dealer plays, and does so without exchanging, the dealer may not pass but has a choice of play. (a) He may play on his own account, with or without exchanging, or (b) he may 'defend miss', in which case he has no part in any transaction at the end of play, the other player settling only with the pool according to the result.

PLAY Eldest hand leads. He must lead the Ace of trumps if he has it (or the King if the Ace is the trump turn-up). If not, he must still lead a trump if he has more than one, and it must be his highest if he is playing against only one opponent. Strict rules of trick-play apply. Each in turn must follow suit if possible and head the trick if possible; if not, he must trump if possible, and only otherwise may he renounce. The trick is won by the highest card of the suit led or by the highest trump if any are played. The winner of a trick leads to the next and must lead a trump if he has one.

SETTLEMENT Each trick taken earns its winner one-third of the pool. If a player is looed (takes none) he pays three counters to the pool, which is then carried forward as a 'double'.

OPTIONAL RULES If the pool is a single, nobody may throw his hand in. In Unlimited Loo the amount contributed to the pool by one who is looed is not necessarily three counters but the amount already in the pool at the start of that deal. (This is where it starts to mount up.)

NOTE ON PLAY What makes this essentially a gambling game is the fact that strict rules of trick-taking make the play virtually mechanical, the only skill left lying in deciding whether or not to stay in. A measure of judgement may be introduced by relaxing these rules to a previously agreed extent.

Loo Variants

BOURRE A modern cross between Ecarté and Loo for two to seven players, using a 52-card pack with Ace high and Two low. Everyone contributes equally to the pool and receives five cards dealt one at a time, the next card being turned for trump. Each in turn may drop out or elect to play, thereby undertaking to win at least one trick. Anyone who plays may discard any number of cards face down and receive replacements from the top of the stock. First active player left of dealer leads. Strict rules apply: follow suit if possible and head the trick if possible; otherwise trump (and overtrump if possible); otherwise play anything. Anyone holding A, K or Q of trumps must lead his highest trump as early as he can. The pool goes to the winner of the most tricks, being shared equally in the event of a tie. Anyone who fails to take a trick contributes to the next pool the same amount as in the pool when he lost.

FIVE-CARD LOO Ante five counters, deal five each (3 +2) but no miss, upturn and remove the next card for trumps. Each in turn may drop, play his hand pat, or discard as many as he likes in return for the same number dealt from the top of the pack, in which case he must play. The ♣J, known as Pam (short for Pamphilus), is the highest card in play, beating everything including the Ace of trumps. If anyone before or after exchanging cards has a flush, holding either five cards of the same suit or four of the same suit plus Pam, he 'looes the board' immediately – i.e., is deemed to win all five tricks without play, no opponent being allowed to drop. If more than one has a flush the order of priority is: a flush with Pam, a flush in trumps, the flush with the highest top card or cards. A player with a flush beaten in this way is exempt from payment, as is any other player holding Pam. Play as at Three-card Loo. If the Ace of trumps is led its leader may say 'Pam be civil,' in which case the holder of ♣J may not play it if he has any other trump. Each trick earns one-fifth of the pool. Variant: Under 'club law', if clubs are trumps, nobody may drop.

IRISH LOO Deal three each but no miss. Instead, as at Five-card, each in turn may drop, stay, or exchange up to three cards. There is no Pam. If clubs are trump no one may drop. Dealer is obliged to defend the pool against a single opponent. All other play as at Three-card Loo.

RAMS Not so much a Loo variant as a substantially similar

game, Rams is for three to five players and uses a 32-card pack with Ace high, Seven low. Ante five to the pool, deal five cards each (3 +2) plus a spare hand of five, and upturn the next card to establish trumps. Each in turn may pass or play, the latter promising to win at least one trick; but when the pool contains only five units nobody may pass. One player only may exchange his hand for the spare, sight unseen, but must then play. A player may bid *rams*, which is an undertaking to win all five tricks, and in this case everybody must play. (He must announce this fact before any player after him has declared his intentions.) If everybody passes, dealer receives five chips from the player on his right and there is no play. If only one player before him offers to play, dealer himself may not pass. Dealer may take the trump turn-up in exchange for any unwanted card. First active player left of dealer leads. It is obligatory to follow suit if possible and win the trick if possible, and to trump, if unable to follow, with a higher trump than any already played if possible. Each won trick earns one-fifth of the pool and a player who takes none adds five units for the next deal. A successful rams bid wins the pool plus five units from each opponent. If lost, the bidder doubles the pool and pays five to each (nothing extra for the player who took the trick that ended the play). Variant games include Rounce, using 52 cards, and Bierspiel, in which ◆7 is always the second-highest trump.

Spoil Five ◎
2–10 players, 5–6 best
1 pack (52)

Spoil Five is, or was, regarded as the national card game of Ireland. It has peculiarities of ranking including the feature whereby, in black suits, the lowest cards are highest and vice versa; but it would be wrong to characterize this as a typical Irishism, as the game is quite clearly derived in large measure from the Spanish game of Ombre. Modern players will probably find these and other pointless complexities not to their taste. But Spoil Five is included here partly for its historical interest (its ancestor, Maw, was much favoured by James I) and partly because it has an unusual and engaging objective not found in other card games. For this reason a simplified variant is appended for those prepared to defy tradition.

PRELIMINARIES Use a 52-card pack and equip each player with at least 20 chips or counters.

POOL Each player chips one to the pool at the start of the game, and if the pool is not taken at the end of a deal each succeeding dealer chips another one to it, so that the pool grows until taken. At that point everybody again chips one to the pool and the same procedure is followed.

DEAL Five each in batches of two then three. Place the remainder face down to form a stock but turn the top card face up to determine trumps.

OBJECT The object is to win at least three and preferably all five of the tricks played. A player unable to do this, however, will try to play in such a way that nobody else can take three. If successful the five tricks are 'spoiled' (hence the name of the game) and the pool remains untaken.

RANK OF CARDS The highest card is always the Five of trumps, followed by the Jack of trumps, followed by the Ace of hearts, followed by the Ace of trumps if not hearts, followed by King, Queen and other trumps in order. 'In order' means from high to low in red suits but from low to high in black. A diagram will make this clearer: see page 150. In this table, ( ) means 'except in trumps', as the cards concerned – Aces, Jacks and Fives – are top in the trump suit. It will be noted that there are 14 trumps except when hearts are trumps, as the Ace of hearts and the Ace of trumps are the same card. In red suits, whether trump or not, Ten is the

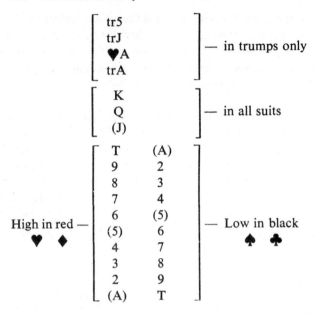

highest numeral card; in black, it is the lowest. The highest card of a non-trump suit is always the King; the lowest Ten in black and either Two or Ace in red depending on the trump suit.

ROBBING THE TRUMP If the turn-up is not an Ace any player who may have been dealt the Ace of trumps must announce this fact before playing his card to the first trick. (He need not announce it until the person before him has played to the trick, but if he himself has the opening lead he must announce it first.) Holding the Ace entitles him to acquire the turned trump in exchange for any other card if he so wishes. If he wants it he passes a card face down to the dealer, who puts it unseen at the bottom of the stock and passes him the trump card instead. If not, he says 'Turn it down', and dealer thereupon turns down the trump card. If the holder of the trump Ace plays it to a trick without having announced it, it is demoted to the status of lowest trump for that deal and the holder may not rob.

If the turn-up is an Ace it may be taken only by the dealer.

If he wants it he discards any card face down before the first trick is led and takes up the Ace just before playing to the first trick. If he does not do so, eldest hand may call upon the dealer to exchange before the first trick is led, and dealer then either exchanges or says 'I play with these.'

TRICKS Eldest hand leads to the first trick; thereafter the winner of each trick leads to the next. Unusual rules of trick-taking apply. If trumps are led others must follow suit if they can; otherwise, they may play any card (but see *Reneging* below). If a plain suit is led others may either follow suit or play a trump as they please, but only if they are unable to follow suit may they renounce. A trick is captured by the highest card of the suit led, or by the highest trump if any are played.

RENEGING The three top trumps – Five, Jack, and ♥A – have the privilege that they cannot be forced out by lower trumps. For ease of explanation we will here call them 'matadors' (as in the game of Ombre). If a low trump is led the holder of a matador is not obliged to play it but may, if he has no other trump, renege by discarding from another suit. Similarly, if a low matador is led, the holder of a higher one need not play it but may renege if he has no other trump. But if a matador is *led* to a trick the holder of a lower matador must play it if he has no other trump. Thus the Five and Jack can force ♥A, and the Five can force the Jack, but nothing can force the Five of trumps (or 'Five Fingers' as it was called in an earlier existence).

Note: In the unlikely event that the holder of ♥A failed to announce it when hearts were entrumped, it not only becomes the lowest trump but also loses its privilege as a matador.

JINKING If a player wins the first three tricks he may either claim the pool immediately, without further play, or continue playing by leading to the fourth trick ('jinking'). If he continues play he must win all five tricks, otherwise he loses the pool.

OUTCOME If nobody wins three or more tricks the game is 'spoiled' and the pool carried forwards. If one player takes three or four tricks he wins the pool. If he takes five he not only wins the pool but also is paid an extra unit by each opponent. If a player who took the first three went on for five, and failed, the game is spoiled and the pool remains untaken.

NOTES ON PLAY

Once the peculiarities of rank and trick-play have been mastered the interest of each deal lies in deciding whether to go for three tricks or to attempt to distribute tricks and so spoil them. The strategy will be partly determined by whether or not the Ace of trumps is announced, the holder of the Ace finding himself in a particularly interesting position from this point of view. Again, having won the first three tricks, the question arises whether to play on for five; a matador is often held back in order to baulk such an attempt. As soon as one player has two tricks the others will naturally combine against him.

SIMPLIFIED VARIANT The following simplification of the ranking of cards only slightly alters the play of the game:

Top three trumps (high to low): tr–5 tr–J ♥A
Then in each suit (high to low): (A)KQ(J)T9876(5)432

VARIANT

FORTY-FIVE This denotes Spoil Five as played by two or by four or six players in two partnerships. Since one side is bound to win at least three tricks there is no pool. Method 1: a side scores 5 points for taking three or four tricks, 10 for taking all five, and game is 45 up. Method 2: the winning side scores 5 points per trick difference between the two sides (thus 5, 15 or 35). If both sides stand at 35 the first to win two tricks wins the game.

Auction Forty-fives

4 or 6 players
1 pack (52)

Auction Forty-fives is a partnership extension of Spoil Five or Forty-Five, said to be popular in Canada and especially Nova Scotia. Bidding is introduced, but the number 45 has no particular significance.

PLAYERS Four or six, in two partnerships, with partners sitting alternately round the table.

DEAL Five each (2 + 3). Do not turn up a trump card.

BIDDING Each player in turn may bid or pass; having passed he may not re-enter. The lowest bid is five, and raises are made in multiples of five up to thirty. If one player bids a number for the first time the next in turn may say 'I hold,' meaning that he takes over the bid at the same number. The player after him must then raise again or pass. The bids refer to points to be scored at the rate of five per trick, plus five for holding the highest trump in play. No suit is mentioned until all have passed save the highest bidder, who then announces the trump suit.

DRAWING Before play, each in turn, starting with eldest, may discard face down any number of cards and receive from the dealer as many as he needs to restore his hand to five.

PLAY The ranking of cards, method of trick-play and privileges attaching to the three top trumps are as for Spoil Five. Eldest leads to the first trick.

SCORE At the rate of 5 points per trick, plus 5 points for having had the highest trump in play, the non-bidding side scores whatever it makes. If the bidding side made at least what it bid it scores all that it made; if not, it deducts the amount of the bid from its score. If the bidding side bid and made 30 it scores 60. Game is 120. A side standing at 100 points may not bid less than twenty.

VARIANT In some circles the dealer, having discarded, may 'rob the pack' by examining all the undealt cards and selecting whatever he likes as replacements. (This feature seems to have been borrowed from High–Low–Jack games such as Auction Pitch and will be rejected by purists.)

Hearts Family

In these games the object is not to win tricks. In fact it is best to avoid taking any tricks at all, as penalties are incurred for capturing thereby certain cards, usually hearts, which count sometimes heavily against their owner. Perhaps better known than the game of Hearts itself is Black Maria, in which an additional penalty is incurred for capturing ♠Q, the eponymous lady herself. Related games include Slobberhannes, in which the chief penalty is ♣Q; Polignac, in which Jacks are to be avoided; Knaves, which improves on Polignac by giving credit for winning 'clean tricks'; and Bassadewitz, in which cards have more varied penalty values.

Omitted from this section is the probable ancestor of them all, a highly complicated eighteenth-century gambling game called Reversis.

Although much skill is required in playing to lose tricks, instead of winning them, it is strange that none of the games embodying that principle has yet emerged as a sophisticated standard as Bridge has to Whist, or Five Hundred to Euchre, or Canasta to Rummy. None has a scoring system that accurately rewards skill. The most promising line of development seems to have petered out in Auction Hearts, wherein players bid to nominate the suit to be avoided; but even that is unpolished and it may be concluded that the ideal member of the family has yet to be conceived.

Black Maria ♙ ◎

3 to 7 players (fewer, better)
1 pack (52)

Probably the most popular game of its type on both sides of the Atlantic, Black Maria is also known as Black Lady, Black Widow, Slippery Bitch, and even worse. No two schools play it with exactly the same rules, and the version described below, though recommended, does not pretend to be exclusive. Three is generally reckoned to be the best number of players as far as skill is concerned, though some prefer four because a more manageable number of cards is dealt.

CARDS Use a standard 52-card pack. For three, remove ♣2; for five, remove ♣2 and ♦2; for six, remove all the deuces; for seven, remove all the deuces except ♥2.

DEAL Deal all the cards around, one at a time. Three each receive 17, four 13, five 10, six 8, seven 7.

OBJECT To avoid capturing in tricks any heart, each of which counts one penalty, and the Queen of spades ('Black Maria'), which counts 13 against.

THE EXCHANGE If three or four play, each player first passes any three cards face down to the player on his right and then takes into hand the three cards passed to him by the player on his left. With more players only two cards are passed on. Cards received may not be looked at before discarding from one's own hand.

TRICKS Eldest hand leads to the first trick and play proceeds clockwise around the table. There are no trumps. Each must follow suit to the card led, if possible, otherwise he may play any card. A trick is captured by the highest card of the suit led and the winner leads to the next.

SCORE At the end of each deal there will be 26 penalty points distributed amongst the players. Play continues until one player reaches a total of 50, when the player with fewest wins. Another deal may be played to break a tie.

REVOKE A revoke may be corrected before the following trick is led: the offender leaves his false card face up on the table and must play it at the earliest legal opportunity, and subsequent players may retract and replay. If discovered too late the offender is penalized 13 for ♠Q, instead of the player who actually took her. If the offender took ♠Q he counts 26 against and the others score zero.

NOTES ON PLAY

It is not necessarily desirable to pass hearts to the right. If you have a good run of low hearts it is best to keep them, as they cannot be forced to take tricks and you may be able to use them profitably to get off play after taking tricks in safer suits. Any high hearts you then receive from the left will be 'guarded' by the low ones, which you throw out, when others lead hearts, so as to be left with the high members of that suit when there are none left for others to lead against you.

Similarly, it is not necessary to pass on Black Maria if you have sufficient spades to avoid being forced into capturing a trick with her. The Ace and King of spades are good hand-outs, and for this reason it is normally essential to keep hold of all spades lower than the Queen, otherwise the receipt of Ace/King may force you to capture the eponymous lady.

Most penalties are usually taken towards the end of the trick-play by players who take over the lead late in the game and then find themselves unable to lose it. To avoid this danger it is normally best to lead Aces and Kings of safe suits as soon as possible – in general, to take all the tricks you have to take early in the game, so as to thwart attempts to put you in the lead later.

When able to discard do not automatically put on penalties but look over the hand first and use the opportunity to get rid of cards that may put you badly in the lead later. This applies especially to cards of middling rank when you have none lower.

Much information can be gained from the cards you receive from the left, and built up during the play by observation of opponents' discards and preferred leads. Experts can usually place every remaining card by half-way through the tricks. A method of reducing the effectiveness of opponents' deductions is to play from sequences in such a way as to avoid revealing the lie of key cards, such as the highest from 4–3–2 or the lowest from A–K–Q.

Here is an illustrative three-hand deal with ♣2 out of play. Charlie dealt, so Abel has the lead after passing cards to the dealer and receiving three from Baker. The hands as dealt are:

Abel	♥Q87 ♠QJ9752 ♦A94 ♣AKT83
Baker	♥KJ932 ♠T843 ♦JT853 ♣Q76
Charlie	♥AT654 ♠AK6 ♦KQ762 ♣J954

Abel has some dangerously high cards. He passes his three hearts to Charlie after reflecting that, as the others have probably about five each including low ones, he is unlikely to get any back and will start from the rare position of being void in the penalty suit. His ♠Q is well guarded.

Baker has some promisingly low cards, and voids clubs in order to make an outlet for his embarrassing hearts.

Charlie is weak in all suits. He must keep ♠6 in case he is given ♠Q but must throw ♠A and ♠K in case he is not. He also throws ♦K as being the worst card of his worst suit.

At this stage Abel can assume that Baker is void in clubs, and Charlie that Abel has only safe, low hearts or none at all.

A	B	C	
♦A	♦K	♦Q	Play high in safe suits first
♦9	♦J	♦7	
♦4	♦3	♦6	Baker pretends to void diamonds
♠J	♠A	♠6	
♠9	♠T	♣J	Charlie discards from a weak suit
♠7	♠3	♣9	
♣8	♦T	♣5	Baker's pretence is revealed . . .
♣3	♦8	♣4	. . . and confirmed . . .
♠Q	♦5	♦2	. . . and stunningly exploited
♠2	♠4	♥A	Baker hoped ♠5 and ♠2 were split
♠5	♥3	♥Q	The rest is mechanical
♣A	♥K	♥4	
♣K	♥2	♥T	And Baker takes the others
0	22	4	Resultant penalty scores

VARIANTS

Many aspects of the game are subject to different rules in different circles of play.

In the exchange some pass cards to the left instead of to the right and some make it illegal to pass on the Queen of spades and/or any hearts.

Some make it illegal to lead hearts before the fourth trick, in order to reduce the advantage that accrues to the holder of safe, low hearts. A more elegant rule to the same effect is to prohibit the lead of hearts until at least one player has discarded a heart to the lead of another suit.

Some insist that the holder of ♠Q discard her as soon as a suit is led in which he is void. A similar restriction is to insist that a player unable to follow suit must play a heart (or other penalty) if he can.

As to the penalty scores themselves the following variants are worthy of mention:

1. ♠Q counts 5 instead of 13 against.
2. ♠A counts 7 and ♠K counts 10 against when captured in tricks, in addition to the 13 for ♠Q.

3. ♥Q – known as 'Pink Lady' – counts 13 against, as well as ♠Q, instead of merely one penalty for being a heart.

4. Additional penalties may be incurred by the capture of top hearts. Two such schedules are (a) J11, Q12, K13, A14 and (b) JQK15 each, Ace 20.

5. ♦T, when captured in a trick, gives a *plus* score of 10 (or 13) to the player winning it, thus reducing the number of penalties against him.

6. A player who succeeds in taking *all* the penalty cards in the pack in tricks scores their aggregate value as a plus count in his favour.

Hearts ⊚

Various numbers of players (2–10)
Normally 1 pack (52)

In the basic game of Hearts, of which Black Maria is an extension, there is no exchange of cards before play begins and the only penalty cards are the 13 hearts, counting one each against their takers. Each deal is a complete game and is immediately settled in chips, counters or coins. The basic method is for each player to pay one unit to the pool for each heart he has taken, the whole pool being taken by the player who takes none, or shared between them in the event of a tie. If every player takes one or more hearts, or if one has taken all thirteen, the pool is designated a 'Jack' and is carried forward. The Jack pool can only be taken on a subsequent deal when one player takes no hearts and all his opponents take some, and is increased by 13 units for each deal when this fails to happen. (An American variation, known as Howell's Settlement, makes the following refinement. For each heart he has captured, each player pays in one unit for each player in the game apart from himself, and then draws out again one unit for each heart he captured less than thirteen. To put it another way, he scores $(13 - ♥) - ♥P$, where $♥$ = number of hearts taken and P = number of opponents.)

The following variations on a theme of Hearts are additional to those of Black Maria described separately above.

Hearts Variants

2–10 players
Normally 1 pack (52)

AUCTION HEARTS For four to six players. The penalty suit is not necessarily hearts; instead, each player bids for the right to nominate the penalty suit. The player who bids highest pays the amount of his bid into the pool, which is divided as in the basic game of Hearts, and leads to the first trick.

CANCELLATION HEARTS For seven to ten players. Use two packs (104 cards) and deal cards round as far as they will go. Any undealt cards are laid aside face down as a 'widow', which is taken by the winner of the first trick. There is no exchange, and eldest leads. If two identical cards are played to a trick neither can win the trick, which instead is taken by the player of the highest unduplicated card of the suit led. If all such cards are duplicated the trick is left ôn the table and taken by the winner of the following trick.

DOMINO HEARTS For two to seven players. Deal six each and place the remainder face down to form a stock. Eldest leads. A player unable to follow suit must draw cards from the top of the stock and add them to his hand until he can; but as soon as the stock is exhausted the rules change, and players unable to follow may discard anything. A player who runs out of cards ceases to play, and, if it was his turn to lead, the player next in turn to the left leads instead. The last player left with cards in hand adds them to those won in tricks. Captured cards are then scored in the usual way. This is one of the most interesting variants.

DRAW HEARTS For two players. Deal 13 each and place the remainder face down to form a stock. The winner of a trick draws the top card of the stock and adds it to his hand, and leads to the next trick when his opponent has done likewise. When the stock is exhausted the remaining 13 cards are played out. Captured cards are counted in the usual way. A Cribbage board is a useful adjunct.

GREEK HEARTS A form of Black Maria in which the penalties are one per low heart, ten per court heart, 15 for ♥A and 50 for ♠Q.

HEARTSETTE For three or more players. Each player is dealt the same number of cards, but a certain number (preferably three) are not dealt but laid aside face down as a widow. The widow is taken by the player who wins the first trick, and he is permitted to see what it contains before leading to the second. In some localities the widow is taken by the winner of the last trick instead of the first. This is more appropriate if the widow contains four or more cards.

JOKER HEARTS Obsolete variant of basic Hearts in which ♥2 is replaced by the Joker, ranking between Ten and Jack. If discarded to a non-heart lead it wins the trick. On a heart lead it falls to any higher heart. If, however, a non-heart is led and another player throws a heart honour, the holder of the Joker may discard it whether he can follow suit or not and, in this event, the highest heart *wins* the trick and the Joker. It counts 5 against. R. F. Foster (see Select Bibliography) described this as 'a most exasperating game'.

OMNIBUS HEARTS Variant of Hearts or Black Maria in which ♦T (or sometimes ♦J) counts +10 to the player winning it in a trick.

PINK LADY Variant of Black Maria in which ♥Q also counts −13 to the player winning it in a trick.

SPOT HEARTS Variant of Hearts or Black Maria in which ♥J counts −11, ♥Q −12, ♥K −13, ♥A −14.

WIDOW HEARTS Any form of Hearts or Black Maria played with a batch of undealt cards – see Heartsette.

Slobberhannes ○⅄○

3 to 6 players, 4 best
1 short pack (32)

The elegance of this delightful game is regrettably belied by
its ugly and unexplained title.

CARDS 32, ranking AKQJT987 in each suit. If three, five or
six play, delete the two black Sevens.

DEAL Deal all the cards around, one at a time.

OBJECT To avoid winning the first trick, the last trick, and
the trick containing ♣Q.

TRICKS Eldest leads. There is no trump. Follow suit to the
card led if possible; if not, play anything. The trick is captured
by the highest card of the suit led and the winner of one trick
leads to the next.

SCORE One penalty each is scored for taking the first trick,
the last trick and ♣Q, and if one player takes all three
penalties he counts an extra one, making four in all. The first
to reach a total of ten is the loser.

REVOKE One penalty is exacted for each revoke.

Polignac ○⅄○

3 to 6 players, 4 best
1 short pack (32)

A French game similar to Slobberhannes and alternatively
known as Quatre Valets or Four Jacks.

CARDS 32, ranking AKQJT987 in each suit. If three, five or
six play, delete the two black Sevens.

DEAL Deal all the cards around, one at a time.

OBJECT To avoid capturing any Jack and, particularly, ♠J, known as Polignac.

TRICKS Eldest leads. There is no trump suit. Follow suit to the card led if possible; if not, play anything. The trick is captured by the highest card of the suit led and the winner of one trick leads to the next.

SCORE Two penalties are scored for taking ♠J, and one each for taking any of the other Jacks.

VARIANTS

CAPOT A player who thinks he can win all the tricks may announce *capot* before the first card is led. If successful he cancels five penalties from his score. If not, he adds five penalties and opponents are penalized as usual for taking any Jacks.

RANKING This being a French game the Ace should rank between Jack and Ten in each suit. Anglo-American play has promoted it to top position. This alters the strategy of the game. To restore authenticity either demote the Ace or penalize the capture of Queens instead of Jacks.

Bassadewitz ∘°∘

3–5 players (4 best)
1 short pack (32)

A German relative with more interesting card values, also known as Bassarowitz, and still popular as a family game. It may be compared with *ramsch* in the game of Skat.

CARDS 32, ranking AKQJT987 in each suit.

DEAL Dealer antes 12 units to a pool and deals eight cards each if four play, ten if three play or six if five play. Any cards left over are laid face down to one side and belong to the winner of the last trick.

OBJECT To avoid winning penalty-scoring cards in tricks, the values being Ace 5, King 4, Queen 3, Jack 2, Ten 10, others nothing, making 96 in all. (Variant: each Ace counts 11, making 120 in all.) An alternative objective, for a player with a majority of high cards, is to win *every* trick.

PLAY Eldest hand leads and normal rules of trick-taking apply. There is no trump, and the trick is won by the highest-ranking card of the suit led. If three or five play, the winner of the last trick adds the two undealt cards to it.

SETTLEMENT The player who took the smallest number of penalties draws 5 units from the pool, the second smallest 4 units, and the third 3 units. The player with the highest penalty count pays 4 units to each opponent. In the event of a tie, priority goes to the tied player nearest dealer's left. If one player takes all the tricks he receives 4 units from each opponent. If three or five play, adjust the amount of the pool and the winnings accordingly.

Knaves ♂

2 to 6 players (3 best)
1 pack (52)

This game is something of a hybrid – and all the better for it – as it gives credit for winning tricks but is still characterized by the need to avoid taking certain penalty cards. Its invention has been credited to Hubert Phillips (see Select Bibliography) who describes it as being particularly good for three players.

CARDS A standard 52-card pack ranking normally from Ace high to Two low.

DEAL If three play, deal 17 cards each, one at a time, and lay the last card face up to one side. The suit of the turn-up is the trump suit for the deal. If more play, see Variants.

OBJECT To win tricks for a score of one point each but to avoid capturing any of the Jacks. Points are subtracted for each Jack according to its suit, as follows:

♥J −4   ♦J −3   ♣J −2   ♠J −1

TRICKS Eldest leads to the first trick. Normal rules of trick-taking apply. Follow suit to the card led if possible; if not, trump or renounce *ad lib*. The trick is captured by the highest card of the suit led, or by the highest trump if any are played, and the winner of one trick leads to the next.

SCORE Each player scores 1 point for each trick he won, less the appropriate number of points for each Jack he has taken. Game is 20 points up.

VARIANTS

The only authority known for this game is Hubert Phillips, who omits to explain how more may take part and what happens (if anything) when the turn-up is a Jack. The following variants are suggestions made by the present writer.

JACK TURNED UP If a Jack is turned for trump it is captured by the winner of the last trick and counts against him accordingly. (It will be noted that if the turn-up is an Ace, King or Queen, the Jack of trumps will be the third highest card in play instead of the fourth, and hence harder to lose. An amusing variant would be to play at no trump whenever the turn-up is a Jack or higher.)

ALL-IN A player who succeeds in taking all four Jacks is not penalized for them but scores 1 point per trick without reduction.

FOR OTHER NUMBERS OF PLAYERS If four play, deal 13 each and turn the last card for trumps before taking it into (dealer's) hand. Since the knowledge of one of dealer's trumps could work to his disadvantage, a better system is to add a Joker to the pack and turn up the last (53rd) card for trumps. Whoever holds the Joker uses it exactly as if it were the turned card. If the Joker itself is turned, play at no trump.

For five, deal 10 cards each and face one of the undealt two for trumps. The two undealt cards are taken by the winner of the last trick, and any Jack between them counts against him. Won tricks score 3 each.

For six, deal eight each, turn up one of the undealt four for trumps, and give them to the winner of the last trick. Tricks count 3 each.

DRAW KNAVES Two may play as follows. Deal 13 cards each and place the remainder face down to form a stock. Turn the top card of the stock face up. During the first half of the game the winner of each trick draws the top card of the stock and adds it to his hand, waits for his opponent to draw the next (face-down) card, turns up the next card of the stock, and leads to the next trick. There is no trump and no obligation to follow suit, the trick being won by the higher card if both are of the same suit, or the first played if not. Jacks, however, may not be lost by discarding. Any Jack played to a trick wins it, unless the other card is of the same suit and higher in rank (Ace, King, Queen). When the stock is exhausted the last 13 tricks are played under slightly different rules: it is now obligatory to follow suit if possible, but, if not, a Jack may be discarded without winning the trick. Won tricks count 1 point each and the penalty value of captured Jacks is increased to:

♥J −7 ♦J −5 ♣J −3 ♠J −1

All Fours Family

Most of the games in this section credit a player with one point each for capturing, in tricks, the following four items:

1. *High*, meaning the highest trump in play.
2. *Low*, meaning the lowest trump in play.
3. *Jack*, the Jack of trumps.
4. Game, meaning the greatest value of scoring-cards, assessed at the rate of 4 per Ace, 3 per King, 2 per Queen, 1 per Jack, and 10 per Ten.

Since not all the cards are dealt out the highest and lowest trumps in play are not necessarily the Ace and Two respectively; the Jack may lie out of play as well. Or, if in play, it might conceivably also be both highest and lowest trump and so worth three points. Originally, 'low' was scored for being dealt the lowest trump but modern practice prefers the reward for capturing it. The highest, of course, cannot be captured from the player to whom it was dealt.

Games of this family seem to be English in origin, the earliest – All Fours – being described in 1674 as 'much play'd in Kent'. It remained popular into the nineteenth century, achieving a mention in *Pickwick Papers* and providing a presumably widely understood title for a not very highbrow play called *High, Low, Jack and the Game* by one Mr J. R. Planché. Nowadays the games are not much played in their country of origin (except in pubs around Blackburn, according to one researcher) but still thrive in such former colonies as the West Indies and the United States. For this reason much modern terminology is American. All are worthy of revival, especially Auction Pitch, which is a particularly good non-partnership game for four.

All Fours (Seven Up) ⚇ ⚈ ⚉

2–4 players, 2 best
1 pack (52)

Seven Up, denoting the number of points constituting game, is the American name for the old English game of All Fours, which is ancestral to all games described in this section. Charles Cotton had this to say about it in his *Compleat Gamester* of 1674: 'All Fours is a game very much play'd in Kent . . . and although the Game may be lookt upon as trivial and inconsiderable, yet I have known Kentish Gentlemen and others of very considerable note, who have play'd great sums of money at it, yet that adds not much to the worth of the Game . . .'

PLAYERS 'Eldest' means non-dealer if two play, or player left of dealer if three or four, four usually playing in partnerships. The third and fourth players, if any, play no part in the determination of trumps.

DEAL Six each in two batches of three; turn the next card as the prospective trump. If it is a Jack, dealer scores 1 point.

OBJECT Each player's object is to win as many as possible of the four points for high, low, Jack and game (see p. 169).

TRUMP-MAKING Eldest may accept the turn-up as trumps by saying '(I) stand', in which case play begins, or refuse it by saying 'Beg'. If he begs, dealer may accept by saying '(I) give you one,' in which case eldest scores 1 point and play begins, or else 'Refuse the gift', in which case the turn-up is turned down and the cards are 'run'.

RUNNING THE CARDS If the first turn-up proves abortive three more cards are dealt to each player (who should keep careful track of which three he gets) and the next is turned up, the dealer again scoring 1 point for a Jack. If this turn-up is of a different suit from the first it automatically becomes the trump, whereupon discards are made and play begins. If it is the same it is turned down, the three cards dealt to each are discarded face down, and the cards are 'run' again. This continues until a trump is established or there are not enough cards to go round in which case all cards are thrown in and the same dealer deals again.

DISCARD AND PLAY If the cards were run each player reduces his hand to six by discarding the extras before play begins. Eldest leads to the first trick; thereafter the winner of each leads to the next. Following players may either follow suit or trump as they please (both, if trumps are led) but may only renounce if unable to follow suit. The trick is won by the highest trump or by the highest card of the suit led if no trump is played.

SCORE One point each is scored for 'gift' and turning a Jack, if applicable, and another each for high, low, Jack, and game. Game is seven points up; in the event of a tie the winner is the first to reach seven as the result of counting high, low, Jack or game in that order of priority.

REVOKE If a player renounces, although able to follow suit, he may not score for Jack or game and each opponent scores 2 points if the Jack is in play, 1 point if not.

VARIANTS

ALL FIVES A two-player game, basically the same as All Fours but with additional scoring features. The winner of each of the following trumps, as soon as he captures it, scores the value shown:

Ace	4	Jack	1
King	3	Ten	10
Queen	2	Five	5

At the end of the game additional points are scored as usual for high, low, Jack and game. (In counting for game the trump Five is 5 and *all* Aces, Kings, Queens, Jacks and Tens respectively 4, 3, 2, 1 and 10 each.) Game is 61 up, to which end it is convenient to use a cribbage board.

CALIFORNIA JACK A two-player game. Deal six each in threes. Square the rest into a pile and place it face up on the table. The suit of the top card is trump for the whole of the deal. Non-dealer leads. The second to a trick must follow suit if he can, and either trump or discard otherwise. The winner of a trick draws the top card of stock; the loser draws the next. When the stock is finished the last six tricks are played out as usual. At the end of play either player scores 1 point for high, low, Jack or game. Game is 10 points up. (Another variant is Shasta Sam, in which the stock is placed face down instead of face up. This removes the desirable feature of playing with a view to drawing or ceding the top card of stock, which, in California Jack, is the best part of the game.)

Auction Pitch ○⚇○ ◎
2–7 players, 4 best
1 pack (52)

The basic game is also known as Setback. It admits of numerous optional extras, as detailed at the end of the following description, many of which give rise to versions with different names, such as Smudge, Pedro and so on.

CARDS 52 with normal ranking (AKQJT98765432 in each suit).

DEAL Highest cut deals first and the deal passes to the left. Deal six each in batches of three and place the remainder face down out of play.

OBJECT Up to four points are played for in each deal, one

each for high, low, Jack and game (see p. 169). The player bidding to take most of these chooses trumps by leading them. Each player scores any of the four points he may make and the bidder (pitcher) is penalized if he fails to make what he bid. Game is usually set at 7 points, taking several deals to achieve.

BIDDING Starting at dealer's left, each in turn may pass or bid one, two, three or four, each new bid being higher than a previous one. No suit is named.

PITCHING Highest bidder becomes the pitcher and 'pitches' by leading any card of his trump suit.

PLAY Unusual rules of trick-taking apply. If trumps are led it is obligatory to follow suit if possible, but when a plain suit is led a subsequent player may either follow or trump as he pleases. (But he may only play another suit if unable to follow.) The trick is won by the highest card of the suit led, or by the highest trump if any are played, and the winner leads to the next.

SCORE The points for high, low, Jack and game (see page 169) go to whoever earns them, except that there is no point for game if two players tie for the highest value of counting cards. The pitcher only scores if he makes at least as many points as he bid, in which case he scores what he makes; if not, he is set back by the amount of his bid and may therefore find himself 'in the hole' with a minus score.

GAME The game is won by the first to reach 7 points (or 11 or any other agreed total). If two players reach 7 in the same deal, the pitcher wins if he is one of them, regardless of actual score. If neither is the pitcher, that player wins who reached 7 first, counting points strictly in order: high, then low, then Jack, then game. Each loser pays the winner one unit, or two if his score is zero or negative.

VARIANTS

DEALER'S RIGHT This rule is frequently applied and may be recommended. It permits the dealer to take the previous bid over at the same level. (Example: if the bidding goes 'one', 'two', 'three', the dealer may also bid 'three' and can then only be overcalled by 'four'.) But if the first three pass, dealer is obliged to bid at least one.

SMUDGE A player who is not in the hole may bid four by announcing 'smudge'. If he then makes four he immediately wins the whole game. Dealer cannot take over a bid of smudge.

RACEHORSE PITCH This is Auction Pitch played with a short pack of 32 cards, nothing lower than Seven. Game is usually 11 up.

JOKER ADDED If a Joker is added it usually ranks as a trump below the Two. It does not, however, count as 'low' but scores an additional (fifth) game point to the player winning it in a trick, this point being counted after Jack but before 'game'. If the Joker is 'pitched' it counts as a spade.

SELL-OUT In this version eldest hand (player left of dealer) either pitches, which is an automatic bid of four, or offers the pitch for sale to the highest bidder. If he offers it the others bid. Eldest may then either pitch himself for the amount of the highest bid, in which case the bidder immediately scores the amount of the bid and play proceeds, or else allow the bidder to pitch, in which case he (eldest) immediately scores the amount of the bid before play begins. But an important restriction applies. No player, if invited to bid, may bid as many points as would give eldest the game if he sold it; conversely, eldest must sell if the high bidder would otherwise mark enough points to win immediately.

NOTES ON PLAY

The first two players should bid conservatively, but dealer stands in a strong position and may err on the side of boldness. Three cards of the proposed trump should be sufficient to assure the point for 'game', but non-trump Aces, though a strengthening factor, will need to be established by a preliminary drawing of adverse trumps. How safely one may reckon a King as the highest trump in play, or a Three as the lowest, depends on the number taking part. If two play, the odds are 4–3 in favour of one's Jack being the highest or Five the lowest; if three play, it is 5–3 against King high or Three low; if more than four play, do not bid for 'high' without the Ace or 'low' without the Two, as both cards are more likely to be in play than not. Any plain Ten in the pitcher's hand is a weakness as far as the point for 'game' is concerned, unless he can rely on drawing trumps first and leading the Ten last.

The first trump pitched should normally be the highest, then work downwards. The Ten, of course, is a dangerous pitch because of its high value towards the point for 'game', and the Jack equally for its own game point. Holding a weak card in a plain suit, the pitcher should be alert to any opportunity of throwing it to a trick which is unlikely to benefit an opponent, as illustrated in the sample game.

To a certain extent the pitcher's opponents may play co-operatively, especially if the pitcher will win the game by fulfilling his bid. Throwing the Jack or lowest trump to an *ad hoc* 'partner' is an obvious manoeuvre; more subtle is the matter of piling up cards counting towards 'game', especially Tens, on one player at the expense of the pitcher.

North: ♠9 ♥2 ♣AQT4
East: ♠AQ73 ♦6 ♣J
South: ♠85 ♥3 ♣K8 ♦2
West: ♠6 ♥Q74 ♦T7

North bids two on the strength of probable points for 'high' and 'game'; East overcalls with three for the same reasons plus the hope of either 'low' with his Three or, more desperately, the win of the Jack if in play. South passes. East pitches the Ace:

N	E	S	W	
♠9	♠A	♠5	♠6	
♣4	♣Q	♠8	♥4	
♣A	♣J	♣K	♦T	West throws his high counter away from pitcher.
♥2	♦6			If East now trumps he will later have to lead this Six and possibly to his disadvantage. He therefore abandons it to a trick which so far contains nothing of value to his opponents.
		♥3	♥7	
♣Q	♠3	♦2	♦7	
♣T	♠7	♣8	♥Q	

No point in holding the Three back; if South can win it now he can equally well win it on the last trick.

Result: East gains his points for high, low, and game, having taken cards to the value of 20 against North's 18. Had he trumped at the fourth trick he would have lost the point for 'game' by North's subsequent discard of ♣T to his losing lead of ♦6.

Pitch Variants

The following may be regarded as extensions of Auction Pitch and follow the same rules except as specifically indicated below.

SANCHO PEDRO The highest bid is 18 and players may keep raising until all but one pass. Points are scored for capturing the following trumps:

High	1	'Game'	1	(Ten of trumps)
Low	1	Sancho	9	(Nine of trumps)
Jack	1	Pedro	5	(Five of trumps)

Game is 50 up. Deal either six each or as many as the pack will allow, so long as all have the same number.

DOM PEDRO As above, but with the addition of 3 for winning the Three of trumps, known as 'Dom'. Highest bid is 21.

SNOOZER As Sancho Pedro or Dom Pedro but with the addition of a Joker (the *Snoozer*). This ranks as a trump below the Two for trick-taking purposes. It counts 15 to the player winning it in a trick but does not count as 'low' for the winning of that point, which still applies to the otherwise lowest trump in play. Highest bid is 33 without Dom or 36 with; game is 100 up.

NINE-CARD DON A Midlands pub game, played by four in partnerships, and scored for convenience on a Cribbage board, game being 91 up. Deal nine each. Player left of dealer leads, and whatever he leads establishes trumps. Points are pegged for the following cards as and when captured in tricks:

trump Ace	4	trump Jack	1
trump King	3	trump Nine	9
trump Queen	2	trump Five	10, any other Five 5

At the end of play, each side counts for 'game' at the following rate: each Ace captured in tricks 4, King 3, Queen 2, Jack 1, Ten 10 regardless of suit. Whichever side has taken the majority (out of 80 possible) pegs a further eight towards game.

PHAT An even more complex extension of Don, played on a league basis around Norwich according to pub-game researchers. All cards are dealt out, 13 to each player. Peg for the following cards, as and when taken in tricks:

trump Ace	4	trump Jack	1
trump King	3	trump Nine	18, any other Nine 9
trump Queen	2	trump Five	10, any other Five 5

The side capturing a majority of the 80 counters, reckoned as Nine-Card Don (above), pegs an additional eight towards game, which is 121 up (twice round a normal cribbage board or once round a specially made phat board).

Cinch ⣿

2–6 players, four best
1 pack (52)

Cinch, also known as High Five or Double Pedro, represents another extension of Pitch and is usually played as a four-player partnership game. Characteristic of Cinch and its close relatives is the addition of extra scoring features, coupled with a change in the definition of 'game', which now comes to mean the Ten of trumps and counts to the player who wins it in a trick. To 'cinch' is to play a trump high enough to prevent an opponent winning with a Pedro.

DEAL Nine cards each, in batches of three.

RANK OF CARDS Cards rank normally, with Ace high and Two low, except that between the Five of trumps (the 'Right Pedro') and the Four there ranks a card called the Left Pedro, which is the other Five of the same colour as trumps Thus there are 14 cards in the trump suit, 12 in the other suit of the same colour, and 13 in each of the others.

OBJECT The highest bidder announces trumps and seeks to win, with his partner, at least as many as the amount of his contract. Points are scored for:

high	1	game	1	(Ten of trumps)
low	1	right pedro	5	(Five of trumps)
Jack	1	left pedro	5	(other Five of colour)

making 14 in all.

BIDDING Starting with eldest, each in turn has one chance only to make a numerical bid (without mentioning a suit), each being higher than any gone before. The highest possible bid is 14.

DRAW AND DISCARD Highest bidder names the trump, and each player, except the dealer, then discards from his hand all except trumps. A player with seven or more trumps must reduce his hand to six and any trump he discards be shown to the others. Dealer then deals enough cards to bring each person's hand up to six cards. Finally, dealer himself 'robs the pack' by discarding his own non-trumps, sorting through the undealt cards and selecting from them whichever ones he pleases to restore his own holding to six cards. (If it later transpires that an opponent of the bidder has discarded a scoring trump it counts for the bidder as if he had won it.)

PLAY High bidder leads any card to the first trick and the winner of each trick leads to the next. Following players may either trump or follow suit as they please (both, if trumps are led) but only if unable to follow may they renounce. The trick is won by the highest trump or by the highest card of the suit led if none are played.

SCORE If the bidding side fulfils its contract, whichever side took the higher number of points scores the difference between the two totals. (It is therefore possible for the bidding side to lose even though it made its bid.) If not, the opponents score 14 plus the number of points by which the bidding side fell short of its bid.

GAME Won by the first side (or player) to make 51 game points.

VARIANTS

AUCTION CINCH (RAZZLE DAZZLE) For five or six players. Each receives six cards and bids (maximum 14) independently but on the assumption of a partner's aid. Highest bidder then chooses a partner by naming a specific card – often the highest trump – whose holder becomes bidder's partner for that round only. The partner may not reveal himself except by playing the called card, and scores the same as the bidder. Play as at Cinch.

BLIND CINCH For four, each playing alone. Deal nine each plus a packet of four each, which remains face down until a high bidder has been established. Highest bidder (maximum 14) adds the four extra cards to his hand *before* announcing trumps, then discards seven, reducing his hand to six. Each opponent then does likewise. Play as at Cinch.

WIDOW CINCH For six players, three partnerships of two sitting opposite each other. Deal eight each and a face-down widow of four. This is taken by the highest bidder (maximum 14) before naming trumps, who discards six to reduce his holding to six. Others discard two each. Play as at Cinch.

SIXTY-THREE As Cinch but with a maximum of 63 game points to be bid and played for by the addition of 25 for winning the King of trumps, 15 for the Three, and 9 for the Nine. Players may bid higher as often as they like. Game is 150 points.

Italian Games

Of all card-players throughout the world, the Italians are the most violent, and a pack of modern cards can have an almost antique appearance at the end of a short train journey.

(Sylvia Mann, *Collecting Playing Cards*, 1966)

These three Italian trick games can be grouped together conveniently because they share the same card values, and in many ways may be regarded as variants of the same game – Calabresella for three, Mediatore for non-partnership four, and Tressette (also played in America), the four-hand partnership equivalent.

All are played with a 40-card pack lacking Eights, Nines and Tens and with the distinctive feature that the deuce and trey are removed from their low position (leaving Four as the lowest card) and elevated in status above the Ace. The traditional Italian 40-card pack has suits of Cups, Coins, Swords and Batons, and court cards representing King, Knight and Valet – the latter sometimes replaced by a girl (Donna). But ordinary cards will serve as well.

Calabresella   ⚇

3 players
1 short pack (40)

Travelling in Italy . . . one could never fail to be struck with the
number of priests in proportion to the population . . . But, see,
those priests enter a café . . . They call for cards, and sit down to
their national game. The glassy eyes become bright, and the dull
countenances full of life. They are playing Calabrasella, which we
mentioned last month, and which we now proceed to explain.

('Cavendish', *The Westminster Papers*, 1 Nov. 1870)

Calabresella is an interesting Italian trick-taking game
which Whist enthusiasts tried to introduce to Britain in the
1870s, though with little success, especially in the matter of
spelling it correctly. It is well worth incorporating into one's
repertoire of three-hand card games. The form described
below is a slightly simplified version. If played strictly, the
deal and all play pass to the right, not the left.

CARDS A 40-card pack lacking Eights, Nines and Tens.

RANK AND VALUE The order of cards for trick-taking
purposes is as shown below, from high to low, together with
the point-value of certain cards when captured in tricks:

3	2	A	K	Q	J	7	6	5	4
1	1	3	1	1	1	0	0	0	0

DEAL Cards are dealt in batches of four at a time as follows:
four each, four face down to the table to form a widow, four
each again, and another four each so that everyone has 12
cards.

OBJECT Whoever becomes the soloist exchanges up to four
cards with the widow in an attempt to improve his hand, then
plays tricks at no trump against the combined opposition of

the other two. As there are 8 card points to be won in each suit, and another 3 for winning the last trick, making 35 in all, the soloist must take a clear majority of 18 or more in order to win.

BIDDING Eldest hand may declare himself the soloist or pass to the next player who, in turn, may pass this privilege to the dealer. If all pass there is another round of options and this time anyone who offers to become the soloist has the additional advantage of calling for a Three not already in his hand. If all pass again the hands are thrown in.

EXCHANGING If the bid was taken on the second round the soloist specifies any Three not in his hand (or Two if he has all four and, in this case, he must reveal his Threes). Whoever has the called card gives it to him, receiving in exchange and unexposed to the third player, any card the soloist chooses to give him. If nobody has the called card, it lying in the widow, he may not call another. Next (or first, if he did not call a card), he rejects from his hand at least one, and up to four, cards which he leaves face down and out of play. Finally, he turns the four widow cards face up so that all may see them and selects as many of them as he needs to restore his hand to twelve. The others are turned down and left.

PLAY The opening lead is made by eldest hand, regardless of the soloist's position. There is no trump suit but otherwise normal rules of trick-taking apply: follow suit to the card led if possible, otherwise throw any card away. The trick is captured by the highest card of the suit led and the winner leads to the next.

SCORE Each side counts the value of cards taken in tricks. Whoever took the last trick adds 3 for last plus the values of any scoring-cards in the four left out of play. If the soloist has 18 or more he scores the difference between the two totals; if not, *each* opponent scores the difference. If one side takes all 35 the score is doubled to 70.

FOUR-HAND CALABRESELLA (MEDIATORE)

Mediatore is Calabresella for four players, each playing for himself. Deal nine each and a widow of four. Whoever bids to win most of the 11 possible points takes the widow and rejects four cards in its place. The 11 points are scored for the following features: 1 for each Ace captured in tricks, 1 for winning the last trick, and 1 for every complete set of three honours captured in tricks, honours being 3, 2, K, Q, J. (There being 20 honours in the pack the highest possible score for honours is 6, scored whether 18, 19 or 20 of them are captured. This scoring system, which also applies to the following game of Tressette, should properly apply to Calabresella – the version actually described above is one devised by those who first introduced the game to Britain.) The bidder may play solo or call for a partner by nominating the holder of a particular Ace lacking from his own hand.

Tressette

4 players
1 short pack (40)

A popular Italian partnership game of long standing, originating in the Naples area. In America, where it was introduced by Italian immigrants, the spelling drops an S and (for explicable but long-winded reasons) the Jack ranks higher than the Queen in each suit. If played strictly, play passes to the right instead of to the left.

CARDS 40, ranking from high to low in each suit as follows: 32AKQJ7654.

DEAL 10 each in batches of 3–4–3.

OBJECT To score points for winning high cards in tricks, especially Aces, and for melding sets and sequences.

MELDS Before play each may declare and score for his side any combination he may hold. A combination is a set of three or four Threes, Twos or Aces, or a sequence of 3–2–A in one same suit. The score for any such combination is 1 point per constituent card.

GIVING INFORMATION When playing to a trick a player may announce that he holds a void, singleton or doubleton in some other suit, but may not say which suit. The leader to a trick may instruct his partner to play the highest card he has, or the Ace. When following to a trick a player may state how many cards he holds in the suit he is playing from.

SCORE I addition to melds there is a score of 1 point for taking the last trick and 1 point for each Ace captured in tricks. Furthermore, 1 point is scored for every three honours captured, the honours being 3, 2, K, Q and J. An odd one or two honours count nothing. Game is 21 points up (or 31 in America).

Skat Family

In most trick-taking games known to English players all that counts is the number of tricks taken. But there is a large group of trick-taking games in which the object is to capture cards that have a scoring value and a trick is worthless if it contains none. Most of these games are of German origin, and all are based on the following card values: Ace = 11, Ten = 10, King = 4, Queen = 3, Jack = 2, the rest nothing. This makes 30 pips (card-points) in each suit, and 120 in the whole pack, and the object in most games is for the highest bidder to capture the majority of them, i.e., at least 61. Because the Ten has such a high value it is usually promoted in tricktaking power to a position between Ace and King.

The 'Ace 11, Ten 10' system is to be found in games other than those described here – for example, in all the Jass games and in many Bézique relatives such as Pinochle. This section, however, is chiefly devoted to the German national game of Skat, together with its American equivalent. Skat is acknowledged by all who know it as one of the world's great games, many rating it higher than Contract Bridge, and its neglect in England can only be described as a national scandal. Admittedly, it looks difficult to grasp at first reading, and, for this reason, it might be a good idea for beginners to start with a simpler relative such as Six-bid.

This section covers Skat in its German and American forms, both of which are for three active players. Four may play, and usually do, but the dealer takes no cards and sits his hand out. It is followed by Schafkopf (Sheepshead), which is for four players and might be described as the Solo Whist of its family. Six-bid is a simpler three-hand game of much the same type; the section concludes with the rather unusual Ukrainian game of Tyzicha, which is easy to learn and fun to play. (*Note: 'skat' rhymes with 'cart'.*)

German Skat ⚃

3 active players
1 short pack (32)

Skat was developed between 1810 and 1820 by members of the Tarock Club of Altenburg, some twenty miles south of Leipzig. Based on the Wendish game of Schafkopf, it was extended by the incorporation of features borrowed from Tarock, Ombre and German Solo. By the end of the century it had become Germany's favourite card game, spreading largely through the enthusiastic medium of the soldiery and studentry and acquiring countless local rules and variations. A 'pure' form of the game was adopted with the formation of the German Skat Congress at Altenburg in 1886 and was considerably modified in 1928–32. Altenburg remains the Mecca of all Skat players, though the modern Deutscher Skatverband has its headquarters at Bielefeld. Thousands of local Skat clubs exist and annual national tournaments are held. The game is played also in Austria and Switzerland and, particularly, in America, where it was introduced by German immigrants a century ago. (As the American game therefore reflects an older form of the German it is dealt with separately below.) It is estimated that there are some 20,000 players in Australia. An International Skat Players Association was formed at Aachen in 1976. The form of Skat presented below is that prescribed by the Deutscher Skatverband for tournament play. Although the association likes to be strict about its rules few people abide by them in practice, and a select list of common variations is appended to the basic account below.

CARDS 32, consisting of AKQJT987 in each suit.

DEAL Ten each in batches of 3–4–3. Immediately before dealing the batch of four deal two cards face down to form the *skat*.

RANK AND VALUE OF CARDS The normal ranking of cards for trick-taking purposes is ATKQ987. The four Jacks or *wenzels* are the four permanently highest trumps, ranking higher than the basic seven cards of the trump suit and lengthening it to eleven cards. Certain cards have a pip-value when captured in tricks. Rank and value may be shown as follows:

in the trump suit	♣J	♠J	♥J	♦J	A	T	K	Q	9	8	7
card pip-values	2	2	2	2	11	10	4	3	0	0	0
in each plain suit					A	T	K	Q	9	8	7

Note that in each plain suit the Ace and Ten are highest and second highest cards, whereas in the trump suit they are only fifth and sixth highest. When there is no trump suit as such, the wenzels form a four-card trump suit of their own with ♣J highest and ♦J lowest. This trump situation is called *grand*. Note also that the total pip-value of the pack is 120.

OBJECT Whoever bids to play the highest valued game becomes the soloist. His object is normally to capture in tricks more than half the pips in the pack, i.e., at least 61. To help him he has the advantage of nominating trumps and the option of exchanging two cards with the skat. If he succeeds he scores the value of his game; if not, he loses that value and may incur other penalties. His opponents combine to beat him by capturing between them at least 60 pips. The turn to deal passes to the left; a game is of any length so long as each player deals the same number of times; and the winner is the player with the highest cumulative total. It is possible for scores to be negative (*in the hole*).

GAME VALUATION Before players can bid they must calculate the prospective value of the particular game they propose to play. The value of a game is:

1. the *base value* of the suit selected as trump *multiplied by*
2. the number of *matadors* (top consecutive trumps) held or not held, plus
3. one or more additional *game factors*.

Note that matadors and game factors are added together first and it is their total which multiplies the base value. These terms are explained as follows:

1. *Base value*. Each player bids on the expectation of becoming the soloist and nominating the trump suit, giving him one of the following base values:

diamonds	♦	9	clubs	♣	12
hearts	♥	10	grand (Jacks)		24
spades	♠	11	grand ouvert		36

Grand means playing with only the Jacks as trumps. Ouvert means playing with one's hand of cards exposed on the table – a difficult feat suitably rewarded.

2. *Matadors*. This means the number of top consecutive trumps, from ♣J down, either held by the bidder/soloist or lacking from his hand. If he holds ♣J then he is playing 'with' as many matadors as he holds. For example:

holding ♣J but not ♠J = with 1
holding ♣J, ♠J but not ♥J = with 2
holding ♣J, ♠J, ♥J, ♦J, Ace but not Ten of prospective trump = with 5

If he lacks ♣J then he is playing 'without' as many top consecutive trumps as lie above the highest card in his hand. For example:

highest card ♠J = without 1
highest card ♥J = without 2
highest card King of proposed trump = without 6 (lacking four wenzels and the Ace and Ten of trumps)

In reckoning matadors all that counts is the *number* concerned – whether playing 'with' or 'without' does not affect the game valuation. When there is a trump suit the maximum number of matadors is 11; at grand, the highest number is 4. (Warning: the two cards of the skat belong to the soloist even if he does not take them into his hand. If he is bidding 'without' several matadors, and the skat proves to have contained a top wenzel, the final value of his game will be reduced. If the final value is less than the amount he bid, he loses that game.)

To the number of matadors concerned is next added one or more of the following game factors.

3. *Game factors.* Each of the following factors, if applicable to the prospective soloist's bid, adds one multiplier to the number of matadors being counted.

Game This denotes the undertaking to win at least 61 pips. Since a bidder expects to do this by definition on becoming the soloist, he automatically counts '1 for game'.

Hand This means playing from the hand, as dealt, without touching the two cards of the skat until the end of the trick-taking. Add one multiplier for undertaking to do so.

Schneider (rhymes with 'spider'). This denotes the capturing of at least 90 pips instead of the normal minimum of 61.

Schneider declared If, and only if, playing from the hand, the soloist may declare his intention of winning schneider. The declaration counts another multiplier in addition to the one for schneider itself.

Schwarz This denotes the winning of all ten tricks and is additional to the 1 for schneider that such a feat would also earn.

Schwarz declared If, and only if, playing from the hand, the soloist may declare his intention of winning all ten tricks. This increases the game valuation by a sixth multiplier, as it automatically includes all those listed above.

Ouvert This means that the soloist plays with his hand of cards fully exposed on the table, which he may only do if he plays from the hand and also guarantees to win all ten tricks – i.e., it increases the game value by a seventh multiplier, as all those listed above must be included. However, a seventh multiplier is not added if the game is played at grand, which, instead, has an increased base value of 36.

The complete range of possible game values is from 18 to 360. The lowest would be with or without one, game two, times diamonds nine = 18 (on a hand such as ♠J ♦J ♦AQ7 ♥AK ♠T7 ♣T), the highest with, or – improbably – without, four, game five, hand six, schneider seven, declared eight, schwarz nine, declared ten, times grand ouvert 36 = 360 (on a hand such as ♣J ♠J ♥J ♦J ♦ATKQ98, which could be played ouvert in diamonds but would then be worth only 153 or 162 if the eleventh trump – ♦7 – turned up in the skat).

NULL There is a special bid of *null* which is an undertaking to win not a single trick. For this purpose there are no trumps at all and cards revert to their 'traditional' ranking order AKQJT987 in each suit. Null may be played with the skat, or from the hand, and ouvert if desired. These bids have fixed and invariable game values as follows:

23	null	46	null ouvert
35	null hand	59	null hand ouvert

BIDDING The player on dealer's left is called forehand, and on his left is middlehand. Dealer himself is rearhand, unless four are playing, in which case he sits out and the player on his right is rearhand. Forehand has an automatic right to become the soloist, so the purpose of bidding is for each opponent to relieve him of that right by offering to play a game higher (not equal) in value. Middlehand starts by naming successive game values from the lowest up, i.e., 18, 20, 22, 23, etc. (see Table 3, p. 196). To each of these forehand replies 'yes' if he intends to play a game equal or higher in value, or 'pass' if not. Middlehand may pass immediately or at any time when he dare not make a higher bid. When one of them passes, rearhand may take over and raise the bidding against the survivor, starting at the next bid above the last one stated. Whoever survives becomes the soloist and must play a game that is not lower in value than the last bid named. If both middle and rearhand pass without naming a value, forehand may declare himself the soloist or pass. If he also passes, the cards are thrown in and the next player deals.

ANNOUNCING THE GAME If using the skat the soloist picks it up and adds it to his hand, then rejects any two cards face down and announces the trump suit, or grand or null as the case may be. If not, he puts it to one side unseen and announces trump, grand or null, followed by the announcement 'hand' and – if applicable – '*schneider declared*', '*schwarz declared*', '*ouvert*'. If playing ouvert he lays his hand of cards face up on the table before the first card is led. (If, after taking the skat, the soloist feels that he cannot justify his bid he may concede the game but will not gain credit for doing so.)

Whether he plays with the skat or from the hand, the two cards out of play remain face down and may not be consulted by anyone throughout the period of trick-taking. At the end of this period the two cards are revealed, and any pips they contain count towards the soloist's total – except in a null game, when they play no part at all.

TRICKS Regardless of who the soloists may be, forehand always leads to the first trick. Normal rules of trick-taking apply. Follow suit to the card led if possible; if not, trump or renounce *ad lib*. The trick is captured by the highest card of the suit led, or by the highest trump if any are played, and the winner of one trick leads to the next. For convenience all cards won by the partners are kept in a common waste pile.

(Note: it must be understood that Jacks belong to the trump suit, not necessarily to the suits marked on their faces (except in null). The lead of a Jack or a trump calls for the play of another Jack or trump. If spades are trumps and diamonds are led the ♦J may not be played if its holder can follow suit to diamonds; but, if he is void in diamonds, he may trump with any spade or Jack. When the game is played at grand the lead of a Jack calls for the play of a Jack, and a player unable to do so may discard anything regardless of suit.)

Each deal must be fully played out, unless one side concedes defeat and the other accepts the concession. A concession need not be accepted if the winning side (soloist or opposition considers that it can make schneider or even schwarz with further play. A null, of course, is lost as soon as the soloist wins a trick.

SCORE For the soloist to have succeeded in his game two conditions must apply:

(a) he must have taken at least 61 pips, or 90 if he announced schneider, or all ten tricks if he announced schwarz, or none if he played null; and
(b) the value of the game he played must be not lower than the value at which he won the bidding.

Condition (a) is usually obvious, but condition (b) has to be recalculated in the light of what happened in the play.

First, he must count the number of matadors he was play-ing with or without. This may be different from the number assumed in his bidding, as one or two trumps may have appeared in the skat. For example, if he was playing without three, the appearance of ♠J in the skat would revalue his game 'without one', thus reducing its value. This may have caused him to overbid; if so, he will have lost his game. This applies even if he played from the hand and did not know about the ♠J until afterwards. If playing 'with', how-ever, a wenzel in the skat can only increase the value of his game.

Next, if playing for a simple game (61 +) he must check his result to see if, in fact, he took 90 +, which increases his game by a multiplier, or even all 10 tricks, for another.

If both conditions are fulfilled he scores the value of the game actually made, which may be higher than what he bid but cannot be lower. But if he failed to win his game, or the game he won turns out to be lower in value than what he bid, then he is set back. The amount of his setback must be not less than the amount he bid and must be an exact mul-tiple of the appropriate base value (except null). It must take account of all the applicable matadors and game factors which he would have counted had he succeeded. If, in addition, he is schneidered by his opponents – i.e., fails to take 31 pips – his value is increased by another multiplier, or two if his opponents won schwarz against him by taking all ten tricks. The lowest number fulfilling all these requirements is the amount to be subtracted from his score. Furthermore, if he played after exchanging through the skat, this amount is doubled before being subtracted. This doubling also applies to null, after exchanging.

The penalty for conceding a game is calculated on the same basis. But if he conceded before announcing his game, he may announce himself lost on a cheaper game than the one he was actually planning, so long as it still justifies his bid. Example: soloist takes the bidding at 23, proposing to play a game in diamonds worth 27. He takes the skat, finds it useless and concedes. Instead of losing 27 doubled for a diamond game, however, he announces null, which is just enough to cover his bid, and loses only 23 doubled.

GAME Game should consist of a previously agreed number of deals, the number being a multiple of the number of players participating (three or four). If played for stakes the usual method of determining who pays whom how much is by means of the following illustrated calculation.

Players	A	B	C	D	
Final score	376	190	0	–84	= total
					482
× number of players (4)	1504	760	0	–336	
Compare with total (482)	482	482	482	482	
Result (r = receive, p = pay)	r1022	r278	p482	p818	

It will be noted that a player whose multiplied score lies above the total receives the difference between those two figures, and one whose score lies below it pays the difference. The final result, of course, balances out to zero. English stakes equivalent to German ones would be between 10 and 100 points per penny.

TABLE 3: GAME VALUES AT SKAT

These are all the possible game values in orthodox German Skat and the bidding should be raised strictly in this order. Against each value is shown the suit or game and the number of multipliers applicable. G = grand, GO = grand ouvert.

18 ♦2	70 ♥7	144 ♦16 ♣12 G6
20 ♥2	72 ♦8 ♣6 G3	150 ♥15
22 ♠2	77 ♠7	153 ♦17
23 Null	80 ♥8	154 ♠14
24 ♣2	81 ♦9	153 ♣13
27 ♦3	84 ♣7	160 ♥16
30 ♥3	88 ♠8	162 ♦18
33 ♠3	90 ♦10 ♥9	165 ♠15
35 N. hand	96 ♣8 G4	168 ♣14 G7
36 ♦4 ♣3	99 ♦11 ♠9	170 ♥17
40 ♥4	100 ♥10	176 ♠16
44 ♠4	108 ♦12 ♣9	180 ♥18 ♣15
45 ♦5	110 ♥11 ♠10	187 ♠17
46 N. open	117 ♦13	192 ♣16 G8
48 ♣4 G2	120 ♥12 ♣10 G5	198 ♠18
50 ♥5	121 ♠11	204 ♣17
54 ♦6	126 ♦14	216 ♣18 G9
55 ♠5	130 ♥13	240 G10
59 N.H. open	132 ♠12 ♣11	252 GO7
60 ♥6 ♣5	135 ♦15	288 GO8
63 ♦7	140 ♥14	324 GO9
66 ♠6	143 ♠13	360 GO10

ILLUSTRATIVE DEAL

The basic mechanics of Skat may seem forbidding at first reading, but everything is quite logical once you know it. It may help to illustrate the mechanics of play before going any further. Counting Jacks as a separate suit, the players receive cards as follows:

	Forehand	Middlehand	Rearhand
J	–	♠♥	♣♦
♣	T987	AKQ	–
♠	K7	T	AQ
♥	T	–	AKQ987
♦	Q87	ATK9	–

The skat contains ♠9 and ♠8, as yet unknown.

Forehand has a risky null, enabling him to go up to 23. He needs the skat as an escape for his ♥T and ♠K and must bank on its not containing even more dangerous cards.

Middlehand has several possibilities. With two Jacks he has a five-card trump if he nominates clubs, or six if diamonds. If he plays from the hand he has the advantage of a void suit but the disadvantage of a vulnerable Ten in spades. If he takes the skat he can not only guard or discard that Ten but may also draw cards suitable for a game in grand. Whatever his game he has the disadvantage of lying second to the first trick. He bids 18, the value of his diamond game, and forehand accepts. Middlehand now raises towards his club game, worth 24, at which forehand passes. Had forehand accepted, middlehand could have decided to play from the hand, increasing his diamond game to 27 or club game to 36.

Rearhand must now start at 27 if he wishes to relieve middlehand of the game. The obvious trump is hearts, and he would be a fool not to play from the hand, giving him a game valuation of with one, game two, hand three, hearts 30. He bids 27, then 30, both of which middlehand accepts. How can rearhand increase his prospective game value to keep in the bidding? He might count on taking 90+ pips and so winning schneider for an extra multiplier, increasing his game to 40. By declaring schneider he could get up to 50. If he switched his bid to 'grand, hand' his game value would be with one, game two, hand 3, times grand 72. But he is sitting in the wrong position for this. He needs the lead in order to run down his hearts and force out an adverse Jack.

He bids, and middlehand accepts, 40, 44, 45, 46, 48. At 50, middlehand passes, as he is not prepared to bid higher than the game in grand. Rearhand therefore has the game and announces 'hearts, hand, schneider declared'.

Forehand leads. He and his partner must take at least 31 pips to defeat the contract. With (+) denoting a pip value to the soloist and (−) a pip value to the opponents, the game begins:

Fore	*Mid*	*Rear*	
♠7	♠T	♠A	+ 21
♥T	♥J	♣J	+ 14
♣T	♣J	♦J	− 14
♠K	♦A	♠Q	+ 18

The remaining tricks belong to the soloist, who captures 90 pips for schneider and so wins a game worth 50.

NOTES ON PLAY

A simple bid in suit normally requires at least five trumps and two other cards which may be trumps, or Aces, or a bare Ace-Ten holding. If the trump suit contains Ace and Ten they must be adequately guarded to prevent their falling to adverse Jacks, unless you can bank on using them to ruff leads in a void suit. If it lacks both Ace and Ten you should have two or preferably three wenzels with which to catch at least one of them. Remember that there are 11 trumps and, if you hold an odd number, never assume that the others are evenly split – they only rarely are. Similarly, remember that plain suits contain only seven cards each. They can always be ruffed on the third round, and often are on the second. Calculate how many Aces and Tens the opponents are likely to win, whether by throwing to each other's tricks, or leading, or ruffing from your own hand.

Do not look to the skat as a source of 'good' cards such as Jacks and Aces. More often than not the skat contains two low cards in suits you are hoping to void. The main purposes of exchanging are (a) to create a void suit and (b) to lay aside high-counting cards that may be vulnerable to capture, such as a singleton Ten. If your dealt hand contains a void suit and is free of vulnerable Tens, the skat is more likely to ruin than assist it.

The typical hand to be played without exchanging contains at least six trumps, a void suit, and two Aces or an unaccompanied Ace/Ten. You must be sure of winning the Ace or Ten of trumps, and if the hand contains more than three losers regard it as risky. A plain suit headed by the Ten is a marked weakness.

The average game in grand requires two wenzels, but beginners tend to overestimate their value: a grand with four is easily lost, and a grand without four perfectly feasible if all four plain suits are short and headed by Aces. Nor does a grand depend solely upon top cards in all suits. A six or seven card suit is as good for grand as for a suit bid if accompanied by at least as many Jacks as you hold voids. To play 'grand hand' you should generally hold at least five cards which are Jacks or Aces, or four if you also have the lead.

To make schneider you should expect to lose not more than two tricks. The task is more difficult if you play from the hand and declare schneider, as your opponents are then more likely to take calculated risks in order to prevent it. It is reasonable to act on the principle that, if a game can be bid with schwarz declared, it can be played ouvert, and if it can be played ouvert in suit, it can equally well be played grand. Such hands are rare but easily recognizable.

To play null, the hand should contain no suit lacking the Seven, though one Eight is an acceptable risk if the suit is short. So long as you are not required to lead from it a suit consisting of 7–9–J etc., i.e., of alternating ranks from the Seven up, is absolutely undefeatable. The same applies if any of them are concertinaed, e.g., 7–9–T–Q etc.; but a gap of two, such as 7–T etc., is a distinct danger. It is unsafe to plan null if you need to lay away two losing cards, as the skat itself may well contain a third.

As the soloist in a suit game your plan should normally be to lead trumps at every opportunity until your opponents are denuded of them, after which they will not be able to trump your plain suit leads while you will be able to trump theirs. To start by leading plain suit Aces and Tens is a beginners' habit referred to in Skat circles as 'visiting the villages'. This does not mean to say it is always wrong. If playing a four-card or otherwise weak trump, for example, it may be necessary to cash Aces and Tens in short suits while the opponents can still follow, and pursue longer suits in order to force out trumps. Trump leads, however, are nearly always best. What to lead from trumps depends largely on the length of your holding and the position of the Ace and Ten. If you lack the Ace and Ten but have seven trumps it is worth fishing for them by leading top Jacks; but, if there seems little chance of catching them in that way, it will be safer to lead low and force them out before they can carry other big scoring cards with them. A rule of thumb for an average five or six card trump holding is to lead high, then low, then high. The first high lead either forces out a Jack or captures a singleton Ace or Ten (with luck, of course); the low lead forces out more trumps without giving too many pips away; and the third lead, high, endeavours to win a trick on the assumption that one opponent will be void in trumps and waiting to throw an Ace or Ten to his partner's trick. With three Jacks it is sometimes acceptable to lead the Ace or Ten of trumps in order to clear the fourth out and leave you in command. With four Jacks, always lead a red one, as there is a good chance that your left opponent will throw the Ace or Ten in the expectation that his partner will win with a black Jack. Do not fear to lead the Ten from a plain suit in which you lack the Ace (unless, of course, your whole game is touch and go). Against good players it is difficult to win the Ten yourself in any case, so you may as well use it to force the Ace out before the other opponent is void in the suit and so able to throw a high scoring card to it. It is not unknown for the soloist to play from the hand and lead a singleton Ten, winning the trick and finding the Ace in the skat.

The soloist's lead of trumps is so statutory as to be embodied in one of many sayings in which the game abounds, namely, 'Trumps is the soul of the game.' This being so, it may be countered that Aces and Tens are its backbone. Note that these eight cards together account for 84 of the 120 pips in the pack. The side that takes the majority of these, i.e., five at least, expects to win. One of them misplaced can lose the game.

The method by which the opponents chiefly seek to win pips is by *swarming*, each throwing high-counting cards to tricks won by the other. If one leads the Ace of a plain suit the other will drop the Ten rather than hang on to it for an unlikely second trick. In playing against the soloist it is always desirable to put him in the middle, i.e., force him as often as possible to play second to the trick. The leader then leads into the soloist's void, so that the partner may swarm if the soloist passes the trick, or throw a worthless card, or even overtrump if the soloist ruffs it. If the soloist is not forehand the opening lead to a suit contract is governed by the saying 'long route, short suit – short route, long suit'. The route is long if you have the lead and the soloist sits at your right, short if he is playing second. This procedure is consistent with the object of eventually putting the soloist in the middle, and even if it does not work, incidentally gives information about your suit distribution, which is more useful to your partner than to the soloist. If an opponent leads a Ten it may be assumed to be a singleton.

7. SKAT Middle- or rear-hand may unhesitatingly play spades from the hand, valuing the game as 'without two, game three, hand four, times spades 11, bid up to 44'. It holds six out of 11 trumps, and a lead of ♥A would be captured at once with ♠T to secure at least a third of the winning requirement. Forehand, having the lead, should bid grand, without two, game three, hand four, for a possible 96 valuation (hoping the skat does not contain a black Jack, which would reduce it to 72). Strategy would be to lead up from ♠Q until the Ace is drawn, retrieve the lead with an Ace or Jack as soon as possible, pursue spades until a Jack is drawn, then follow the same procedure.

In playing a grand the soloist must be careful not to waste his Jacks. The most valuable feature of a grand hand is a long suit with top cards, which should be led downwards. It does not matter if the Ace or Ten falls to a Jack, as this only strengthens the soloist's trump holding and subsequently enables him to run through the rest of the suit uncontested when he retrieves the lead.

The great attraction of Skat is that it lends itself to the exploitation of 'freak hands'. It is the only game in which the soloist can nominate as trumps a suit in which he is void. For instance: ♠A987 ♥AT87 ♦AT87 (after taking the skat). The soloist discards both Tens and announces clubs trump. With 20 in the skat he needs to make 41 in tricks. By leading the Aces for a total of 33 he cannot fail, unless one opponent has a void suit, to capture less than three Queens and ♠K for a 13-point surplus, giving him 66 of the 120 pips in all for a game valued 'without 11, game 12, times clubs 144'. This example requires the lead, of course.

GERMAN SKAT VARIANTS

Skat is rich in local variations which are frowned upon by the Deutscher Skatverband but popular everywhere. For example:

BIERLACHS A method of play designed to result not in a winner but in a loser, who then has to pay for the drinks (*Bier* = 'beer'). If the soloist wins his bid, its value is deducted from each of his opponents' scores instead of being added to his own. If he loses, its value is deducted from his own score. Thus only minus points are recorded, and the first to reach 501, or to exceed it by the greater amount, is the loser.

BOCK A *bock* round is three successive deals in which all scores are won or lost double. It follows an 'agreed event', such as a game in which the soloist loses 60/60, or wins a game worth 100 or more. Strictly for gamblers.

DOUBLE An opponent may 'double' the soloist's bid by saying '*kontra*' and the soloist may '*rekontra*', i.e., redouble. Purists can find good reasons for rejecting it, but it remains popular.

GRAND is quite widely valued at 20 instead of 24, and grand ouvert 30 instead of 36, following rules extant before 1932. This variation is to be commended. It reduces the incidence of grand bids, which are too frequent and less interesting than bids in suit.

MIT SPITZE(N) A bid *mit Spitze* is an undertaking to win the tenth trick with the lowest trump, i.e., the Seven in suit or ♦J in grand, and adds one multiplier to the game valuation. Some add the multiplier for doing it and a second for having bid it. Some add another multiplier for also successfully bidding to take the penultimate trick with the second lowest trump, and so on. If declared beforehand, the appropriate card is either reversed in the hand or laid face up on the table to remind everyone of the object, since the game is lost if the soloist fails to achieve it, even though he may fulfil every other requirement.

MOLOTOV A 'compendium' game based on Skat. The deal rotates in the normal way, but at each deal forehand is obliged to undertake a game. He may nominate a suit game, grand, null, or ramsch. Whichever of these four he chooses the first time round is deleted from his record, so that next time he is in that position he must play one of the other three. This continues until four rounds have been played (twelve deals if three take part, sixteen if four), each player having undertaken one game in each category. The game can be extended by introducing other bids, such as spitzengrand (see below).

OFFIZIERSKAT Skat for two players. There are several methods. In one form, the players receive ten cards each, and bid and play as at standard Skat. When ten tricks have been taken, the remaining ten cards are dealt out one at a time, and the winner of the tenth trick leads to the first of the 'last five' tricks. If null is played, the last five are not played. Alternatively, the bid of null is replaced by a bid of schneider, the object being to capture less than 31 in fifteen tricks. In another version, a third hand is dealt face up, acting as the soloist's second opponent, and is played from by the live opponent in proper rotation.

RAMSCH A game played when all three players pass. It is so widely followed that its neglect in the official rules is hard to understand. Basically, only Jacks are trumps and each plays for himself with the object of taking the fewest pips in tricks. There are several different versions. The best is as follows. Forehand takes the skat, passes two cards face down to middlehand, who passes two face down to rearhand, who rejects two face down to form a new skat. This goes to the winner of the last trick. Whoever captures the largest number of pips subtracts that number from his score. In some circles a round (three deals) of *ramsch* automatically follows an 'agreed event' such as a lost bid of grand. In this respect, compare *bock* (above).

SPITZENGRAND A bid like grand, in which only Jacks are trumps, but in which the ranking of cards is reversed. Thus in each plain suit the Seven is high and Ace low, even though retaining its normal pip-value, while of trumps the highest is ♦J and the lowest ♣J, though matadors are counted from ♣J in the usual way. The base value of the game is 16. Strict players condemn it for crowding out bids of null, which require similar card holdings, though it could be represented as more in keeping with the spirit of the game than null itself, which derives from Whist.

UNO Rarely played nowadays but, in the author's opinion, only because it is overvalued. Played as grand (only Jacks trump), the soloist's object is to take exactly one trick, neither more nor less. Purists condemn it as out of keeping with the pip-counting spirit of the game – but then, so is null. The actual value is 100 if played after the exchange.

American Skat ♙

The chief difference from German Skat lies in the fact that
there is no bid to nominate one's own trump suit after taking
up the two skat cards. Instead, the lowest bid is a *tournee*.
The soloist who announces a tournee undertakes to play as
trump a suit turned up in the skat as follows. He first takes up
either card of the skat. If he is content to accept this as trump
he shows the card, announces its suit to be trump, and adds
both skat cards to his hand, discarding any two to reduce his
hand to ten again. If he does not like the suit of the first card
he adds it to his hand without showing it and must then
expose the second card and accept its suit as trump instead,
taking and discarding again in the usual way. If the card he
turns is a Jack he may either accept the suit on its face as
trump or announce that he will play grand. If he loses his
game on 'second turn', i.e., after rejecting the first card as
trump, his penalty is doubled before being deducted from his
score.

The only occasion on which the soloist may take up both
cards at once and exchange without showing them is if he
intends to play grand, in which case the announcement is
'grand *guckser*'.

All other bids are played 'solo', which is the equivalent of
'hand' in German Skat. This includes null, which may not be
played with benefit of the exchange. Grand ouvert may only
be played solo, and no suit game may be played ouvert.

The base values of the various possible bids and games are:

Tournee		*Solo*		*Grand*		*Null*	
in ♦	5	in ♦	9	tournee	12	simple	20
in ♥	6	in ♥	10	guckser	16	ouvert	40
in ♠	7	in ♠	11	solo	20		
in ♣	8	in ♣	12	ouvert	24		

As at German Skat, these base values are multiplied by the number of matadors played with or against (without), plus 1 for game, 1 for schneider made, 1 for schneider declared (only permitted if played solo), 1 for schwarz made, and 1 for schwarz declared (solo only). The two null values are fixed and invariable. There is no extra multiplier for playing ouvert, as the only ouvert games permitted, grand and null, have special values to start with. Game values progress as follows: 10, 12, 14, 15, 16, 18, 20, 21, 22, 24, 25 etc., to a maximum of 192.

If all players pass, the hands are not thrown in but a game called *ramsch* is played. Only Jacks are trumps and each plays for himself with the object of capturing in tricks the smallest number of pips. The skat cards remain unseen but are taken by the winner of the last trick who counts whatever pips they may contain. The player who takes fewest pips scores 10, or 20 if he takes no trick at all. If two tie for low, the one who did not take the last trick wins. In any other tie forehand wins. But if one player takes all the tricks he subtracts 30 from his score and nobody scores plus.

Although the strategy of play is affected by the tournee bid, which leads to more bids on four-trump holdings, the mechanics and basic principles of play and scoring are the same as at German Skat with the exception that *schneider* is 91 points instead of 90. American Skat has a simpler and more logical system of scoring but the bid of tournee introduces a greater element of chance than is allowed to exist in the German game.

ROBBER SKAT

Properly Räuber Skat, a slightly simplified German Skat played in Texas. Base value of grand is 20. Null hand is fixed at 23 and null hand open at 46 – null may not be played after exchanging. Any other game played ouvert has a fixed value of 59 regardless of base value and multipliers. Schneider requires 91 as at American Skat, not 90 as German. If all pass, simple Ramsch is played (see above).

YUKON

Said to have been a game of the Klondike gold rush, Yukon is clearly influenced by Skat if not necessarily a direct descendant. It is played with a full pack by two to four players – three must discard one of the deuces; four may play in partnership. Each player is dealt five cards and the rest are stacked. After a trick is played, each in turn draws the top card of the stock starting with the previous trick-winner. The object is to capture scoring cards in tricks as follows:

Grand Yukon (♠J)	15	Each Ace	5
Other Yukons (Jacks)	10	Each King	3
Each Ten	10	Each Queen	2

This gives a total value of 125, and the winner is the first to reach 250 after as many deals as it takes. Tricks are played in the usual way, except that Yukons are trumps and do not belong to the suits marked on their faces. It is obligatory to follow suit if possible; if not, a Yukon must be played if possible; if not, play anything. A trick is won with the highest card of the suit led or a Yukon if any are played. If more than one Yukon falls to the same trick the first beats the second, except that the Grand Yukon always wins.

Schafkopf o୪o

4 players
1 short pack (32)

Schafkopf means Sheepshead and is apparently so called because the nine game points to which the original version was played up were chalked or scratched as lines arranged in the crude representation of a sheep's head. There are several different versions of the game, which is the principal ancestor of Skat. That most widely played in Germany today is Doppelkopf (Doublehead), while the North American Skat

League promotes a basically three-hand game streamlined under the name of Shep. But the most characteristic version is Wendish Schafkopf, a popular German home game forming a good introduction to Skat. It is described below as the main game, others following as variants.

PLAYERS Four, each playing for himself in the long run, though *ad hoc* partnerships may be formed from deal to deal. Each contributes 50 counters, chips or coins to a pool.

CARDS 32, consisting of AKQJT987 in each suit.

RANK AND VALUE The pip value of cards when captured in tricks is Ace 11, Ten 10, King 4, Queen 3, Jack 2, making 30 in each suit and 120 in the whole pack. All Queens, Jacks and diamonds are trumps, ranking in this order:

♣Q ♠Q ♥Q ♦Q ♣J ♠J ♥J ♦J ATK987

In each plain suit cards rank ATK987. The two black Queens, as top trumps, are known as the Old Women (*die Alten*).

DEAL Eight cards each in two batches of four.

OBJECT Basically, the two players dealt the old women are partners, and aim to win at least 61 of the 120 pips available in tricks. They may not identify themselves to each other except by the play of cards. But a player can override this if he thinks he can play solo, capturing 61 or more without the aid of a partner, while a player who is dealt both old women has the choice of calling for a partner or playing a solo, whichever suits his hand better.

If one player has both old women he may do one of the following:
1. Call for a partner by naming any card he does not hold. Whoever has that card automatically becomes his partner but may not identify himself except by the play.
2. Play a secret solo. In this case he says nothing, and the opponents only deduce that he is playing solo from the progress of play.

3. Play a declared solo. In this case he announces before play that he is playing alone. Furthermore, he may either accept diamonds as the trump suit or change it to some other suit. So, for example, if he announces 'Heart solo' the permanent Queen and Jack trumps are followed by hearts instead of diamonds.

If a player has one black Queen only, he may play a secret or declared solo as described above. If he plays secretly, however, he must declare himself as soon as the other old woman is played to a trick, in order not to mislead its player into thinking himself a partner.

A player without a black Queen may not play solo.

PLAY Eldest hand leads to the first trick. Throughout play, if a non-trump is led everybody else must play a card of the same suit (other than Queen or Jack) if possible; if not, they may play any trump or other card. If a trump is led, whether Queen, Jack or in suit, everybody else must follow with a Queen, Jack or trump *ad lib* and may only discard from a plain suit if they have no trumps. The trick is captured by the highest card of the suit led, or the highest trump if any are played, and the winner of one trick leads to the next.

SETTLEMENT If the Queen-holding partners win, taking 61 + pips between them, each draws 5 units from the pool, or 10 if they make *schneider* (90 + pips), or 15 for *schwarz* (winning all ten tricks). If they lose, each opponent wins 10 for game, 15 for schneider, 20 for schwarz (or 10–20–30 in some circles). Solo games are settled without reference to the pool, the soloist receiving 5 from each opponent if he wins and paying 10 to each if he loses, increased as above for schneider or schwarz.

NOTE ON PLAY Partners will try to discover each other as soon as possible. A common convention is that one of them, at the earliest opportunity, leads ♦A or ♦T, and the other reveals himself by winning the trick – not necessarily with a black Queen if he can safely do so with a lower trump.

VARIANTS

DOPPELKOPF Basically as Schafkopf, but played with two identical 24-card packs shuffled together, with Nine the lowest rank. In each plain suit cards rank ATK9, but there are two of each. All Queens, Jacks and diamonds are trumps as in Schafkopf, but again there are two of each. If two identical cards are played to a trick the first one beats the second. The 'old women' are the two Queens of clubs. Optional extra bids exist.

DREIWENDSCH = three-hand Wendish Schafkopf. Each player receives 10 cards, dealt in batches of 3–4–3, and two are laid aside to form a skat. The player dealt ♣Q (or, in some circles, the player at dealer's left) has the option of taking the skat, rejecting any two cards, and playing against the other two with the object of capturing at least 61 pips, including any that may be in the skat. If he does not wish to play he may pass this privilege to his left-hand neighbour, who may himself pass it on.

GERMAN SCHAFKOPF Played by four in permanent partnerships, the two sitting opposite each other being partners for the whole game. Eight cards each are dealt from a 32-card pack. The four Jacks are permanent trumps, ranking from high to low ♣J ♠J ♥J ♦J, and these are followed by the seven cards of the trump suit, which changes from deal to deal. In each suit cards rank AKQT987. The Ten is still worth 10 when captured in a trick, even though demoted in trick-taking power to beneath the Queen. Each in turn states how many trumps he would be playing with if he were allowed to nominate the trump suit. The minimum number is five (including Jacks) and whoever has most declares the trump suit for the deal. If two have the same number, the one whose trumps total the higher pip value has priority. If no one has more than four it is declared by the player who holds ♣J ('the old man', as it is also called in Skat). In this event, as the game was forced, it is not doubled if lost. The player who nominated trumps leads to the first trick. Play as at Skat, except that you must trump if unable to follow suit.

SHEP, a revised form of Sheepshead or American Schafkopf for three active players, but with variants for other specific numbers. Played as Dreiwendsch (above) but with forehand given first option to take the skat and play. If all pass, ramsch is played as at (American) Skat. Winner is paid 3 units by each opponent, or 4 for schneider, 5 for schwarz, and pays each opponent equivalent amounts for losing. Ramsch winner gains 2 from each opponent or 3 if he takes no tricks.

Tarock ♘

3 players
1 short pack (36)

Original or Austrian Tarock lies outside the scope of this book, as it cannot be played with ordinary cards, but its derivative, Bavarian Tarock, a popular family game in that part of the world, is not so restricted. It may be regarded as intermediate between the Skat and the true Tarock families.

CARDS 36, ranking ATKQJ9876 in each suit.

VALUE Ace counts 11, Ten 10, King 4, Queen 3, Jack 2, totalling 120 pips in the whole pack.

GAME Each player contributes an equal amount to a pool and the game ends when it is empty.

DEAL Eleven each in batches of 4-3-4, with an extra batch of three face down to the table forming the *stock*.

OBJECT Whoever bids highest opposes the other two in an attempt to capture at least 61 pips in tricks, or as many more as he may have bid. In a 'simple' game the soloist may exchange three cards through the stock before announcing trumps; in a 'hand' game he plays without using the stock and may also raise his bid beyond 61. In either case any pips lying in the three cards out of play count for him at the end.

BIDDING Anyone who passes may not bid again, and if all three pass the cards are thrown in and the deal rotates. Forehand (on dealer's left) may announce 'pass' or 'play'. If he passes, the next in turn has the same option and so on. 'Play' is a bid to play at least a simple game. The next in turn may overcall by offering to play from the hand, announcing 'Play, too'. Forehand may then pass if he does not wish to play from the hand; otherwise, he can accept the challenge by saying 'Hold'. If the next player still wishes to contest he can raise the bidding by saying 'Five more', which is an undertaking to win at least 66 pips. Again the first may pass or hold, and if he holds, the next can only overcall by bidding 'ten more' (71 pips), 'fifteen more' (76) and so on. When one of them passes, dealer may enter the bidding by raising further against the survivor. Note that bids of over 61 can only be for 'hand' games.

STOCK If playing a simple game the soloist takes the stock cards without showing them, adds them to his hand, rejects any three face down, and announces the trump suit. If playing hand, he does not look at the stock cards until play is over.

PLAY Forehand always leads. Strict rules of trick-taking apply. Each player must not only follow suit but also play higher than the previous card if he can. If unable to do either he must trump if he can. Only otherwise may he play any other card. The trick is captured by the highest card of the suit led or by the highest trump if any are played, and the winner leads to the next.

SETTLEMENT For winning a simple bid the soloist draws from the pool one unit if he took 61 or more, two for 66 or more, three for 71 or more and so on. If he loses he pays out of his own pocket to one opponent one unit for taking 56–60, two for taking 51–55 and so on, while the other opponent draws the same amount from the pool. A hand bid, won or lost, is always settled out of pocket and the pool remains untouched, the soloist paying each opponent if he loses and receiving from each if he wins. The appropriate amount is two units basic, plus two units for every five pips taken above the number he bid. (Example: if he bid 'fifteen more', promising at least 76 pips, and took 83, he wins four from each.) Losses are similarly calculated below the number bid, i.e., two to each opponent for each additional five pips short.

VARIANT In some accounts of the game, bids of simple may be raised beyond 61 in increments of 5, but any hand bid beats a simple. The strict rules of trick-taking described above may also be found superseded by 'normal' rules (see p. 21).

Six-bid ⚇

3 players
1 short pack (36)

Six-bid is a relative of Skat once popular in the states of the American frontier, and is also known as Six-bid Solo, or just Solo, Slough or Sluff.

CARDS 36, ranking ATKQJ9876 in each suit.

CARD VALUES Ace 11, Ten 10, King 4, Queen 3, Jack 2, giving 30 in each suit and 120 in the whole pack.

DEAL Eleven each in batches of 4–3–4, with three dealt face down to the table to form a blind immediately before the last batches of four.

OBJECT Whoever names the highest valued game plays it against the combined efforts of the other two. From lowest to highest the bids are:

1. *Solo.* Bidder undertakes to win at least 60 of the 120 pips after announcing as trumps any suit except hearts. The blind remains unseen, but any pips it may contain count towards his total at the end of play.

2. *Heart solo.* Same, but hearts are trumps.

3. *Misère.* Playing at no trump, the bidder undertakes to lose every trick. The blind remains out of play.

4. *Guarantee solo.* Bidder undertakes to capture at least 74 pips if he plays in hearts, or 80 if he entrumps any other suit.

5. *Spread misère.* Same as *misère*, but bidder plays with his hand of cards exposed on the table and the lead is made by the player on his left.

6. *Call solo.* Bidder chooses trumps and undertakes to capture all 120 pips (not necessarily taking all the tricks). Any contained in the blind belong to him at the end of play. Before play, he may call for any card not in his hand, and whoever has it must give it to him in exchange for any card the bidder does not want. If the called card is in the blind he may not exchange or make another call.

BIDDING The player at dealer's left bids or passes. If he bids, the next in turn may pass or overbid. If he overbids, the first may pass or bid even higher. The next in turn then bids against the survivor in the same way. A player who has once passed may not bid again. If all pass, the cards are thrown in and the deal rotates.

PLAY The opening lead is made by the player at dealer's left, except in spread misère, where it is made by the player at bidder's left. Strict rules of trick-taking apply. Follow suit to the card led if possible; if not, trump if possible; only discard from another suit if unable to follow or trump. The winner of one trick leads to the next.

SCORE Settle in counters or record transactions in writing. Bidder receives the appropriate amount from each opponent,

if successful, or pays it to each if not. In the two lowest bids
there is no payment if the result is a 60/60 tie.

Solo	2	⎫ per pip captured over or under 60
Heart solo	3	⎭
Misère	30	
Guarantee	4C	
Spread	60	
Call	100	(150 if ♥ trump)

FROG

A simplified form of Six-bid popular in Mexico, where
it is also known as Rana. (Rana is Spanish for Frog, though
'frog' itself has nothing to do with amphibians but comes
from German *Frage* = 'question', denoting the lowest
possible bid in games of this type.) There are only three bids:
(a) Frog: bidder undertakes to capture at least 60 pips,
accepting hearts as trump but first taking the three cards of
the blind, adding them to his hand, and then discarding
three face down, any pips they contain counting for him at
the end of play. He wins, or pays, one chip per point taken
over or under 60. (b) Solo or Chico: as above, but bidder
nominates any other suit as trump and plays without
exchanging three cards, though anything in the blind counts
for him afterwards. Payments are double those of Frog.
(c) Heart solo or grand: as above, but with hearts as trump.
Payments are treble those of Frog. Rules of play otherwise
exactly the same as Six-bid.

Tyzicha ⚇

3 players (or 2)
1 short pack (24)

A delightful 'Ace 11, Ten 10' game, for three, which may be
represented as a cross between the serious game of Skat and
the hilarious game of Pip-Pip. Its first English description (in
Games & Puzzles magazine) ascribes it to the Ukraine –

where they are not supposed to play cards – and says that *tyzicha*, meaning 'thousand', is short for *tyzicha odin*, meaning 'a thousand and one' – which, as they say, figures. The spelling has been criticized but pronounce it tizzy-cha with the stress on the first syllable. An equivalent game for two players follows the main description.

CARDS 24, ranking ATKQJ9 in each suit.

VALUE Ace counts 11, Ten 10, King 4, Queen 3 and Jack 2. The Nine has no value. There are 30 pips in each suit and 120 in the whole pack.

DEAL A batch of three to each player, three face down to the table to form a blind, and the rest round one at a time until everyone has seven cards.

OBJECT Whoever bids highest becomes the soloist, whose object is to win as many points as he bid against the opposition of the other two. Points are scored for (a) winning value cards in tricks and (b) making or changing the trump suit.

TRUMPS The game starts at no trump, but any player holding K–Q of the same suit may declare that suit trump when he is about to lead one of them to a trick. Making a trump scores for that player according to the suit named, as follows:

♠ = 40   ♣ = 60   ♦ = 80   ♥ = 100

BIDDING The lowest permissible bid is 100, and all bids are made in multiples of 10, though bids may be raised by any number of tens at a time. Eldest hand must start the bidding: he may not pass. Thereafter each in turn must pass or raise the previous bid. A player who has passed may not re-bid and when two have passed the third becomes the soloist.

EXCHANGING If eldest hand took the bidding at 100 he may not increase his bid but now takes the three cards of the blind and adds them to his hand without showing them. If he, or anyone else, took the bid at a higher level, the soloist reveals the three cards of the blind before adding them to his hand and may then, if he wishes, raise his bid to a new high or concede the game if he thinks it hopeless. If he concedes (announcing 'forty each'), each opponent scores 40 and the soloist is set back by the amount of his bid. If not, he concludes the exchange by passing from his hand one card face down to each opponent. Now everybody has eight cards and play begins.

PLAY The soloist leads to the first trick. Normal rules of trick-taking apply: follow suit if possible; if not, trump (if any) or renounce *ad lib*. The winner of one trick leads to the next. Each player keeps his tricks separately. A player may make or change the trump suit by revealing the King and Queen of the suit concerned and leading one of them to a trick. The trump cannot be made by a player who is merely following to a trick, and is therefore lost if either of the cards is captured before they can be used.

SCORE If the soloist wins at least the amount of his bid in cards and trumps he scores the value of his bid – not more. If not, that value is deducted from his score. In either event, each opponent scores what he personally took in cards and trump announcements. Game is won by the first player to exceed 1000 points, but this may only be done by a soloist. If an opponent reaches 1000 his score is pegged until he becomes the soloist and makes another score. (Scores are usually rounded down to the nearest five, in which case an opponent pegs his score at 995.)

FOR TWO PLAYERS   O
                       O

There is a similar Austrian game for two players, called Tausendeins and also played up to 1001. The same 24-card pack is used and cards have the same rank and values. Eight each are dealt in batches of 3–2–3 and the last eight laid aside face down to a stock. There is no bidding and the object is to score for winning value-cards and making trumps. Play starts at no trump, and after each trick the winner draws the top card of stock and adds it to his hand, leading to the next when his opponent has also drawn. When no more are left in stock the remaining cards are played out, and there is a bonus of 10 for taking the last trick, making 130 card points available all together. Whenever a player is about to lead to a trick he may declare a marriage, announce that suit as trumps, score accordingly, and then lead one card of the marriage to the next trick. Regardless of the actual suits involved the first marriage/trump declaration scores 40, the second 60, the third 80, and the fourth – if it gets that far – 100. Interesting situations arise because both players seek to hold back declarations until they are worth more, a practice which can easily be self-defeating. This game is clearly a close relative of Sixty-Six (see p. 249).

Jass Games

Jass, pronounced Yass, denotes (a) a large family of closely related games of which the three described here are most representative, and (b) any game played with Jasskarten, i.e., the 36-card Swiss pack with traditional suits of acorns, bells, flowers and shields, and ranking Daus (deuce), King, Over, Under, Banner, Nine, Eight, Seven, Six. In this chapter we are only concerned with (a), as (b) are largely adaptations of other games described elsewhere.

True Jass games include a two-hander popular all over the world in slightly differing forms under varying names, including Klabberjass, Clobiosh, Kalabriasz and that denizen of bistrots, Belote. They are characterized partly by the 'Ace 11, Ten 10' card-value system of Skat and its relatives, but with the added feature that the Jack of trumps, called Jass, is promoted to highest position with a value of 20, and is followed by the Nine of trumps, which has a value of 14 and is known as Menel, or just Nel (no doubt from the card called Manille in Ombre and related games). Furthermore, additional scores are introduced for holding or acquiring certain combinations of cards, such as a marriage, consisting of the King and Queen of trumps.

Jass games are particularly associated with Switzerland but the Swiss ascribe them to the Dutch, whose soldiery are thought to have introduced them into the cantons in the last decade of the eighteenth century. Klaverjass, described below, remains a national game of the Netherlands.

Handjass ⚇

2 to 4 players, 3 best
1 short pack (36)

It is a very simple game, well fitted to amuse these mountaineers when they are fatigued with their cheese-making.

(Rev. S. Taylor, *The History of Playing Cards*, 1865)

Of the thirty and more varieties of Jass played in Switzerland and western Austria, the following may be recommended as one of the most basic, and most satisfactory, for three players or four if each wishes to play for himself. Handjass is also known as Sack-Jass, as a player who fails to take a minimum number of pips in the play is penalized by being put 'in the sack'. An unusual feature of the game is that winning players drop out until only one is left 'in'. The one left in is the loser and has to pay for the drinks. For authenticity, Jass should be played with traditional Swiss Jass cards with suits of acorns, bells, flowers and shields and ranks of Daus (Deuce), King, Over, Under, Banner and numerals from Nine to Six.

CARDS 36, consisting of AKQJT9876 in each suit.

RANK AND VALUE For trick-taking purposes, cards rank and are valued as follows:

trJ	tr9	A	K	Q	(J)	T	(9)	8	7	6
20	14	11	4	3	2	10	0	0	0	0

In trumps the highest cards are the Jack and Nine, known as the Jass and Menel respectively. In other suits the Ace is the top card, and the Ten, though counting high when captured in a trick, ranks in trick-taking power only between Jack and Nine (or Queen and Eight in trumps).

ORDER Swiss Jass games are played from left to right, anti-clockwise around the table. In this case eldest is the player on dealer's right.

DEAL Nine cards each, in batches of three. When four play, show the last card to determine trumps. When three play, lay the remaining cards face down as a spare hand but turn up the top card to establish trumps. When two play, deal two extra hands of nine: one is 'spare' and may be taken as described below; the other is 'dead' and is used only to establish trumps by turning up the top card.

OBJECT To score for having the best meld in hand and for capturing value-cards in tricks; in particular, to avoid scoring less than 21 for melds and tricks.

EXCHANGE When two or three play, whoever has the Six of trumps may exchange it for the turn-up. Thereafter, each in turn, starting with eldest, has the right to throw his hand in if he thinks it bad and take up the spare hand in its place – without examining it first and without being able to change his mind after seeing what it contains. Only one player may make this exchange. The first to do so therefore cuts the others out.

MELDS A meld is three or more cards of the same suit and in sequence (for which purpose, in trumps, the Jack and Nine rank above and below Ten respectively), or four cards of the same rank if higher than Eight, or a marriage, i.e., the King and Queen of trumps. The values of these melds are:

Sequence of three 20, four 50, five or more 100
Four Queens, Kings, Aces 100, Nines 150, Jacks 200
Marriage 20

Only the player with the best meld in hand may score for melds, but he may score for every meld he holds. No card may count as part of a sequence and of a quartet in the same hand, but the trump King and Queen may count both as a marriage and as part of a sequence or quartet as well.

As each player contributes a card to the first trick he announces the best meld he has, but need give no more information about it than is necessary to establish its superiority over someone else's. (For example, eldest may merely say

'100' and only be forced into saying more about it as and when other players whose best melds are also worth 100 rise to the challenge.)

As between apparently equal hands, the 'best' is the one which:

1. scores most; or, if equal,
2. contains most cards; or, if equal,
3. is in the trump suit if applicable; or, if not,
4. was declared first, for which purpose eldest declares first and dealer last.

TRICKS Eldest leads to the first trick, and the winner of each subsequent trick to the next. A trick is captured by the highest card of the suit led, or by the highest trump if any are played. Simplified rules of trick-play (but see Variants) are as follows: each subsequent player must follow suit if possible and head the trick if possible; if unable to follow, it is obligatory to trump if possible.

SCORE The two players making the most in melds and tricks count one game point each. A player who has failed to make 21 in melds and tricks is 'in the sack'. He has a figure nought marked against his name, and any opponent who is not himself in the sack counts one game point for each player who is. A player who is in the sack at the end of one deal does not gain a game point for being one of the top two in the next deal but merely cancels his previous sack, though he still counts a game point for any opponent who finds himself in the sack. As soon as one player has made five game points he drops out and the others continue playing. The last one left in loses.

VARIANTS

TRICKS The strict rules of trick-play are somewhat complicated. If a trump is led you must follow suit if you can, unless your only trump is the Jass, in which case you may play anything. If you can follow suit to a plain suit lead you may either do so or trump, and if you cannot follow you may either renounce or trump; but, in either case, if you play a trump it must be higher than any other trump already played to the trick, unless you have only trumps in hand, in which case you may play any one.

SCORE By another system only the player taking most in melds and tricks scores a game point, and a player taking less than 21 loses a point. Players drop out of the game when they have amassed seven points. A player with a bad hand may throw it in and decline to play, in order to avoid the risk of losing a game point.

Klabberjass ⚇

2 players
1 short pack (32)

Pronounced 'Klobiosh', spelt 'Kalabriasz' in another incarnation (especially in the world of Damon Runyon), sometimes shortened to Clobby, Klabberjass is probably one of the most widely played two-handers in the world, certainly in Europe, where every country seems to have its own version – Belote in France, Alsös in Hungary, Clobiosh in the East End, to name but the better known. It is particularly associated with Jewish culture, and the name is German for 'Jack of clubs'.

CARDS 32, consisting of AKQJT987 in each suit.

DEAL The turn to deal alternates. Deal six cards to each player, three at a time. Turn up the next card for trumps and place the remainder of the pack on top so that it projects from underneath.

OBJECT To score for melding certain combinations and for taking valued cards in tricks. The first to reach 500 points over several deals wins.

RANK AND VALUE OF CARDS The Jack and Nine are high in the trump suit only:

Rank:	trJ	tr9	A	T	K	Q	(J)	(9)	8	7
Value:	20	14	11	10	4	3	(2)	0	0	0

In non-trump suits, Ace then Ten are the highest cards, and Jack and Nine fall into their proper place.

BIDDING Elder speaks first. He may (a) *take it*, meaning that he accepts the turned card as establishing trumps, or (b) *pass*, meaning that he rejects it as trumps, or (c) *schmeiss*,* which is an offer to accept the turn-up as trump or to throw both hands in, as dealer wishes. In case (c) dealer may refuse the schmeiss, in which case the game is played with the turned suit as trump, or accept it, in which case there is a new deal.

If elder passes, dealer has the same options: to take, to pass, or to schmeiss.

If both pass there is a second round of bidding. Elder may (a) nominate another suit as trump, or (b) pass, or (c) schmeiss – the latter being an offer to nominate another suit or to throw both hands in, as dealer prefers.

If he passes, dealer may nominate another suit, or pass. If he passes, there is a new deal.

When a suit has been established as trump the person who did so becomes the maker. If it was established through a schmeiss, the maker is the player who offered the schmeiss, not the one who accepted it.

REDEALING Dealer deals three more cards to each player from the top of the stock, one at a time. If the suit of the turn-up has become the trump a player holding the Seven of trumps may exchange it for the turn-up. Traditionally, but pointlessly, the top card of the stock is then turned face up merely to show that the deal has been completed. This turn-up has no part to play, but its appearance may affect the players' tactics in certain situations.

* Rhymes with *mice*.

MELDS A meld is a sequence of three or more cards in the same suit, for which purpose the sequential order is AKQJT987 regardless of suit. A sequence of three counts 20, of four 50. Elder announces whether or not he has a sequence by saying 'None', '20' or '50' as the case may be. If dealer can do better he says 'Not good'; if not, he says 'Good'. If he has a sequence of the same value as announced, he asks 'How high?' and elder then names the top card of his sequence. Again, dealer says 'Not good' if his top card is higher, 'Good' if it is lower, or 'Equal' otherwise. A longer sequence beats a shorter, and a trump a non-trump sequence in the event of a tie.

PLAY After the announcements elder leads any card to the first trick and dealer follows suit. At this point the player who proves to hold the longer or higher sequence may now show and score for *all* sequences of three or more cards that he may hold. A sequence longer than four counts only 50. Only the player with the best sequence may score. If there was a tie for best sequence (or both had none) neither scores, even if one had more sequences than the other.

BELLA If a player holds the King and Queen of trumps he may score 20 for them by announcing *bella* when he plays the second of them to a trick.

TRICKS Suit must be followed if possible, and a player void in the suit led must trump if possible. If a trump is led the opponent must play a higher one if he can.

LAST TRICK The winner of the last trick scores 10.

SCORE Each player notes the total he made for (a) melds, if any; (b) value-cards taken in tricks; and (c) winning the last trick. If the maker has more points, both score what they make; if there is a tie, the maker scores nothing; if the maker has fewer, he scores nothing and his opponent scores the total made by both combined. (In this case the maker is *bête*.)

GAME The winner is the player with the higher score when at least one of them has reached or exceeded 500 points.

KLABBERJASS VARIANTS

CLUBS PREFERRED Numerous minor variants may be encountered. In one, no card is turned for trump; instead, the 'preferred' suit is clubs, and another suit may only be nominated on the second round of bidding if clubs are not accepted on the first.

BELOTE In the French game, four of a kind can be declared. Only the player with the highest ranking quartet may score, but he may score both in the unlikely event that he has two. Four Jacks count 200, Nines 150, anything else 100 except Eights or Sevens, which are not valid. A sequence of five or more cards scores 100. There is a bonus of 100 for winning all the tricks, which is scored *instead* of 10 for last, and game may be played by two or more players up to 500, 750, 1000 or 2000 points. An optional rule permits one player to knock when he believes that he has taken enough points to win – for example, if, playing up to 1000, he started a deal with 950, declared a sequence of three for 20, led the Jass for 20 and captured the Ace of trumps thereby, he would have gained 51 points and could then end the game and claim the win. If he proves to be wrong he loses the whole game, not just the deal. Two-hand Belote has lost in popularity to Belote Coinchée, a partnership game that has borrowed many features from Contract Bridge.

TATTLE In Tatteln, Törteln or Tartl the game is played in the same way as Bézique, each drawing from stock after playing to a trick. The winner of a trick may declare a *tattle*, which is a sequence of three, but cannot score if his opponent has a better one. The game is of Austrian provenance.

SANS ATOUT, TOUT ATOUT A bid to play other than in the turned or preferred suit may be overcalled by a bid of *sans atout* (no trump), in which there is no trump suit and therefore no Jass or Menel, all Jacks and Nines ranking in their traditional position and with no special scores. This in turn may be overcalled by *tout atout* (all trumps). Here, too, there is no trump suit, but every suit is headed by its Jack and Nine, which are worth 20 and 14 respectively.

JO-JOTTE An extension of Klabberjass invented by Ely Culbertson, of Bridge fame, and named after his wife Josephine. As might be expected, it includes doubling, redoubling, nullo bids, slams, above-and-below-the-line scoring and rubber bonuses. Surprisingly, it does not include a Joker; but, by way of light relief, one announces 'Jo' upon playing the first card of the marriage and 'Jotte' upon playing the second.

CINQ CENTS, known as Senserln or Quinzent in Bavaria, and Zensa in Austria, is a Germanic form of Belote. The significant differences are that there is no bid of *schmeiss*, that the Ten ranks in all suits in its low position (between Nine and Jack in non-trumps, Eight and Queen in trumps) but still counts 10 points when captured, and that a quartet of Nines does not count. Other quartets, sequences and *bella* are as at Belote, and there is a bonus of 100 for winning all nine tricks.

NOTES ON PLAY (ALL FORMS)

A hand containing four or more cards worth at least 10 each should be regarded as the minimum requirement for accepting or making a trump, and length in the trump suit is often of less importance than holding the Jass itself. Do not make trumps unless you are genuinely confident of winning more points, for if you are *bêted* the loss will be immense – apart from melds, your opponent can pick up a hundred or more points from scoring cards alone. The bid of *schmeiss* admits of some bluffing possibilities, as it may be made on a strong hand in the hope that one's opponent will accept; or the first player may pass in the hope that dealer himself may *schmeiss*.

It is not obligatory to declare all one's melds, and it may sometimes be advantageous to hold back or 'sink', say, a sequence such as T–9–8 in trumps if there is the danger that the Nine may be captured by the Jass. Use non-scoring cards to lead in suits of which your opponent has none, as he will then be forced to trump with little advantage. Remember that the game is one of card-points, not tricks. Keep careful count of what you have taken and of the cards that have fallen.

Klaverjass ⊞

4 players
1 short pack (32)

Klaverjass is the Netherlands' most popular card game. There appears to be no authoritative standard form of the game, which varies according to whether you play the Amsterdam or the Rotterdam version and the circle in which you are playing. In one respect Klaverjass differs markedly from its Swiss and other cousins and that is in its preference for making melds on the table rather than in the hand . . . as will become apparent below.

CARDS 32, consisting of AKQJT987 in each suit.

RANK AND VALUE For trick-taking purposes cards rank and are valued as follows:

trJ	tr9	A	T	K	Q	(J)	(9)	8	7
20	14	11	10	4	3	2	0	0	0

The Ten ranks between Ace and King in every suit, the Jack and Nine between Queen and Eight in every suit except trumps, in which they are the two highest cards, known as Jas and Nel, and count 20 and 14 respectively. The total value of cards in the pack is 152, and there is a score of 10 for taking the last trick, making 162 to be played for irrespective of further scores for melds.

DEAL Eight each in two batches of four.

OBJECT Both sides try to win a majority of points for tricks (out of 162) plus melds, but the side that selects the trump suit – the 'bidding' side – has the greater obligation to do so and is heavily penalized if it fails. The game is played up to 155 points.

BIDDING Starting with eldest hand each in turn passes or names a trump suit. As soon as someone names a trump suit the bidding is over and the trump nominator and his partner become the bidding side. If the first three pass, dealer is obliged to name a suit.

MELDS A meld is four cards of the same rank, or a sequence of three or more cards in the same suit (for which purpose only, cards rank AKQJT987 in all suits including trumps), or the King and Queen of trumps (*marriage*). They score as follows:

Sequence of three 20, four 50, five or more 100
Four of the same rank 100
Marriage 20

Melds 'from the hand', i.e., those that may be held by the players amongst the cards originally dealt them, are not recognized by modern players. They are now scored exclusively 'on the table' as and when they are formed by the cards played to a trick, as explained in detail below.

TRICKS Eldest hand leads to the first trick. Unusual rules of trick-taking apply. Each subsequent player must follow suit to the card led if possible; if not, he is not only obliged to trump if he can but must also play a higher trump if someone else (even his partner) has already trumped it. If a trump is led each succeeding player must, if he can, play a trump higher than any already played to the trick. A player may only renounce if he cannot follow suit and cannot play a trump. The trick is captured by the highest card of the suit led or by the highest trump if any are played. The winner of a trick scores for any melds it may contain, and leads to the next.

MELDS ON THE TABLE If the four cards played to a trick include a sequence of three or four in the same suit, the value of that meld is scored by the side winning the trick. If a trump sequence includes the King and Queen the marriage is scored in addition to the sequence. The trick-winner would also score for the quartet if all four cards played were of the same rank, but this happens once in a blue moon.

SCORE If the bidding side scores more points than the other both sides score what they make. If not, the non-bidding side scores the combined total of points made by both sides. Game is 1500 up.

VARIANTS

TRUMP-MAKING The last card dealt (belonging to dealer) is revealed to establish a preferred trump suit, or else a second pack is cut for the same purpose. In one round of bidding each in turn may pass or accept the preferred suit as trump. If all pass there is a second round, in which each in turn may pass or nominate one of the other three suits as trump. If all pass again there is a new deal. (This system appears to be out of use now but has certain advantages.)

MELDS Originally, melds could also be scored from the hand. As each player played a card to the first trick he could reveal any melds his hand might contain and score for them. Most players have since rejected this way of scoring melds because it owes all to chance and none to skill, and could upset the bidding. Some, however, still permit a marriage to be declared from the hand. One effect of abolishing melds from the hand has been the virtual elimination of the quartet as a scoring feature, even though it has been extended to include four of any rank. (Players who regret this may wish to introduce scores for three of a kind or even pairs made 'on the table'.)

TRUMPING In some circles a player is not obliged to over-trump a trick already being won by his partner's trump to a plain suit lead.

DOUBLING In some circles the non-bidding side may double before the first trick is led. All scores made on that deal are thereby automatically doubled.

NOTES ON PLAY

In deciding whether or not to bid look first for a Jack and Nine of the same suit, for unless other cards are outstandingly weak their combined value of 34 for Jas and Nel, plus trick-taking power, almost certainly make the hand biddable. Look next for melding possibilities, especially if you have a potential Jas or well-guarded Nel but not both. For example, if you hold King and Queen of trumps you cannot make a marriage on the table, though you can score it from the hand if following the rule that permits it. If you hold only one marriage partner, preferably the King, it is worth keeping the marriage possibility in mind. A hand devoid of Jacks and Nines is rarely biddable unless it contains length in trumps and good support in plain suits. A hand full of middling cards, especially Tens unaccompanied by their Aces, is weak: you need Aces for winning tricks, Sevens and Eights for leading worthless losers. Middling cards, such as King, Queen and Jack, not only add to your opponents' card count when lost in tricks but also combine more easily into sequences, thus running the risk of boosting their score even further.

In the play consider each card carefully from the viewpoint of swarming (throwing counters, especially Tens, to tricks won by your partner), and especially *not* swarming when your opponents seem likely to take the trick. At the same time consider its potential as part of a sequence. If playing to a trick containing your partner's Jas and an opponent's Nel, play the Ten if you have it and score for the sequence; but play something else if it contains an opponent's Jas and your partner's Nel.

In the following game North dealt and East bid diamonds, preventing South from bidding hearts and West spades. The hands are:

East: ◆JAK ♠87 ♥A ♣97
South: ◆7 ♠KQ ♥TQJ ♣J8
West: ◆T8 ♠AJ9 ♥9 ♣KQ
North: ◆9Q ♠T ♥K87 ♣AT

East leads. Winning tricks are underlined. The trick value is marked (+) if won by the bidders, (−) if won by opponents, and where there are two values the second is for a meld made on the table.

	E	S	W	N	Value
1.	♠7	♣Q	♠A	♠T	+24
2.	◆J	◆7	◆T	◆9	+44, 20
3.	◆K	♣8	◆8	◆Q	+7, 20
4.	♠8	♠K	♣9	♥K	−8
5.	♥A	♥J	♥9	♥7	+13
6.	♣9	♣J	♣Q	♣T	−15, 50
7.	◆A	♥Q	♣K	♥8	+18
8.	♣7	♥T	♠J	♣A	−23, 10 for last

East/West score 146, North/South 106.

East's lead of a low non-trump at trick (1) is conventional: it calls for partner to lead his highest trump as soon as possible. At trick (2) West obliges by leading the Ten. North's Nel gives the bidders 20 for a sequence of three after West plays the Jas. At trick (3) East leads the King to marry the Queen, virtually a foregone conclusion. At (4) East gets off play with a worthless spade. North might reasonably have been expected to swarm the Ace or Ten of clubs to his partner's trick instead of a comparatively cheap King. At (6) the bidders play badly and donate a sequence of four to their adversaries. East should have led the Seven rather than the Nine, as the Eight had already gone, and West should have played the King instead of the Queen in order to restrict any possible sequence to a three-card rather than a four. With proper play North/South would have made no

meld at all. At (7) West is obliged to trump by the rules of
the game, otherwise he might have preferred to throw the ♣7
and add a second worthless card to the trick. At (8) North is
fortunate to have made his Ace of clubs as well as his earlier
Ten, as there was a good chance that either would fall to the
last trump or a lead in the 'wrong' suit.

Bézique/Pinochle

Bézique is a two-player game of French origin still widely played in Europe by the *cognoscenti*. Pinochle, a development of the still popular German Binockel, is essentially an American game, which, though losing ground in recent years, has long been in the top five of the popularity stakes among card games in the U.S. The two games are closely related, and the names of both of them denote a particular card combination, consisting of the ♠Q and ♦J, to which a special score is attached. A fanciful explanation of the name *bézique* derives it from the Spanish *besico* meaning 'a little kiss', in allusion to the supposed relationship between a Queen and Jack of different suits. A more plausible explanation of *binockel*, which under its French spelling *binocle* means much the same as 'binocular', relates it to the fact that in the commonest Franco-German pack design ♠Q is the only Queen and ♦J the only Jack to be depicted in profile, thus exhibiting only two eyes between them.

These and other obviously related games, notably Sixty-Six and Gaigel, involve tricks and pip-counting cards as in Skat and Jass games, but go even further than Jass in extending the range of melds or combinations for which scores may be made. Bézique, indeed, has dropped the value-cards and attaches little importance to tricks, and has become almost entirely a game of combinations, for which purpose it may be played in grandiose versions requiring more and more packs of cards to enable more and more combinations to be formed.

Bézique 8

2 players
2 short packs (64)

He felt it was his turn to speak,
And, with a shamed and crimson cheek,
Moaned: 'This is harder than Bézique.'

(Lewis Carroll, *The Three Voices*, 1869)

Played in the nineteenth-century gaming establishments of
Paris, Bézique first made itself known to Britain in 1861 and
failed to win many converts. By 1869, however, it had been
picked up in his travels by Alfred, Duke of Edinburgh, and
achieved rapid popularity through this bestowal of royal
favour – just as his late father, the Prince Consort, had
unwittingly popularized Patience (Victoria, herself, preferred
Poker, strange as it may seem. As a home game it gave rise
to elaborate versions played with more and more packs of
cards simultaneously, while, in the clubs, it found itself
squeezed into the straitjacket of rules and laws codified by
the Portland and other clubs. Like most games for fewer
than four players Bézique has since been pushed into the
background by Bridge. It is easy to learn, fast to play, and
makes more demands on table-space than on brainpower.
Start with the two-pack version and work upwards.

CARDS 64, consisting of two 32-card packs (certainly of the
same size and preferably of the same back design and
colour) shuffled together. Cards rank in this order for trick-
taking purposes: ATKQJ987. Note the position of the
Ten.

DEAL Higher cut deals first, eight cards to each player in
batches of 3–2–3. Place the rest face down to form a stock,
then take the top card and lay it face up underneath but
projecting from the stock. The suit of this card is the trump
for that deal. If it is a Seven, dealer scores 10 for it.

OBJECT Tricks are played, each drawing from the stock after each trick to restore his hand to eight. The winning of a trick entitles that player to declare and score for any card combinations he may hold, as described below. Otherwise there is no merit in winning tricks except that *brisques* (Aces and Tens) captured in tricks score 10 each at the end of play.

SCORING COMBINATIONS The combinations that may be declared and scored are shown in Table 4. The combinations are divided into various classes: sequences, quartets and *béziques*. A card used and scored in one combination may not subsequently be counted in a lower combination of the same class. But, for example, a Queen used in a marriage may subsequently be counted as part of a quartet or bézique.

TABLE 4: COMBINATIONS AND SCORES AT TWO-PACK BÉZIQUE

Sequences

Sequence	A–T–K–Q–J of trumps only	250
Marriage, royal	K–Q of trumps	40
Marriage, common	K–Q of plain suit	20

Quartets

Hundred Aces	Any four Aces	100
Eighty Kings	Any four Kings	80
Sixty Queens	Any four Queens	60
Forty Jacks	Any four jacks	40

Béziques

Bézique (single)	♠Q with ♦J	40
Double bézique	♠Q–♦J–♠Q–♦J	500

Other Scores

Dix*	7 of trumps	10
Brisques	Each Ace and Ten won	10

* Pronounced *deece*, though it is hardly mentioned in practice.

A royal marriage may not be declared if either card has already been declared in a trump sequence, but may be declared first and subsequently converted to a sequence by the addition of A–T–J.

If one card of a quartet has been played out, the quartet may not be reformed by the addition of its duplicate, though any cards left of it may be used in combinations of a different class. Similarly, a widowed monarch may not remarry.

Double bézique only counts if all four cards are on the table simultaneously. It is permissible to declare single bézique for 40, then later declare another for 40, and later still declare them double for 500, provided that all four cards are on the table.

PLAY Non-dealer leads to the first trick. Unusual rules of trick-play apply: the second player is not obliged to follow suit but may follow, trump or discard *ad lib*. The trick is won by the higher card of the suit led or by the higher trump if any are played. The winner of the trick may declare any one combination he may hold, within the seven cards left to him by laying those cards face up on the table before him and marking the appropriate score. He then takes the trick, draws the top card of the stock, lets his opponent draw the next card, and leads to the next trick. Cards declared in combinations remain face up on the table but continue to form part of their owner's hand and may be played out to tricks as and when desired. Only one combination may be scored at a time. If its owner is able to convert it into a higher one he must win another trick before doing so.

DIX Whoever holds or draws a Seven of trumps may declare it for 10 points, and the first to do so may exchange it for the trump turn-up. The *declaration and exchange* of the Seven may only be made upon winning a trick and instead of any other declaration; but the *declaration only* may be made and scored at any time, usually upon playing the Seven to a trick. (This is a recommended compromise between various different rules governing this point.)

END-GAME At the end of the 23rd trick there will remain untaken only the turn-up (Seven) and one card of stock. The winner of that trick takes the top card, leaving the Seven to his opponent, and has this last opportunity of making a declaration. Both players then take into hand any cards they may have on the table before them, and the winner of the last trick leads to the first of the 'last eight' tricks. Now, however, the rules of play change. The second to play *must*, if able, play a higher card of the suit led; if unable, he must nevertheless follow suit; if unable, he must trump if possible; and only otherwise may he discard from another suit. Finally, the winner of the last trick of all scores 10 for it.

SCORE Each player then sorts through his cards won in tricks and scores 10 for each Ace and Ten amongst them. (For this, of course, the two players' scores will total 160.) The winner is the first to reach 1000 points, which usually takes several deals, and he wins double if the loser fails to reach 500.

VARIANTS

TRUMPS Some dispense with the turn-up and play at no trump until a marriage or sequence is declared, its suit automatically becoming the trump. In this case the Seven of trumps has no special power or value.

BÉZIQUE If spades or diamonds are turned for trump, some redefine bézique as ♣Q–♥J.

DIX Some permit either trump Seven to be declared at any time.

LAST TRICK It may be preferred to score 10 for winning the last trick before the stock is exhausted (the 23rd) instead of the last trick of all. (Also, in the original game, the 'last eight' were played as at Whist, i.e., with Ten ranking between Jack and Nine.)

NOTES ON PLAY

Do not bother to win tricks except for a purpose – e.g., to declare a combination, or to prevent your opponent from declaring one (especially if approaching the end of the stock with the possibility of denying him any further declarations at all), or, at the least, to win a brisque. A brisque counts only 10 but is worth 20 – the price of a common marriage – to the difference between scores.

Study your opponent's declarations in order to discover what cards are not available to you. Clearly, you cannot save up for a double bézique if he has declared 'forty Jacks'. Similarly, prefer to play a card from the table to one from the hand, as this reduces your opponent's information as to cards not available to himself.

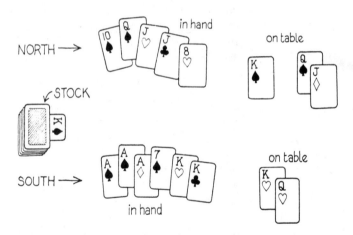

8. BÉZIQUE (TWO-PACK) North has declared a royal marriage (40) and single bézique (40). He needs to draw ♠J for '40 Jacks', plus ♠A for the sequence (250) and/or ♦J for double bézique (500). If he held the trump Seven, he could exchange it for the turn-up and declare a second royal marriage. South has just declared a marriage (20) and drawn ♠7. If he leads a trump Ace he can exchange ♠7 for the King (for 10) and hold '80 Kings' for subsequent declaration. This means breaking up his potential '100 Aces' but is probably worth it. Alternatively, he could lead ♥Q and hope to be given the trick.

As there is no such scoring feature as a quartet of Tens, reserve them for winning tricks when needed. If in a quandary as to what to discard without breaking up a potential combination, prefer to throw a non-bézique Jack to a Ten or other high card, as the score for 'forty Jacks' hardly repays the inconvenience of collecting them, and a trump sequence is rarely obtainable. (It is, however, worth aiming for a sequence if dealt three towards it at the outset.)

Do not be over-anxious about making early declarations. Any declaration gives your opponent valuable information about card availability, which is denied him the longer it is held back. A fine judgement is called for in deciding when to make declarations: too early and they give too much away; too late and you may not be able to win enough tricks in time for them all.

Rubicon Bézique ⚇

2 players
4 short packs (128)

Two may play extended versions of Bézique with four, six or eight 32-card packs shuffled together. The following rules apply to the four-pack game, which is called Rubicon Bézique. They also apply for the most part to the six- and eight-pack versions, any differences being noted at the end of the following account.

DEAL Nine each in ones or threes. The rest form a face-down stock, no card being turned for trump.

CARTE BLANCHE If either player is dealt a hand devoid of courts (KQJ) he may declare *carte blanche* for 50, proving the fact by rapidly playing his cards one at a time face up to the table. Thereafter, if, after playing to a trick, he draws a card which is not a court he may show it and score 50 again. This privilege ends as soon as he draws a court.

TRUMPS Play as at two-pack Bézique, except that the game starts without a trump suit. As soon as one player declares a marriage (or a sequence, though it is more profitable to declare the marriage first and convert to a sequence later) the suit of that marriage becomes trump for the rest of the game, scoring 40. No special power or score attached to the trump Seven.

PLAY As at two-pack Bézique, non-dealer leads to the first trick and each trick-winner leads to the next after drawing the top card of the stock and waiting for his opponent to draw the next. The follower need not follow suit but may trump or discard *ad lib*, the first of two identical cards beating the second. Before drawing, the winner of a trick may declare *one* combination by laying it face up on the table before him, where its constituent cards continue to be played as part of his hand. The combinations and their scores are given in Table 5. Substantial differences of procedure from two-pack Bézique are noted below.

DECLARATIONS In sequences, note that it is possible to declare a sequence in a non-trump suit for 150 as well as for 250 in trumps. If a sequence is declared the marriage it contains may not be declared later; but, if a marriage is declared, it may later be converted into a sequence and scored as such.

In quartets, note that the four cards may be of any combination of suits, not necessarily one of each.

To score for double, treble or quadruple bézique, all four, six or eight cards must be on the table at the same time. But, with two or more béziques in hand, it is permissible to declare them one at a time (after duly winning tricks) for the individual as well as the cumulative scores.

A card may be declared twice in the same combination (unlike two-pack Bézique) so long as at least one card of that combination is played to a trick. Thus, if 'hundred Aces' is declared, and one of them is played out, another Ace may be added to the three on the table and 'hundred Aces' scored again. Similarly, if (say) three marriages in the same suit are on the table, and one of the cards is played out, its marriage partner may be declared for another marriage score in conjunction with one of the remaining monarchs. As many such rearrangements may be made and scored as are distinct from one another. A King or Queen in a sequence may be married to a Queen or King added from the hand. The latter may then subsequently be used to re-form the sequence after its double has been played out. Bézique Queens and Jacks may not be rearranged with one another on the table, but if one is played to a trick, it may be replaced by a double from hand and the whole bézique combination scored again.

At any point a player may have several visible combinations yet to score, but he may only declare *one* each time he wins a trick. Any left undeclared when the last card of the stock has gone remain unscored.

END-GAME When the last card of the stock has been taken, and the last combination declared, the players take up their cards and play to the last nine tricks. Now it is obligatory to follow suit and to win the trick if possible; if unable to follow it is obligatory to trump if possible. The winner of the last trick scores 50.

SCORE Brisques (Aces and Tens won in tricks) do not count except to break a tie. Each player reduces his score to the nearest hundred below, and the winner scores the difference plus 500 for game. If the loser has less than 1000 he has failed to cross the 'rubicon', and the winner scores an additional 500 even if he himself failed to reach it.

If the rounding down results in a tie (e.g. 1290 and 1200 reduce to 1200) then brisques are added in at 10 each and the new totals are rounded down. If this still produces a tie the player with the higher actual score rounds *up* instead of down to produce a difference of 100. The loser is permitted to count in his brisques, if this enables him to cross the rubicon, in which case the winner also takes his brisques into account. If it is apparent at the start of the 'last nine' tricks that one player will be rubiconed, and that neither his capture of any brisques nor his win of the last trick will affect the other's game score, the last nine need not be played out.

Chinese Bézique ⚇

2 players
6 short packs (192)

Six-pack differs slightly from what used to be known as Chinese Bézique. Rules of play are essentially the same as for Rubicon Bézique but with these additional and alternative features.

DEAL Twelve each, in ones. The following feature is optional but fun: after cutting, the dealer lifts a packet of cards from the top of the pack and his opponent estimates (out loud) how many are in it. If the dealer has taken exactly 24 he scores 250 and if non-dealer's estimate is correct the latter scores 150.

CARTE BLANCHE, which some players omit, counts 250, and may be scored and re-scored as described under Rubicon Bézique.

TRUMPS AND BÉZIQUES The suit of the first marriage (or sequence) establishes trumps. If bézique is always defined as ♠Q–♦J then the same suit may be trump in consecutive games. A major variant, however, is that the same suit may not become trump in two consecutive games, in which case the cards constituting bézique consist automatically of (a) the Queen of trumps and (b) a Jack of the opposite colour, such that spades always pair with diamonds, and clubs with hearts. When this rule is followed trumps may be established by the declaration of a bézique – e.g., the declaration of ♥Q–♣J makes hearts trump.

BRISQUES are not counted, even to break ties.

DECLARATIONS and their values are given in Table 5. Note the special score for trump quartets and the inclusion of Tens in this feature. As before, multiple béziques only score the increased premiums if all the constituent cards are visible simultaneously.

TABLE 5:
FOUR-, SIX- AND EIGHT-PACK BÉZIQUE FEATURES

	Four	Six	Eight
Deal to each	9	12	15
Carte blanche	50	250	—
Sequences			
Trump sequence (A–T–K–Q–J)	250	250	250
Non-trump sequence	150	150	150
Royal marriage (trump K–Q)	40	40	40
Common marriage (other K–Q in suit)	20	20	20
Quartets, Quintets			
Any four Aces	100	100	100
Any four Kings	80	80	80
Any four Queens	60	60	60
Any four Jacks	40	40	40
Four trump Aces	—	1000	1000
Four trump Tens	—	900	900
Four trump Kings	—	800	800
Four trump Queens	—	600	600
Four trump Jacks	—	400	400
Five trump Aces	—	—	2000
Five trump Tens	—	—	1800
Five trump Kings	—	—	1600
Five trump Queens	—	—	1200
Five trump Jacks	—	—	800
Béziques			
Single	40	40	40
Double	500	500	500
Treble	1500	1500	1500
Quadruple	4500	4500	4500
Quintuple	—	—	9000
Winning last trick	50	250	250
Rubicon	1000	3000	5000
Add for game	500	1000	1000
Add for rubicon	500	loser's total	loser's total

SCORE After rounding down to the nearest hundred in each case, the winner scores 1000 plus the difference between the two scores. If the loser fails to reach 3000 he is rubiconed, and the winner scores 1000 plus the total of the two scores.

EIGHT-PACK BÉZIQUE Played as above but with the differences noted in Table 5. Carte blanche is not recognized. Note the addition of trump quintets and quintuple bézique. It is permissible to score for a trump quartet , then add a fifth card (after winning a trick) and score also for the quintet.

Bézique Variants

THREE-HAND BÉZIQUE Use $3 \times 32 = 96$ cards. Only the trick-winner may declare. Score 1500 for triple bézique, valid only if all six cards are simultaneously visible. In the last eight tricks each must win the trick if he can and trump or overtrump if unable to follow. Game is 2000 up.

FOUR-HAND BÉZIQUE Use $4 \times 32 = 128$ cards. The game is best played in partnerships. A trick winner may himself declare, or invite his partner to declare, or may declare one or more cards which convert any of his partner's visible cards into a combination of different class or higher value. Score 500 for double and 1500 for triple bézique, but valid only from the hand of one partner. In the last eight, each player must seek to win the trick if he legally can, even if his partner is already winning it. Game is 2000 up. (For four players, a better game of this family is Gaigel.)

CHOUETTE Three or more may play Four- or more-pack Bézique as follows. Highest cut is 'in the box' and plays a two-hand game against second highest, who represents the others as their captain. All may advise the captain on play but he has final decision. If the soloist wins he collects in full from each opponent and plays again, the captain being replaced by someone else. If he loses he pays everyone else in full and joins the others as least in order of precedence to the captaincy. The captain who beat him becomes the new soloist, and the new captaincy is taken over by the next in line to it.

Fildinski ⚁ ⚃

2 (or 4) players
2 short packs (64) (or more)

Fildinski is more usually known as Polish Bézique and will be easily picked up by anyone who already plays two-pack Bézique, as there are so many resemblances. Its fundamental difference from Bézique, however, imparts so distinctive a flavour to the game that its earlier name is retained in order to emphasize its originality. Many Bézique players consider it a finer game.

GENERAL PROCEDURE Play as at two-pack Bézique to the following extent. Deal eight each and turn the top card of stock for trump, against which the first holder of the trump Seven may exchange and score 10, and the second may merely declare and score 10. Play tricks, either following suit, trumping or discarding *ad lib*, and drawing the next card of stock to restore the hand to eight. When the last card of stock has been drawn the last eight tricks are played with strict rules of following (follow suit and head the trick if possible; if unable, trump if possible; only otherwise discard from a plain suit).

DECLARATIONS Declarable combinations and their scores are as at two-pack Bézique (Table 4) but declarations are not made from the hand to the table. Instead, the winner of each trick immediately scores 10 for any brisque it contains, and lays face up on the table before him any card of the trick which is capable of combining. (In effect, this simply means that the Eights and Nines captured in tricks are thrown aside to a common waste pile and all others are kept.) Any one or more combinations formed by the addition of either or both cards taken in the trick may be scored immediately. Cards thus lying in front of a player do not form part of his hand and play no further part in tricks. Furthermore, no such card may be used again in another combination of the same sort.

The first to win a Seven of trumps in a trick scores 10 and may exchange it for the turn-up. The second merely scores 10. The player who draws the exchanged Seven at the end of the stock may not declare it again.

END-GAME The winner of the last trick before the stock is exhausted scores 10 for it. During the play of the last eight tricks declarations may continue to be made and scored in the usual way.

SCORE The winner is the first to reach 2000 points, which may take several deals.

VARIANTS

BÉZIQUE may be defined as ♣Q–♥J when either spades or diamonds are trumps.

THREE PACKS (96 cards) may be used, in which case triple bézique scores 1500 and the game should be played to a higher target such as 2500 or 3000. (It may be found preferable to lower the scores for sequence, double and triple bézique to 150, 300 and 1000 respectively.)

FOUR PLAYERS may undertake Fildinski in partnerships, using four or five 32-card packs. Triple and quadruple bézique are declarable for 1500 and 4500 respectively. Each player may declare only combinations made by himself. It may be agreed, however, that if one player has a bézique before him, and his partner subsequently makes a bézique of his own, the latter may additionally score for double bézique (or triple, etc., as the case may be); but no bézique may consist of one player's Queen and his partner's Jack. In the last eight tricks the partnerships divide – i.e., the winner of the trick before the last eight plays eight tricks against the opponent on his left, his partner simultaneously playing eight tricks against the other. Game is 2000 up with four packs or 3000 with five; in either case a quadruple bézique wins the game. (If both sides exceed the target score the winning partnership is not that which makes the higher total but that which reached the target first, i.e. on the earlier trick. This problem only arises because of the split partnerships on the 'last eight'.)

Four-hand Fildinski will be found to give rise to some splendid opportunities for partnership cooperation as each tries to donate cards needed by his partner for a declaration – provided his partner can be sure of winning the trick bearing the donation.

Sixty-six 〇〇

2 players
1 short pack (*24*)

This popular German game is also played in America. Good two-hand games being rare, its neglect in Britain is surprising. It may be regarded as a cross between Bézique/Pinochle games and those of the Skat family, being rather more like the former even though it does not recognize any Queen–Jack combination. Tradition ascribes the invention of Sixty-six, in 1652, to a particular inn at Paderborn in Westphalia, where even today there is a society devoted to promulgating official rules.

CARDS 24, ranking ATKQJ9 in each suit.

DEAL Higher cut shuffles, offers for cut, and deals six cards each in two batches of three. The thirteenth card is laid face up beside the stock and its suit becomes the trump.

OBJECT To score 66 or more points for capturing counting-cards in tricks, declaring marriages and winning the last trick, as follows:

Taken in tricks		*Other scores*	
each Ace	11	royal marriage (K–Q of trumps)	40
each Ten	10	marriage (K–Q of other suit)	20
each King	4	for winning last trick	10
each Queen	3		
each Jack	2		

(It may be noted that 66 is one more than half the total points available for counters (120) plus 10 for last.)

PLAY So long as any cards are available from the stock, tricks are played as follows: non-dealer leads to the first, and the winner of each leads to the next after drawing the top card of the stock and waiting for his opponent to draw the second. The second player to a trick need not follow suit but may follow, trump or discard *ad lib*, the trick being won by the highest card of the suit led or the highest trump if any are played.

A player holding a marriage may declare it only when it is his turn to lead. He must show both cards and lead one of them to the trick. If dealt a marriage, non-dealer may declare it and lead either card to the first trick, but he may not score it until he has won a trick.

A player holding the Nine of trumps may exchange it for the turn-up at any time provided that he has won at least one trick and that at least one face-down card remains in the stock.

END-GAME Unless the stock is 'closed' (see below) the end-game begins when a trick-winner has taken the last face-down card of stock and his opponent the upturned trump. In the play of the last six tricks it is obligatory to follow suit to the card led. Marriages may still be declared (unless previously agreed otherwise). The winner of the last trick scores 10.

CLOSING Before the stock is finished either player may, if he thinks it to his advantage, announce '(I) close,' and/or indicate closure by turning the upturned trump face down. He may do so before or after drawing. In this event no more cards may be drawn from stock, and the last six (or five) are played exactly as described above except that there is no score for winning the last trick. If the player who closes does not win he is penalized.

CLAIMING If either player announces during play that he has reached a score of 66 the game is 'closed' and no more tricks are played. The claimant is penalized if he has not made 66.

SCORE The first to reach 66 scores 1 game point, or 2 if his opponent has failed to make 33 (*schneider*), or 3 if his opponent has taken no trick (*schwarz*). If neither makes 66, or both have done so by the time one player notices the fact, nothing is scored now but an extra game point goes to the winner of the next deal.

If a player 'closes' and then fails to reach 66 in the deal, or ends the game on a claim of 66 but proves mistaken, his opponent scores 2 game points, or 3 if he has taken no tricks.

The winner is the first to make 7 game points.

VARIANTS

THREE-HAND GAME Each deals in turn and the player who deals sits that hand out, scoring the same number of game points as the winner of it. If the dealer has six game points he may not score the seventh except as an active player. If the result is a carry-over (both making or exceeding 65), the odd game point is credited to the dealer instead of being carried forward and he is permitted to count this as his seventh game point.

FOUR-HAND GAME Use 32 cards ranking ATKQJ987 in each suit and play as partners. Deal eight each (in batches of

3-3-2) and reveal the last card for trump before taking it into hand. Player left of dealer leads. Each player must not only follow suit but also, if possible, play a higher rank than any already played to the trick – even if this means overtaking his partner. A player void of a plain suit led must trump if possible and furthermore play a higher trump than any that may have gone before. Marriages do not count, but cards captured in tricks count at the usual rate (A11, T10, K4, Q3, J2), and 10 for winning the last trick makes 130 available in all. The winning side scores 1 game point, or 2 if it scored 100 or more, or 3 for winning all eight tricks. In the event of a tie (65/65) the game point is held over and credited to the side winning the next deal. (Alternatively, the game may be played with a value of 11 for the Ten of trumps instead of 10, making 131 in all and hence preventing a tie.) The game is won by the side first making 7 game points.

AUCTION SIXTY-SIX for four players enables the trump suit to be established by bidding. Use either 24 cards (Ace high, Nine low) and deal six each (3-3), or 32 cards (Seven low) and deal eight each (3-2-3). Bids are made in multiples of six from 66 upwards, no suit being stated until a bid is established. If the first three pass, dealer must bid at least 66. The successful bidder names trumps and leads. Normal rules apply: follow suit if possible; if not, trump or discard *ad lib*. If the dealer was forced into a bid after three passes, each side scores what it makes. Otherwise the bidding side scores what it makes provided that it has not fallen short of the bid, the other side scoring nothing; or, if it fails to reach the amount bid, the opposing side scores what it makes *plus* the amount of the bid. If the bid was 130 the winning side scores 260. Game is 666 up. (In one variant marriages are scorable at at two-hand Sixty-six, the highest bid becoming 230 – i.e. 130 plus three common marriages at 20 and one in trump at 40.)

Gaigel ⚅⚅

4 players best
2 short packs (48)

This popular German game is usually played in partnerships but can also be played by two to eight players, each for himself.

CARDS, RANK AND VALUE Cards rank in the following order from high to low and have the values shown:

A	T	K	Q	J	9
11	10	4	3	2	–

A double 24-card pack is used, making 48 in all, and of two identical cards played to a trick the first played beats the second.

DEAL Deal five each in batches of three and two, and place the remainder face down to form a stock. Face and lay the top card beside it to determine the trump suit.

OBJECT To be the first side (or player, if non-partnership) to reach 101 points made for (a) counting-cards captured in tricks, and (b) making declarations from cards in hand as follows:

Common marriage	(K–Q in suit)	20
Royal marriage	(K–Q of trumps)	40
Double marriage	(K–Q–K–Q in suit)	40
Double royal marriage	(K–Q–K–Q of trumps)	80
Any five Nines in hand at one time		101

Winning the last trick additionally scores 10.

Each Nine of trumps also scores 10. The first may be exchanged (at any time) for the upturned trump; the other may be shown and scored as soon as it is drawn.

PLAY Player left of dealer leads. Others may follow suit, trump or discard *ad lib*, and the trick is won by the highest card of the suit led or by the highest trump if any are played.

The winner of a trick may declare or pass this privilege to his partner. Only one declaration may be made, and the appropriate cards are laid face up on the table in front of the player making it, remaining there as part of his hand until they are played out to tricks. Two marriages in the same suit may only be scored simultaneously as double marriage; otherwise, if only a single marriage is declared, the second marriage in the same suit is not declarable. After any declaration has been made, each in turn, starting with the winner of the trick, draws the top card of the stock, and the trick winner leads to the next.

END-GAME When all cards have been drawn from stock (the turned trump going to the player on the right of the last trick-winner) the last five tricks are played with 'strict' rules of play, i.e., it is obligatory to follow suit if possible and to play higher if possible; if void of a plain suit led it is obligatory to trump if possible, and to play a higher trump than any so far played.

SCORE Neither side may keep a written score or tally but must count its points mentally. As soon as a player thinks he or his partnership has taken 101 he knocks on the table and the game ends. He is permitted, before knocking, to look back at the last trick but not at any earlier ones to check his calculation.

If everything is in order the side that knocks and wins counts a single game. A double game or *gaigel*, however, is counted in any of these circumstances:

1. For counting 101 + before the opponents have scored
2. By the other side if one side wrongly claims to have made 101
3. By the other side if one side makes 101 + and fails to knock
4. By the other side if one side wrongly claims an error

For example, if one side fails to knock after taking a high-valued trick and a member of the other thinks it has thereby made 101 +, the latter may claim a gaigel for reason (3), which it scores if correct. But if the claim was false, then the accused side wins a gaigel instead, for reason (4).

Auction Pinochle ⚇

3 active players
2 short packs (48)

In its many and varied forms Pinochle is one of America's most popular games, and its failure to attract a following in Britain will ever remain one of life's mysteries. The form selected for major treatment here is technically known as 'Auction Pinochle with Widow', which many rate the finest of all versions of Pinochle. It has the rare merit of being a particularly good game for three players, although, in American practice, it is usually played by four, each taking it in turn to deal and 'sit out'.

CARDS 48, consisting of two 24-card packs shuffled together, no card lower than Nine.

DEAL Deal a batch of three cards to each player and another face down to the table to form the 'widow' (or 'blind'). Deal the remainder around in batches of three until each player has 15.

RANK AND VALUE From high to low, cards rank in the following order for trick-taking purposes, and score the values shown to the players capturing them in tricks:

A	T	K	Q	J	9
11	10	4	3	2	0

If two identical cards are played to a trick the first beats the second.

OBJECT The player making the highest numerical bid announces trumps and plays with the object of scoring the amount he bid against the combined efforts of the other two to defeat him. Points are scored for (a) capturing counting-cards in tricks as shown above, plus 10 for winning the last trick, making 250 the maximum possible under this heading; and (b) holding certain scoring combinations at the start of the game. For this purpose the soloist takes the three cards of the widow and makes melding declarations from all 18 cards he holds, then rejects any three in their place before tricks are played. Any counters contained in the rejects are credited to him at the end of the play.

Declarations and their scores are shown in Table 6.

TABLE 6: PINOCHLE DECLARATIONS AND SCORING FEATURES

Sequences		
Flush	A–T–K–Q–J of trumps	150
Royal marriage	K–Q of trumps	40
Common marriage	K–Q of non-trump suit	20

Quartets		
Hundred Aces	One Ace of each suit	100
Eighty Kings	One King of each suit	80
Sixty Queens	One Queen of each suit	60
Forty Jacks	One Jack of each suit	40

Others		
Pinochle	♠Q–♦J	40
Dix	Nine of trumps	10

Optional*		
Roundhouse	Four marriages, one per suit	240
Double pinochle	♠Q–♦J–♠Q–♦J	80
Grand pinochle	♠K–♠Q–♦J worth, if spades trump	80
	if spades not trump	60

* Double and grand pinochle tend now only to be recognized in two-hand play. Strictly, double pinochle must be melded in one turn to count 80 and is therefore not more profitable, only quicker, than melding singles on two separate turns. If agreed, one may be melded for 40 and another added for a further 80 (120 in all) provided that the first has not yet been broken up. Grand pinochle was originally worth 80 regardless of trump.

BIDDING Player left of dealer opens the bidding at any level and each in turn must pass or make a higher bid. A player who passes may not re-enter. If all three pass the cards are thrown in and the next player deals. All bids must represent multiples of 10. The lowest bid is 300 (in strict circles; but 250 or even 200 are optional variants), and the highest is 650 (unless the roundhouse is recognized, in which case 790).

MELDS The highest bidder becomes the soloist and must make the amount of his bid in order to win. He turns up the three cards of the widow so that all can see them before adding them to his hand. He then scores (and shows, if requested) all the valid melds he can make from his 18 cards. No card may be counted twice in the same combination or in another combination of the same class – e.g., if a flush is scored, the royal marriage it contains may not also be scored.

BURYING After scoring for melds the bidder 'buries' three cards by laying them face down before him. He may not bury a card that he used in a meld; and if he buries any trumps he must announce the fact that he has done so, without specifying which.

CONCEDING At any point up to the play of the first trick the bidder may concede defeat without further play, or his opponents may concede him the game if both agree to do so (as they will, for example, if he makes his bid on melds alone).

PLAY Having announced his trump, if it was not already clear from his melds, the bidder leads to the first trick. Each in turn must follow suit to the card led or, if unable to follow, must trump. If a trump is led each succeeding player must, if possible, play a higher trump than the previous player.

SETTLEMENT Scores may be kept (see below) but settlement is usually made in chips. If the bidder succeeds he receives the appropriate amount from each opponent; if he concedes without play he pays the appropriate amount to each opponent; and if he plays but fails he pays twice the appropriate amount to each opponent. If four play, the dealer is included in the settlement. The 'appropriate amount' varies according to which schedule is being followed and whether the lowest bid is 200, 250 or 300. Here are some examples:

Bid	I	II	III	IV
250+	1	2	1	—
300+	2	3	2	1
350+	3	4	4	3
400+	4	5	6	7
450+	5	6	8	10
500+	6	7	10	13
550+	7	8	12	16
600+	8	9	14	19

If 200 is the minimum bid, count 1 for a bid of 200–240 and follow column II. If 300, follow column IV.

SCORING A simulated score may be kept by recording settlements made on the basis given above. Alternatively, the bidder scores the amount of his bid if he makes it, loses that amount once if he concedes, or twice if he plays and fails, and the game is played up to 1000.

NOTES ON PLAY

In assessing the hand assume as trump the longest suit held but do not be blinded to the prospect of other opportunities that may arise from the contents of the widow. Remember that there are 12 cards in each suit and two of each rank, so a holding of A–T–K–Q–J–9 (without regard to its melding value of 160) is only a run of alternate cards. A top sequence of six would be A–A–T–T–K–K. A short non-trump holding headed by two Tens is weak: two guards are needed to throw to the Aces before the Tens can be led, and there is a strong chance that the second will be trumped if not the first.

The average value of counting cards captured in tricks is

5 each, but it is optimistic to assume a value of 15 for each prospective won trick as the opponents will tend to throw high counters to tricks won by each other and low to those won by bidder. Nevertheless, a not unreasonable assessment of the hand may be made at this rate by virtue of one's advantage in nominating the trump suit and exchanging cards through the widow, which may on average be expected to add about 25 to the playing value of the hand.

As for melds, it is unreasonable to expect the widow to complete a high-scoring combination unless any one of four cards will suffice, as the chances of drawing one of four are slightly better than evens. Experienced players rarely count towards game more in melds than they hold on the initial deal.

A fair assessment of one's maximum bid may therefore be made by assuming as trump a holding of at least five and preferably six cards, counting the actual melding value of the hand but not more (unless one of four or more cards will do it), plus 10 to 15 per prospective trick won, plus an improvement of 20 to 30 by virtue of the exchange.

Having taken the bid and turned the widow consider first whether some other suit may now make a better trump, especially if you have drawn cards producing a *flush* (i.e. sequence). Then take into account the fact that no card declared in a meld may be buried: it may well prove better to forgo 20 for a marriage or even 40 for Jacks in return for the ability to void a suit. Not that a void suit is a great advantage in Pinochle, as the opponents can lead low from it in order to weaken bidder's hand by forcing out his trumps; but the Jack would be a good discard from a holding of, say, A–A–J as it will then be possible to trump the probable lead of a Ten after the Aces have been cashed.

In discarding consider the shape of the playing hand rather than the possibility of stashing counters away. There is no point in discarding non-trump Aces that are virtually certain to win tricks; but Tens from plain suits lacking an Ace make good discards, partly to prevent their being captured by Aces or subsequently trumped when led, and partly because, having no melding value, they are not restricted by the burying prohibition. Short plain suits with uncertain top cards are readily dispensable. The ideal playing hand contains at least six trumps, a long plain suit with which to force out adverse trumps, and one or two unaccompanied Aces in other suits.

Usual procedure in the play is for bidder to cash his on-the-side Aces and then lead his longest plain suit at every opportunity in order to force out adverse trumps. The opponents will naturally swarm on each other's tricks by playing high counters to tricks won by the other. In particular, it is conventional for one opponent to throw the other Ace to a plain-suit Ace led by his partner. It is frequently possible for the opponents to play the bidder's own game by turning the tables and leading plain suits in which he is void in order to weaken his trumps.

Here is a sample hand for assessment:

♠ TKKQJ9
♥ AAQJ
♣ AKQ
♦ AQ

With spades as prospective trump, this hand melds 40 for the royal marriage, 10 for the dix, 20 for the marriage in clubs, and 60 Queens, total 130. As it stands it may be assessed at seven tricks for not more than 105 in counters, plus perhaps 25 for general improvements. A bid of up to 260 is justifiable.

The draw of an Ace of spades (remember there are two available) would increase the value of the melds considerably, adding 150 for the flush and 100 for the Aces. Discounting the royal marriage, which would not then be declarable, the bid made on this hope would reach 370. But the chance of drawing one of two cards is only about 1 in 3, and no sensible player would bid on that hope. On the other hand several cards would make melding improvements of at least 20, such as any red King for a marriage, or either ♦J for pinochle, or the other ♠Q for a second royal marriage. The bid may therefore be increased to 280 and perhaps 300 at the outside.

Let us suppose that the widow turns up ♥K ♥J ♣T, producing:

♠ TKKQJ9
♥ AAKQJJ
♣ ATKQ
♦ AQ

The only meld added is that of a marriage in hearts, but now there are two suits to consider as trumps. With spades trump the meld value is 150 by the addition of the heart marriage. With hearts trump the meld value is exactly the same except that it lacks the dix, making 140. In either case it will be difficult to find legal discards, as so many candidates – such as ♦Q – will have been used in melds.

Hearts make by far the stronger trump as they are headed by the Aces. The lead of the second stands a good chance of drawing one of the Tens, and the long spade suit can be used to draw trumps where necessary. A way of playing this hand that should justify a bid of 280 would be to bury the two black Tens and ♠J (keeping the Nine as a cheap leader) for 22, count 140 for melds, and go against normal practice by leading both Aces of trump. This should drop at least one Ten, and another trump lead will bring out the other, leaving the hand with three winning trumps. If spades are returned two of the outstanding top three will probably fall to the same trick, leaving this hand with both Kings high. The lead of side-suit Aces from this hand would rapidly leave three suits weak for exploitation by the lead of other high cards followed by low ones to force out trumps.

Pinochle Variants

Three-hand Auction Pinochle with Widow as described above is probably the best introduction to numerous versions of Pinochle that have been devised for various numbers of players from two to eight.

Common to all of them (unless otherwise stated) are the following features:

1. Games are played with two or more 24-card packs shuffled together with no card lower than Nine. Of two identical cards played to a trick the first beats the second.

2. Cards rank in the following order for trick-taking purposes and have the stated values when captured in tricks: A–11, T–10, K–4, Q–3, J–2, Nine 0. There is a score of 10 for taking the last trick, giving a total possible value of 250 'for cards' (plus 120 per additional pack if more than two are used).

3. Scores are also made for declaring certain melds from the hand: they are explained and valued in Table 6.

4. A trump suit is established either by upturning the last card dealt (or the top card of the stock) or as nominated by the highest bidder in auction varieties of the game.

5. There may or may not be a widow of three or so undealt cards, which the highest bidder may take into hand, discarding a like number in their place. (For details, see Auction Pinochle as described above.)

6. Strict rules of trick-play apply (unless otherwise stated): if unable to follow to a plain suit lead it is obligatory to trump if possible; and, if trumps are led, each subsequent player must (if possible) play a higher trump than any that have already been played.

7. Simplified card values are employed in many versions, typically A = 10, T = 10, K = 5, Q = 5, J = 0, or A = 10, T = 10, K = 10, others zero.

TWO-HAND PINOCHLE Deal 12 each in threes and fours, lay the rest face down to form a stock, turning up the top card for trump and laying it next to or under (but projecting from) the stock. The play is virtually identical to that of two-hand Bézique, from which the game derives, except that (a) double pinochle, if recognized, counts 80; (b) grand pinochle (♠K ♠Q ♦J, if recognized) counts 60, or 80 if spades are trumps; and (c) the game is played up to 1000 and the player first to reach that total calls 'out' to end the play (losing the game if he is wrong). If both have over 1000, a new target of 1250 is set, and this increases by 250 every time such a tie occurs.

THREE-HAND PINOCHLE This forerunner of Auction Pinochle for Three may well be preferred as it gives everybody a chance to meld. For this reason it is recommended for beginners, to gain basic experience faster.

Deal 16 each in batches of four (no widow), turning the last card for trump. The first player left of dealer holding a dix (Nine of trump) may exchange it for the turned card, the dix then being taken by dealer. This scores 10 (provided that player subsequently wins at least one trick). Players declare their melds and note the scores. Eldest leads and tricks are played in the usual way, each playing for himself and the last trick counting 10. Each player counts towards game the value of his melds plus the value of cards captured in tricks. If a player fails to take a trick, however, he may not score for any of the melds he noted at the start of the deal. Game is 1000 up, increasing by 250 each time two players reach the target score in the same deal.

THREE-HAND PINOCHLE WITH WIDOW Played like Auction Pinochle, the highest bidder making his melds from 18 cards including the widow. Each opponent, however, also scores for melds he makes and separately for counters captured in tricks. The 'partners' keep their tricks separate, and if either takes no tricks he may not score for his melds. The bidder scores the value of his bid if he succeeds, zero if not. Game is 1000 up, bidder's score is counted first, and the others only if he fails to reach the target. If bidder exceeds the target he wins, even if one opponent reaches a higher score on the same deal. If both opponents reach the target but bidder does not, the target is increased by 250 and increases every time the same thing happens.

FOUR-HAND If four wish to play each for himself, as opposed to partnership, the usual game is as three-hand Pinochle without a widow. Each receives 12 cards and the game is played up to 1000. A player taking no tricks, which is a more frequent occurrence than with three, may not score for melds.

PARTNERSHIP PINOCHLE is played by four players in predetermined partnerships. There are several methods of play, to all of which the following optional 'bonus melds' may be applied:

Double flush (2 × A–T–K–Q–J of trumps)	1500
Eight Aces	1000
Eight Kings	800
Eight Queens	600
Eight Jacks	400
Double pinochle (♠Q–♦J–♠Q–♦J)	300

Such scores are rarely made, since not more than 12 cards are dealt to each player and a meld must be made in one player's hand (i.e. may not consist of cards held by both partners).

In the auction game, each receives 12 and bids are made in the usual way, rising in tens and with no suit being stated. The highest bidder nominates trumps, and the bid (and trump) is binding on his partner. Both sides count melds. Highest bidder leads (or player left of dealer, if previously agreed). The bidding side, if successful, scores what it makes; if unsuccessful, it loses the amount of its bid. Game is 1000 up. Should both sides reach it on the same deal, the bidding side wins regardless of the actual total.

The same may be played 'with widow', each receiving 11 cards. Highest bidder takes the widow, melds from 15 cards, then buries four, which count to his side at the end of the game.

In the 'one-bid' version, each player may make only one bid in the auction and must therefore either pass or bid his hand to the limit.

Firehouse Pinochle is an extension of the 'one-bid' game in which each bid from 200 to 300 conveys previously agreed information to one's partner. For example, 200 = barely biddable; 210 = good trump suit but less than 60 in melds; 220 = good trumps, 60 to 120 in melds, but not holding four Aces; and so on. If the first three pass, the dealer must take the game at 200.

Check Pinochle, an extension of Firehouse but not

restricted to 'one bid', introduces a bonus feature comparable to above-line scoring at Bridge. Each partnership has a number of checks (chips or counters) which it pays to the other at agreed rates for certain scoring features in addition to those recorded in the scoring. Certain melds made by either partner are immediately rewarded in checks by the opponents as follows:

roundhouse (four marriages)	5
flush (trump sequence)	4
four Aces	2
double pinochle	2
four Kings, Queens or Jacks	1

But these checks are returned if the partnership then fails to make its bid. If the bidding side wins it collects a number of checks appropriate to the bid made as follows:

200+	2
250+	4
300+	7
350+	10

and thereafter 5 extra for every 50 jump. If the bidding side fails it pays the opponents twice the appropriate amount. Additional checks are paid for yet other feats as follows:

10 for game (1000 up) plus 1 per 100 extra scored over 1000
  5 additional if the losers finish with a minus score
  5 for winning all 12 tricks, or
  4 for taking 250 for cards though not all the tricks

If the bidding side justifies its bid it scores what it makes; if not, it loses the amount of its bid, the value of its melds, *and* the total value of counters won in play.

A player may not bid unless he holds a marriage, but this requirement does not apply to the dealer if the first three players pass, since he is then obliged to make a bid and is permitted to do so at any level.

Numerous bidding conventions have been devised. For example, 250 implies four Aces held, 290 a roundhouse, 300 a flush.

CONTRACT PINOCHLE Deal 12 cards each. The lowest bid is 100 and higher ones must be multiples of 10. Each bid must also mention a prospective trump suit, as at Bridge (e.g. '100 spades – 150 diamonds – 160 hearts', etc.), but all suits are equal and all new bids must be numerically higher. A bid may be doubled by an opponent and redoubled by a defender. The bidding ends when three players have passed.

The opponents do not meld, but the bidding partner lays his melds on the table and scores for them and his partner does likewise. Scores may then be made for melds made between the partners. Thus the bidder may lay out one or more cards which, considered in conjunction with those of his partner, form valid melds; after which, his partner may then lay out more; and so alternately until neither can make any further improvement. At that point the bidder may nominate one card which he needs for another meld – for example, holding ♠Q he may call for ♦J or ♠K to make a pinochle or marriage respectively. If his partner can oblige the meld is made and scored and bidder may call for another desired card. This continues until his partner cannot oblige. It is then the partner's turn to call for a card and, as before, more melds can be made so long as the bidder can supply a nominated card or either partner can add to the cards already melded. As soon as he cannot, the melding is over.

The cards are then taken into hand and, if the bid has not yet been fulfilled by melds alone, the high bidder leads to the first trick. Won cards are counted in the usual way. If the bidding partnership succeeds it scores the amount of its bid; if not, that amount goes to the opposing side. The score may be double or quadruple as a result of doubling or redoubling earlier.

ARMY AND NAVY PINOCHLE for three, four or six players dispenses with the Nines and uses 80 cards (two-pack) or 120 (three-pack). Multiple melds with inflated scores are recognized as follows: four Aces, Kings, Queens or Jacks at 100, 80, 60, 40 as usual; eight Aces, etc., score 10 times those values; twelve score 15 times; sixteen score 20 times (thus, for example, sixteen Jacks count 800). Pinochles count 40 single, 300 double, 600 triple, 3000 quadruple. With 120 cards, 20 Aces count 2500, Kings 2000, Queens 1500, Jacks 1200, quintuple pinochle 4000, sextuple pinochle 5000.

Three play with 25 cards and a five-card widow; four (partnership) with 20; six (three teams of two each) with 20. Trumps may be established by turning, by one-bid or by free auction.

PINOCHLE FOR SIX OR EIGHT PLAYERS These realms of addiction are entered with a $4 \times 24 = 96$-card pack and the following scores:

Flush, single 150, double 1500, triple 3000
Royal marriage 40, double 300, triple 600, quadruple 1200
Common marriage 20, double 300, triple 600, quadruple 1200
Aces, four 100, eight 1000, twelve 2000, sixteen 3000
Kings, four 80, eight 800, twelve 1600, sixteen 2400
Queens, four 60, eight 600, twelve 1200, sixteen 1800
Jacks, four 40, eight 400, twelve 800, sixteen 1200
Pinochle 40, double 300, triple 600, quadruple 1200

Dixes count 10 each. Four, eight, twelve and sixteen of a kind are only valid if represented by an equal number of each suit.

Six receive 16 each and play as three teams of partners. If a trump is turned the first holder of a dix left of the dealer exchanges it for the last card and counts 10 for it; otherwise, trumps are established by one-bid or free auction. The last trick may be set at 20 instead of 10 to give a maximum of 500 for cards (instead of 490). Game is 3000, 4500 or 6000 up.

Eight receive 12 each and play as four teams of partners. Quadruple melds cannot be made.

RELATED GAMES

BINOCLE A form of one-pack Bézique played in Switzerland. The 32 cards rank ATKQJ987 per suit, and have the usual pip-values. Two start with eight cards each and play as at Bézique, the first marriage determining trumps. The ♠Q–♦J combination, *binocle*, counts 40; grand binocle is ♠K–♠Q–♦J for 80. If four play, all cards are dealt and the holders of ♠Q and ♦J are automatically partners. Strict rules of trick-play apply (follow suit and head the trick if possible; otherwise trump/overtrump if possible). Only the winner of a trick may meld.

BINOKEL The still popular German game from which Pinochle derives is played, if by three, as at Auction Pinochle but with some differences. Melds are: *family* (ATKQJ of a suit) 100, *trump family* 150, *double family* 1500, *marriage* 20, *trump marriage* 40, *diss* (trump Seven) 10, *binokel* (♠Q–♦J) 40, *double binokel* 300, four Aces 100 or Kings 80 or Queen 60 or Jacks 40, eight of a kind 1000, *roundhouse* (four marriages, one in each suit) 240. A marriage may not be scored separately if forming part of a family or roundhouse. Bidding starts at 200 or 300 as agreed. Besides taking the widow, highest bidder may call for any card not in his hand. Whoever has it must give it up in exchange for whatever the soloist gives him. Opponents of the soloist may meld as well, but if a player takes no tricks his meld score is cancelled. A player who takes all 15 tricks scores a bonus of 1000; this may be bid beforehand. In some localities a bid of *bettel* (misère) is recognized. Strict rules of trick-play apply. If the soloist makes his bid he scores everything he makes; if not, he loses twice the value of his bid. Game is 1500 up. Four play as partners with 11 cards each and a widow of four. Two play as at two-hand Bézique/Pinochle with 12 cards each.

BRISCAN A two-hand 32-card forerunner of Bézique, lacking a ♠Q–♦J combination but with extensive scores for sequences.

BRUSQUEMBILLE A 32-card forerunner of Briscan, counting Ace 11, Ten 10, etc. but lacking declarations.

CINQ CENTS or 'Five Hundred Bézique' is effectively Bézique played with a single (32-card) pack. Captured cards count Ace 11, Ten 10 etc.; ♠Q–♦J is called *binage*; a trump sequence scores 250, plain sequence 120; royal and common marriages count, but not quartets.

ELFERN An elementary and possibly ancestral German game played by two with 32 cards but without scoring for combinations. The winner is the player capturing the majority of honours – i.e., at least 11 out of A–K–Q–J–T cards only. Method of play as at Bézique.

MARIAGE Forerunner of Sixty-six. Virtually identical but with a score for *amour*, consisting of the Ace and Ten of a suit; 30 plain, 60 in trumps.

MARIAŠ Modern version of Mariage, played in Czecho-slovakia.

MARJOLET An old form of one-pack Bézique from Spain and south-western France, *marjolet* consisting of the Jack of trumps in combination with any Queen for 20, or Queen of trumps for 40. Marriages and quarters count, but not sequences.

PENCHANT A Bézique derivative apparently invented in England in the late nineteenth century.

SCHNAPSEN A still popular Viennese game, virtually identical to Sixty-six but played with a 20-card pack.

ULTI Popular Hungarian three-hander combining elements of Sixty-six with those of Skat and Tarock. *Ulti* itself is a bid to take the last trick with the lowest trump – compare the *mit Spitze* variant of Skat. An interesting feature is that each time a player makes a bid he takes the two undealt *(skat)* cards and rejects any two from his hand, so that they keep changing before the final bidder gets them. (For description, see *Journal of the Playing Card Society*, Vol. IV, No. 4.)

Piquet

I hope . . . that you will have better luck at Piquet than I have with Harry Bennet at Cribbage.

(Charles II, letter included in *Clarendon State Papers*, Vol. 3, 1656)

Like Bézique, Piquet is a two-hand card game of tricks and combinations, but it has so many unusual features as to belong in a class on its own.

Although no longer popular, in the strict sense of the word, Piquet retains a well deserved reputation among card lovers as the greatest and most skilful of two-handers. Certainly it is one of the oldest, one of the earliest references to it occurring in Rabelais's list of games played by Gargantua in his early sixteenth-century epic of that title. Its origins have been ascribed variously to the Spanish and to the Germans, though it was long regarded as the national card game of France and is entirely French in flavour and terminology. In English the name is pronounced, and used to be spelt, 'Picket', but the French pronunciation ('P.K.') is widely preferred, possibly to avoid unpleasant associations. If the game attempted a transatlantic crossing it must have got lost at sea. American writers tend to dismiss it as a museum piece, or else describe an out-of-date version of the game.

Piquet looks complicated at first reading but is perfectly simple in mechanics once the logic is grasped. Versions exist for more than two players but are not recommended. A similar game called Imperial is appended to the main description.

Piquet ⚇

2 players
1 short pack (32)

The version now played is that standardized under the name Rubicon Piquet.

If the loser fails to reach the 'rubicon' of 100 points he is penalized more heavily.

CARDS From high to low, AKQJT987 per suit.

GAME A *partie* is six deals, each dealing alternately, and is won by the player with the higher score. Points are counted throughout play and are traditionally announced verbally as the deal progresses. But use may be made of a mechanical scorer or even a crib board. Only the resultant score of each deal need be recorded.

DEAL Higher cut decides whether or not to deal first. Deal 12 each in batches of two or three – not both, and whichever arrangement you use for your first deal you must stick to for your next two. Lay the remainder face down and slightly spread in the middle of the table. They constitute the *talon*. Note that the dealer is known as *younger*, his opponent *elder* hand.

CARTE BLANCHE If either player has been dealt a hand devoid of courts – a rare occurrence – he may claim 10 for *carte blanche* and must prove his claim by rapidly playing his cards one by one face up to the table. If younger has it he announces the fact immediately but waits until elder has discarded before proving his claim and making his own exchange. If elder has it he announces the fact immediately and tells younger how many he intends to exchange. Younger then exchanges up to as many as he is entitled to, then elder proves his claim and makes his own exchange.

THE EXCHANGE Each player rejects unwanted cards face down from his hand, then draws the same number from the talon – sight unseen – to restore his hand to 12. The purpose of the exchange is to 'improve the hand' by (hopefully) drawing cards that make up scoring combinations and/or are good for playing tricks at no trumps. The scoring combinations are:

point – greatest number of cards in any one suit
sequence – longest run of consecutive cards in one suit
set – three or four cards of the same rank, Ten or higher

Elder exchanges first. He must discard at least one and not more than five. He then draws a like number from the top of the talon downwards, strictly in order. Being entitled to five, he may, if he exchanges fewer, look at any cards he was entitled to but did not take, without showing them to younger.

Younger, in turn, must discard at least one and up to as many as are left – usually three, but more if elder took less than his due. If younger takes fewer than are left, it is his choice whether the untaken cards be faced or left concealed, but it is not permitted for one player to see them and not the other. If younger is to exchange first because elder declared a carte blanche, he draws from the top of the talon, the number he is entitled to being eight less the number that elder said he was going to exchange himself.

After the exchange, the eight cards not held in the players' hands remain unused and out of play, though each is permitted to refresh his memory by referring to his own discards during the play.

DECLARATIONS If either player had a carte blanche he announces his score as 10 before declarations begin. Elder announces, strictly in this order, his best point, his best sequence, and his best set. To each announcement younger replies 'not good' if he can beat it, 'good' if he cannot, or else 'equal'. If his combination is acknowledged 'good', elder scores for it immediately. Furthermore, if his sequence is good he may score for any other sequence(s) he may hold, and if his set is good he may score for any other set(s) he may hold.

The combinations and their scores are:

point   = 1 for each card in the suit
tierce   = 3 for a 3-card sequence
quart*   = 4 for a 4-card sequence
quint   = 15 for a 5-card sequence
sixième   = 16 for a 6-card sequence
septième   = 17 for a 7-card sequence
huitième   = 18 for an 8-card sequence
trio   = 3 for three of AKQJ or T
quatorze   = 14 for four of AKQJ or T

* pronounced *kart*.

In announcing point, elder merely states how many cards he has in his best suit. If younger replies 'equal', elder then declares the combined pip-value of his point suit, counting each Ace 11, each court 10, and others at face value. Elder then scores for his point if younger declares it 'good', and not if 'not good'. If younger can equalize on this basis, neither player will score for point.

If younger has a sequence equal in length to the one announced by elder, the winning sequence is the one with the higher top card. If there is still equality, neither player may score for any sequences.

Having made his announcements and totalled his score so far (if any), elder leads any card face up to the table and adds one point 'for leading'.

Before replying to that card, younger scores for any combinations he may hold which are better than those announced by elder – i.e., in all those classes which he declared to be 'not good'. If he scores for sequence or set he may score for any other sequence or set he may also hold. Having declared and scored any combinations to which he is entitled, younger plays to the first trick.

PIQUE, REPIQUE If either player reaches a score of 30 before his opponent has scored anything he adds a bonus of 60 for *repique*. For this purpose it should be noted that declarations are counted strictly in order: carte blanche, point, sequence, set. Thus if one player scores for carte blanche, the other cannot score repique, even if he makes 30 for point and sequence, as the carte blanche is reckoned first. On the other hand, if there is no carte blanche and one player makes 30 or more on point and sequence alone, the other cannot prevent it by scoring for set, as point and sequence have priority. Finally, equality does not save the repique. Even if both equalized on point, and neither scored for sequence, a player could score repique on two quatorzes and a trio (14 + 14 + 3 = 31, plus 60 for repique 91). Elder's 1 for leading does not save him from repique if he previously made nothing and younger reaches 30 in declarations.

After elder had led his first card, and younger has replied, neither player can score repique. Elder, however, can score 30 for pique if he reaches 30 during the trick play and younger still has yet to score. (It is impossible for younger to score pique because elder counts 1 for leading and cannot therefore enter trick-play with a zero score.) If elder makes 29 in combinations, his 1 for leading may give him pique but not repique.

TRICKS Tricks are played at no trump. Suit must be followed; the trick is won by the higher card of the suit led; and the winner of one trick leads to the next. The winner of a trick scores 1 point if he led to it, or 2 if his opponent led to it.*

THE CARDS, CAPOT If both players take six tricks the cards are said to be divided and neither scores a bonus. If one player takes more than six tricks he counts a bonus of 10 'for the cards'. If one player wins all 12 tricks (a rare occurrence) he scores a bonus of 40 for *capot*. The bonus for cards or capot does not count towards a pique.

SCORE At the end of each deal the players note their scores for that deal and their cumulative score for the partie so far. If the result is a tie at the end of a partie, two more hands are played, each dealing once more. The winner scores the

---

* This comes to the same thing as the usual way of describing it, which is '1 for leading to a trick, 1 for winning a trick, and an extra 1 for winning the last trick'.

difference between the two players' totals, plus 100 for game.
If the loser has failed to reach 100 he is rubiconed (even if
the winner also failed to reach it), and the winner scores 100
for game plus the *sum* of the two totals.

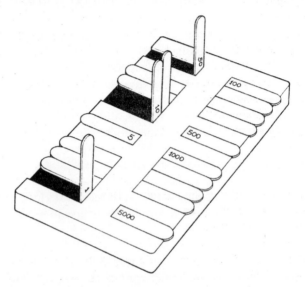

9. PIQUET Markers for recording Piquet or Bézique scores,
common at the turn of the century and still to be found in antique
or junk markets, were made in pairs, one of light and one of dark
wood. Spring-loaded pegs were of ivory-substitute. A workable
substitute can be made by using scissors or artist's scalpel to cut
appropriate strips in the sides of an unwanted playing card.

SINKING AND PROVING Neither player is obliged to declare
a combination or to declare the whole of one. Holding back
part of a combination – e.g., declaring only a trio when you
hold a quatorze – is called *sinking* and is a legitimate
manoeuvre to make when wishing to hide the fact that you
hold a particular card. On the other hand, any combination
declared by either player must be considered known to his
opponent. If, therefore, you have declared a sequence of five
and your opponent asks which suit it is in, or what the
highest card is, you must tell him. But you are not obliged to
reveal anything you have not declared (*sunk*).

VARIANT: POINT/SEQUENCE OF NOUGHT This optional extra, introduced by the present writer, adds another element of interest. After the exchange a player holding a void (no cards in a given suit) may call it a point and/or sequence of nought, and score for it in either capacity if acknowledged good.

A point of nought has an imaginary pip-count of 50½ and is therefore only beaten by a point of five worth 51 or a point of six or more. If good it scores 5.

A sequence of nought beats a quint to the King, or any shorter sequence, but is beaten by a quint major (to the Ace) or any longer sequence. If good it scores 10 and entitles its holder to count any lower sequence he may also hold.

NOTES ON PLAY

Having the lead and the greater exchange, elder is always in the stronger position and should play an attacking game, even to the extent of taking risks provided he is not too far behind in the score. It is advisable to pass the first deal if you win the cut and be elder on the first hand, but not for this reason. As elder on the first hand you will be younger on the sixth. If, at that point, you are in danger of being rubiconed you are in a better position to sink combinations and declare equality to anything your opponent announces, thus preventing either of you from making a score which, in the event of a rubicon, will only go to the winner in any case.

Most of the skill lies in the discard. Elder should nearly always exchange his full entitlement of five cards, even if it means throwing an uncombinable Ace or the guard to a King. The only good reason for taking fewer than five is generally to avoid breaking up a ready-made combination worth 14 or more. Even then, if you hold a quatorze of Tens but are void of any higher rank, it may be worth breaking them up in order to prevent younger from taking an extra card and so finding the fourth Jack, Queen or whatever.

It is usually best to keep your longest or strongest potential point suit and find five discards from amongst the others.

Sequences that lack courts often make good discards. Given a quart to the Ten, for instance, it is three to one against drawing the Jack for the quint. Having picked on a weak suit to discard from it often pays to void the suit altogether. The sure signs of a novice are (a) frequent failure to exchange five cards, and (b) automatic discard of Sevens, Eights and Nines from miscellaneous suits.

Although younger should also keep his most promising point suit, and avoid breaking up high or potentially high combinations, he must be more concerned than elder to ensure coverage in all four suits. It is highly dangerous for younger to unguard Kings or Queens, or to void a suit by throwing a low sequence, as he must retain every opportunity to take a trick somewhere and get his own top cards into play. The fact that elder leads means that he can play his long suits out first and weaken younger's hand by putting him to the discard. It is quite easy for younger to be capoted, despite holding a top quart or quint, if elder is void in that suit and has top cards in all the others. Unlike elder, younger may well exchange less than his full entitlement in order to avoid creating dangerous gaps in his hand. Having done so it is usually to his advantage to leave the untaken cards of the talon unseen.

Here are some practical examples:

	Elder		Younger	
♠	. . Q . T 9 . .		. K 8 7	
♥	A . Q J . . 8 .		. K . . T . . .	
♣	. . Q		A K . J T . 8 7	
♦	A K . . . 9 8 .		. . . . T . . .	

Elder must keep his three Queens, and draw for the fourth, while retaining either of his two four-card suits for point. Since he is playing for a specific card – the ♦Q – he must discard his maximum of five, which necessitates throwing out either ♥A or ♦K. He opts for the latter, making hearts his intended point suit.

Younger has a long point in clubs, but no sequence, and it is not 'good against the cards' as there is every likelihood that elder will be strong in diamonds. His only hope of salvation lies in drawing the fourth King (the fourth Ten would not be good against the cards, as elder may have four Queens to beat it), or either of the two outstanding clubs. A club would give him a quint, which *would* be good, as it is clear from his own holding that elder cannot possibly hold better than a quart in any suit. With three possibilities open to him younger throws ♦T and both low spades. (In other circumstances it would be wiser to keep the Ten as a guard on the possible draw of the King and to throw one or two low clubs in order not to unguard the King of spades.)

Elder draws the fourth Queen, as hoped, together with two cards of his intended point suit. Younger successfully draws ♣9 and is fortunate in also finding ♠A to cover his unguarded King. The hands after the exchange are now:

	Elder	*Younger*
♠	. . Q J	A K. . . . . .
♥	A . Q J . 9 8 7	. K. . T . . .
♣	. . Q	A K. J T 9 8 7
♦	A . Q 7	. . . J . . . .

Elder announces a point of six which younger declares 'not good'. Elder's tierce minor (♥987) is not worth mentioning, so he keeps quiet about it and declares 'quatorze' (of Queens) which younger is bound to acknowledge 'good'. Having no other set to add to that, elder announces his score thus: 'Fourteen, and one for leading, fifteen', playing ♥A to the table.

Younger now declares his goods: 'Point of seven, seven, plus a quint minor fifteen, making twenty-two'. Having no lower sequence to add to the quint, he says no more but plays to the first trick, his card being ♥T.

Elder wins the trick, scoring one and announcing '16', then leads ♦A. Younger plays ♦T. Elder announces '17', leads ♦Q. Younger replies ♣7. Elder announces '18', leads ♦7. Younger plays ♣8. Elder announces '19'. No matter what he leads younger takes the trick and wins the rest. Since this is a foregone conclusion he lays his cards face up and claims 'Eight for nine' (i.e., the next eight tricks, scoring two for the first and the rest one each). Elder concedes, repeating his final score for the deal as 'Nineteen'. Younger's final score is 31, made up of 22 for combinations, nine for tricks, and ten for the cards (i.e. taking the majority of tricks). The result is slightly untypical, as younger rarely wins more than once in three or four deals.

In the play of tricks elder follows the principle of leading his strongest suit (hearts), hoping that younger will not hold both King and Ten, for if the King falls to this trick elder will make six hearts and three diamonds, scoring ten for the cards. But younger has the King guarded, and throws the Ten. This gives elder no option but to make his diamonds while he can, for once he loses the lead he may never regain it. His Ace–Queen are top cards because he himself discarded the King and he knows younger cannot have more than two – the Jack and/or Ten. Younger correctly discards from the bottom end of his point. After the first four tricks younger cannot lose.

Here are a few more sample hands:

♠ . . Q J T . . .
♥ A . Q . T 9 . .
♣ . . Q . T 9 8 .
♦ . . . J . . . .

Elder should keep his spade sequence and heart point, throwing to this end his clubs and diamonds. The trio of Queens is not worth keeping, especially as there are four Kings against.

♠ . K Q . . . . .
♥ A K Q . . . . .
♣ . . Q J . . . .
♦ A . . . T 9 8 7

Elder should not waste high cards in drawing to the low point in diamonds, but should throw the diamonds out and aim for a quatorze of Queens. Younger, however, should discard ♥AK and ♣J. This gives him every opportunity to defend against elder's winning the cards by means of his long suits while preserving his own outside possibilities of a quatorze (Queens) or good quint (diamonds).

♠ A . Q J . 9 . 7
♥ A . Q . . . . .
♣ . . Q . . 9 . 7
♦ . . . J . 9 . .

Elder must choose between retaining his point in spades and going for the fourth Queen. If he keeps the point *and* the Queens he must either throw the ♥A, thus assuring younger of at least 20 for tricks (as against his own 14 for Queens if successful), or discard only four, thus reducing his chances of improving the point or drawing the fourth Queen. He will probably do better to forget the Queen and discard all his clubs and diamonds. Younger, with his hand, would be justified in giving up the point, discarding the three low spades in order to keep himself covered in all suits. (Note: in order to make a good quatorze of Queens he would need to draw the fourth Queen, *and* a King in his three cards, except in the unlikely event of elder's having discarded a King.)

Piquet Variants

AUCTION PIQUET

According to the pseudonymous 'Rubicon', in *Auction Piquet* and elsewhere, this variant originated in Oxford and was developed by prisoners of war in 1914–18.

BIDDING After the deal, but before the exchange, each player in turn beginning with elder may bid 'seven' or more or pass. (If both pass there is a new deal but this happens rarely.) A bid of seven is an undertaking to win at least seven tricks in the play-off – or, if so stated, to *lose* at least seven tricks (i.e., to force one's opponent to take at least the stated number). Since plus and minus bids are equal in value a bid can only be overcalled by raising the number of tricks to be won or lost. A given bid may be doubled by the opponent and redoubled by the maker but the effect of doubling is cancelled if the next player then shifts to a higher number.

EXCHANGE The exchange takes place in the usual way except that neither player is obliged to exchange at least one card if he is satisfied with the hand as dealt.

DECLARATIONS In a minus bid the bidder scores everything good in his opponent's hand so the exchange should be made with this in mind. Point, sequence and set are declared and scored in the usual way except that they may be declared in any order (with a view to making the *repique*). Sinking, of course, is not permitted in minus deals.

PIQUE AND REPIQUE In a plus deal *pique* or *repique* is made upon reaching a count of 29 (instead of 30); in a minus deal it is made at a count of 21.

SCORE FOR TRICKS Score two points for a trick led to by oneself, one point for a trick led to by the opponent (the reverse of normal Piquet). Re-expressed in the manner normally used for tricks at Piquet the rule is: score one for leading to a trick only if you win it and one for winning a trick anyway, but there is no extra point for last.

In addition, the bidder scores 10 points for each trick made above his contract, or 20 if doubled or 40 if redoubled, or loses the same amount for each trick by which he falls short of his contract. For example, if he bid (plus) seven and took ten he would score 30 extra, but if he took only six tricks he would lose 10 to his opponent. Had he bid minus seven, and taken seven, he would be down 20 points as his bid was an undertaking not to take more than five. Doubling and redoubling affect only the score (if any) for overtricks or undertricks.

GAME The rubicon is set at 150 points. In the event of a tie a seventh deal is played, but if this is also tied the partie ends.

PIQUET AU CENT

Or Hundred Up Piquet, or Sant or Saunt as it used to be called, may (if desired) be played much as the standard rubicon game, the essential difference being that the first to reach or exceed 100 points wins a single game, or a double game if his opponent has failed to reach 50. The partie is won by the player who wins three games out of five (a double counting as two games). There are also minor differences of procedure but they are not essential to the play and many are optional in any case.

Elder does not lead until all announcements and scores have been made. The scoring for tricks differs from that of Rubicon Piquet as follows: count 1 point for leading a card higher than Nine, and one point for winning the opponent's lead by playing a card higher than Nine. Count an additional 1 point for winning the last trick, unless also scoring for capot. As in Rubicon Piquet, there is a score of 10 for cards (i.e. winning the majority of tricks) or 40 for capot (winning all twelve).

The winner is the first to reach or exceed a total of 100 points, and his game score is the difference between the two totals. If the loser fails to reach 50 points he is rubiconed, or in the lurch, and his opponent's game value is twice the difference.

MULTI-PLAYER PIQUET

PIQUET CHOUETTE (3) This is not really three-hand Piquet so much as two-hand Piquet played by three players in rotation. Highest cut has choice of deal and plays against the other two in combination (the latter playing *à la chouette*). Lowest cut sits out and participates in his partner's hand by advising him on play and making the same score. If the single player wins the partie he continues to play the other two, who then swap their active and passive roles. When the single player loses a partie his place is taken by the passive opponent and the active opponent becomes the new soloist. The soloist always has choice of deal and, if the game is played for stakes, plays double.

PIQUET NORMAND (3) Three take part in play, all against all. Deal 10 each and lay the last two aside. Dealer (but nobody else) may discard two and take the undealt cards in their place. Eldest announces first: only the player with the best point, sequence or set may score it, and, in the case of sequence or set, may score any lower ones he may also hold. There is a bonus of 90 for repique for reaching 20 in combinations before either opponent has scored, or 60 for pique for reaching 20 in combinations and tricks before either opponent scores. There is a bonus of 10 for taking more tricks than either opponent, and 40 for taking all twelve. If two players take twelve between them, each scores 20 for capot. The winner is the first to reach or exceed 100 points.

PARTNERSHIP PIQUET (4) Deal eight each. Eldest announces his best combinations in all classes, and leads. His left-hand opponent follows, announcing any better combinations that he may have. This establishes which side may score in each category. As the rest of the first trick is played, the partner of the player scoring for sequence or set may announce and score for any sequence or set held by himself. Repique of 90 is scored for making 20 in combinations before the opposing partnership has anything to count, or pique of 60 for reaching 20 in combinations and play before the opponents score.

DUPLICATE PIQUET A and B are partners against Y and Z. With the aid of a fifth person to deal identical hands and talons at both tables, A plays elder against Y's younger at one, while B plays younger against Z's elder at the other.

ROUND PIQUET Three or more may play a series of two-hand games, each playing a hand first as elder against the player on his right, then as younger against the player on his left. When all have played an equal number of times, each pays any with a higher score the difference between their two scores.

Imperial ⚇

2 players
1 short pack (32)

Also known as Piquet Imperial, this unjustly neglected game
has just enough typological and historical features to warrant
inclusion in the same chapter as Piquet. It has, because of its
curious scoring system, been described as a cross between
Piquet and tennis, though the resemblance to Piquet is
somewhat far-fetched. The classical form of the game is
described first.

DEFINITIONS To avoid confusion it is helpful to distinguish,
from the outset, between an imperial with a small 'i' and an
Imperial with a capital. An *imperial* is made when a player
reaches a total of six points, at which stage any odd points
made by his opponent are cancelled and play continues. The
winner is the first to score four (or six) imperials in this way.
An *Imperial* is the name given to one of several scoring
combinations that may be dealt or otherwise arise in play:
some Imperials score a single imperial to their holder or
maker, and others are worth double.

CARDS 32 ranking from high to low KQJAT987 in each suit.

DEAL Twelve each, in twos, threes or fours (not mixed). The
undealt eight are laid face down and remain out of play, but
the topmost is faced to establish the trump suit. If it is an
honour (K,Q,J,A or 7) dealer scores 1 point for it.

IMPERIALS IN HAND If either player has been dealt an
Imperial he declares and scores for it. There are three types
of Imperial:

1. Sequence of KQJA in one suit: scores one imperial, or
two if in the trump suit
2. Set of four Kings, Queens, Jacks, Aces or Sevens: scores
one imperial
3. Carte blanche (a hand devoid of courts): scores two
imperials

IMPERIAL DE RETOURNE Next, elder hand may score for an Imperial if able to make one by counting the trump turn-up as part of his own hand (though he may not actually take the card).

POINT The player holding the most or strongest cards in any one suit now scores one for *point*, which goes to elder in the event of equality. Elder starts by announcing the total pip-value of cards comprising his best suit, counting for this purpose Ace 11, courts 10 each, others face value. Younger replies 'not good' and scores if he can beat it.

TRICKS Elder leads to the first trick, marking one point if he leads an honour (K, Q, J, A or 7 of trumps). Strict rules of trick-taking apply: you must follow suit if possible and win the trick if possible. If unable to follow you must trump if possible. Only otherwise may you play anything else. Score 1 point for leading an honour to a trick and 1 point for capturing an honour in a trick.

IMPERIAL DE RENCONTRE This rare feat is achieved by winning all four high honours (KQJA) of the same suit in two tricks, not necessarily consecutively.

MAJORITY OF TRICKS The player who took a majority of tricks scores 1 point for each trick he has taken above six. If he wins all twelve he scores two imperials for capot instead of one point per overtrick.

SCORING IMPERIALS Whenever a player scores an imperial, or makes an imperial by bringing his point score to six, his opponent cancels any odd points that he may currently have. Play is not interrupted, however, but continues from a point-score of zero for each player. The game ends as soon as one player has made three imperials, and the value of his game depends on the loser's standing at that point as follows:

Nothing at all : quadruple
Odd points, but no imperial : treble
One imperial, 3 − points : double
One imperial, 4 + points : single

ORDER For the purpose of counting imperials and cancelling odd points it is important to observe the order in which scoring features apply, namely:

1. Trump turn-up   5. The point
2. Imperials in hand 6. Honours
3. Carte blanche   7. Tricks over six
4. Other imperials   8. Capot

SCORE-KEEPING WITH COUNTERS It is usual and most convenient for each player to record his score by means of three red and six white counters. For each point scored he transfers one white to his pool. Upon scoring an imperial he takes his six whites back and transfers a red to his pool. When cancelling his odd points he takes back any whites currently lying in his pool.

NOTES ON PLAY

An imperial feature of the game is 'playing to the score' by attempting to delay the making of an inevitable imperial until one's opponent has more odd points to lose upon being set back, as the following example shows.

	Elder	*Younger*
♠	K Q	. . J A . 9 8 .
♥	K . J . . . 8 .	. Q . A T 9 . .
♣	K Q . . T 9 . .	. . J A . . . .
♦	. Q J . . . 8 .	K . . . . 9 . .

Elder has four points to younger's two, the latter having scored for turning a trump honour (♠7). Elder announces a point of 39 in clubs, which is not good as younger has 40 in hearts, giving him the point and bringing his score to three. Elder could now make two and the imperial by leading his top trumps (♠KQ). But then younger would have two to score for his Jack and Ace after taking down his points. Instead, elder forces him by playing ♣K, ♣Q and ♣T; younger is now obliged to trump the latter, bringing his score to four. Elder is bound to win the next or subsequent trick, whereupon he forces younger again by playing ♣9.

Younger trumps for five, but, thereafter, elder can lead his top trumps to complete the imperial and younger will end the deal with no points, having already played his two honours.

It would be disastrous for him to trump the club leads with the Eight and Nine, for then elder would draw Jack and Ace with King and Queen and score an imperial *de rencontre*!

VARIANTS

ACCORDING TO CAVENDISH As proposed by Cavendish in his treatise on the game (1880s), the following differences may be observed:

1. An Imperial *de retourne* is available to both players
2. The Imperial *de rencontre* is discounted.
3. In the event of a carte blanche both may score for Imperials, but there is no contest for point and the hand is not played out
4. Tricks are played as at Whist, it being obligatory to follow suit but optional whether to win, trump or discard where the choice exists.

ACCORDING TO MARABOUT According to the *Guide Marabout* the modern French version of the game embodies the following significant features:

1. Cards rank AKQJT987 in power of trick-taking
2. The sequence Imperial is K–Q–J–T (not Ace)
3. If the trump turn-up is an Ace or King the dealer may exchange it for the Seven of trumps if he has it.

Rummy Games

Almost anyone who knows an ace from an elbow can probably play Rummy in one or more of its many incarnations. Counting such offshoots as Gin and Canasta it has become one of the most popular games of the twentieth century, the modern counterpart of Victorian family favourites like Pope Joan and Snap. Received opinion derives it from the mid-nineteenth century Mexican game of Conquian, known in Texas as Coon Can, though another school of thought swims bravely upstream to trace its source back to Poker.

Rums or Rummies tend to be family and social games rather than forms of intellectual masochism like Bridge, a fact which does not prevent some of them from being as complicated as you like, if you happen to like being complicated. Nobody has pointed out, though I think it worth observing, that Rummy is essentially American, and as much South as North, if not more. This means it has been played over many square miles and by millions of people in that part of the world, and has consequently given rise to numerous variations which, though faithfully recorded in all the English-language textbooks, are probably less relevant and more confusing than need be to the majority of non-American players. For this reason it seems reasonable to concentrate on a few central games and relegate others to the status of 'honourable mentions'.

Whereas most card games are based on the playing of tricks, tricks play no part at all in the family of Rums, which instead are entirely based on the business of collecting *melds*. A meld is a number of cards which 'go together' according to the rules of the particular game. Typically, a meld is either (a) a *group* of three or more cards of the same rank (e.g., 2-2-2 or K-K-K), or (b) a *sequence* of three or more cards of the same suit (e.g., ♠A-2-3 . . . or ♥ . . . J-Q-K-A).

Players achieve a turnover of cards in hand by continually

drawing from a stockpile and discarding to a waste pile. When, by this means, a player's hand contains a valid meld he lays it on the table, thus reducing his hand. A game usually ends as soon as one person has 'gone out' by either melding or discarding the last card in his hand. In some games the main object is to go out first, the winner scoring the total value of unmelded cards (*deadwood*) left in opponents' hands. In others, melds themselves have values and the main object is to make the highest possible score for melds rather than to get out quickly.

The games are dealt with in more or less related groups: first, Rummy and Gin, representing the basic forms of the game in which the sole object is to go out, plus the ancestral game of Conquian (now known as Coon Can) and its gargantuan derivative, Panguingue, which is hardly worth playing with under 240 cards.

Next, Continental and Contract Rummy require particular melds to be made before anyone can go out. These are followed by Michigan/Five Hundred Rum, Arlington/ Oklahoma, then Canasta and all its progeny. These embody a trend to using more and more packs, and the emphasis lies on making melds that score rather than on going out.

The only noteworthy omission is of a cross between Rummy and Poker called Pif Paf, a South American game that was a temporary fad some time before Canasta, and a similar Italian game, Ramino. Some might also classify Calypso as a Rummy game, but see p. 436 instead.

TECHNICAL TERMS

Certain terms and features common to nearly all Rummy games should be known in advance.

DEADWOOD Unmelded cards left in hand at the end of a game, counting against their holder.

DISCARD To play an unwanted card from the hand to the table. Discards are invariably made face up to a discard pile, which in some games is kept squared up so only the top card is visible, in others is spread out so that all are identifiable.

DRAW To take the top card of the (face-down) stockpile and add it to one's hand, or to appropriate any other card which the rules of a particular game may permit.

GO OUT To get rid of one's last card, whether by melding, laying off or discarding it, and so end the hand, or otherwise to end the hand as the rules of the particular game may specify.

GROUP Three or more cards of the same rank (e.g. 2–2–2, K–K–K, etc.).

LAY OFF To play a card from the hand to a meld already made on the table, whether one's own or somebody else's (as the particular game prescribes), provided that it matches the meld, either by being of the same rank if it is a group or by continuing the sequence otherwise.

MELD A meld is a set of three or more cards related by rank or sequence (e.g., 2–2–2 or 2–3–4); to meld is to lay such a set face up on the table. (Confusingly, a card which is 'laid off' to a meld is often said to be 'melded'.)

SEQUENCE Three or more cards of the same suit and forming part of the sequence A–2–3–4–5–6–7–8–9–T–J–Q–K–A. In very few games a sequence may *turn the corner* by including the sequence . . . K–A–2 . . ., i.e., Ace counts high and low simultaneously.

STOCK (PILE) The undealt portion of the pack, which is placed face down on the table. Each player in turn may draw the top card of the stock and add it to his hand.

WILD CARD One which may be used to stand for any desired card. Jokers are frequently introduced as wild cards. For example, ♥ 2–3–Jo–5 would be a valid sequence. Certain ranks are sometimes wild. In Canasta, for example, deuces are wild, so that K–K–2–2–2, is a valid group of Kings.

Although the strategy and tactics of any game are dictated by the particular objectives and mechanics of that game alone, some notes generally applicable to all forms of Rummy may be made here to avoid repetition later.

For example, a major characteristic of Rummy games, unlike most trick-taking games, is that everyone tends to be playing against the pack rather than against the other players. Only in two-hand Gin and partnership games such as Canasta does it become possible – and essential – to keep track of what everyone else is doing and so play as to make use of that knowledge. Even then it is difficult to do anyone else any positive harm: you can usually only hope to do yourself some good, or at most avoid playing to the advantage of an opponent. In games of four or more where everyone is playing for himself, it is hardly worth concentrating on any but one's immediate left- and right-hand opponents – the former to avoid discarding anything he might wish to pick up, the latter to note what he is tending to discard and shape your own melds accordingly. For this reason three is a good number of players for any but an essentially two-sided game like Gin or Canasta.

Observation is the first requirement of a good Rummy player. You start the game with positive knowledge only of what you hold and may form some plan on the basis of that knowledge as to which potential melds to concentrate on. This you may do on the assumption that the cards you need are in the stock. But, as the game progresses, you have the opportunity of observing other cards in opponents' melds, and in what they discard, and from this may learn whether or not to pursue your plan. For example, given ♣5 ♣7 in your initial hand you may think in terms of catching ♣6 to make a sequence, though it is twice as difficult to fill a sequence with a gap in it than one based on two consecutive cards (♣6 ♣7 or ♣5 ♣6 each require either of two cards to fill, but ♣5 ♣7 can be filled with ♣6 only). As soon as you observe an opponent drawing a Six from the discard pile, even though not of clubs, you can drop the whole sequential idea in case he is collecting a group of Sixes and may therefore already hold ♣6. Or again, if you hold ♣6 ♣7 and note that one opponent has taken two Fives from the discard pile and another has taken two Eights, you can drop that idea as well. Observation, therefore, is but the means to an end. The qualities that derive from it are those of fluidity and flexibility. Good Rummy players are continually changing their intentions in the light of changing conditions. It is a game for tacticians rather than strategists.

In one-pack games it is useful to construct a mental picture of a 4 × 13 rectangle representing the 52 cards arranged by suit and rank. Note that sequences and groups interfere with each other, and that the pack tends to polarize into one or the other type of combination. Thus, if you have the choice of building a group or a sequence, and only sequences have so far been melded, you are more likely to make the sequence.

Individual games may extend these basic opportunities for skill and modify some of the principles outlined above. For example, in a game like Rummy, in which penalties for deadwood constitute the sole or major basis for scoring, you will almost certainly give up a high gappy sequence like ♥J ♥K, for fear of incurring their penalty value if the Queen fails to materialize, whereas a low one like ♥2 ♥4 may be safely kept for some time – perhaps even after ♥3 has gone –in order to finish with a low count. Or again, in Canasta, there are positive opportunities for bluffing by discarding cards you really want and feel confident of winning back again.

A final, practical point: Rummy games, more than most, tend to put the pack in order. Really thorough shuffling is essential between deals.

Rummy ◎

2 to 6 players
1 pack (52)

Rummy is deservedly popular because it is easy to learn, fast to play, suitable for all ages, playable by any number (more than six play Double Rummy, see below), and as suitable for gamblers as for missionaries – though perhaps not both at once. As now understood it first appeared about 1910, since when it has given rise to countless variants. By 1950 a survey carried out by the United States Playing Card Company showed it to be the most widely known card game in America and the foremost family game. Almost certainly the name indicates the drink, rum, rather than the then current English use of the word as a synonym for 'odd' or 'queer'. It is said, by the Poker-origin school of thought, to have first appeared in the 1890s as Rum Poker and been named by the same process that gave Whisky Poker and Gin Poker. The origins of Rummy would therefore appear to be lost not so much in the mists of time as in the alcoholic haze of history.

CARDS One standard 52-card pack.

DEAL If two play, ten each; three or four receive seven each; five or six receive six each. Deal cards face down and one at a time. Place the remainder face down to form a stock. Take the top card of stock and place it face up on the table to start the discard pile.

OBJECT To go out by laying down melds of three or more cards at a time. A meld is a group of cards of the same rank, or a sequence in the same suit, for which purpose Ace is low (A–2–3 only). If not the first to go out, a secondary object is to reduce the total face values of cards left in hand (deadwood). In this respect Ace counts one and court cards ten each.

PLAY Each in turn must (a) draw the top card of either the stock or the discard pile and add it to his hand; (b) meld or lay off one or more cards if able and willing to do so; then (c) discard one card face up to the discard pile. A player who has drawn the top discard must discard something different.

MELDING AND LAYING OFF One or more melds and/or lay-offs may be made at the same time. A meld is placed face up on the table in front of the player making it. A card that extends any meld on the table may be laid off against that meld regardless of who made it. For example, an Ace may be played to a meld of A–A–A, or ♥5 ♥9 to a meld of ♥6–7–8.

END OF STOCK It may happen that no one goes out before the stock has been exhausted. If there are no cards in stock for the player in turn to draw from, he may either take the top discard in the normal way, or turn the discard pile upside down to form a new stock, in which case he must continue his turn by drawing the top card of it.

GOING OUT The winner is the player who goes out by playing the last card from his hand, whether by melding, laying off or discarding. The game immediately ends, and each opponent pays the winner an amount equivalent to the combined face values of all the cards left in his hand (or the winner scores an equivalent amount).

GOING RUMMY A player goes rummy by getting rid of his entire hand in one turn, by any combination of melding, laying off and discarding, but without having melded or laid off a single card in the current deal. In this event he receives or scores double against each opponent.

GAME may consist of any agreed number of deals or be played up to a previously agreed target score.

NOTES ON PLAY See general notes, p. 292.

Rummy Variants

Every variant of Rummy, however trivial, has its own name. Some, such as Kaluki, are so distinct as to amount virtually to separate games; others, such as Round-the-Corner and Queen City, merely denote modifications to the basic rules which can be put together in almost any combination the players wish to accept.

BLOCK RUMMY If the stock runs out, the discard pile is not turned but game ends as soon as all players refuse to take the top discard. Scores or settlements are made between individual players on the basis of differences between their respective amounts of deadwood.

BOATHOUSE RUMMY If a player draws the top discard he must also then draw the top card of stock. (Or, in a common variant, must draw either the top card of stock or the next discard. Either way he takes two cards if he draws from the discards first, but only one if he draws from stock.) He may then meld and must discard one card only. Players may thereby increase the number of cards they hold. Melds may be made round the corner (... K–A–2 ... counts as a sequence) and Ace counts 11 against if unmelded. Nobody melds until one player can go rummy by melding his entire hand, at which point the others meld what they can and the winner scores in the usual way (or, in another variant, one per unmatched card regardless of rank). Cards may not be laid off.

CALL RUMMY This feature may be added to any Rummy variant. If a player discards a card that could be laid off against a meld, any opponent may immediately call 'Rummy!', lay the discard off, and replace it with a discard from his own hand. If two call simultaneously, priority goes to whichever of them is next in turn to play.

DISCARD RUMMY Another additional rule. A player may only go out if he can end his turn by making a discard – he may not play his last card by melding or laying it off.

DOUBLE RUMMY An extension of Rummy for more than six players. Use two 52-card packs and two Jokers shuffled together, and deal ten each. Ace counts high or low and is 11 against if caught unmelded. A group consists of any three or more cards of the same rank. Jokers are wild. If a Joker is used in mid-sequence it must remain whatever it is stated to be, but if lying at one end it may be regarded as either. Thus to a meld of ♥5–Jo–7 one may add ♥4 or ♥8 but not ♥6, but to a meld of ♥5–6–Jo one may add either ♥4 or ♥8 *ad lib*. A Joker counts 15 against if caught in hand.

ELIMINATION RUMMY Deuces are wild, and one or two Jokers (optional) may also be introduced as wild cards. Deal seven each. At each turn a player's first action is to meld. If he does he then draws a card but may not discard. If not, he draws and discards but may not meld after drawing. Melds are collected but may not be made in instalments. The game ends when one player goes rummy by melding all seven cards simultaneously *or* melds six cards and is left in hand with a card worth not more than five. Face values apply as in Rummy (Ace = 1), but wild cards count 25 against. Each player records a penalty score amounting to the total face value of his hand (including the winner if he melded six to go out). If the winner melded all seven he subtracts 25 from his current penalty score. When a player reaches 100 he drops out of the game and pays one unit to the pool. The last player left in takes the pool, or it goes to the player with the lowest score if more than one reach 100 on the same turn.

FREEZE-OUT Another name for Elimination Rummy.

JAVA RUMMY Another name for Freeze-out.

KALUKI (KALOOCHIE, KALOOKIE) An extension of Rummy suitable for those who like the idea of Canasta but find it too complicated or dislike partnership games. Use two 52-card packs shuffled together with four Jokers (108 cards in all). Deal 15 each if two, three or four play, 13 each if five, 11 if six. Play as standard Rummy but with the following major differences:

1. A group of three or four cards of the same rank may not contain duplicates, i.e., two of the same suit, two Jokers, or a Joker and a card of the suit it purports to represent. Ace counts high or low in a sequence, but not both.

2. Jokers count 25, Ace 11, pictures 10, others face value.

3. A player may only draw from stock, not from discards, until he has made at least one meld. But a player who has not yet melded may take the top discard if (a) he immediately uses it in a meld and (b) the total face value of his initial meld(s) is at least 50.

4. No player may lay off cards to other melds until he has made at least one meld himself.

5. Whether a player has melded or not he may, during the course of his turn, remove a Joker from a meld and add it to his hand if he can immediately replace it with a card which the Joker may properly be said to have represented.

Going out, going rummy and scoring are as at standard Rummy.

KINGS AND QUEENS Two-pack (104 cards) version of Seven-card Rummy with all Twos wild. A player goes out by melding all seven cards in sequences and/or sets of three or more, or melding six cards provided that the seventh, which counts against, is not higher than a Seven. Play ceases when one player goes out, and if he has a card unmelded then opponents may lay off their own unmeldable cards of the same rank against it to increase his deadwood. The point of the game is that any King forming part of a valid meld reduces a player's penalty score by 5 points, and any Queen similarly by 3 points. Players drop out when they reach 100 penalty points, the last two in sharing the pool between them in proportions of 3:1; or else the game ends when one reaches 100, and the winner is the player with lowest count (which may be negative).

KNOCK RUMMY Basically standard Rummy, with the variation that a player who feels he has less deadwood than anyone else may end the game and have a countdown, instead of waiting to go out. Nothing is melded during play. Any player in turn, having drawn a card, may knock on the table to indicate the end of the hand. He then makes all the melds he can, discards one (if he has any left over), and shows his deadwood. Opponents also make all the melds they can but without laying off cards against others' melds. The player with the lowest count receives the difference between his count and that of each opponent in turn, plus 25 if he went rummy (no deadwood). The player who knocked is obliged to win. If an opponent ties with him, that opponent wins instead; or, if an opponent has the lowest count, he not only wins but also gains a ten-point bonus from the player who knocked. In some circles a player may not knock with more than 15 in deadwood.

ONE-MELD RUMMY A form of Rummy in which a player may only go out by going rummy, i.e. melding all his cards in one go, with or without a discard. The amount he wins from each opponent is the total face value of his melds, regardless of anyone else's deadwood value.

POKER RUMMY Same as Knock Rummy.

QUEEN CITY RUMMY Same as One-meld Rummy.

ROUND-THE-CORNER RUMMY Any form of Rummy in which sequences may turn the corner, i.e., incorporate K–A–2. Ace always counts 11. (Also called High-low Rummy.)

SEVEN-CARD RUMMY Basic Rummy with seven cards dealt to each, regardless of how many play.

TWO-MELD RUMMY Basic Rummy with the restriction that no player may go rummy. Any player able to do so must hold back one meld for his next turn. Melding with the apparent threat of going out on the next turn may therefore be used as a form of bluff.

WILD-CARD RUMMY Deuces are wild as are one or more Jokers (optional). Nobody melds until someone can end the game by going rummy. Wild cards left in hand count 25 against.

Gin Rummy ⚇

2 players (adaptable for more)
1 pack (52)

The realm of card games seems more fraught with origin-myths than almost any subject save folk cosmology. Gin Rummy, for example, is said to have been invented in 1909 by a Philadelphian Whist tutor called Elwood T. Baker, and named 'gin', by analogy with Rum, by his young son, who would appear to have been weaned somewhat intemperately. This is pooh-poohed by the Poker-origin sect who point out that Gin Poker, or Poker Gin, was being played at least a decade earlier, and hardly differed from Gin Rummy. Against this, the Conquian-originists quite legitimately observe that neither Gin Rummy, nor Gin Poker, nor even Poker Gin, is substantially different from the yet earlier Conquian except in the number of cards used.

Baker's contribution may have been to polish up the scoring of a two-hand version of Knock Rummy and promote it amongst his students. He succeeded better than he might have foreseen. Gin rose in popularity until the 1920s, went into a decline (perhaps at the hands of Bridge), then burst forth, like a supernova, in a blaze of brilliance in the early 1940s amongst the stars, starlets and lesser luminaries of Hollywood. Ten years later it was to be eclipsed by Canasta, since when it has settled down to a period of quiescence.

In short, it has become a modern classic.

CARDS Standard 52-card pack.

DEAL Ten each, in ones. Place the rest down to form a stock. Take the top card of stock and lay it face up to start a discard pile. Throughout play the discard pile is kept squared up, and its top card is the upcard.

OBJECT Melds are collected, but are not revealed until one player ends the hand by 'knocking' whenever his deadwood (unmeldable cards) totals ten or less in face value, counting Ace one and pictures ten each. The knocker then wins and scores, unless his opponent ties or undercuts him, in which case the latter wins with a bonus.

MELDS Valid melds are groups and sequences of three or more cards. In sequences, Ace counts low.

PLAY To start, non-dealer must either take the upcard or pass. If he passes, dealer must also either take the upcard or pass. If he passes too, non-dealer begins by drawing from stock. Thereafter, each in turn either draws from stock or takes the upcard, then plays a card to the discard pile. If the upcard is taken the discard must differ. This continues until one player knocks and there is a showdown. If neither has knocked by the time only two cards remain in stock, the game is a draw and the same dealer deals again. The two bottom cards of stock may not be taken.

KNOCKING Either player, upon drawing a card, may end the game by knocking, provided that he can meld enough cards to be left in hand with cards whose total face values do not exceed 10. He signifies this by discarding (usually face down), then laying his hand of cards face up on the table and divided clearly into melds and deadwood. His opponent similarly melds all that he can, lays off any cards that may match the knocker's melds, and reveals his own deadwood. If the knocker went *gin*, his opponent may not lay off any cards against the knocker's melds. (This is not always observed.)

SCORE If the knocker's deadwood is less than his opponent's he scores the difference between the two totals. If he melds all his cards ('goes gin'), having no deadwood, he adds a bonus of 25. If, however, the opponent has an equal or lower count for deadwood, he not only scores the difference himself but also adds a bonus of 25 for *undercut*. By definition, only the knocker can go gin, and he scores the bonus for it even if his opponent manages to reduce his count to zero.

GAME Deals alternate. Each hand score is added to its maker's previous total and a line is drawn beneath it. Game ends when one player reaches or exceeds 100 points. He then adds a bonus of 100 for game. Furthermore, if he won every hand (i.e. his opponent has scored nothing) he doubles the resultant total for *shut-out*. Finally, each player adds a total *line* or *box* bonus, equivalent to 25 points for each hand he won during the course of the game.

SCORING VARIANTS The bonuses have now settled down to 25 each (for gin, undercut and box), and doubling for shut-out. An older system was 10 for undercut, 20 for gin, 20 for box, and a straight 100 for shut-out. Other combinations may be encountered. See also Hollywood Gin.

NOTES ON PLAY

Gin ('Gin Rummy' is basically a contradiction in terms) is about the purest and most concentrated form of Rummy for the application of skill by observation, calculation and flexibility. By observation of his opponent's discards and upcard-draws the expert player soon forms a good picture of the adverse hand and adjusts his play accordingly. It is even possible to make fairly accurate inferences about an adverse hand by noting the *non*-appearance of certain cards both from stock and from discards. Nor need observation be confined to cards alone. Habits of play can reveal as much if not more. In the words of one commentator, 'Every element of your behaviour during the play of the hand is a clue to a clever opponent.'

When drawing from stock add the card to your hand and discard something else: nothing gives more useful information than drawing the stock-card and transferring it straight to the waste heap. Since a good opponent will be watching every transaction between yourself and the discards it is inadvisable to draw a speculative upcard. Positive reasons for taking the upcard include (a) to complete a meld in hand; (b) to exchange an unmatched high card for an unmatched low card with a view to reducing deadwood; and (c) to fool your opponent into thinking (a) or (b) applies when it does not. (Obviously, (c) is useless against a non-observant opponent.)

It is obviously preferable to keep low unmatched cards and throw high ones; on the other hand, since your opponent is doing the same thing, it may be easier to complete high melds than low ones by taking his high discards. If dealt a pair of high cards, or two in sequence, it may therefore be worth hanging on to them for several turns in the hope that your opponent will discard a match. When to give up waiting is a matter of judgement. Many hands end well before half the stock is exhausted.

Players are often tempted to keep interlocking combinations too long for safety – a particularly dangerous practice with high cards. An example would be ♠9 ♥9 ♣8 ♣7. The basic chances of filling either meld (modified, of course, by the actual state of play) are 12 to 1 against, and even then the other two cards will be deadwood.

The bonus for gin should be regarded as just that, not as an objective. It is generally best to knock as soon as you can. In the long run the box bonuses (25 for each hand won) are far more profitable.

Gin Variants

Gin may be (and has been) varied in all sorts of trivial ways, such as by permitting Ace to turn the corner in sequences (and counting 15 if unmelded), by granting a bonus of 50 if the opponent of the player who knocks can lay off all his cards on to the knocker's melds, by the introduction of wild cards, and so on *ad nauseam*. Worthy of specific mention are:

HOLLYWOOD GIN This is a scoring device whereby two players may play three different games simultaneously. Each game is scored separately. The score for the first hand won by a player is entered under his name in the first game; that for his second win is entered in both game one and game two; his third and subsequent wins are entered in all three games, until each game is ended and scored (with appropriate bonuses) upon one player's reaching the required 100 points or whatever other total is agreed.

OKLAHOMA GIN This variant, better known as Cedarhurst Gin to avoid confusion with Oklahoma Rummy, is justly regarded by many as the standard form of Gin. Instead of calling the knocking requirement 10, it is set at whatever is the value of the first upcard – e.g. 9 if a Nine is turned, 2 if a deuce. If it is an Ace, you can only knock by going gin. Optional extra: if the upcard is a spade, all scores for that hand are doubled.

OPEN OR DOUBLING GIN This incorporates the doubling principle of Le Truc (p. 440) or, better known, Backgammon. Before drawing, a player may offer to double. If his opponent accepts, play proceeds as usual but the winner's score for that hand is doubled, or redoubled if already doubled, and so on. If the double is refused, that double does not take effect, but the doubler must knock immediately. There are variations on this theme.

THREE-HAND GIN Highest cut deals, next highest sits at his left. Play as at two-hand Gin, with the following differences.
1. Eldest must take the first upcard or pass; if he passes, next in turn must take it or pass; if he also passes, eldest draws from stock and play begins.
2. At each turn a player may take *either* of the two top cards of the discard pile, unless one of them was taken by the previous player, when he may only take the upcard.
3. The winner scores the difference between his own hand and that of *each* opponent.

4. There is no bonus for undercut; instead, the knocker subtracts 25 from his score.

5. Opponents may only lay off cards against the knocker's original melds – not against each other's, and not against a card already laid off by the other.

6. The bonus for gin is 50.

7. None of the bottom three cards of the stock may be taken. If no one has melded by then it is a draw.

8. Game is 200 up.

There are also versions by which only two players are active at a time, but it seems pointless for three players to play a two-hand game. Even more pointless are forms of partnership Gin for any even number of players whereby all play is two-handed but scores are lumped together in teams.

CAROUSEL Use a full pack plus Joker, doubled if three play (106 cards). Jokers are wild and count 25; melds in the two-pack game may not include duplicated cards. There is no discard. Each in turn draws a card and melds, for which purpose he may steal required cards from opponents' melds provided that no meld is left invalid (e.g. from 9–8–7–6 you may steal 9 or 6 but not 8 or 7). If unable to meld, draw again, and so on if still unable, up to four cards, after which the turn passes. Knock at 10 or under in turn but before drawing. There is no laying off. Lowest deadwood wins; if not the knocker, he pays a bonus of 10 (each). Tied players divide equally. Gin bonus 25. Game set at 150. Winner adds 100 for game. Player with nothing loses double.

TUNK Full pack for two or three; doubled if four or five play, but no meld may contain duplicates, and the maximum meldable group is four of a kind. Deuces are wild, but a group must contain two natural cards. Play as at Gin, but knock ('tunk') with deadwood of 5 or under. Others have one more turn, and may lay off on tunker's melds unless he went gin. Tunker's count is doubled if anyone undercuts him. Players drop out as their penalties reach 100; last left in is the winner.

Coon Can (Conquian) ⚇

2 players
1 short pack (40)

The Mexican game of Conquian, widely held to be ancestral to all Rummy games, received its first complete description at the hands of R. F. Foster in 1898 along with the note that it was also a great favourite in the bordering American States and particularly Texas. It survives practically unchanged under the name Coon Can and remains especially popular among negroes. Word for word, Conquian relates to *¿con quién?*, meaning 'with whom?', which leaves the problem of explaining the meaning of the meaning. (Those who derive Coon Can from Poker and Conquian from Coon Can still have to explain what the latter means.) To add to the confusion Coon Can is also used as an alternative name for 106-card Double Rummy, which is quite different.

CARDS 40, representing the Spanish pack, lacking Eights, Nines and Tens, with cards running in sequence thus: A234567JQK. (Some prefer to remove the court cards instead and play with the ten numerals. Do not play with a complete 52-card pack, as the game is spoilt by the possibility of going out with a single sequence.)

DEAL Ten each in ones. Place the remainder face down to form a stock, with cards slightly spread.

OBJECT To go out by melding eleven cards in matched groups or suit-sequences of three or more each. The eleventh card is necessarily one drawn (technically *plucked*) from stock or table, so a player with only ten cards melded, even though he has none in hand, must continue play until he gets and adds the eleventh. Ace and King are not in sequence with each other; Seven and Jack are.

PLAY Note first that neither player may ever take a card and add it to his hand: any card taken must be melded immediately. Non-dealer starts by plucking the top card of stock and exposing it beside the stock. He may then meld it by placing it on the table before him in conjunction with two or more matching cards from his own hand, at the same time making any other complete melds that may be available from hand. He completes his turn by playing a discard face up in place of the card he plucked. If he cannot meld he must pass.

Thereafter each player in turn will be confronted by a faced card, and has two choices. First, he may (if able) take the card and meld it, along with any other melds he may have, and finally make a discard exactly as described above. Alternatively, he turns the card face down and plucks the next card of stock, laying it face up on the discard pile. In this case he may then meld it and discard, as described above, or else pass the turn to his opponent, who may himself meld it or turn it down and pluck.

Discards once turned down remain unavailable for the rest of the game. If no one goes out when the last card has been plucked and discard made, the game is a draw.

HITTING A player in turn may *hit* a meld of his own by laying a card or card off against it from the hand, for which purpose he may rearrange (*switch*) melded cards. (For example: having melded four Threes, a player holding ♥2 and ♥5 and finding himself able to take ♥4 from the table may take ♥3 from the group and meld ♥2–3–4–5.) No card may be switched, however, if it reduces a group to fewer than three or a sequence to fewer than three consecutive cards.

FORCING A player in turn may hit one of his opponent's melds by laying a card off against it, the card he laid off counting as his discard for that turn. In this case the opponent has no option but to compensate for the extra card by discarding one from the hand face up to the table. He may do nothing else, and the discard ends his turn. There is another way in which an opponent may be forced. If a player in turn is able to take the card available to him and lay it off against one of his melds, but declines to do so and simply passes (as is sometimes necessary for tactical reasons), his opponent may insist that he take it, in which case he must.

GAME Play ceases as soon as one player has melded eleven cards. (If a player has melded ten, having none in hand, he continues until able to hit one of his melds with an available card.) Each deal is a complete game and settled accordingly. If neither has gone out the result is a tie (*tab*, or *tableau*) and each pays an agreed amount into the kitty, which is taken by the next player to win a game. The loser deals to the next game.

NOTES ON PLAY

Coon Can is one of the few Rummy games that enables you to spoil an opponent's hand, by hitting and forcing. In an extreme case you can prevent him from going out at all. Suppose he has melded a nine-card sequence, from ♥A to ♥Q, and is holding a middling rank such as ♠8. His only way of going out is to take another Eight and meld them both together with ♥8 (leaving two valid heart sequences). If you hold ♥K you can hit his long sequence with it, forcing him to discard the ♠8. Now he has a 'ten-card hole' – no possible eleventh card will match it. Similarly, if he passes up ♥K you can force him to take it.

Pan (Panguingue) ◎

6 to 15 players
6 to 12 short packs (40 each)

Pan- (so called for short) guin- (as in be*gin*) gue (as in *geyser*) is a multi-player extension of Conquian, whose mainly west American aficionados are catered for in special gaming establishments. It is hardly worth playing with fewer than six people or packs, eight of each being a good round number. Traditionally, all play proceeds to the right – i.e., anti-clockwise around the table.

CARDS Approximately eight 40-card packs, cards ranking A234567JQK in each. Ace is low, Seven and Jack consecutive as at Coon Can.

DEAL Shuffle thoroughly (in relays) and deal 10 each in two batches of five. Turn the next card to found a discard pile. Place some of the remainder face down beside it to form the *head* of the stock, from which cards are drawn, and the rest (the *foot*) somewhere else to replenish the stock when exhausted.

OBJECT As at Coon Can, to go out by melding 11 cards: 10 from hand and one eventually drawn from stock. Certain melds (called *conditions*) carry bonuses which are paid for as soon as they are made.

MELDS Any meld when made must consist of exactly three cards, but others may be added on subsequent turns. The three must form a sequence in the same suit or a group of the same rank. Sequences may be extended to the maximum of ten cards. A group of three Aces or Kings (*non-comoquers*) may be of any suits, and may subsequently be extended by the addition of any of the same rank regardless of suit. A group of three of any other rank (*comoquers*) must be either all the same suit, and therefore identical cards, or of three different suits. A group of identical cards may only be extended by the addition of more identical cards, but any other group may take additional cards of the same rank regardless of suit.

PLAY Before play, anyone dissatisfied with his hand may drop out, his cards being returned to the bottom of the foot (and a penalty sum, if any is agreed, placed on top of it). Each in turn may meld the discard with two cards from his hand, or lay it off against one of his own melds, and completes his turn by playing a discard to the face-up pile. If he does not take the discard and no one forces him to, he turns the top card of stock, melds it or lays it off if he can, and finishes by discarding, If a player in turn *can* take the discard to lay off

against his meld he *must* do so if any other player insists. In
no circumstance may a player add any card to his hand. If he
cannot meld the card drawn from stock he must discard it.
He may not increase an opponent's meld. He may rearrange
or split cards from his existing melds in order to create new
ones so long as the melds remain legal.

CONDITIONS When a player melds a *condition* he immediately receives a prescribed number of chips from every
player (except any who dropped out). The conditions and
their appropriate payments are listed below. So-called *valle*
cards are Threes, Fives and Sevens; all other ranks are
non-valle.

Three valle cards, different suits	1
Three valle cards, same suit	2 (4 in ♠)
Three non-valle cards, same suit	1 (2 in ♠)
High or low sequence (A–2–3 or J–Q–K)	1 (2 in ♠)

A condition is paid again each time a card is added to it, or if
made or remade by rearrangement (*splitting*).

ENDING When a player melds his tenth card he cannot discard and can only go out by melding a discard or top card of
stock. The winner is paid once again for each of his conditions, plus one chip from each player who dropped ˅ut (and
takes their penalties, if any).

NOTES ON PLAY

As in Coon Can the original hand cannot be improved –
hence the 'dropping out' option. Conditions are profitable;
lose no opportunity to make one. Suppose you have melded
three different Jacks and added a fourth. You hold ♠K, and
turn ♠Q from stock. You can now meld ♠K and ♠Q
together with ♠J split from the Jacks (still leaving a legal
meld of Jacks). This brings you 2 chips per player for the
high spade sequence, and will do so again if and when you
extend it with ♠7, then ♠6 and so on.

Continental Rummy ◎

2–12 players (5–8 best)
2–4 packs (52 each)

This has been described, rather cattily, as 'at one time the most popular form of Rummy in women's afternoon games, until in 1950 it lost out to Canasta', and may be regarded as forming a transition from basic Rummy to Contract Rummy. It has the particular merit of being suitable for a large group of players.

CARDS If not more than six play, use two 52-card packs well shuffled together, each containing one or two Jokers to taste. Use three such packs if up to nine play, or four if up to 12 take active part.

DEAL Deal 15 each in batches of three. Deal the next card face up to found a discard pile, and place the remainder face down beside it to form a stock.

OBJECT To go out by melding all 15 cards in sequences of the same suit (groups of the same rank do not count), and only in one of the following patterns: 3-3-3-3-3, 3-4-4-4, or 3-3-4-5.

RANK Ace counts high or low but not both, i.e., sequences may not turn the corner. All Jokers and deuces are wild; each may be used to represent any card its owner pleases, regardless of suit. Because deuces are wild a low sequence may run A-3-4 . . .

PLAY As at basic Rummy, each in turn draws from stock or discards and rejects one card face up to the discard pile, which must be kept squared up. Melds are not revealed until one player goes out by drawing a card, melding all 15 in one of the required patterns and making a final discard.

SCORING The cards melded by the winner determine how much he receives from each opponent, namely:

1 for winning
1 for each deuce melded
2 for each Joker melded
7 for going out on first turn (after one draw)
10 for going out without having drawn
10 for using no wild cards in melds
15 if all non-wild cards are of the same suit

If appropriate, two or more such bonuses may be collected simultaneously.
Note: other rules as for basic Rummy.

Contract Rummy ◎
3–8 players (5+ best)
2–3 packs (52 each)

This heading refers not so much to a single game as to an inbred family of games based on a single idea – namely, that a game consists of seven deals, each imposing a specific pattern of melds (the contract) to enable a player to go out. The original form appears to have been invented during the 1930s under the name Zioncheck. Other names, each denoting a more or less trivial variant, include Hollywood Rummy, Joker R, King R, Liverpool R, Progressive R, Seven-deal R and Shanghai R. It seems to be the prerogative of each compiler to describe the version that most appeals to his own taste.

CARDS If three or four play, use two packs shuffled together with two or four Jokers; if more, three, with up to six Jokers. Jokers are wild. So may deuces be, if agreed beforehand.

DEAL A game consists of seven deals, the first four of ten cards each, the last three of twelve. Deal the next card face up to found the discard pile, and place the rest face down beside it to form a stock.

OBJECT In each deal the object is to be the first to go out by melding and laying off all one's cards. But a player may not lay any melds face up on the table until he can exactly match the contract required for that deal, which varies as follows (g3 = group of three cards of the same rank, s4 = sequence of four cards in the same suit):

1st deal:	g3	g3	(melding 6 of 10 cards)
2nd deal:	g3	s4	(7 of 10)
3rd deal:	s4	s4	(8 of 10)
4th deal:	g3	g3	g3	(9 of 10)
5th deal:	g3	g3	s4	(10 of 12)
6th deal:	g3	s4	s4	(11 of 12)
7th deal:	s4	s4	s4	(all 12)

Ace counts low or high in a sequence, but not both at once. Where two sequences are required they may be of the same suit but must not be consecutive (e.g., ♠2–3–4–5 ♠6–7–8–9 are not valid). Having melded, a player goes out by subsequently laying off any cards remaining in hand.

PLAY The method of play differs somewhat from basic Rummy. The player in turn may take the upcard, meld or lay off if he can and will, then make a different discard to end his turn. If he does not want the upcard he announces that fact, whereupon each player in turn round the table from his left may himself take the upcard and must also take the top card of the stock with it, thus increasing his hand by two cards. Only one player may take the upcard, and may not discard since he is not properly in turn. When the upcard has been taken, or refused by all, the player in turn completes his turn by drawing the top card of stock, melding or laying off, if able and willing, and making a single discard.

LAYING OFF No player may lay cards off until he has made his contractual meld, nor may he do so in the same turn as melding. Thereafter he may lay off one or more cards against his own or other players' melds as and when he can, but may not himself open new melds.

EXCHANGING If a player who is entitled to lay off holds a card which is currently being represented by a Joker in any meld on the table, he may, during his turn, exchange it for the Joker and immediately lay the Joker off against another meld. In some circles this is not permitted if the Joker forms part of a group.

GOING OUT The hand ends as soon as one player plays the last card from his hand by laying it off or discarding. If nobody goes out before the stock is exhausted, the discards are shuffled and placed face down to form a new stock.

SCORE When a player goes out, all play ends and each opponent scores (against himself) the total face value of cards remaining in his hand, counting Aces and wild cards 15 each, pictures 10. At the end of the seventh deal the player with the lowest total wins.

VARIANTS

All sorts of variants and bonuses can be and have been introduced. Originally, all contract melds were required to consist of exactly three cards, sequences as well as groups. Frequently, players are permitted to make additional melds besides laying cards off after they have fulfilled the contract.

Michigan Rum ⚬⚭ ◎

2–6 players
1 pack (52)

This series of games, which some regard as the best of the rummies for skill and simplicity, represent a transition from basic Rummy to Canasta by (a) permitting players to draw any number of discards, or even the whole pile, and (b) giving credit in the score for the value of cards melded besides the usual penalties for deadwood. Michigan and its variant Polish Rummy are the simplest and ancestral forms.

Five Hundred Rummy is particularly good for three players, and its extension, Persian Rummy, is a good partnership game. Michigan appears first, being the simplest form.

CARDS Standard 52-card pack.

DEAL Ten each if two play, seven if three or four, six if five or six. Face the next card to found a discard pile and lay the remainder face down beside it to form a stock.

OBJECT To meld as many cards as possible, preferably high-scoring ones, and either to go out first or to be left with as low deadwood value as possible. Valid melds are groups and sequences. Ace ranks high or low, not both at once. Pictures count 10 each (plus if melded, minus if deadwood), others face value. Ace counts 1 if melded in a low sequence (A–2–3 . . .) but 15 otherwise.

PLAY Each in turn may draw the top card of the stock, then makes any melds that he can and will, and rejects a card face up to the discard pile. This pile is kept spread so that all cards in it are identifiable. A player need not draw the stock card but may instead draw *any* card from the waste pile provided that (a) he immediately melds or lays off the card he draws, and (b) he also takes all the other discards lying above it, adding them to his hand or melding or laying them off as the case may be. Cards may be laid off against one's own or opponents' melds. Having taken discards and melded, the player completes his turn by making any discard in the usual way. Whenever a player melds or lays cards off, their scores are credited to him and kept in a running total.

GOING OUT All play ceases as soon as one player plays his last card, whether by melding, laying off or discarding, or as soon as the last card of stock has been drawn if no one has gone out. (Variant: If the stock runs out, which rarely happens, it may be preferred to turn the discards face down in a pile to form a new stock and let play continue.)

SCORE Each player keeps whatever score he has made for melds, and calculates his total value of deadwood, which is added to the score of the winner. The game continues until one or more players have amassed 500 or more points, the highest being the winner.

VARIANT In a variant called Polish Rummy a player in turn may take the whole of the discards pile whether he can use the bottom card or not (but he may not take part of it except under the conditions prescribed above).

FIVE HUNDRED RUM (PINOCHLE RUM)

In essence, this differs from Michigan Rum only in the scoring. No running score is kept. Whenever a player lays a card off against another's meld, he merely announces that fact but plays the card face up before himself, so that it will count in his favour at the end of play. (It therefore becomes important to keep careful track of extended melds, so as not to miss any opportunity to lay off.) When a player goes out, play ends immediately. Each player scores the total value of cards he has melded less the total value of cards left in hand, resulting in a plus or minus score as the case may be. Scores are kept cumulatively in successive deals, and the winner is the first to reach 500 or exceed it by the highest amount.

PERSIAN RUMMY (500 JOKER RUM)

This extension of Five Hundred Rum is a good partnership game.

CARDS 56, consisting of a 52-card pack and four Jokers, which should be of the same back design and colour as the other cards.

DEAL Deal seven each, turn the next face up to found the discard pile, and place the remainder face down beside it as a stock.

OBJECT To meld and lay off cards in groups and sequences until one player goes out, at which point scores are made as at 500 Rum, the partnership score for each side being that of its two partners combined. Ace ranks high only and always counts 15. Jokers are not wild but may be melded as a group of three or four, counting 20 each (for or against).

SCORE A group of four, if melded intact, scores double its face value. This does not apply if it is merely made by adding the fourth to a meld of three. If a player goes rummy (melds all his cards without having previously melded or laid off) his side scores a bonus of 25. Game is two deals, and the winning side adds a bonus of 50 before settlement is made on the basis of the difference in scores.

Arlington (Oklahoma) ⚇ ◎

2–5 players (good for three)
2 packs (104)

Arlington, a name preferable to Oklahoma to avoid confusion with Oklahoma Gin, continues the trend towards greater elaboration in the scoring for melds. As such it may be described as more complicated than the Michigan rummies but less interesting than Canasta; or, less complicated than Canasta but more interesting than Michigan.

CARDS Two packs shuffled together, with or without a Joker (104 or 105).

DEAL Thirteen each. Deal the next card face up to found the discard pile, and place the remainder face down to form a stock.

OBJECT To score as much as possible for melds, and then go out, or be left with as little deadwood as possible if somebody else goes out.

MELDS Group of three or four cards (but not more) make valid melds, as do sequences of three or more in the same suit, for which purpose Ace may rank high or low, but not both at once, though two Aces may be used to make a sequence of 14 cards. The Joker and all deuces are wild, and the Joker (but not a deuce), when melded, may be reclaimed by any player who has the natural card it represents in exchange for it. The owner of a meld containing ambiguous wild cards must indicate what ranks they are intended to represent, either verbally or by arrangement (e.g., 6–7–X must be read as 6–7–8), as this determines what cards may be laid off against it.

SPADE QUEENS Special value attaches to both Queens of spades. They are melded in groups or sequences in the normal way, but it is a rule of the game that a player may not discard ♠Q unless he has no other card to throw.

PLAY To start, each in turn may take the upcard and then discard or pass. When somebody has taken it, or all have refused, the next in turn begins play proper. At each turn a player may draw from stock, meld and lay off *ad lib*, and must then discard one card face up to the discard pile, which is kept squared up. Instead of drawing from stock, however, he may take the upcard provided that (a) he immediately melds with it or lays it off, and (b) he takes the *whole* of the discard pile into hand, finishing his turn by making any more possible melds and lay-offs, and returning any discard to restart the pile. Each player may lay off cards only against melds of his own, not against anyone else's.

GOING OUT Play ceases as soon as one player goes out by playing his last card, whether by melding, laying off or discarding. There is a bonus for going out *concealed*, i.e., melding one's whole hand in one turn, having made no previous melds, and with or without a final discard. But this does not apply if the player is able to do so on his first turn.

SCORING Each player scores the difference between the total value of cards he has melded and that of cards remaining in his hand, and the player who went out also gains a bonus.

	plus value if melded	minus value if in hand
Joker	100	200
♠ Queen	50	100
Ace	20	20
High card (8–K)	10	10
Low card (3–7)	5	5
Deuce (melded, scores value of card represented)		20
Bonus for going out	100	
Bonus for going out concealed	250	

(This bonus is not added to the player's running total but is held in abeyance until the end of the game.)

GAME The turn to deal passes to the left. Play continues until one or more players reach or exceed 1000, the winner being the player with the highest score. He adds 200 for game before settlement is made on the basis of differences. If two tie for most, they split the 200 bonus.

NOTES ON PLAY

Unless your hand is a dead certainty for going out in a few turns do not start by thinking in terms of the going out bonuses. Instead, concentrate on increasing your hand, and therefore your melding possibilities, by refraining from too long or too early melds and taking the discard pile as soon as you can make use of it.

Meld groups of three rather than four, as four cannot be extended but three can conveniently take a fourth card for the purposes of going out. Since neither ♠Q can be discarded it is usually advisable to keep hold of other Queens and high spades so that she may be melded if drawn.

Pairs are easier to turn into melds than two-card sequences.

Canasta ⚭

4 players
2 packs (104 +)

Legend has it that Canasta was 'invented by the ladies of
Montevideo as a counter-attraction to Poker, which, in their
opinion, took up far too much of their menfolk's time'* –
which, if true, says little for the feminine attractions of
Montevideo. From Uruguay it 'developed in Argentina,
reached the US in 1949, and from 1950 to 1952 was the
biggest fad in the history of card games'.† Its popularity
with the royal family ensured equal success in Britain. By
the time it pervaded the rest of Europe practically every
other South American state had got in on the act by develop-
ing more and more elaborate variations under such names as
Chile, Bolivia, Mexicana, and all stations north of Tierra del
Fuego.

Technically, Canasta is an extension of Rummy, via the
Michigan group and Arlington, in which all the emphasis lies
on scoring for melds and comparatively little on 'going out'.
Though more or less playable by any number, it is unique
amongst Rummy games in being essentially designed for
four-hand partnership play, for which reason (plus the
attraction of inflatable scoring values) it has long been
popular with Bridge players.

The name of the game is the Spanish word for 'basket'.
Various explanations have been proposed to account for its
precise significance.

CARDS 108, consisting of two preferably identical packs
shuffled together with four Jokers.

DEAL Eleven each in ones. Turn the next face up to found
the discard pile, and place the remainder face down beside it
to form the stock. Throughout play the discards are kept face
up in a squared up pile, which is known as the *pack* (or, in

---

* Ostrow, *The Complete Card Player*.
† Morehead & Mott-Smith, *Hoyle's Rules of Games*.

America, the *pot*). The top card of the pack is called the upcard. If the upcard is wild or a red Three it must be covered by the next card of the stock, and so on until the upcard is natural. If anyone is dealt a red Three he must lay it face up before him and draw a replacement.

OBJECT Players sitting opposite each other are partners. Each side's object is to score as much as possible for making melds and laying cards off against them, the two partners' melds being kept together on the table. Play continues until one player, with his partner's permission, goes out by playing his last card. Each side then scores positively for cards it has melded (the most valuable melds being *canastas*) and negatively for cards left in hand. There is a bonus for going out, but this does not constitute the main objective of the game.

VALUE OF CARDS All four Jokers and eight deuces are wild, standing for any desired 'natural' card. Threes have special uses and are not melded except in a sense to be explained later. The values of cards (plus or minus as the case may be) are:

Joker	= 100 each	7654	= 5 each
Deuce	= 20 each	Black Three =	5 each
Ace	= 20 each	Red Three = 100 each	
KQJT98 =	10 each	doubled if all four drawn	

MELDS A meld is a group of cards of the same rank (sequences do not count) and is made by taking the matched cards from the hand and laying them face up on the table. It must contain at least three cards, of which at least two must be natural and not more than three may be wild. Melds may be increased by the addition of one or more cards at a time, either of the same rank, or wild to a limit of three. One side may not make more than one meld of the same rank. A meld of seven cards, whether made at once or gradually built up, is called a *canasta*.

CANASTAS A canasta carries a bonus value of 500 if it consists entirely of natural cards, or 300 if mixed, i.e.,

containing one or more wild cards. When a canasta is made
it is squared up into a pile, with a red card on top if it is
natural or a black card if mixed. Squared up canastas may
be extended by the addition of any number of wild or matching cards, but if a wild card is added to a natural canasta its
bonus value is reduced, and the top card must be changed
from red to black to indicate that fact. Canastas are important not only for their bonus values, for neither side is permitted to go out without melding at least one canasta.

PLAY Each player in turn normally draws the top card of
stock and adds it to his hand; he may then make as many
melds as he legally can and wishes, and/or lays off cards
against melds already made by his side, and completes his
turn by playing a card face up to the pack. In certain circumstances he need not draw from stock but may instead
draw the upcard, provided that he immediately melds it and
also takes the rest of the pack. The whole procedure is
modified by special rules relating to (a) minimum initial
meld requirement, (b) taking the pack, and (c) use of red and
black Threes.

INITIAL MELD REQUIREMENT The first meld or melds made
by a side, regardless of which partner melds, must meet a
minimum face value requirement. The required value varies
throughout the game depending on how many points that
side has so far accumulated – as follows:

side has so far scored	minimum initial meld requirement
negative	no restriction
less than 1500	50
1500–2995	90
3000 or more	120

TAKING THE PACK According to circumstance the pack
may be *frozen* or *unfrozen*. When it is unfrozen the player in
turn may, instead of drawing from stock, take the upcard
and either lay it off against one of his side's existing melds or

canastas, or meld it in conjunction with two or more cards from his hand (but not with two unaccompanied wild cards). Having done so he must then take up the rest of the pack, may make as many more melds and/or lay-offs as he wishes, and ends his turn by discarding one to start a new pack.

FREEZING THE PACK When the pack is frozen the player in turn may only take it if he can make a new meld by taking the upcard and adding to it at least a natural pair from his own hand. Furthermore, the resultant meld must meet the appropriate initial meld requirement if his side has not already made a meld. He then takes the rest of the pack, melds and/or lays off, and finally makes one discard. The pack is frozen in the following circumstances:

1. To either side if that side has not yet made a meld.

2. To both sides if it contains a wild card. Whenever a player discards a deuce or a Joker to the pack he should place it at the bottom of the pack, and projecting sideways from it, so as to mark the pack as frozen.

3. To one player only if, on his turn to play, the upcard is a black Three. Technically, the pack is then described as *stopped* rather than frozen, as there is no way at all in which he can take the upcard. He must then draw from stock, and his discard automatically unstops the pack to his left opponent (unless he also discards a black Three).

BLACK THREES Black Threes may not be melded during the course of play. As described above, the main use of a black Three is to 'stop' the pack to one's left-hand opponent for one turn only. A player cannot go out if he holds two black Threes, but if he holds one he can go out by melding all his other cards and discarding the black Three last; and if he holds three or four he can meld them together as part of the process of going out. Wild cards may not be included in a meld of black Threes.

RED THREES These odd cards contribute to the score but not to the play. Whenever a player draws a red Three from the stock he must immediately lay it face up on the table and draw the next card to replace it. (If the initial upcard was a red Three, whoever takes it along with the pack also lays it face up on the table.) Red Threes may not be kept in hand or discarded. At the end of the game each side scores for its red Threes, unless the side has failed to meld, in which case it is penalized for them. If the last card of the stock is a red Three it may not be drawn, and the game ends immediately.

END OF STOCK If no one has gone out when the last card has been drawn from stock, play proceeds as follows. Each in turn *must* take the previous player's discard if he can legally add it to a meld, or *may* take the discard if he can legally use it to form a new meld. However, a player with only one card in hand may not take a pack consisting of a single card. Play ceases as soon as one player in his turn has failed to take the upcard, whether because he cannot lay it off or because he cannot (or will not) meld it.

GOING OUT A player goes out by voiding his hand of cards with or without discarding to the pack. No player is permitted to go out unless his side has at least one canasta, though it is permitted to make an initial canasta in the process of going out. It is proper (but not obligatory) for a player who is in turn and able to go out to ask his partner's permission to do so. If he does ask he is bound by his partner's reply and penalized for disregarding it.

GOING OUT CONCEALED A player goes out concealed, or blind, if he melds his entire hand of cards without having previously melded or laid cards off to his partner's melds. In doing so he must meld a canasta himself and may not add cards to any of his partner's melds; but he is not bound to meet the minimum initial meld requirement, and he may discard one to the pack but is not obliged to do so.

SCORING The amount to be scored by each side consists of (a) premiums, plus (b) total face values of cards melded, *minus* (c) total face values of cards left unmelded. Face values have already been given. Premiums are credited for:

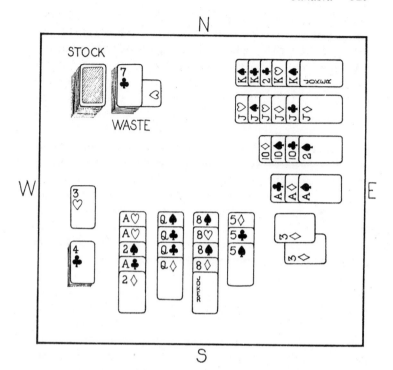

10. CANASTA IN PROGRESS South is looking after his side's melds and East after his. North–South have a canasta of Fours, mixed (as indicated by the black Four on top), and will be wanting to go out, as East–West have yet to complete their first canasta but are threatening to make a 'natural' canasta of Jacks. The pack is frozen, as indicated by the red deuce projecting from beneath it. As bonuses, North–South have one red Three and East–West two. For exercise, calculate the scores accruing to each side so far as can be seen on the table.

Going out (unconcealed)	100
Going out concealed	200
Each natural canasta	500
Each mixed canasta	300
Each red Three	100
or if all four held	200 each

If one side has made no meld at all, the value of any red Threes it may have taken is subtracted.

GAME The turn to deal passes to the left. Play continues until either side has reached or exceeded 5000, and settlement is made on the basis of the difference between both totals.

IRREGULARITIES

A game of such ritual as Canasta is particularly prone to procedural errors and unusually sensitive to their effects. No description would therefore be complete without a note of penalties. Some players prefer to apply the procedural rectifications without the point-penalties, but point-penalties are probably more effective than anything in correcting sloppy habits.

DRAW OUT OF TURN 100, and put it back. Or, if the card is added to the hand, 200, and leave it there.

TOO MANY DRAWN 50, and on subsequent turns discard without drawing until the hand is correct.

TAKING THE PACK 200 for (a) illegally taking the discard pile or (b) taking the upcard into hand instead of properly using it on the table and in constant view.

EXPOSED CARD If a player exposes a card of his hand which is not properly meldable he must leave it face up on the table and on each subsequent turn either meld it or discard it.

ILLEGALLY MELDING 100 for melding in an opponent's turn, 200 in one's partner's turn. For adding to a meld more wild cards than it may legally include, transfer excess wild cards to other melds if legally able; if not, treat them as exposed cards.

INSUFFICIENT MELD COUNT If a player's initial meld fails to reach the appropriate value requirement he may continue melding or adding cards until it does. If unable or unwilling to do so he retracts all exposed cards and his side's initial meld requirement is increased by 10 points.

FAILURE TO DECLARE A RED THREE 500 points for being caught with a red Three in hand at the end of play.

IRREGULAR GOING OUT A player may be forced to go out by his opponents if he asks his partner's permission to do so, is told 'yes' but fails to do so; or if he exposes any of his cards before his partner has replied; or if he (or his partner) gives any indication of cards held, by word, deed or implication, in requesting permission or answering it.

INABILITY TO GO OUT If a player starts to go out and finds he cannot properly do so he must meld what he can, leave other cards on the table and treat the latter as 'exposed cards' (above).

IMMUNITY A player who may have committed an irregularity is immune from penalty as soon as his left-hand opponent draws a card for his turn, and the irregularity stands.

NOTES ON PLAY

The main object of Canasta is not to go out, which is often a defensive manoeuvre, but to score as much as possible for melds, and particularly for canastas. The side that first melds a canasta is in a *position* to go out, a threat which becomes more effective as it continues to increase its score. The other side must equalize as soon as possible, or, if hard pressed, aim to go out as a form of resignation to keep the adverse score low.

In order to make melds it is important to take a large pack as early as possible, and – both before and immediately after that point – to refrain from laying off or melding too many cards. It is the player with the greatest number of ranks in hand, especially pairs, who stands the best chance of taking the pack.

To make an initial qualifying meld is vital and must be striven for, but not at the expense of crippling the hand by over-reducing it. Meld economically, using no more cards than legally necessary, and preferably by taking the pack rather than playing entirely from hand. This gets harder as your initial requirement increases, but it is still best to use no more than four cards from hand to make 90, or six to make 120 if at all possible.

Having melded, make as many more as possible and add to them as much as possible so long as this can be done without drastic reduction of the hand. Points for melds are like profits from investments: you must constantly weigh the value you are getting against the payment for the privilege. Canastas are worth having, whether mixed or natural, and it is generally best to put wild cards to use rather than hoard them.

Don't freeze the pack for the sake of it. A good time to do so is when your opponents have melded and your side has not, as the greater difficulty of taking the pack should tell against them rather than you. The side better able to take the pack at any time is the one with the greater number of cards in hand, a point to remember when discarding. A good time to 'stop' the pack with a black Three is when you have just made an initial meld from the hand, as it prevents your left opponent from taking it before your partner has an opportunity to use it.

Discard low, at first, and ranks which your left opponent also appears to be discarding. But be prepared for the ruse which you yourself may try on the right opponent who is similarly watching you. By discarding from a set of three you may induce him to discard one of the same rank, thus enabling you to take the pack with your remaining natural pair and so regaining the sprat that caught the mackerel.

There are several factors favourable for going out: one is when your side has melded a canasta and made a lot of profit from it, and it now seems likely that your opponents are about to make one as well; another, of course, is when they have masses more cards in hand than yourself or partner. Again, a side with no hope of catching up may think of going out to end the play before the opponents have had time to reach astronomical figures.

Canasta Variants

If card games were planets, Canasta would be a belt of asteroids. It will be convenient to consider adaptations of basic Canasta under this head, then list derivative games individually.

TWO-HAND CANASTA Follow the main rules except the following: deal 15 each, and at each turn draw two but discard one. Two canastas are required to go out. Penalties need not be so rigidly enforced, as there is no partner to benefit from illegally acquired information.

THREE-HAND CANASTA Follow the main rules except the following: deal 13 each (or 11), and at each turn draw two but discard one. Each plays for himself. This version should be described as Cut-throat Canasta, but the term is actually reserved for what properly should be called Solo Canasta and plays as follows: the first player to take the pack becomes the lone player and the others play as partners against him. The initial meld requirement is fixed by the melder's individual score to date, and red Threes are scored separately instead of in partnership (except that one player is not penalized for red Threes if he has not melded but his partner has); otherwise, each scores the amount made by the partnership. Two canastas are required to go out, and game is 7500. If no one takes the pack each scores individually. If no one goes out play ends when the stock runs out. If one goes out before the pack is taken he scores as the lone player and the others as partners.

FIVE-HAND CANASTA There is an awkward system by which the two who cut high play as partners against the other three, a different one of whom sits out each succeeding hand; this is not a true five-hander. Experimenters may like to try a version in which all five play and the first to take the pack immediately becomes the partner of the player next but one to his left, the other three combining as opponents of the partnership.

SIX-HAND CANASTA One version involving six active players splits them into two partnerships of three each, with partners sitting alternately round the table. Use three 52-card packs plus six Jokers and deal 13 cards each. Two canastas are required to go out. Red Threes count 100 each up to three; four or more count 200 each. Game is 10,000 points and the initial meld requirement for a side with 7000 or more is increased to 150. Another version involves three partnerships of two each, with partners sitting opposite each other.

SAMBA This logical extension of Canasta introduces the melding of sequences in addition to groups.

Cards Three 52-card packs with six Jokers, 162 in all.
Deal 15 each.
Play As at standard Canasta, except that each player in turn draws two cards from stock, discarding only one in their place.
Melds Melds of three or more cards of the same rank are made and built up into canastas in the usual way, except that none may contain more than two wild cards or seven in all. In addition, three or more cards of the same suit and forming a sequence may be melded, the lowest being 4–5–6 and the highest terminating... Q–K–A. Such a sequence is called an *escalera* ('ladder'). It may be extended by the addition of natural cards only. A sequence of seven becomes a *samba*, which carries a bonus of 1500 and is turned face down to distinguish it from canastas. Neither a samba nor a canasta may be extended by the addition of extra cards.
Other rules A side needs two canastas or sambas or one of each to go out, and the bonus for going out is 2000 with nothing extra for going out concealed. Red Threes count 100 each up to five; six count 1200 in all. Game is 10,000, and a side with 7000 or more must meld at least 150 initially.

BOLIVIA Played like Samba, except that a samba is called an *escalera*, and with the addition of a meld of from three to seven wild cards. Seven wild cards constitute a *bolivia*, which carries a bonus of 2500. To go out, a side must have made one escalera and a second major combination, which may be another escalera or a canasta or a bolivia. Game is 15,000 points.

BRAZILIAN CANASTA An extension of Bolivia. Game is 10,000 up, and initial meld requirements are stepped up as follows:

5000+ : 150
7000+ : 150 + mixed canasta or better
8000+ : 200 + mixed canasta or better
9000+ : 200 + natural canasta or better

A bolivia counts only 2000. To go out, it is permitted to lay off one or more properly sequential cards to escaleras. At the end of play any incomplete escalera or bolivia counts 1000 against, face values being ignored. Up to four red Threes count 100 each, five or six 200 each; but these scores are deducted if the side has failed to meld a canasta.

CHILE (CHILEAN CANASTA) Three-pack Canasta with escaleras, scoring as at Samba, but with wild-card melds (bonus of 2000 for seven) as an alternative to escaleras – i.e. a side may meld one or the other type but not both.

CUBAN CANASTA (WILD-CARD CANASTA) A two-pack game without sequences but with wild-card melds. Deal 13 each. The pack is permanently frozen. Game is 7500, and a side with 5000+ must initially meld at least 150. Three or more wild cards may be melded for their face values, plus 2000 for a wild canasta, or 3000 if it consists of four Jokers and three deuces, or 4000 for seven deuces. One red Three counts 100, two or three 200 each, the fourth 500, plus or minus as appropriate. Black Threes behave like red Threes, though not in conjunction with them.

HOLLYWOOD CANASTA A cross between Samba and Bolivia. Play as Samba but with these differences. A sequence may contain one wild card, a mixed samba counting 1000 instead of 1500 extra. A meld must contain at least three natural cards, but wild-card canastas may be built for a bonus of 2000. Canastas are limited to seven cards. The up-card of an unfrozen pack may be laid off to a meld, but if it is wild it can only be taken with a matching pair (deuces *or* Jokers, not one of each).

ITALIAN CANASTA A three-pack game with 15 dealt to each. Turn the upcard and then deal face down to the table, from the top of the pack, a number of cards equivalent to the rank of the upcard, i.e., three for a Three, up to ten for a Ten, Jack 11, Queen 12, King 13, Ace or wild card 20. Place the upcard face up on the discard pack, so that the first to take the upcard gets the lot. The pack is permanently frozen; it can only be taken with a matching pair. A wild-card canasta carries a bonus of 2000, or 3000 if it consists of deuces only; in either case the bonus applies only for the side going out, the other scoring only face values. If a wild-card meld is under way any available deuces must be added to it, instead of to other canastas, until the wild canasta is completed and turned down. Game is 12,000. Up to 7500 the initial meld requirement is 160; up to 10,000 it is 180; beyond that 200. Going out counts 300 (nothing extra for concealed) and two non-wild canastas must have been made. Red Threes count 100 each; four or more count 200 each. Optionally, there is a bonus of 1000 for making five canastas, or 2000 if all are natural.

MEXICANA Three-pack Canasta, 13 dealt each, in which the first to meld, or the first in each partnership, immediately draws 13 more cards from stock. Sometimes a canasta of Sevens carries a bonus of 1000 and an upcard Seven cannot be taken. Going out requires two canastas and not less than one red Three per canasta melded.

QUINELLA Four-pack Samba with more elaborations.

TAMPA Three-pack Canasta much like Samba but with wild-card melds instead of sequences. A wild canasta carries a bonus of 2000.

URUGUAY Two-pack Canasta with the addition of wild-card melds, a wild canasta carrying a bonus of 2000. A forerunner of Cuban Canasta.

YUKATAN Eight-pack Samba. Melds of identical cards are permitted. Seven identical cards constitute a *peninsula*, carrying a bonus of 1000 per constituent natural card (minimum five). Game is 25,000 up.

Cribbage

That most English of social institutions – like the pub, where it is chiefly played – Cribbage is traditionally regarded as the invention of Sir John Suckling (1609–42), the poet-soldier, who took his own life in France after being implicated in a plot to rescue the Earl of Stafford from the Tower.

The exact extent of his contribution to the game now called Cribbage is unclear. There was a certain forerunner which went under the name of Noddy, and two other games described in the 1674 edition of *The Compleat Gamester* bear clear resemblances. None of the individual scoring features making up the game are unique to it: the counting up to 31, the recognition of pairs, prials, runs and flushes, even the special attachment to the Jack ('his heels', 'his nibs', 'his nob' etc.) are all to be found elsewhere.

Nothing, however, has the distinctive flavour of Crib other than Crib itself. It is not a particularly deep game, but it belts along at a rattling pace and is full of excitement and variety. It is a very fair game, which always rewards the canniest and most careful player – canniness being a quality born of long experience. It is arguable that more games are lost through error than won by brilliance.

Cribbage is essentially a two-hand game but is playable by

three and in pubs is most frequently encountered as a four-hand partnership game. The crib world seems to be divided into traditionalists, who play the original five-card version, modernists, who play the six-card variety, and occasional freaks who attempt the seven-card extravaganza. In the following account the five-card game is presented first, partly because it claims historical priority and partly because it is preferable for beginners. Then there is Auction Cribbage, apparently the invention of Hubert Phillips, which, for all its merit, has failed to catch on for the perhaps regrettable reason that one cannot tamper with tradition and get away with it. Solitaire versions have also been devised.

A word about the Cribbage board. This is a handy scoring device, as old as the game itself, designed to keep simple but accurate track of the respective scores which are made in dribs and drabs during the actual course of play. The

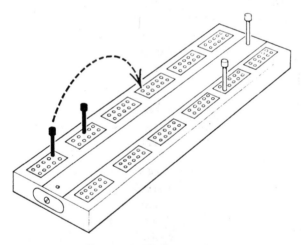

11. CRIBBAGE Traditional Cribbage board designed for play up to 61, or 121 if played 'twice round'. Scores are recorded up the outside and down the inside row of holes on one side of the board for each player. In this illustration 'black' stands at 8 points and is about to increase his score to 16 by transferring his back peg 8 holes in front of his leader, while 'white' stands at 10 points made on one deal, as can be seen from the fact that his back peg has not yet moved from the '0/61' position. The two-peg system guards against inaccurate scoring.

simplest model contains 60 holes on each side plus one extra at each end. Each player sticks a coloured peg (or matchstick) in the end-hole nearest himself, and, throughout the game, he advances it one hole per point scored, up the outside row and back down the inside, returning to the end-hole for the winning count of 61. When the game is played up to 121 the peg travels 'twice round the board' before returning to the end-hole, or else a 121-hole board is used. It is advisable for each player to use two pegs, each new score being marked (*pegged*) by moving the trailing peg in advance of the leading peg by the appropriate amount, as a double-check on accuracy – otherwise it is possible to take the peg out, do the calculation, and then forget where it came from. The posher boards contain storage compartments for the pegs and additional holes in which to record the number of games won.

To save space in the game descriptions, features common to all forms of Cribbage are presented in Table 7.

TABLE 7: SCORING COMBINATIONS AND TERMS
USED IN CRIBBAGE

Cards

Sequence:	A	2	3	4	5	6	7	8	9	10	J	Q	K
Pip-value:	1	2	3	4	5	6	7	8	9	10	10	10	10

Scoring Combinations

Pair: Two cards of the same rank (e.g. Q–Q) scoring	2	
Pair royal: Three cards of the same rank	6	
Double pair royal: Four of the same rank	12	
Run: Three or more cards in sequence	1	per card in sequence
Flush: Three or more cards of the same suit	1	per card in suit
Fifteen: Any two or more cards totalling 15 (e.g. 5–Q)	2	

Other Scoring Features

For 'last': To non-dealer, five-card game only	3	
His heels: To dealer only if Jack turned up	2	
His nob: For holding Jack of same suit as start	1	
Go: For playing the last card towards 31	1	if under 31 or 2 if 31 exact

Five-card Cribbage 8

2 players
1 pack (52)

The game is usually played up to 61; the first to reach or exceed this figure wins, and may (by agreement) win double if his opponent is *lurched*, or *in the lurch*, by failing to reach a score of 31. (If played up to 121 a score of 91 + is needed to save the lurch.)

DEAL Lowest cut deals first (Ace low) and the turn to deal alternates. Either may shuffle, but dealer may shuffle last and must offer to cut before dealing. Deal five cards each, one at a time, face down, to non-dealer first. Non-dealer immediately pegs '3 for last', but only on the first deal of a new game.*

THE GENERAL IDEA In the first part each player discards two cards face down to form a *crib* of four cards. This belongs to dealer at the end of the deal, and any scoring combinations it may contain will count to his credit – thus forcing non-dealer, in his own interest, to discard the most uncombinable cards he can manage. The second part is the play-off. Each lays a card face up and announces the cumulative total of cards so played. Points are scored for making the total 15 and 31, for being the last to play without exceeding 31, and for any scoring combinations that may be made between both players' cards on the way. Finally, non-dealer scores for combinations contained within his own cards, and dealer for combinations contained first within his own cards and then within the crib.

DISCARDING Each player discards two cards face down. These four cards form the crib, which belongs to the dealer, but remain face down until later in the play.

* The purpose of this score is to compensate slightly for the dealer's initial advantage in the game.

THE START Non-dealer next lifts the top half of the pack and dealer turns up the top card of the bottom half as the *starter*, which remains face up throughout play. If the starter is a Jack, dealer immediately pegs 2 for *his heels*.

THE PLAY Starting with non-dealer, each player in turn lays one of his cards face up on the table before him and announces the cumulative total of cards so played. That is, if non-dealer starts with a Three he announces 'three'; if dealer then plays a Six he announces 'nine', and so on. Pictures count 10 each; other cards face value.

If either player brings the total to 'fifteen' or 'thirty-one' in this way, he pegs 2 points. Cards so played may not exceed a total of 31. If either cannot play without exceeding this number, he says 'Go', and the other may then play as many cards consecutively as he can so long as he does not exceed it. Whoever plays the last card pegs '1 for last', or 2 if he makes 31 exactly.

During the course of this play points are also pegged for laying cards that make pairs, pairs royal or runs (sequences) in conjunction with immediately preceding cards (see Table 7 for scores). For instance, if one plays an Ace, and the other immediately follows with an Ace, he pegs 2 for the pair. The first may then play another Ace and peg 6 for the pair royal; and the second may play the fourth Ace and peg 12 (an infrequent event).

If a card is played which forms a run when considered in conjunction with the two previously played cards, its player pegs 3 for the three-card sequence. It does not matter exactly in which order the cards were played, so long as no other card intervenes which does not belong to it. Thus the play of a Five immediately following a Six and a Four makes a valid run, but not following (for instance) 6–J–4.

If one player pegs 3 for a run the next may add a fourth card to the sequence and peg 4; the next fifth for 5; and the next – most improbably – a sixth for 6. It is possible for a higher run to be scored without a lower having been made. For example, 3–4–6–7 contains no sequence, but the subsequent addition of a Five pegs 5.

During this part of the play suits have no significance and flushes are not counted.

THE SHOW After the play, dealer gathers up his cards while non-dealer 'shows' his three cards and scores for any scoring combinations they may contain. For this purpose he also considers the starter (the upturned card of the pack) as part of his hand, though without removing it, and is thus able to score for combinations made on a hand of four cards instead of only three.

From amongst these four cards he pegs 2 for each and every distinct combination of cards which together total 15, counting, as he does so, 'Fifteen 2, fifteen 4, fifteen 6' and so on. For example, if the four cards were ♠A ♥7 ♣7 ♦8 he would count 'Fifteen 2, fifteen 4' for each Seven taken in conjunction with the Eight, and announce 'Fifteen 6' for the two Sevens and the Ace $(7 + 7 + 1 = 15)$, pegging six points in all.

Next, he pegs 1 for each card belonging to a sequence of three or more cards. Thus, with 3–4–4–5 he pegs 3 for one 3–4–5 and 3 for the other.

Next, he may score for a flush if his three cards are of the same suit, pegging 3. If the starter is of the same suit as the three in his hand he counts this too and pegs 4 instead.

Next, he pegs 2 for each distinct pair of cards of the same rank. For example, with ♠7 ♥7 ♣7 he pegs a total of six (which explains the valuation of 6 for a pair royal and 12 for a double pair royal). Note that it is not enough for two cards to be of the same pip-value: they must be of the same *face* to count as a pair. Thus Q–Q–K–K is only two pair for 4, not a double pair royal for 12.

Finally, if his hand of three cards contains the Jack of the same suit as the starter he pegs a further *one for his nob*.

DEALER'S SHOW AND CRIB Unless non-dealer has 'pegged out' and thus won the game on his show of cards, dealer now reveals his three cards and scores for any combinations contained within them, also counting the starter as part of his hand. The scoring is exactly the same as for non-dealer, as described above. He then turns his crib of four cards face up and scores on the same basis for any combinations they contain – this time counting the starter as a fifth card in his hand. Fifteen, pairs, runs and 'his nob' are counted in exactly the same way as before. A flush, however, is only scorable if it contains five cards (pegging 5). It is not enough for the four cards of the crib to be of the same suit: the starter must also be of the same suit in order to make the flush.

NOTES ON PLAY (ALL FORMS)

Skill at any form of two-hand Cribbage lies first in discarding to the crib and second in the play up to 31. It may be noted, by the way, that in Five-card Cribbage there are 10 ways of discarding two cards and six of playing the hand, making 60 possible ways of managing any given hand, while in Six-card there are 15 ways of discarding and 24 of playing, giving 360 possibilities altogether. Theoretically, therefore, Six-card is six times more complicated than Five-card, though it doesn't feel that much in practice.

In discarding to his own crib, dealer will naturally try to lay aside either ready-made combinations, such as a pair or a fifteen, or readily combinable cards. Fives and tenths (i.e., cards counting 10) are combinable for potential fifteens. For example, if you are dealt a Five but no tenth, there is an approximately 1 in 4 chance of turning a tenth as the starter. Tenths are also combinable for possible runs. In discarding a Five you can often reasonably hope that your opponent will have been forced to donate a tenth to the crib; otherwise, however, there is no point in discarding towards any particularly hoped-for card from non-dealer's hand.

Non-dealer, of course, will seek to throw uncombinable cards to his opponent's crib. Avoid throwing Fives or tenths, or pairs, or any two cards belonging to a run. Widely spaced cards are good, especially an Ace and a King, as they do not easily form runs. Do not spoil your playing hand for the sake of avoiding the discard of two cards to a flush, as dealer must have discarded two of the same suit as yourself *and* requires a starter of the same suit in order to score. The danger is minimal.

Both players will also assess their discards with a close eye on what is left in the playing hand, both for the count up to 31 and for the scoring features. Low counters are particularly useful in the play. The lead of a card lower than Five, for instance, prevents the making of fifteen on the next card, while the possession of a low counter when the upper twenties are reached needs no advertisement. A flush may be retained if the hand has little else of promise and the consequent discards are suitable for the crib. If it proves impossible to discard, without breaking up a good combination, prefer the retention of a pair to that of a fifteen, as it may enable you to score for a pair royal in the play.

In the play, never lead a Five or bring the count to 21, as the opponent only needs a tenth to score, and tenths are the commonest cards. Twenty-two is a good count to make – but not with a Nine, as the play of another Nine pegs 2 for the pair as well as 2 for last. Similarly, avoid making 23 with an Eight, 24 with a Seven, and so on. If you have an Ace spare, 20 is a good count, as your opponent will rarely resist making it up to 30 if he can. Given a choice of pairing or making fifteen with the previously played card, prefer to peg 2 for the fifteen rather than make the pair and perhaps give your opponent a pair royal. If your opponent appears to be playing for a run, go along with it if you have possibilities of turning his run of three into one of four, but break it up if not – and remember, the higher the cards, the shorter the possible run. You will never, for example, be able to extend a three-card run containing a Ten.

Similar considerations apply to the three- and four-hand versions but with less flexibility. In the four-hand game don't forget to discard favourably when your partner is 'in the box' (has the crib) – not that the one card you have to throw allows very much scope in this respect.

NUMBER LORE As in Poker, there are 2,598,960 different five-card hands and hence that number of different possible cribs (and initial deals in the five-card game). Of these, about one tenth contain no scoring combination at all, being *bust* hands, and only 624 include a double pair royal (four of a kind).

The highest-counting five-card crib consists of a Five turned starter and a box of three Fives and the Jack of the same suit as starter. This counts 'Fifteen 16 (i.e., four lots of 5 + J and four lots of three Fives), double pair royal 12 for 88, and one for his nob, 29'. In order to get it, however, your opponent must have been daft enough to discard a pair of Fives or a Five and a Jack. If he makes his ideal discard of an Ace and a King your best result will be to throw a pair of Fours, and have a Four turned starter, producing 'Fifteen 6 (for each combination of A–4–K) and pair royal 6, making 12'. Higher counts than 12 are not infrequent because of the element of chance involved in the discard. In six-card Cribbage the average hand counts 8 and the average crib 4. Counts of 19, 25, 26 and 27 are impossible. (Claiming a count of 19, therefore, is a common euphemism for pegging zero.)

It is essential, especially for beginners, to study every hand and crib carefully, physically rearranging cards if necessary, in order not to miss a pegging combination. To facilitate counting, and to avoid being taken for 'muggins' (an excellent optional rule which tends to concentrate the mind wonderfully), it is advisable to check the hand in the following order: fifteens, runs, flushes, pairs and royals, and one for his nob.

MUGGINS This feature is optional and must be agreed beforehand. If a player overlooks a scoring combination in his hand or in the crib, his opponent may draw attention to it (with a cry of 'Muggins!') and peg its value to his own credit; it is a similar technique to 'huffing' in Draughts, only more sensible.

Cribbage Variants

SIX- (AND SEVEN-) CARD CRIBBAGE

Follow the rules of Five-card but with these differences:

GAME 121 up, requiring 91 to escape the lurch. (Seven-card is 181 up.)

DEAL Six (seven) each. Non-dealer does *not* peg 'three for last'.

DISCARD Discard two each to form a four-card crib, leaving four (or five) cards in hand for the play.

THIRTY-ONE When neither player is able to play a card without exceeding 31, the play-off does not end. Instead, after one player has pegged one for 'Go' (or two for making 31), both turn their played cards face down, and the one who scored last leads off again to a new count. This continues until all eight (or ten) cards have been played out. It is thus possible for 'Go' to be scored twice in Six-card and three times in Seven-card Cribbage.

THE SHOW As before, the starter counts as part of each player's hand, thus considerably increasing the scoring potential. The crib, however, continues to contain four cards, augmented by the starter. A flush in the hand is valid only if all the cards are of a suit, and in the crib only if all are of the same suit as the starter.

AUCTION CRIBBAGE

The purpose of Auction Cribbage, which was designed for the Six-card game but may be applied to any standard form of Cribbage, is to give both players the opportunity of taking the crib instead of automatically giving dealer this advantage as of right. The game is played as normal but with the following difference and its consequences:

BIDDING After the deal, but before a card is turned as the starter, each player, beginning with the dealer, may bid for the right to take the crib. Dealer may bid one, non-dealer must raise or pass, and so on until one player passes. The other then subtracts from his score the amount of his bid as 'payment' for the privilege of the crib. The crib-winner leads first (after both have discarded in the usual way) and also has first show – a fact which makes the winning of the crib a matter of some importance to the player who is in the lead towards the end of the game. If both players pass, the hands are thrown in and there is a new deal. (At the start of the game, indicate the deduction of bid-points by placing the bidder's peg the appropriate number of holes in arrears of the starting point.)

THREE-HAND CRIBBAGE

Three-hand Cribbage may be played cut-throat or solo. In cut-throat each plays entirely for himself at each deal; in solo, two play in partnership against the dealer.

CUT-THROAT Deal five cards each, and a sixteenth face down to start the crib. Each lays aside one card to the dealer's crib so that, at the end of the deal, each player counts a hand of four cards plus the starter; dealer's crib is of the same constitution. The player at dealer's left leads to the play and has first show. Dealer shows last. Each scores what he himself makes.

SOLO Five cards are dealt to each opponent and six to the dealer. Each opponent discards one card and dealer adds them both to his hand. He then lays aside any four of his eight cards to form the crib. The player at dealer's left cuts for starter, leads, and has first show. Each partner scores the total made between them; dealer scores from hand and crib in the usual way.

PARTNERSHIP CRIBBAGE

PRELIMINARIES Partnerships may be determined by cutting, the two lowest against the two highest. Partners sit opposite each other and play alternately. Lowest cut deals first and the turn to deal passes to the left. The crib board is placed between dealer's right-hand opponent and partner, who alone are responsible for pegging.

DEAL AND CUT Dealer shuffles last and, after offering for cutting to the right, deals five cards each, singly. Each player lays aside one card to the crib, which, as usual, belongs to dealer. Dealer's left opponent cuts for starter, leads to the play, and has first show.

PLAY AND SHOW The play is exactly as two-hand six-card Cribbage, all sixteen cards being played out and 'Go' being scored as often as necessary.

CRIBBAGE SOLITAIRES

Various forms of Cribbage solitaires and patiences have been devised, and one of each may be mentioned for completeness. (The distinction drawn here between a solitaire and a patience is that the former denotes a one-player adaptation of the game whereas a patience is not so much a game as a puzzle.)

CRIBBAGE SOLITAIRE The method usually described is to deal yourself six cards and a crib of two (either 3–2–3 or 2–1–2–1–2). Discard two to the crib and turn a starter. Score for your own hand and then for the crib. For the next deal reject the first eight cards and deal the starter as the first card of a new hand.* Play six hands in this way (leaving four cards unused) and consider yourself to have 'won' if you reach 120 points for all hands and cribs. This exercise affords valuable practice for the real thing.

CRIBBAGE PATIENCE Deal sixteen cards one at a time from the top of the pack, placing each one face up and adjacent to

* Returning the starter to the bottom of the pack, as some accounts recommend, reduces the element of skill by virtue of the fact that you know which four cards are out of play at the end.

any card already showing until you have formed a square of 4 × 4 rows and columns. Turn up the seventeenth card and count it as the starter. Score then for each of the four rows and each of the four columns as if it were a Cribbage hand, counting the starter as the fifth. (Only five-card flushes are valid, not four-flushes.) Score 61 or more to 'win'.

Cassino Games

Cassino itself has long been a popular home game in America and is often recommended for children, though several related games are much easier to grasp in principle and no less worthy of serious attention. The family as a whole, all of whose members closely resemble one another, are distinctly Mediterranean in background – the best of them, Scopone, being of sufficient importance to count as the national card game of Italy. Their early history is obscure, but Cassino first appears in an edition of Hoyle in 1808.

The unusual feature of the family is that they are neither trick-taking nor meld-making games. Like Cribbage and Pontoon they attach little importance to suits and are based instead upon the arithmetical properties of the ranks in their capacity as numerals. In short, they are adding-up games. This may be why they are recommended for children and this, in turn, may be why their potential depth has gone unnoticed, especially in Britain.

The chief games described here are Cassino for two and Scopone for four. As the former looks somewhat complicated at first sight, beginners may prefer to start with Scopone and work backwards. Of the related games outlined between the two of them, Royal Spade Cassino may be recommended for its variety, Tablanette for its high scoring potential, Sbarazzina for its neatness and comparative simplicity.

Cassino

2 to 4 players (2 best)
1 pack (52)

The basic form of the game is presented first. Experts tend to prefer one or more of the advanced 'variants' appended to this account, but even the simplest form is complicated to describe and beginners are advised to walk before they can run. It has become fashionable to point out that Cassino is a mis-spelling and to revert to the original form Casino with one S. But it seems useful to observe two different spellings for words with two different meanings, especially when used in similar contexts (a Cassino game is certainly not a casino game); the mis-spelling has been perpetuated long enough to have acquired a sort of common-law status. One might as well say that Shakespeare was really written by another man called Shakspere.

PLAYERS Two, three or partnership four, but it does not work well for three, and four would be better off playing Scopone. It is assumed below that two play, except where special rules apply to different numbers.

CARDS A standard 52-card pack is used. Cards from Ace to Ten are regarded purely as numerals from one to ten respectively.

DEAL Deal two to each opponent, two to the table and two to the dealer, then similarly another two each so that everyone has four. Turn the four table cards face up in a row. Place the rest of the pack to one side. When everyone has had four turns, thereby voiding his hand, deal another four each in batches of two, and so on throughout the game. No more cards are dealt to the table, however, at any time. When the stock is exhausted, dealer should announce that fact, as it affects the strategy of the end-play.

OBJECT At each turn, players seek to capture cards from the table in conjunction with a card from the hand. Cards so captured are placed face down before their winner and remain out of play. At the end of the game, points are scored for having captured:

the most cards	3
the most spades	1
big *cassino* (◆T)	2
little *cassino* (♠2)	1
each Ace	1

During play, anyone who in one turn captures all the cards on the table scores 1 point for a *sweep* (but this is often discounted when only two play). Apart from the object of capturing spades and two special cards, the suits of the cards are of no significance in the play: only their ranks count.

PLAY Each player in turn plays one card to the table, then either turns it face down before him together with any table cards it may have captured, or leaves it face up with the table cards. The card he plays is thus used either to *capture* or to *build*, or, if neither is possible, simply to *trail*.

CAPTURING A card played from the hand captures one or more single cards of the same rank by *pairing*. Thus an Ace may capture one or more single Aces, a Three one or more single Threes, and so on. A court card can only be captured by pairing – Jack takes Jack, Queen Queen and King King, and only one may be paired in a turn (i.e. with two Kings on the table a player with a King may capture only one of them. But it may be agreed beforehand that *three* courts of the same rank may be simultaneously captured by the fourth).

Similarly, a card from hand may be used to capture, by *combining*, two or more single cards whose combined values total that of the capturing card. Thus a Ten may capture, besides a Ten, an Ace and a Nine, or a Two and an Eight, or Two-Three-Five, or Ace-Two-Three-Four, and so on.

A single card in one turn may make as many captures by pairing and combining as may be possible, provided that the cards captured are all *single* (in the sense of not forming part of a *build* as described below), and that none of them appears in more than one combination simultaneously. But a build itself may be captured, as a whole, by a card equal in value to it.

BUILDING This means to play a card to the table for the purpose of forming a combination which can be captured by another card from hand on the next turn. A player may only build if he holds a card enabling him to make the subsequent capture, and if he does build he may not trail on the next turn (unless his build is taken by someone else).

The simplest build occurs when a player holds two cards of the same numerical rank and there is a third on the table. If he captured immediately he would win only two cards instead of three. Instead, he plays one from the hand on top of the table card it matches, and announces 'Building Fives' (or whatever the rank may be). On his next turn he may play his other Five and capture them by pairing, unless an opponent captures them first with the fourth Five.

A player may also build by adding a card from his hand to one or more table cards and announcing their combined value, thereby declaring his ability to capture them all on his next turn with a card equal to the value of that build. For example, with

```
table cards    2 3 8 9
in hand        A 4 6 9
```

he could play the Ace to the Eight, announce 'Building Nines', and capture that build with his Nine on his next turn (along with the table Nine, captured by pairing). Or, on his next turn, he could play the Four to the Three and add the table deuce to it to make nine, and then, on his next turn, sweep the board by playing his Nine and capturing the Ace-Eight build, the Two-Three-Four build, and the Nine by pairing. Of course, this sweep would take two turns to achieve, so doubling the danger that an opponent may capture the build with a Nine from his hand, or increase it to Ten.

Any player may increase a build by adding another card to it and announcing the new total, provided (a) that he holds a card equal in value to the new total so that he is in a position to capture it on his next turn if still available, and (b) that it does not form part of a multiple build. A multiple build is illustrated by the example given above. On his first turn the player adds the Ace to the Eight and announces 'Building nine'. Before he plays again an opponent could add another Ace to it and announce 'Building ten', thereby threatening to capture it with a Ten on his next turn. But if the nine is left intact, the first player would, on his next turn, add his Four to the Two and Three, announcing 'Building nines', and place that build on top of, or next to, his first build of nine. This turns it into a multiple build and it cannot be increased – the two builds can now only be captured with a Nine.

12. CASSINO If North is to play, he may (a) capture the Queen by pairing, (b) capture both Threes with his Six, or (c) add his Three to the others and announce 'building nine' for subsequent capture with his Nine – a move that would prevent South from capturing the Threes by pairing. If South is to play, he may (a) capture both Threes by pairing with his own, (b) build eight by playing his Two to both Threes and capturing them all with his Eight, together with the Eight by pairing, on his next turn, (c) build eights by adding an Eight to the table, for subsequent capture of both by pairing with the other in his hand, or (d) build 2+3+3 on this turn and 8 + 8 on his next, and hope to capture both builds with an Eight on the turn thereafter.

A possible source of confusion in building cards must be avoided by clearly announcing the total. For example, a player may add a Three from his hand to a Three on the table. If he announces 'Building threes', the two cards may only be captured with a Three (by multiple pairing). But if he announces 'Building six', the build may be captured only by a Six. Furthermore, the build of six could be increased by the addition of another card to make a higher build, but the build of Threes could only be increased by the addition of another Three (which, of course, would only happen in the four-hand partnership game).

TRAILING A player who is unable or unwilling to capture or build must *trail* by playing any card from his hand face up to the table, where it becomes available for subsequent capturing or building like any other table card. But he may not trail if any build he made or increased on his last turn is still available for capture; he must either capture it, or increase it, or make any other build or capture that may be possible.

SWEEPING THE BOARD Except (optionally) in two-hand play, a player who sweeps the board by capturing all the cards on the table in one turn scores 1 point. It is convenient to mark this fact by leaving the capturing card face up in the pile of won cards and to count it along with the rest of the score at the end of the game. When a player has made a sweep the next in turn has no option but to trail.

END PLAY The last player to capture a card from the table also takes all the cards left on the table if and when all those playing after him were forced to trail. This does not, in itself, count as a sweep, though the game may end with a sweep if the last card played happens to capture all the remaining table cards by pairing and/or combining.

SCORE Players sort through their won cards and score 1 point for each sweep, Ace and the little cassino (♠2), and 2 points for big cassino (♦T). The player or side with the greatest number of captured spades scores 1 point, and, for the majority of cards (counting everything), 3 points. The 3 for cards is not counted in the event of a tie.

GAME There are several methods of determining the game score or pay-off. (a) Each deal is a complete game and the higher score wins. (b) The first player or side to reach 11 points wins, and their score is doubled if achieved in two deals or quadrupled if achieved in one, the loser's score being subtracted to determine the margin of victory. If both exceed 10 the higher score wins, but in the event of a tie there is no pay-off. (c) Game is 21 up. In the event of a tie the winner is the side with the majority of cards, or of spades if that does not break it.

Cassino Variants

These are played like Cassino unless otherwise stated or obvious from the context. A 40-card pack, where mentioned, is one lacking all Eights, Nines and Tens.

CALLABRA A fast and simple forerunner of Cassino for two or three players, using a 52-card pack. Deal three each and five to the table. The rest remain out of play and the simple object is to capture a clear majority of the cards in play – i.e., six if two play, eight if three. Numerals count face value, plus J11, Q12, K13. Each in turn (passing to the right) plays a card face up to the table and leaves it there unless able to capture one or more table cards with it. A card played from the hand may capture one or more cards of equal value, and/or one or more card combinations totalling the value of the capturing card. The game ends when (a) one player has captured a majority of cards, or (b) one player has run out of cards and no one has won, or (c) no more cards are available for capture.

DIAMOND CASSINO Italo-American version of Scopa. Two or more players use a 40-card pack, dealing three each and four to the table. Game is 11 up, counting 1 for cards (capturing 21 or more if two play), 1 for diamonds (capturing six or more of them), 1 extra for ♦7, 2 for capturing all four Sevens or Sixes or Aces, and 1 per sweep.

DRAW CASSINO Any two-hand version of Cassino played in the following way: after playing a card, each completes his turn by drawing the top card of stock to restore his original number of cards. There are no extra deals. When the stock is exhausted the last cards are played out in the usual way.

DRY GAME Curious name for a curious game quoted by Harbin (see *Select Bibliography*) from a Greek source. Two to four players, 52 cards, six each. The next four are dealt face up in a pile so that only the top card is available. When players run out of cards there is a new deal, including four to the pile. Each in turn plays a card face up to the pile. If it matches the top card by rank it captures the whole pile, and the next in turn has no option but to start a new one by playing any card face up. If not, it is left on top. Any Jack captures the whole pile regardless of the top card. A player capturing a pile consisting of only one card immediately scores 10 points for a *dry trick (sic)*. Score 3 for cards, 3 for capturing the most clubs, 2 for ♦T, 1 extra for ♣2, and 1 per Jack.

HURRICANE Italian game here quoted from a German source. Two (or more) players, 40 cards, six each, four to the table. Play as Cassino, but without building, and score as follows: 1 for cards, 1 for hearts (majority of), 1 extra for ♥7, 1 for *primiera*. To determine the point for primiera each player takes from his won cards, the highest-valued card in each suit, for which purpose J = 8, Q9 K10 A11, 2 = 12, 3 = 13, 4 = 14, 5 = 15, 6 = 18, 7 = 21. The point goes to the player whose top cards have the highest aggregate value. Game is 16 up, and won double if the loser fails to reach 8. (A *hurricane* is a sweep.)

LADIES' GAME Another oddity reported by Harbin. Two or more players, 52 cards, six each, four to the table. Play as Cassino except that all court cards have a numerical value of 10 and there is no building, cards being captured only by pairing or combining. Score as at the Dry game (see above).

PAPILLON A French member of the family, probably defunct, characterized by an elaborate system of side-payments for special coups and by its almost exclusive suitability for three players. Fifty-two cards, three each, seven to the table (or only four if four play). Each in turn plays one card and captures by pairing or combining, with certain restrictions. One K, Q, J or T will capture as many cards of the same rank as may be available, but any lower card may pair with not more than one of its rank. On the other hand, lower cards may capture by combining, e.g., an Eight will capture 2–3–3, etc. A player unable to capture must trail. When all hand cards have been played three more each are dealt. When all table-cards have been taken, seven (or four) more are dealt. The last to capture a card takes any left over at the end of play. Payments were made as follows: 1 to the pool each time a card is trailed, from each opponent 2 for capturing an Ace with an Ace, 4 for capturing two Aces with a deuce, 6 for capturing three Aces with a trey, 8 for capturing four with a Four, 1 for capturing any three cards of the same rank with the fourth (a feat known as *hanneton*, meaning 'cockchafer'), 1 for a sweep (called *sauterelle* or 'grasshopper') – after which the next in turn must lay out his remaining cards to form a new table – 1 for winning a majority of cards (not counted in the event of a tie, but the winner of the next counts 2), and various other payments, which are not 100 per cent clear but may easily be extended by exercise of the imagination. The name of the game means 'butterfly' and it is clear that all variants must be named after arthropods.

PISHTI An apparently Turkish member of the family, again reported by Harbin. Played exactly as Cassino except that cards are captured only by pairing or combining, and a Jack

may be used to sweep the board. Score 3 for cards, 3 for
♦T, 2 for ♣2, 1 per Ace and Jack.

ROYAL CASSINO Basic Cassino but counting each Jack 11,
Queen 12 and King 13, so that court cards may be built or
captured by combining as well as by pairing. As an optional
extra, Ace may count 1 or 14 *ad lib*.

SBARAZZINA As Scopa (below) except that cards may only
be captured which, together with a card from the hand, total
15. For example, if the table cards include 2–7–K they may
be captured by, and together with, a Six played from hand –
bearing in mind that court cards have a positive count of
zero. A player unable to capture in this way must trail. Any
Ace may be used to sweep the board provided that no other
Ace is on the table. Scored as at Scopa but with the addition
of 1 for capturing ♦K (*re bello*).

ROYAL SPADE CASSINO A mixture of Royal Cassino and
Spade Cassino.

SCOPA Two-hand equivalent of the superior four-hand
Scopone, still much played in Italy. Two or more players, 40
cards, three each, four to the table. Court cards count Jack
8, Queen 9, King 10. Capture by pairing or combining.
Score 1 for cards, 1 for majority of diamonds, 1 for ♦7
(sette bello), 1 for *primiera* (as explained under Scopone,
page 361), 1 per *scopa* (sweep).

SPADE CASSINO Standard Cassino except that 1 point is
scored, not for taking the majority of spades, but for *each*
spade captured, with an additional point for ♠J, ♠2 (little
cassino) and ♠A (by virtue of the score for Aces).

TABLANETTE Said to be of Russian provenance. Two
players, 52 cards, six each, four to the table. Capture by
pairing or combining. Ace counts 1 or 11 *ad lib*, Queen 13,
King 14. A player holding a Jack may use it to sweep the
board regardless of pip-count. Sweeping the board – i.e.,
taking all the table cards available in one turn – is known as

making a *tablanette* (possibly from French *table nette* or 'clean table'), and entitles the player to score the combined pip-count of all the cards so captured, including the one used to capture it, except that a Jack in itself has no value. Apart from the potentially huge scores for tablanette, players score 1 for each A, K, Q, J and T captured, an extra 1 for the ♦T, 1 for ♣J, and 3 for the majority of cards. Game is 251 up.

Scopone ♋

4 players in partnerships
1 short pack (40)

This excellent and unusual partnership game, the national card game of Italy, deserves fuller treatment than a simple listing in the Cassino variants described above. Players looking for something quite different from the usual run of trick-and-trump games, easy to learn but of considerable depth, may confidently be recommended to look into it. Scopone is thought to have originated in the Naples area, where it is still played with a traditional 40-card Italian pack whose court cards represent King (*Re*), Knight (*Cavallo*) and a sort of female Jack (Jill? – actually called *Donna*, meaning just 'lady'). The earliest account of the game is a full treatise on it in Macaronic Latin by an early eighteenth-century writer, Chitarella.

PLAYERS Four, with partners sitting opposite each other. Traditionally, all play passes to the right (anti-clockwise around the table).

CARDS 40, consisting of A234567JQK in each suit. Cards from Ace to Seven count their respective face values, plus Jack 8, Queen 9 and King 10.

DEAL In batches, three to each player, two to the table, three more each and two to the table, and finally three more each. Thus everybody has nine cards, four are laid face up on the table, and none remain.

OBJECT Each side's object is to capture as many cards as possible, particularly diamonds and high numeral cards (not courts). If the table cards include three Kings, it is usual (but not official) to deal again.

PLAY Each player in turn plays a card face up to the table. If it is of the same rank as a table card he thereby captures it and places both cards face down in the pile of cards won by his side. Or, if it is equal in value to two or more table cards added together, it captures those cards in combination and all are added to the pile of winnings. If a card is played which can capture either by pairing or by combining, it may be made only by pairing. (Example: if the table cards are 2–4–6–J the play of a Six captures the Six but not the 2–4.) A sweep *(scopa)* is made when there is only one card on the table and a player captures it by pairing, or when all the cards on the table are captured in combination by a single card equalling their aggregate value. This is a scoring feature and is marked by placing the capturing card face up instead of face down in the pile of won cards. If a player is unable or unwilling to capture, he must merely *trail* by playing any card face up to the table. It is not permitted to trail a card which is able to capture, and if such a matching card is played the capture must be made. When a player makes a sweep the next in turn has no option but to trail. Play continues until no cards are left in hand. Any cards remaining on the table then go to the side that last made a capture but this does not count as a sweep. Nor does it count as a sweep if the last card of all played from the (dealer's) hand validly captures all the cards left on the table.

SCORE The appropriate side scores as follows:

1 for cards (21 or more captured)
1 for diamonds (six or more captured)
1 for the gold (the ♦7)
1 for the *prime (primiera*; see below)
1 for each sweep

The point for prime is determined as follows. Each side

extracts from its won cards the highest-valued card it has taken in each suit, counting for this purpose,

Seven	21	Four	14
Six	18	Three	13
Ace	16	Two	12
Five	15	K, Q, J	10

The side whose top cards have the highest aggregate value scores 1 for the prime. It is possible for both sides to tie for cards, diamonds or prime, in which case neither scores the point at issue.

GAME The deal passes to the right and the winning side is that which reaches or exceeds 11 points first or with the greater excess. In the event of a tie the points made on the last deal are counted strictly in order: cards – diamonds – the gold – the prime – sweeps; and the first to score on that basis wins.

VARIANT

TEN-CARD SCOPONE Ten cards are dealt to each player and none to the table, thus forcing the first player to trail. This is the version usually described in American books but is regarded by Italian experts as 'unscientific'.

NOTES ON PLAY

Scopone lends itself to considerable strategic and tactical skills which can hardly be touched upon in the space available.

If at the start of the hand each player were to capture exactly one card, the dealer would score a sweep, eldest would be forced to trail, and there would be a strong tendency for the dealer's side to be continually sweeping while the opponents continually trail. (This tendency is even stronger in Ten-card Scopone, which explains the weakness of that variant.) It is incumbent upon eldest's side to break up this potential pattern. Suppose the table cards dealt are

A–3–4–J. Eldest plays a Five and captures two cards, i.e., $5 = 1 + 4$. This makes life difficult for dealer's partner. He is confronted with 3–J, a combination worth 11 and so unsweepable. If he pairs either card he leaves one, and the chance of a sweep, to his next opponent, though his own holding will give him some idea of the extent of risk. For example, if he held two Jacks and a Three he could take the Three on the basis that it is two to one against the next player's holding the other Jack. Otherwise, his safest play is to trail, which scores nothing.

After the first move ($5 = 1 + 4$) there remain in play three cards each of the ranks Ace, Four and Five, and these ranks are consequently said to be unpaired (*sparigliato*). Generally, it is to the non-dealers' advantage to maintain as many ranks as possible unpaired. In order to redress the balance, dealer's side should seek to trail the lower cards of three or more unpaired ranks so that they may capture by combining – an attempt which the opponents will try to frustrate by trailing the highest unpaired rank before the others can get both of the lower ranks into play. In the above example, dealer's side will now seek to trail a Four and an Ace so as to capture both with a Five of their own. But if the non-dealers can themselves trail a Five before a Four and Ace are got into play then the dealer's side will not be able to catch them, since, by the rules of the game, a player must capture by pairing instead of by combining where the choice exists.

Another common sequence of play is known as *il mulinello* ('whirlwind'). Suppose the table cards are A–3–4–5 and eldest has two Threes. Trusting that his next opponent does not have the fourth, he plays $K = A + 4 + 5$, leaving the Three *in situ*. Dealer's partner does not have the Three and must trail a court card in order to prevent the next from possibly sweeping. Let us suppose it is a Jack. Now third-hand, who does have the fourth Three, pairs the Jack, thus leaving dealer in exactly the same fix as his partner. As the fourth Three is a constant threat this painful situation can be dragged out for some time.

When forced to trail it is natural to choose a rank of which two or three are held, a fact which can give useful information to one's partner and possibly enable him to reap a whirlwind as described above. For example, suppose the first move is $6 = 2 + 4$. Second-hand trails one Four from a pair. If now his partner, dealer, has the other Four, the two of them can set up a whirlwind based upon that rank. (Borrowing from Bridge terminology, the situation could be described as a 'squeeze'.)

The single most important card in the pack is ♦7 – the *sette bello* or Golden Seven (bearing in mind that the Italian suit equivalent to diamonds is coins or pieces of gold). It is worth a point in itself, counts towards the majority of diamonds and is worth most in the point for prime. Much of the play is directed towards catching this card, or at least preventing the opponents from catching it too easily. Next in importance are the other three Sevens, as the prime point can be won on three Sevens provided that the fourth card is a Three or better. A side which has already lost a majority of Sevens must chase after the Sixes, then the Aces, and so on down the scale.

Poker/Brag

Fields: Poker? Is that the game where one receives five cards? And if there's two alike that's pretty good, but if there's three alike, that's much better?

Gambler: Oh, you'll learn the game in no time.

(W. C. Fields)

Poker is America's national card game and one of the most popular games in the world. In both respects it is of comparable status to Bridge and is to no lesser extent a contest of skill, in that the best players always win in the long run, and usually in the short run too. On the other hand it is an entirely different type of game from Bridge, the expert practitioner at both being as rare as a professional cricketer and footballer combined. Unlike Bridge, it requires no skill at card play in the usual sense of the word. Quite rightly, Poker has been described as '... not a card game (but) a game of money management. Cards are merely the tools for manipulating money' (David Spanier, *Total Poker*). Poker, Brag and relatives are essentially gambling games to the extent that they are pointless unless played for real stakes. But it must be emphasized that they are not 'gambles' in the loose sense of the word, implying that all is won or lost on the turn of a card at Dame Fortune's dictate. Those who win do so because they are better money managers than those who lose, a fact which makes it expensive to become a good player. Chance enters into the picture, but only as a servant – not as a master.

Poker and Brag owe their superiority over other gambling games by operating on what might be called the 'vying' principle, which enables a good player to win by superior play over the player who may hold better cards but fails to convince his opponents of that fact. Vying consists of progressively raising the amount it costs to stay in the game, until some drop out and others will raise no further but merely pay to 'see' the highest raiser. If it comes to a show-down the player actually showing the best hand wins the *pot* (the total amount staked during play); but if all save one drop out, the one left in wins the pot without showing his hand, which may in fact have been good, bad or indifferent. The point is that each player knows his own hand and knows what action others are taking on theirs. He must therefore balance his own probability of winning against the amount it will cost him to stay in the game and size of pot he would win if successful.

Poker (general) ◎

3–10 players
1 pack

First recorded by name in 1829, Poker evolved in New Orleans and spread along the Mississippi in the steam-boat saloons. It was at first played with twenty cards, but increased to fifty-two within a decade, and without recognition of straights or flushes, which only became an integral part of the game in this century. Although Draw Poker had developed by the start of the Civil War, and Stud apparently during it, the game as a whole did not reach the pages of *The American Hoyle* until the 1880s, while, as late as 1897, one commentator noted that 'The best clubs do not admit the game to their rooms.' It soon reached England, where G. Eliot referred in 1855 to the 'game of Brag or Pocher', and Queen Victoria later confessed herself amused by it. American Ambassador Schenk is said to have taught it to the whole Court of St James.

The name derives either from a French game Poque, whose details are unrecorded, or from the German Pochspiel, in which a player passed by knocking on the table (saying 'Ich poche'). The distinguishing features of the game are, first, the system of raising and calling bets, and, second, the fact that players bet on a hand of five instead of the previously more common three cards. Five is also characteristic of an old Persian game called As Nas, which could have reached America via French settlers who had been in the Persian service. For this reason, Poker has been represented as the direct descendant of an ancient oriental game. But the theory is somewhat far-fetched, as the oldest known Persian cards do not antedate 1700. They contain only five ranks or suits (not both), and the method of play could as well have been borrowed from Europe as vice versa.

FORMS OF POKER Poker is a living game that by its nature invites and receives constant variation in everyday play. Many variations are *ad hoc* and go unrecorded; others become popular over various periods of time and often acquire different names. Thus the game does not lend itself to being pinned down in books, and it must suffice here to describe the most basic forms, together with the broad lines along which variations occur.

The original game was Straight Poker, or Cold Poker, in which five cards were dealt to each player; one period of betting ensued, and the winner of that took the pot. From this developed Draw Poker, in which, after the first betting interval is over, each player can seek to improve his hand by rejecting some of his cards and 'drawing' (= being dealt) replacements, a process followed by a second betting interval before the winner is determined. Draw is still regarded as the basic game for home play and is recommended for beginners, but serious players are now devoted to various forms of the next development, Stud Poker. In these, each player receives five or even more cards, from which he selects any five as his eventual playing hand. Some of these are dealt face down (= hole cards) for his eyes only, others face up (= upcards) for all to see. There is no draw, but betting intervals follow the deal of successive cards, giving more opportunity for betting and for the application of skill.

Both Draw and Stud may be combined with a major variant called Lowball, in which the pot is won by the lowest hand, or, more popularly, High-Low Poker, in which it is shared between the highest and the lowest hand. These and other variants follow the main descriptions of Draw and Stud.

The reason for so variegating the basic game is usually given as a desire to speed up the action by increasing the relative frequency of 'good' hands, which otherwise rarely occur. Though true, this is only half the story. Each variant also introduces its own schedule of mathematical probabilities. These can hardly be learned by rote, but the skilled player, experienced in several forms of the game, starts out at a considerable advantage over the player whose knowledge stops short at orthodox Draw Poker. It is for this reason that the most popular form of the game is Dealer's Choice, in which each dealer announces exactly what game is to be played on his own deal, or for the round of deals initiated by himself. He is even at liberty to invent new variations and to name them as he pleases. In this way the mathematical variety of the game is given full play almost from deal to deal.

POKER HANDS All forms of Poker recognize the same range and relative ranking of card combinations which determine who has the best or worst hand. A Poker hand by definition consists of five cards (more may be dealt, but ultimately only five count). If some of these are related by rank or suit in certain prescribed ways, they form a Poker combination. This may, but need not, involve all five cards. Any that do not form part of the combination are *idle* or *dead*, though they may be called into account to decide between competing combinations of otherwise equal value. The rank of individual cards from highest to lowest is always AKQJT98765432, with Ace alternatively lowest on certain occasions. From highest to lowest, orthodox Poker combinations are as follows. The figures following each are, first, the number of such combinations possible in a 52-card pack with none wild, and second the probability (expressed as a percentage, i.e., number of times out of 100) of being dealt such a combination straight from the pack.

STRAIGHT FLUSH (40 = 0.0015 per cent) Five cards in suit and sequence. Ace may count high, as in A–K–Q–J–T (*royal flush*), or low, as in 5–4–3–2–A. As between two straight flushes, the one with the higher-ranking top card wins. A tie is possible.

FOUR OF A KIND (624 = 0·0240 per cent) Four cards of the same rank, the fifth idle. One with a higher-ranking set of four beats one with a lower, and ties are impossible.

FULL HOUSE (3744 = 0·144 per cent) Three cards of one rank plus two of another. One with the higher-ranking set of three beats one with a lower. Ties are impossible.

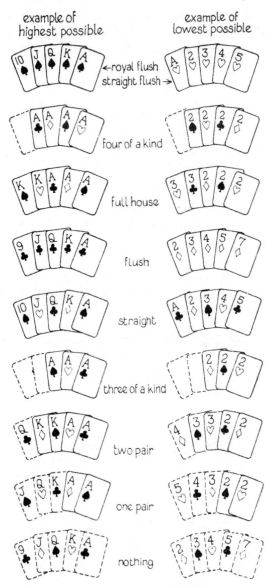

example of highest possible / example of lowest possible

←royal flush
straight flush→

four of a kind

full house

flush

straight

three of a kind

two pair

one pair

nothing

13. STANDARD POKER HANDS Dotted cards are not essential to the combination and may be anything, though they may be called into account to break ties. Ties are not possible between fours or threes of a kind, or full houses.

FLUSH (5108 = 0·1956 per cent) Five cards of the same suit not in sequence. As between flushes, the one with the highest-ranking top card wins, or second highest if equal, and so on. An all five-card tie is possible but extremely unlikely.

STRAIGHT (10,200 = 0·392 per cent) Five cards in sequence but not of one suit. Ace counts either high (A–K–Q–J–T) or low (5–4–3–2–A). One with a higher top card beats one with a lower. Ties are possible.

THREE OF A KIND (54,912 = 2·13 per cent) Three cards of the same rank, the other two idle and unrelated. Three of a higher rank beats three of a lower. Ties are not possible.

TWO PAIR (123,552 = 4·75 per cent) Two cards of one rank, two of another, the fifth idle. To break ties, the one with the highest ranking pair wins, or the second highest if equal, or the higher idle card if still equal.

ONE PAIR (1,098,240 = 42·2 per cent) Two cards of the same rank, the other three idle and unrelated. Ties are decided in favour of the highest-ranking pair, or best unmatched card if equal.

NOTHING (1,302,540 = 50·1 per cent) Also called a 'high card' hand because competition between combinationless hands is decided in favour of the one with the highest-ranking top card, or second highest if equal, and so on. (This is consistent but illogical, since combinationless hands with Ace high are over 120 times commoner than those with Seven high, others ranking *pro rata*.)

WILD-CARD HANDS A *wild* card is one that may be used by its holder to represent any card he wishes. Originally the Joker was added as a wild card, but it is now more usual to specify as wild all cards of a particular rank, most frequently deuces. The effect of even only one wild card is to introduce additional combinations as follows:

Five of a kind: for example A–A–A–A–W or A–W–W–W–W represents five Aces. Five of a kind beats everything, though some schools artificially rate a royal flush higher.

Double Ace flush: for example, ♥A–J–9–3–W, in which the wild card is held by its owner to be another ♥A in order to beat, say, ♠A–K–J–9–3. It beats an ordinary flush. Although five of a kind is universally accepted, some players refuse to recognize the Double Ace flush. This point should be agreed before play.

As between tied combinations of the same rank, the one with fewer wild cards wins. Thus 9–9–W–5–2 (three Nines) beats 8–8–8–5–2 (three Eights) but is beaten by 9–9–9–3–2 (three natural Nines) or J–W–W–3–2 (three Jacks). Some hold that any combination with wild cards is inferior to any of the same type without, by which reckoning the order of those quoted would be, from best to worst, 9–9–9–3–2, 8–8–8–5–2, 9–9–W–5–2, J–W–W–3–2. The first method of assessment is more logical, the latter more satisfying, and the point must be decided before play.

COMPETITIVE LOW HANDS In Lowball and High-Low Poker it is necessary to determine who has the lowest Poker hand. The basic method is simple: decide which of two hands is higher as explained above, and it loses to the other. By this method the lowest possible hand is a non-flush 7–5–4–3–2 (*seventy-five*). But it must be agreed before play which practice to follow in respect of Aces and straights. For example, is A–5–4–3–2 a combinationless hand with Ace high, or is its owner obliged to declare it a low straight (5–4–3–2–A) and inevitably lose? Here are the options: (a) Ace is automatically high unless its owner wishes to call it low, which he may only do to make a straight. (b) Ace may be counted high or low as its owner pleases. In this case he may count a pair of Aces lower than any other pair, and the lowest combinationless hand is a non-flush 6–4–3–2–A. (c) Straights and flushes play no part in the game, and Ace is high or low *ad lib*. In this case the lowest possible hand is 5–4–3–2–A (a *Wheel*, or *Bicycle*) even if flush. Option (a) is for purists; (b) is most suitable for High-low, and (c) for Lowball, in which there is no competition for high hands.

WILD CARD LOW HANDS Wild cards in low hands are usually held to create pairs. Hence A–K–Q–J–9 would beat 7–5–4–3–W, which must be a pair of Threes at least.

FREAK HANDS Unorthodox Poker combinations such as the *blaze, flash, zebra* etc., are now little used in serious play. See p. 388 for examples.

STAKES Poker is properly played with counters or chips as follows:

white = 1 unit
red = 5 (or 2½ or 2)
blue = 25 (or 20 or 10)
yellow = 100 (or 50 or 25)

Yellows are optional and therefore blue chips are usually highest (hence the phrase 'blue chip'). Proper practice is for players to buy a fixed amount before play from the banker, i.e., the host or person running the game. Two hundred chips each should suffice; more, if needed during play, should be bought from the banker, not from other players. Throughout play, each player must keep all his chips on the table in full view of the others. Before play it is important to agree limits on permissible bets. These vary from Draw to Stud and are therefore dealt with separately below.

CARDS Standard Poker cards are wider than the so-called Bridge cards used for most other games, and have extra large numerals. Their use is a convenience but not an essential. It is also convenient to use two packs of contrasting backs, with the understanding that any player may call for a change of pack at the end of a hand.

Draw Poker ◎

5–7 players best
1 pack (52)

The distinguishing feature of Draw Poker is that, after the
first betting period, players may exchange any or all of their
cards in the hope of improving their hand (the draw), after
which there is a second period of betting before the pot is
claimed.

PRELIMINARIES Agree a time limit for the game, on the
understanding that all players should deal an equal number
of times and that any dealer after the time limit may declare
that deal to be his last. Agree the form and details of the
game to be played, and the extent (if any) to which they may
be determined by the current dealer. Agree limits on permissible stakes as explained below. Other matters for agreement are noted as they occur, including penalties for
irregularities. All play proceeds clockwise, i.e., the turn to
deal, order of dealing, order of betting and so on.

STAKE LIMITS To be agreed are (a) the minimum amount a
player may bet at any one time and (b) the maximum he may
bet. These may be fixed values, e.g., 1 and 5 units respectively.
The amount of the ante is usually the same as (a), but may
be less, e.g., ante 1, minimum 2, maximum 5. If *pot limits* are
played, the maximum a player may bet at any time is the
amount in the pot at the time he bets. If *jackpots* is played
(only applicable after a deal in which all players passed
without betting), the minimum bet is raised to the amount
in the pot at the start of the deal. If *table stakes* or *freeze-out*
is played, each player, after a showdown but before the next
deal, sets aside a particular amount, which fixes his own
maximum betting limit for the next deal. He may 'call' for
this amount even if it is less than the previous raise, but if he
wins the pot after others have called for higher amounts, the
difference goes to whichever of those others has the best
hand.

ANTE Before each deal an agreed amount, the *ante*, is staked by every player. Alternatively, and especially if the game is dealer's choice, the dealer alone puts up stakes on behalf of all the players. The ante and all subsequent payments are made by pushing chips towards the centre of the table to constitute the pot, which eventually goes to the winner of the deal. At every stage it should remain clear how much has been staked by each player individually.

DEAL Choose first dealer by any agreed means, after which the deal always passes to the left. Shuffle thoroughly, offer to cut, and deal five cards to each player, one at a time and face down.

OPENERS It may be agreed that no player may open the betting unless he holds a pair of Jacks or higher. (This is often called Jackpots, as it is invariably applied when the staking method of that name is followed.) It may also be agreed that a four-card flush qualifies as a minimum opening requirement. The alternative, if agreed, is to allow an opening on anything.

FIRST BETTING INTERVAL From the left around the table, each in turn may drop, pass, bet, stay or raise. A player *drops* by throwing his hand in face down and remaining inactive for the rest of the deal. Whatever he has staked so far stays in the pot, which he cannot win; but no other charges are incurred by him. He may drop at any time when it is his turn to play, and should announce clearly what he is doing. A player *passes* if no one has yet opened the betting and he wishes to remain in the game but does not hold the minimum opening requirement of Jacks or better. As soon as someone has opened, no subsequent player may pass. If all pass without betting, the hands are thrown in and the next deal ensues. A player opens the *betting* if no one else has yet done so by paying a certain number of chips to the pot and announcing that figure, which must accord with previously agreed limits. He must be able to meet the minimum opening requirement. The amount of the opening bet fixes the sum which subsequent players must pay if they wish to *stay* in the game, unless, and until, it is raised by somebody else. A player *raises* by staking the amount it costs to stay, plus an additional amount in accordance with agreed limits. He should state clearly 'Stay for x, raise y.' This increases the amount (to $x + y$), which succeeding players must pay to stay. As soon as one player's raise has been followed by a round of play in which no one else re-raises but either drops or stays, the bets will have been equalized and the first betting interval ends.

Example In a five-hand game player A passes, B opens for 2 units, C drops, D stays for 2, E stays for 2 and raises 3. Now A stays for 5, B stays for 3 and raises 4, D stays for 7 (the combined amount of the two previous raises), E stays for 4 and A drops. At this point all bets are equalized, the pot containing 32 units plus the antes, with three active players left in the game.

If all players drop save one, he wins the pot without showing his hand – unless he opened the betting, in which case he must show enough of it to prove that he was qualified to do so.

THE DRAW Now the dealer asks each active player in turn whether he wishes to exchange any cards. Each may either *stand pat* (play with the hand as dealt), or reject from one to three cards face down, receiving the same number dealt from the top of the pack. Dealer serves himself last, clearly announcing how many he is taking. The player who opened the betting is permitted to *split openers*, i.e., to throw out one or more of the cards which qualified him to open, but he must announce that he is doing so and keep the relevant rejects to one side for subsequent examination should he win the pot. If there are not enough cards to go round, dealer gathers up all rejects (except any that may be needed to prove split openers), shuffles them together, and continues the deal from this reconstituted pack. Variant: if more than five play it may be agreed that all players exchange any desired number of cards – even all five.

SECOND BETTING INTERVAL Whoever opened the betting in the first interval speaks first in the second. As before, each in turn may drop, check, bet, call (= stay) or raise. A *check* is the equivalent of a pass, but is made for a different reason. The first to speak need not bet first but may pass this privilege on without dropping from the game. In effect, it is a bet of zero units, made with the object of gaining position over the others. Each in turn may do the same, but as soon as someone starts the betting no subsequent player may check. If all players check, the first to do so must open the betting when his turn comes round again. Play continues as before. As soon as one player's raise has been followed by a round in which others either drop or call, but do not re-raise, the second interval is over. If more than one active player remain there is a showdown.

THE SHOWDOWN Starting with the player who was called (made the last raise), each in turn reveals and announces his hand. Whoever has the best hand wins the pot. In the event of absolute equality the pot is shared between the tying players, any odd amount going to the player who was called. If all players dropped save one, he wins the pot without showing his hand (except, if necessary, to prove that he opened legally).

DRAW POKER VARIANTS

Almost any of the rules quoted above may be altered by agreement, or as part of dealer's choice, and one or more cards may be made wild (see pp. 371 and 384). Nearly all such variants have special names. For example, if players are not allowed to check, the game is *pass-out*; in *blind openers* there is no minimum requirement for opening. The following are worth mentioning separately.

ENGLISH POKER Roughly the same as American Blind and Straddle, which went out of use around 1900 in the U.S. After the deal, but before players look at their cards, eldest hand must ante one chip, called the *blind*, and the next in turn put up two, making the *straddle*. Now players look at their cards, and those following the straddle may drop, or stay by paying the same amount as the previous straddle, or straddle again by doubling the previous straddle. When the turn comes round to those who started, they may drop, increase their stakes to the amount of the previous straddle, or double again. Some limit should be agreed to the number of straddles permitted. In one system, doubling ceases at 16 and then proceeds by eights, i.e., 24, 32, etc. The purpose of straddling is to gain position, because after the draw it is the player to the left of the last straddler who has to speak first, thus putting the last straddler in the advantageous position of hearing everybody else before deciding how to proceed. Unless this rule is observed, the point of straddling is lost. (The freak hands named after cats and dogs are particularly associated with this variant; see p. 389.)

LAINO (ROLL 'EM) After the draw (of not more than two cards) players simultaneously reveal one of their cards. There is a betting interval, after which another card is turned, or *rolled*; and so on. After the fourth interval players declare whether they are playing for high or low or both (see High-low, below), and the fifth card is then revealed.

OPEN POKER Each player receives five cards face up. There is a betting interval, and the player with the best hand after the draw wins the pot.

POTS Either on certain specified deals, or throughout the game, a round of pots may be played. If the game is Jack pots, a player may not open on less than a pair of Jacks; if no one is qualified to open, the stakes are left in for the next deal, and so on until the pot is won. If the game is Ace pots, no one may open on less than a pair of Aces, which means that the pot will usually be that much larger by the time someone is qualified to open. In Progressive Pots the round is Jacks to start with, then Queens if no one opens on Jacks, then Kings, then Aces. If still no one opens on Ace pots, the requirement drops back to Kings, Queens, Jacks and so on, like a switchback, until someone has opened.

SHOTGUN Deal three cards each, followed by a betting interval, then a fourth and a fifth, each followed by another betting interval. Then there is a draw, followed by the final betting interval.

SPIT IN THE OCEAN This has given rise to a whole family of variations on the same theme, some of which are shown in fig. 16. In basic spit, each player is dealt four cards, and an extra card, the spit, is dealt face up to the table. This counts as the fifth card in every player's hand, and the game proceeds as usual. The spit and others of its rank may be declared wild.

NON-DRAW VARIANTS

FLAT POKER Originally Straight Poker, the basic game. Players are dealt five cards each; there is a betting interval but no draw; and the winner takes the pot, either by having the best hand at a showdown or by frightening the others into dropping.

SHOWDOWN (COLD HANDS) A pure gamble. Players ante a fixed amount; five cards each are dealt face up; and the player with the best hand wins the pot.

STRAIGHT POKER Similar to Shotgun, but without a draw. Five cards each are dealt, but a betting interval follows the deal of each, making five in all.

LOW HAND VARIANTS

These may be combined with any of the above games and also apply to Stud Poker. To determine the best of competing low hands, see p. 372.

DOUBLE BARREL The pot is won by either the lowest or the highest hand as follows. Minimum openers are specified – say a pair of Jacks. If the game is opened it proceeds as normal, the highest hand winning the pot. If no one can open, however, it changes to Lowball, and the lowest hand wins after a betting interval.

HIGH-LOW POKER The most popular form, in which the pot is shared between the highest and the lowest hands. Play proceeds as normal up to the showdown, except that no openers are specified. Before the show, players announce simultaneously whether they are playing for high or low. (A convenient method is to conceal in the fist a white chip for low, a red chip for high, or both to compete for both. When ready, fists are opened all together.) It is usual for Aces, straights and flushes to count high or low *ad lib*.

LOWBALL The pot is won only by the lowest hand. There is no opening requirement, and it may be agreed to ignore straights and flushes, in which case the lowest possible hand is 5–4–3–2–A.

Stud Poker ◎

7–10 players best
1 pack (52)

The distinguishing features of Stud Poker, a game played for real money and preferred by the experts, are that there is no draw, so that, at Five-Card Stud, ten players are easily accommodated with two cards left over, and most of the cards are dealt face up. This increases the scope for strategic skills, and, as there are more betting intervals than at Draw, the pot is generally much larger. Five-card Stud may be regarded as the basic game, and is described first.

PRELIMINARIES As at Draw, agree the game to be played, a time limit for the last round of deals, rules covering irregularities, and the applications of stake limits.

STAKES Decide whether each player should ante an agreed amount before the deal, or the dealer should ante on behalf of all, or that no ante should be required. Decide the minimum and maximum amounts a player may bet at any one time, and whether or not intervening quantities may be bet. By agreement, a limit may be modified according to circumstance: e.g., (a) the maximum may only be staked by a better showing of at least a pair of Jacks, or (b) a maximum may not be bet until the third or fourth betting interval, or (c) a player may bet any amount up to the size of the pot *(pot limit)*. If *jackpot* is played, the procedure when one player opens and the others all fold is that on the next deal those who folded must each ante the amount bet by the previous opener, which remains in the pot. If this exceeds the maximum limit, it establishes a new one for that deal.

DEAL Shuffle thoroughly, offer to cut, and deal one card face down to each player followed by one card face up.

FIRST BETTING INTERVAL After each player has secretly examined his hole-card (that dealt face down), the player dealt the highest upcard (face up) opens the betting by staking an amount according with the limits agreed. If more than one player ties for rank, the one of them who is first left of the dealer opens. Each succeeding player in turn must then either fold, stay or raise. A player *folds* by throwing his cards in and remaining inactive for the rest of the deal, *stays* by increasing his stake to the same total as that of the previous active player, or *raises* by increasing his stake to the requisite amount and adding an additional amount. Each player should state clearly what he is doing and how much he is paying. When one player raises and the turn reaches his right-hand active player without any other raises made, all bets are equalized and the first betting interval ends. If all have folded save one, he wins the pot without further play, unless he was the only one to bet and jackpot stakes are being played (see above).

FURTHER PLAY The dealer now deals another card face up to each player, and a second betting interval is opened by the player showing the two best upcards. For this purpose a pair beats a non-pair, a higher beats a lower rank, and ties are decided as before. In this and subsequent intervals, players may not only fold, stay or raise but also *check*. To check is to stay in the game without paying. The player due to open may check instead, passing the turn on to his left-hand active player, and this privilege rotates until someone opens the betting. As soon as it is opened, no succeeding player may check. If all players check, the interval ends and the next cards are dealt. Otherwise the interval ends when bets have been equalized. Thereafter a fourth and a fifth card are dealt face up to each player, and each is followed by a betting interval initiated by the player showing the best combination (four of a kind, three of a kind, two pair, one pair, highest card etc.).

SHOWDOWN If, at any stage of the game, all players fold save one, he wins the pot. Otherwise the game ends when all bets have been equalized in the fourth interval (i.e., all players having five cards each). For this purpose each player reveals his hole card, and the best hand wins the pot. If wild cards are used, each player must state what his combination is intended to be, and may not change his first announcement.

STUD VARIANTS

There are numerous variants. The most basic forms are described below. The first betting interval usually follows the deal of the first upcard. Even in Five-card, the last card may be dealt face down instead of up, and the same applies to other forms according to the choice of the dealer. Where more than five cards are dealt, each player selects any five as his final hand in the showdown.

BULL Each player receives three hole cards, arranges them in any order he chooses, and bets. Four upcards are dealt, with betting after each. Each then turns up his hole cards one by one in predetermined order, with betting following each turn.

EIGHT-CARD STUD Two down, four up, one down, the last either way by agreement or dealer's choice, with six betting intervals.

ENGLISH SEVEN-CARD At the end of the third betting interval, when all have two down and three up, each player rejects one card before receiving his sixth and another before receiving his seventh, the sixth and seventh being dealt up or down to match the reject, and followed by a betting interval. A player may stand pat, but if he does so on the sixth he must do so on the seventh. Thus the last three bets are made on a five-card hand.

FOUR FORTY-FOUR Four down, four up, four betting intervals, Fours wild.

MEXICAN STUD (FLIP) The first two are dealt face down, and each player chooses which of his two to turn up. In further extensions, every card is dealt face down, and the player may either turn it up or keep it down and turn up his previous hole card instead.

NINE-CARD STUD Two down, four up, two down, last up or down.

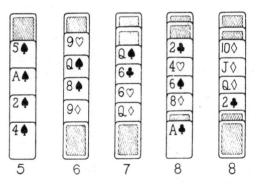

14. STUD POKER Basic forms of Stud. Usually the first betting interval takes place after the deal of the first upcard, and another interval after each subsequent card.

PIG STUD A cross between Stud and Draw. Three down, bet; two up, bet after each. Then players take all five into hand, and draw and play exactly as at Draw Poker.

SEVEN-CARD STUD Has always been more popular than Five-card in England, and for home play has become so in America. Usually two down, four up, one down. In Seven-card Flip, each receives four face down and chooses any two as his upcards. In Seven-toed Pete, Sevens are wild. In Seven-card Lowball (Razz) the lowest hand wins the pot.

SIX-CARD STUD Usually one down, four up, one down, with five betting intervals.

TEN-CARD STUD Two down, four up, three down, last up or down.

THREE FORTY-FIVE Three down, four up, one down, five intervals, Fives wild.

FURTHER VARIANTS (DRAW AND STUD)

As previously indicated, the range of variations permitted under Dealer's Choice is too wide, confused and transient for definitive enumeration. Major lines of variation are here sketched under seven headings for convenience, but even they are not mutually exclusive: rules of one type may be combined in the same deal with features from one or more others, and the result may have several different names. It is up to the dealer to specify the rules of his choice and the name of the game.

WILD CARD VARIANTS One or more cards may be designated wild. Originally the Joker was added as a 53rd card which could be used to represent any other. Later, its use was restricted: as the *Bug* it may represent an Ace or be used to fill a straight flush. Nowadays it is more usually dropped in favour of specified wild cards. Good balance is achieved by nominating one rank as wild, typically deuces. Also

15. WILD CARD POKER If deuces are wild, this hand is at best four Kings, though if the King and Jack were of the same suit it would be a royal flush. If one-eyed Jacks are wild, it is at best four deuces. If all moustaches are wild, it is five deuces. If moustaches *and* deuces are wild, it is anything you care to name.

popular are specified court cards, such as those which are 'one-eyed' (i.e., depicted in profile), or those wearing moustaches (usually three Kings and two Jacks, rarely Queens), or those facing left (varying from pack to pack). Games in which all 12 courts are wild, or even all 13 cards of one suit, are not so much wild as lunatic. In Spit variants (see below) wild cards vary from deal to deal. A player may be permitted to count as wild the lowest rank he holds, or any other of his cards. In Stud Poker, he may count as wild his hole card and any others he holds of that rank. Obviously, the greater the proportion of wild cards, the less skill and more chance comes into play. Four or five is usually enough.

SPIT VARIANTS Spit in the ocean, already described as a form of Draw, has given rise to a whole family of similar variants. Some are illustrated in fig. 16.

PASS-ON VARIANTS Several games have been devised in which a player may pass on unwanted cards to an opponent, a generic title being Pass the Garbage, or Trash. Typically, each receives seven cards, passes three face down to his left

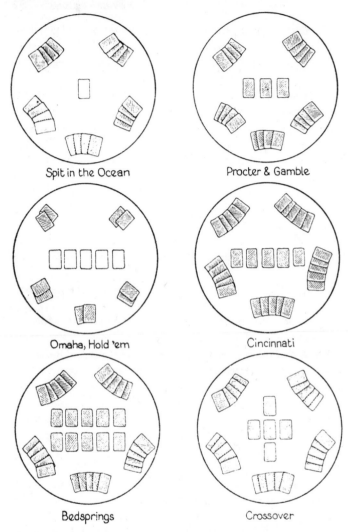

Spit in the Ocean

Procter & Gamble

Omaha, Hold 'em

Cincinnati

Bedsprings

Crossover

16. COMMUNAL CARD (SPIT) VARIANTS The ancestral form is Spit in the Ocean, in which each receives four cards and a communal card is dealt face up. This counts as the fifth card in each player's hand, and it and others of its rank may be designated wild. In Procter and Gamble, three communal cards are dealt face down. They are then *rolled* (faced) one at a time, with a betting interval after each. The rank of the third to be rolled is wild. In Omaha, two each are dealt and a betting interval follows. Then five more are dealt face up one at a time with an interval after

and similarly receives three from his right, then selects five of the seven as his playing hand. In a variant called Anaconda, these are then played as at Laino or Roll 'em (p. 378).

PACK LENGTH VARIANTS One or more ranks, usually from deuces upward, may be stripped out to shorten the pack to 48, 44, 40, etc., cards, or the game may be played, as in Europe, with standard short packs such as the 40-card Italian or 32-card French pack. The fewer the cards, the rarer flushes become, though this is not always taken into account in the relative ranking of hands. One of the earliest forms of Poker was played by four players with only 20 cards (AKQJT), flushes and straights being ignored. In Pinochle Poker, the 48-card Pinochle double pack is used. In this, five of a kind is the top hand, a flush without duplicated ranks is beaten by a flush with one pair, and that by a flush with two pair.

NUMBER DEALT VARIANTS The following may be noted in addition to Stud played with six or more cards.

One-card Poker There is no draw (unless the dealer specifies otherwise), and the highest rank wins, or splits with the lowest in High-low.

---

each. This has developed into the currently popular Hold 'em, in which the first three communal cards are dealt together, cutting out two betting intervals. In Cincinnati, five each are dealt, there is a betting interval, then the five centre cards are rolled singly with an interval after each. In Bedsprings the centre cards are arranged as shown and rolled singly with a betting interval after each. Each player may count any pair of vertically adjacent cards as part of his hand, and any five of those seven as his playing hand. In Crossover, a betting interval takes place after the roll of each arm of the cross, and finally of the centre card. Each player selects as his playing hand any five from the cards he holds plus either the vertical or the horizontal three of the cross. There are countless variations on each of these basic patterns. In all of them, each player selects any five cards from those he holds plus any of the communal cards according to the rules of the particular variation being played.

Indian Poker More of a party game. Each is dealt one card and, without looking at it, places it against his forehead like the feather of an Indian brave with its face outwards so that all but himself may see it. Betting proceeds as usual.

Two-card Poker May be played Stud or Draw; it is known as Hurricane if played High-low and Dynamite if with wild cards. A pair beats a non-pair, a higher rank a lower.

Three-card Poker (Monte) As Two-card. Three of a kind beats a flush but not a straight flush.

Four-card Poker As above, but four of a kind beats a straight flush.

Acey Deucey Two card stud with a draw. Deal one down, one up. Each in turn may draw one card at a time as often as he wishes, dealt up or down to match the card rejected. When all are satisfied, there is a betting interval.

FREAK HAND VARIANTS Non-standard or unorthodox Poker combinations are listed below in order of ranking from highest to lowest, together with standard hands to show which they beat. Any of these may be acceptable in Dealer's Choice, though some are more recognized than others. In so-called Canadian Poker the fourstraight and fourflush are accepted as showdown hands as well as qualifying for openers, and big and little cats and dogs were devised for Blind and Straddle particularly. (Cats are alternatively known as tigers.)

Three pairs In six or more card Stud, a sixth card may be be kept to form three pairs, which beats everything.

Five of a kind Accepted in any form of wild-card Poker.

Straight flush Standard. In some circles a royal straight flush beats five of a kind.

Skeet flush A flush hand containing 9, 5, 2 and two intervening ranks.

Skip flush A flush hand with alternating sequence, e.g., J–9–7–5–3.

Blaze fours Four Jacks, Queens or Kings plus another court card, but beaten by four Aces.

Four of a kind Standard.

Big bobtail Four-card straight flush. If the fifth card makes a pair, the hand beats any unpaired bobtail.

Blaze full A full house consisting entirely of court cards.

Full house Standard.

Double Ace flush Non-straight flush containing an Ace and a wild card representing the same Ace.

Flush Standard.

Big cat Non-flush hand with King high, Eight low and no pair.

Little cat As above, with Eight high and Three low.

Big dog As above, with Ace high and Nine low.

Little dog As above, with Seven high and Two low. (Dogs sometimes rank above cats: agree beforehand.)

Five and ten As above, with Ten high and Five low.

Straight zebra A straight in suits of alternating colour (e.g., ♠9–♥8–♠7–♦6–♠5).

Straight Standard.

Round the corner straight Lower than 5–4–3–2–A is 4–3–2–A–K, then 3–2–A–K–Q, and 2–A–K–Q–J lowest of all.

Skip or Dutch straight Non-flush alternating sequence, e.g., Q–T–8–6–4.

Skeet or pelter Non-flush hand with 9, 5, 2 and two different intervening ranks.

Kilter or pelter Non-flush hand with 9 high, 2 low and no pair.

Zebra or *striped straight* Non-sequential unpaired hand in which colours alternate from high to low (e.g., ♠K–♥9–♣8–♥4–♣2).

Blaze threes Five court cards forming not better than three of a kind.

Three of a kind Standard.

Little bobtail A three-card straight flush. If tied, highest top card wins; if still tied, hand with more pairs wins, or highest odd card if no pairs.

Flash Hand containing one card of each suit plus the Joker, when used, representing an imaginary fifth suit.

Blaze Five court cards forming not better than two pair.

Two pair Standard.

Fourflush Four cards of the same suit but not in sequence. If the fifth card makes a pair, the hand beats any unpaired fourflush.

Fourstraight Four cards in sequence but not flush. If the fifth card makes a pair, the hand beats any unpaired fourstraight.

One pair Standard.

High card = no combination (standard).

Seventy-five Non-flush 7–5–4–3–2, the lowest possible hand in High-low Poker when strict rules apply.

Swinging Ace low Non-flush 6–4–3–2–A, the lowest possible if it is permitted to count Ace high or low *ad lib.*

Wheel or *bicycle* 5–4–3–2–A, the lowest possible hand in Lowball, in which Ace may count low and straights and flushes are ignored.

Yet other methods of comparing hands are employed in some games acceptable as Dealer's Choice; see below.

DEALER'S CHOICE GAMES

The following are not strictly forms of Poker at all, but are recorded as acceptable by Dealer's Choice.

BEAT YOUR NEIGHBOUR Each is dealt five cards in a face down pile. The first faces his top card and a betting interval ensues. The second turns his top card. If it is not higher than the previous player's, he turns his second, and so on, until he reaches a higher card. If he reaches a higher card, a second round ensues. If none of his five is higher, he drops out of play. Each in turn does the same, turning cards until he reaches one higher than any before, followed by a betting interval, or dropping out otherwise. The last player in wins the pot.

BEST FLUSH Draw Poker, in which only flushes and part flushes count. The best hand is the one with the greatest number of cards of the same suit. If equal, highest rank decides.

BUTCHER BOY Cards are dealt one at a time face up around the table. When a second card of the same rank appears, it is given to the player who received the first. He initiates a round of betting, in which players may drop, check, stay or raise. More cards are dealt, starting with the player who was next due for a card when the duplicate appeared. The pot is won by the last left in, or the first to receive four of a kind.

KNOCK POKER Played like Knock Rummy, with five each, a stockpile and a waste pile. As soon as one player is satisfied with his Poker hand, he knocks after discarding. Others are permitted one more draw and discard, and the best hand wins. As there is no betting, the players or (preferably) dealer alone should previously ante.

PUT AND TAKE All but the dealer receive five cards face up. Dealer turns up the top card of the remaining pack, and anyone who has a card of the same rank pays him one chip for it (or for each if he has more than one). Upon turning the second he receives 2 chips for each card of the same rank held, then 3 for the third, 4 for the fourth, 5 for the fifth (or, in some circles, respectively 1, 2, 4, 8, 16). He then turns up the next five, but this time pays out to players with matching cards, following the same schedule as before.

RED AND BLACK (PLUS AND MINUS) Played like Draw Poker, but without Poker hands. Instead, cards have a point value: Ace 1, others face value, courts 10 each. Red cards count plus value, black cards minus. The best hand is the one with the highest total point value. Often played High-low.

WHISKY POKER (Spelt with an 'e' if Irish or Bourbon, without if Scotch.) In this version of Commerce played with Poker hands, five cards are dealt to each player and to a dummy hand – the widow – face down on the table. After anteing and looking at his cards, each in turn from the left around may take the widow up and lay his dealt hand face up in its place. As soon as somebody does so this privilege ends, and play proceeds from the player on his left. If no one exchanges, dealer turns the widow face up and the player on his left begins. At each turn a player may exchange his whole hand for the widow, or any number of cards between the two. As soon as he has made an exchange which gives him a satisfactory hand, he knocks. The others have one more turn each, after which there is a showdown and the best hand wins the pot.

ZEBRA POKER Draw Poker, in which hands count only if they are *zebras* (alternating in colour from high to low; see Freak variants). The one with the highest top card wins, or second highest, etc., to break a tie.

NOTES ON PLAY

Poker is a game of probabilities and personalities, and personalities play a far greater part than in any other card game. At any given stage of play there is always a fixed and precise mathematical probability that you are holding the best hand, but even a player capable of calculating that probability will not always win if he exactly matches his bet to it. A substantial part of that calculation must be based on an appraisal of what lies behind opponents' course of action, and these are rarely based upon logic; more upon habit, whim and deliberate inconsistency – otherwise called psychology. In short, it is not enough to learn the mathematics by heart and follow them blindly. You must also observe and know your opponents, and give nothing of your own game away by predictable habits and methods of play.

The first rule for beginners who think Poker is all chance and bluff is a hard one to abide by, but cannot be overestimated. It is: only stay in the game if you genuinely believe you have the best hand. If in doubt, pull out, and wait for your run of cards to come along. As to whether you have the best hand, this must be determined by both theory and practice. In five-hand Draw Poker, theory suggests that if you are dealt a pair of Aces you probably have the best hand, and should open on them in first position or otherwise first to speak (i.e., if others have passed). In practice, however, you may find yourself lying fourth or fifth to speak and having to follow an opening bet followed by a stay and a raise. The probabilities in favour of your Aces up are now somewhat reduced by the actions that have already taken place. This also demonstrates the importance of position. As last to speak, you have the advantage of being able to assess your hand on the basis of what you have heard and seen from previous players. Conversely, the man *under the gun* (first to speak) is at the greatest disadvantage. In Draw Poker, whoever opens puts himself under the gun after the draw, a fact which makes it all the more necessary to open on an openable hand and pass a poor one.

If you are sure of having the best hand, your next object is to make the most of it. Skill here lies in knowing exactly how to string opponents along with you. Bet too high and there is a danger that all will drop and leave you with a cheap pot; too low, and you may be called too soon. Whether to check, raise or call in this situation cannot be answered by general rules: it depends entirely on how the others are betting.

In five-hand Draw Poker played without wild cards, the average pot is won on three of a kind, or two pair with Jacks or better. In the opening deal, a pair of Jacks will go on to win just under half the time, a pair of Queens just over. This is what sets the limit when jackpots is played, and in any case determines a commonsense minimum hand on which to open even where none is demanded. The commonsense minimum increases if more than four players have to speak after yourself, for example if you are under the gun in a seven-hand game, or if you are in a late position and someone has already opened. Local rules may permit you to open on a four-card straight or flush, but without wild cards it is rarely worth staying on such a hand, let alone opening. The most deceptive opening hand is two low pairs, because it is nearly always the best hand in the game before the draw but rarely so afterwards. As it is not worth backing two pair against more than two opponents, the usual strategy on such a hand is to raise before the draw in order to frighten others into dropping and so reduce the opposition. Two pair or not, raising before the draw generally suggests an attempt to reduce the number of opponents, a fact which will enter into everybody's assessment of the probable situation.

The sensible player does not draw unless he has something worth drawing to, for which reason the exchange of more than three cards is nonsensical. Three are normally drawn against a pair, and two against three of a kind. Some players will sometimes or always keep a high 'kicker' and draw two to a pair, for example by throwing the low cards from A–J– J–4–2. The hope is to draw either a third Jack or a second Ace, in the latter case ensuring a win if no one exceeds two pair. The chances of improving are measurably reduced by the rejection of only two cards instead of three, but against this may be set the possible deceptive value of suggesting one holds three of a kind. The player who stands pat may be lucky enough to have been dealt a straight or better, or may with equal unlikelihood be running a risky bluff on two high pairs or even less. But the most intriguing draw of all is of one card only. This move is most frequently made from two pair, with the object of drawing a full house, and is also justifiable in the rarer event of a four-card straight flush, such as ♠9–8–7–6–♦2, as there are not unreasonable prospects of getting a straight or a flush if not both. It may, however, also be made from a four-card flush or open straight, provided that the player thinks he can afford the risk by reference to how well up he is in the game, what the chances are against him, and the odds offered by the pot. (An outside straight is one that can be filled by either of two ranks, such as J–T–9–8. No player in his right mind draws one card to an inside straight such as Q–J–9–8 or an end straight such as A–K–Q–J, unless they are all of a suit.)

Few guidelines can be offered for the period after the draw, beyond repeating earlier suggestions. If you have failed to improve, have the courage to drop before it is too late, and be wary of backing two pair against more than two opponents. If you believe you have the best hand, keep going, and keep raising just enough to fatten the pot without frightening people out. Don't just keep calling. This procedure is not so much defensive as defeatist, especially if you are being 'sandwiched' – a situation which occurs when players A and C keep raising and re-raising, making it impossible for middleman B to call at a price he can afford.

At Five-card Stud, the average winning hand is lower than at Draw because there is no opportunity to improve the hand. Because there are more betting intervals at Stud, it is rare for much raising to take place before the last round, and not unusual for a round to be passed out entirely by a series of checks. Generally, the object of each round is to establish who is staying in and who is folding.

The most important round of betting is the first, the orthodox opening requirement being a pair back to back or an Ace in the hole. Throughout the play, it is axiomatic to fold whenever you cannot beat anything visible on the table – for example, with (Q)-9-4 against (?)-8-8. At Seven-card, the usual minimum opening requirement is one pair, three cards to a flush or in sequence, or two cards higher in rank than any unpaired card showing.

The introduction of wild cards to any form of the game renders the calculations more complex, the general effect being to raise the level at which the various combinations can compete. Experienced players can be expected to cope with up to four cards wild, such as all the deuces, which is enough to increase the skill factor without going too far. But an excessive number of wild cards renders calculation so inhumanly complex that to all intents and purposes Poker is reduced to merely a game of chance.

Brag ◎

3 or more players, 5–6 best
1 pack (52)

As one of the few games Hoyle really did write about (in 1751) Brag has a long history and is even now evolving faster than most books can keep up with. Its forerunners included Primero, as advertised in Shakespeare, and a game called Post and Pair, while Poker may be regarded as one of its descendants. The form described below may be described as modern Brag as currently played in and around London.

CARDS Use a standard 52-card pack. Individual cards and Brag hands rank as shown in Table 8.

PRELIMINARIES Agree stake limits. The turn to deal passes to the left after each hand, and a game may be of any length so long as all deal an equal number of times.

TABLE 8: THREE-CARD BRAG HANDS

Name	Meaning	Number of possible hands	Probability of being dealt
Prial	three of the same rank (e.g., 7–7–7)	52	0·2%
Flush run	three in suit and sequence (e.g., ♠6–7–8)	48	0·2%
Run	any three in sequence (e.g., 6–7–8)	720	3·2%
Flush	any three in suit (e.g., ♠-♠-♠)	1096	5·0%
Pair	two only of same rank (e.g., 7–7–X)	3744	17·0%
High card	no combination, highest card wins	16,440	74·4%
Total number of different three-card hands		22,100	

Cards rank high-low AKQJT98765432, but Ace may count low in sequence A–2–3. Between identical combinations the highest-ranking top card wins, or second-highest to break a tie. A higher pair beats a lower, but equal pairs are decided on the odd card. Note that a prial beats a flush run even though marginally easier to get. In some schools a prial (= pair royal) of Threes beats any other and the sequence A–2–3 beats Q–K–A. The probability quoted refers to that of receiving the stated hand upon being dealt three cards from a perfectly shuffled pack, though the game is not usually played in that way.

DEAL Dealer antes (stakes a previously agreed amount) and deals three cards each, face down, one at a time. He then stacks the remainder face *up* on his left. Dealt cards remain face down for the time being.

PLAY Eldest hand may bet with or without looking at his cards. If he looks at them he may either bet, by placing his stake on the table before him, or drop out of play. If he drops, he stacks his cards face up on the pack and takes no further part in the hand. If he bets blind (without looking) he should not touch his cards.

The next in turn may bet blind, or look at his cards and either bet or stack as described above. If he bets it must be an amount at least equal to the first player's. But if the first bet blind, and the second open, the second must bet at least double that of the first; or, if the first bet open and the second blind, the second may not bet more than half that of the first. Throughout play anyone who has looked at his cards must bet at least double the amount of the previous blind bettor.

Each player thereafter has the same options. A player who bets blind must increase his stake to at least the same amount as the previous blind bettor, and a player who bets open must increase his to at least that of the previous open bettor. On subsequent rounds a blind player may, at his turn to bet, either continue to bet blind or look at his cards and then either stack them or bet open. In the latter event he must increase his stake to that of the previous open bettor. At any point a player who stacks drops out of play, his stakes being left for the eventual winner.

A player who stakes the least amount required to remain in merely stays and should announce that fact ('Stay for *x* pence'). A player who increases his stake announces 'Stay for *x*, raise *y* pence'.

SHOWDOWN Play continues until all but two have dropped. If both are playing open, either may call to see the other upon matching his opponent's previous stake. The caller may admit defeat without showing his hand, in which case the other wins all the stakes on the table; otherwise, if his hand is better, he must show it to win. There is a rule that 'You can't see a blind man'. If both are betting blind they must continue to raise until one looks at his cards; if the latter then stacks, the former wins everything without showing his hand. If one is betting open, and the other blind, the open bettor must continue to double the blind man's stake. (In some circles one may call for a showdown if both are betting blind – i.e., only a blind man can see a blind man.)

If the stakes are won by a blind bettor, he is permitted to keep the same hand for the next deal provided that he does not look at it before his first turn to bet. (In this event it is customary to include him in the next deal, his new hand being automatically turned up and stacked 'in order to keep the sequence of the cards'.)

The next dealer does not shuffle the cards unless a prial occurred in the previous round.

VARIANTS

AMERICAN BRAG Basically the same as textbook or Classical Brag, as described under that heading below, except that all Jacks and all Nines are braggers or wild cards. A hand with one or more braggers beats an otherwise equal hand with fewer or none, so the highest possible hand consists of three braggers. No bragger is better than another, so ties are more frequent.

BASTARD Brag equivalent of Whisky Poker. All contribute equally to a pool. Deal three cards each and a spare hand face up. Each in turn must exchange either *one* or *all three* of his cards with one or all of the spare hand – not two. When a player thinks he has the best hand he knocks. The others may stick or exchange once more. Best hand wins the pool.

CLASSICAL BRAG Shuffle and deal three cards each. A prial beats a pair and a pair beats three unrelated cards. Runs and flushes do not count. There are three wild cards called braggers, each of which may be used by its holder to represent any desired card: they are ♣J ♦A ♦9. Of two competing hands of the same type, that with the greater number of braggers wins; if still equal, high card decides. Players look at their hands and each in turn may drop out of play or bet. The first player may bet any amount; thereafter each player must increase his stake to at least that of the previous player still in the game, either equalling it or exceeding it (raising). If one player raises and the others either equalize or drop out instead of raising further, there is a showdown and the player with the best hand wins all the stakes, including those of players who dropped. If all players but one drop out, the one left in wins without revealing his hand. This is the form of the game perpetuated in most books, but braggers seem generally to have dropped out with the introduction of runs and flushes.

CRASH A contemporary pub game involving Brag hands; but not a betting game as such.

SEVEN- AND NINE-CARD BRAG To increase the incidence of the rarer hands, which include runs and flushes, players may be dealt seven or nine cards, from which they select three as their betting hand and discard the others face down. Generally, the highest hand in seven-card Brag is a prial of Sevens, and in nine-card a prial of Nines.

THREE-STAKE BRAG An older form of the game, disregarding runs and flushes, and counting only prials and pairs. Before the deal each player puts up three separate stakes. Players are then dealt three cards each, two face down and the last face up. The player with the highest faced card wins the first stake, which, in the event of a tie, goes to the player nearest the dealer's left (himself being farthest from his own left). Next, the other cards are taken into hand and a normal round of Brag betting ensues, the second stakes going to the player with the best hand. For this purpose braggers are included (♣J ♦A ♦9 being wild cards). Finally, all cards are exposed and the third stake goes to the player whose cards most nearly total a combined pip-count of 31, counting Ace 11, pictures 10 and others face value. The total may be under or over; only the difference counts. A player whose cards total under 31 may draw another card, but if this brings him to over 31 he loses. Ties are decided as for the high card round.

POKER-BRAG RELATIVES

Ancestral games based on the same betting principles and similar combinations include the following.

AMBIGU Game of Italian origin popular in eighteenth-century France, played by two to seven players with a 40-card pack (no Eights, Nines, Tens). Four dealt, with an interval after each two. From highest down, *fredon* = fours, *flux* = flush, *tricon* = threes, *prime* = straight, *point* = pair.

AS NAS Persian game said to have been played by four players with 20 cards; five each dealt; straight and flushes not recognized.

BOUILLOTTE (= hot water bottle!) Revised form of Brelan which emerged in early nineteenth-century Paris to overcome prohibitions on that game. Usually played by five with 28 cards (Eight low), or by four with 20 cards lacking Tens and Jacks. A 'spit' game, with three each dealt plus a communal upcard.

BRELAN (from *Berlan*) Dating from the sixteenth century, played by three to five players with a 32-card pack. Three each were dealt and the best hand was three of a kind, with Jacks beating everything.

GILET An old French game similar to Brelan.

GLEEK A curious three-hand game played in seventeenth-century England with 44 cards (lacking Twos and Threes) and involving tricks as well as Poker-like betting. Possibly = Glic, a French game mentioned in the sixteenth-century and said to have been played as late as the nineteenth-century. See Cotton's *Compleat Gamester*.

POCHEN, POCHSPIEL A German member of the family, played by three to six with a 52-card pack. After staking to compartments labelled A, K, Q, J, T, marriage, sequence, *poch*, players received five cards each and a trump was turned. Contents of A, K, Q, J and T compartments went to holders of those trumps, or were carried forward if no one claimed. Holder of King and Queen of trumps collected for marriage as well, while sequence went to the holder of the longest, trumps winning if equal. Anyone with a pair or better then stayed in to compete for poch, with raising, staying or dropping as at Poker. The best three of a kind won, or the best pair if none.

PRIMERO, PRIMIERA Italian game described by Cardano in sixteenth century as 'the noblest of them all'; popular in England under Henry VIII and Elizabeth I (both keen players); said to be still played by Italian Americans. Four play with a 40-card pack carrying point-values thus: Two = 12, Three 13, Four 14, Five 15, Ace 16, Six 18, Seven 21, courts 10 each. Each received four cards. Hands originally ranked from high to low: *chorus* = fours, *fluxus* = flush, *supremus* = A–6–7 of one suit, *primero* = one card of each suit, *numerus* = two or three cards flush. As between equal hands, the one with the highest point count won. Modern accounts describe play like Commerce and omit highest and lowest of combinations described above.

Commerce ◎

3 to 12 players
1 pack (52)

The method of this game, possibly ancestral to Poker and Brag, particularly resembles Whisky Poker and Bastard Brag, not to mention the game of Thirty-One. It can be happily played by children for buttons. If played strictly, the order of play is anti-clockwise, eldest hand being the player on dealer's right.

COMMERCE HANDS The object is to acquire the best Commerce hand, ranking from high to low as follows:

Tricon. Three of the same rank, Aces highest, Twos lowest.

Sequence. Three cards in suit and sequence, from A–K–Q high to 3–2–A low.

Point. The greatest pip-value on two or three cards of the same suit, counting Ace 11, courts 10, others face value. If equal, a three-card beats a two-card flush. If still equal, the tied player nearest in turn after the dealer wins, dealer himself, however, having absolute priority.

Flushes and pairs may be introduced, but one might as well play with Brag hands.

CARDS 52, running AKQJT98765432 (A).

POOL Each contributes an equal amount to a pool.

DEAL Three each and three face up to the table to form a widow.

PLAY Dealer may start by exchanging his whole hand for the widow. Whether he does or not, eldest hand and each in turn after him exchanges one card of his hand for one card of the widow. When a player is satisfied with his hand he knocks on the table and ceases play. When two have knocked all play ceases and the player with the best hand wins the pool.

VARIANT

TRADE OR BARTER No widow is dealt. Starting with eldest, each in turn may trade or barter. To trade, he gives the dealer a card face up and a counter, which does not go to the pool but is profit to the dealer. Dealer then deals him a card face down from the pack and the turn passes. To barter, he offers a card face down to the player next in turn, who must accept or refuse without seing what it is. If he accepts he takes it in exchange for an unwanted card from his own hand and it is then his turn to play. If not, he knocks on the table to indicate that he is satisfied with his hand, and play ceases. Play continues until someone knocks, when the best hand wins the pool. If the dealer does not win the pool he pays one counter to the winner. If he has point, sequence or tricon, and still fails to win, he pays one to every player. A player dealt a good hand may knock immediately and prevent any trading.

Related Games

THIRTY-FIVE An adding-up game, like Pontoon, except that there is no banker. Up to five can play. Cards count face value (Ace 1, courts 10) and the object is to get a number of cards *of the same suit* which total as close as possible to 35, whether under or over that target. Players ante an agreed amount to the pool. Deal one card to each player, face down, dealer last, and then an extra card face down to the middle of the table. Repeat until each player and the table has four cards. Then deal five more cards each so that each player has nine. The four table cards constitute the widow and players now bid for the right to buy it. Each in turn either throws his cards in or offers an amount which is not greater than the pool but not less than the previous bidder's offer. Whoever bids most rejects any four cards from his hand and takes the widow in their place. If he now can produce 35 or more in one suit he wins from the pool the amount of his bid; if not, he pays that amount in. If a player is originally dealt 35 + in suit he wins the pool without play (shared if necessary).

THIRTY-ONE Another numerical game, similar in mechanics to Whisky Poker and Bastard Brag. About half a dozen players are dealt three cards each, and three more are dealt face up to the table as a widow. Ace counts 11, courts 10 and others face value, and the object is to get as close to possible to a total of 31 on cards of the same suit or, failing that, three cards of the same rank, which counts 30½. Each in turn draws one card from the widow and replaces it with a card from his hand. As soon as a player thinks he has the best hand he knocks on the table, and each opponent may then either stick with the cards he has or make one more exchange. Cards are revealed and the player with the highest suit-total wins the pool, unless beaten by three of a kind. Tied hands share it.

TRENTA CINQUE This Italian game, of which Thirty-five is the American version, is played by four players with a 40-card pack lacking Eights, Nines and Tens, counting numerals face value and courts 10 each. The target, as before, is 35 in one suit. Deal nine each and a widow of four face down. Everyone antes five chips to the pool, and each in turn either passes or bids up to five for the privilege of taking the widow. A higher bid supersedes a lower, but two or more may stay in if they bid five each, in which case the widow goes to whichever of them has the highest count in one suit. The purchaser takes the widow, and wins the pool if he can now produce cards of one suit totalling 35 or more. If not, he loses his bid to the pool, which is carried forward to the next deal. If a player was originally dealt a hand lacking any court card, or containing K–Q–J of one suit, he stays in and collects 2 chips from each opponent.

Banking Games

Pontoon, alias Blackjack, Twenty-one, Vingt-Un etc., is the best and most popular member of the family of essentially gambling games distinguished from Poker and Brag by the fact that participants play against the dealer/banker, who usually has the advantage over them. The superiority of Pontoon is due to the fact that it gives players a fair amount of choice in play and so permits the application of skill. Many other games played against a bank are purely betting games and so more appropriate to casino than to home play. Omitted from the following chapter for that reason are such traditional gambles as Card Bingo, Faro, Lasquenet, Racing Aces, Stuss and others of their ilk.

Pontoon ◎

3–10 players, 4–6 best
1 pack (52)

We had a pleasant game of cards, though I lost four shillings and
Carrie lost one, and Gowing said he had lost about sixpence: how
he *could* have lost, considering that Carrie and I were the only
other players, remains a mystery.

(G. and W. Grossmith, The Diary of a Nobody, 1892)

Pontoon was formerly known as Vingt-un or Twenty-one
and is similar to the American game of Blackjack. It is the
best known and best loved, at least in Britain, of an age-old
family of games in which the object is to acquire cards whose
combined face values most closely approach a given total –
in this case 21. Although probably the most popular card
game of the armed forces in both world wars, and now much
played in casinos in its American form, it remains essentially
the small-stake game of home and pub. It is one of the few
banking games to reward skill, and hence one of the few
that can be played for love as well as money. There is no
acceptable 'book standard'. Different schools have different
rules, and that is how it should be.

CARDS Use a standard 52-card pack. Suits are irrelevant:
all that counts is the numerical face-value of the cards.
From Two to Ten count 2 to 10 respectively, court cards
count 10 each, and Ace counts either 1 or 11 at its holder's
discretion. It is convenient to refer to cards worth 10 as
tenths.

PRELIMINARIES Pontoon is a banking game and requires
counters, chips, coins or other manageable objects. The
banker deals and the punters play against him. Agree
beforehand how the bankership is to change hands: e.g.,
each player deals/banks in turns passing to the left, or the
bank goes to a punter who beats the banker with a *pontoon*,

or it may be bought at any time for a mutually acceptable sum. Agree to end play at a particular time.

DEAL Banker shuffles the cards before his first deal, but not thereafter, so the pack remains unshuffled until the next takes over. Deal one card each, face down, dealer's last. All except the banker may look at their card.

OBJECTIVES Everyone will get a second card, and more may be bought thereafter. The object is to finish with a better hand than the banker's. A hand whose cards total over 21 is bust, and loses. A hand totalling 16 to 21 beats the banker only if the latter has a lower counting or bust hand. There are also three special hands:

Pontoon is 21 on two cards, i.e., an Ace and a tenth. This beats the banker, unless he also has a pontoon, and wins double.

Royal Pontoon is three Sevens (= 21). The banker cannot beat this even with a pontoon. Furthermore, only a punter counts a royal pontoon: three Sevens for the banker counts as an ordinary 21 and is beaten by a punter's pontoon. It wins treble stakes.

Five card trick. A hand of five cards that is not bust. This beats anything the banker has, except another five card trick, and wins double stakes.

SECOND CARD Each punter looks at his first card and stakes upon it an amount that lies within previously agreed limits, entitling him to receive a second card. The banker deals everybody a second card, the last going to himself, at which point he now looks at both his cards. If he has a pontoon he shows it and wins, collecting double everybody's stakes. If not, he says 'play'. If now a punter has a pontoon he indicates that fact by turning the Ace face up, and receives no more cards.

SPLITTING If a punter has two cards of identical rank (two different tenths will not do) he may split them and play two hands if he wishes. He indicates this by separating them on the table and staking on the second card the same amount as he staked on the first. The banker then deals another card face down to each hand. Again, if either hand is a pontoon, the punter faces the Ace and, if either is a pair, he is allowed to split again, and so on. The banker may not split his own cards.

ADDITIONAL CARDS The banker now addresses himself to each punter in turn, not proceeding to the next until he has finished transactions with the first. If the punter is satisfied with his cards and requires no more, he says 'stick'; if not, he may acquire more cards until he either does stick, or is bust. In order to stick, at any time, his cards must total at least 16. He may acquire further cards by buying them face down or twisting them face up. He may start buying, and then switch to twisting, but once he has twisted he may not subsequently buy. If he says 'buy' he pays not less than the amount for which he bought his previous card, nor more than his total stakes so far, and receives the card face down. If he says 'twist' he pays nothing but receives the card face up. If he busts he must announce that fact. If he is trying for a five card trick, the fifth card is dealt face up even if he buys it. If he gets a royal pontoon he must reveal his cards immediately.

BANKER'S PLAY The banker does not yet collect the stakes of anyone who has bust but must play first. He turns his cards face up, and deals himself further cards face up until he is satisfied with his total. If he busts he collects the stakes of punters who went bust and pays the others the amount they staked (double for a pontoon or five card trick, treble for a royal pontoon). If he reaches exactly 21 on three or four cards, he pays only those with pontoons or five card tricks. If he gets a five card trick, he beats a punter's five card trick but not a pontoon, and receives double stakes. With anything under 21 he pays those with a higher count or better hand and collects from those with equal, lower or bust hands. Cards are then gathered up and returned to the bottom of the pack.

HOUSE RULES Common variations on these rules are as follows. (a) The banker may look at his first card and, if he likes it, order everybody to double their stake. (b) Banker's five card trick beats anything. (c) Pontoon must consist of an Ace and a court card, an Ace/Ten being ordinary 21. These and similar variations generally favour the banker.

NOTES ON PLAY

The banker has all the advantages, and derives most of his income from the fact that he always wins on equal hands even when bust. As banker you should come out best by sticking when you can, though the fewer the punters you are playing against (i.e., the more who have bust), the higher you can afford to aim.

As a punter it is usually best to stick at 17 or more, 16 being marginal. The worst total is 12 to 15 without an Ace, as roughly one card in three will bust you – don't forget that sixteen cards in the pack count 10. From that position it is best to twist.

It is obviously best to stake high on an initial Ace and almost as high on a tenth. A Seven or higher is not a bad opening card, but lower ranks are unpromising. It is certainly not worth thinking in terms of a five card trick until you have three cards and do not yet qualify to stick.

With a pair, split Aces, Fours, Sixes, Sevens and Eights, but keep a pair of tenths. Nines are a moot point, but a pair of Fives gives a total of 10, which is a good count to buy to. Two and three are unpromising totals to buy to, as the receipt of a tenth puts you in the 12–15 bracket, so you may as well keep a pair of deuces or treys and dream about a five card trick.

Do not be misled or put off by rumours of a winning strategy at Pontoon. An apparent winning strategy was published some years ago for the game of Blackjack, as played in American casinos, but it depended upon a long enough use of an unshuffled pack, complex calculations, substantial capital and an unparalleled degree of avarice.

Related Games

BACCARAT So spelt in England and Nevada, but Baccara elsewhere, this is basically a two-player game like Pontoon but with courts counting zero and Ace one, the object being to get as close as possible to nine on two or at most three cards (anything over merely drops the first figure). It is a casino game, one player, who deals, being put up by the house, the other, putting up the bank, representing everyone around the table. No skill is required, as only one total (five) gives a player the choice of standing or drawing. Varieties of Baccarat, differing only in banking arrangements, include Baccara Banque, Chemin de Fer (Chemmy), and Punto Banco.

BLACKJACK American equivalent of Pontoon. A count of 21 on two cards is a *natural*. Players ante before the deal. If a punter has a natural, banker pays him and collects from the others without further play. Otherwise they may stay (stick) on any total and call for (twist) as many more cards as they wish, dealt face up. Pairs may be split. If his first two cards total 11 a player may double his stake (*double down*); the rule may be extended to totals of 10 or 9. Optional payoff hands, calling for immediate payment from the banker, include five or more card tricks, paying double for each card over four; 21 with 6–7–8, paying double; and 21 with three Sevens, paying treble.

CHEMIN DE FER (CHEMMY) See Baccarat.

FARMER Old European game still played in rural America, played with 45 cards after rejecting all Eights and Sixes except ♥6. The object is to get as close to 16 as possible, but not more, counting Ace 1 (only), others face value, courts 10. Players ante 1 unit to the farm (pool), and the farmer (banker) deals one card each face down. Each in turn must call for at least one card and may request more, all being dealt face down. He may stick when he likes, but does not reveal whether he is bust. Hands are then exposed. Anyone (except the farmer) who is bust pays 1 unit to the farmer. The player with the best total – nearest 16 – collects 1 unit from each player with a lower total but not from a bust hand; in the event of a tie for best, the payment is shared between them. The farm and the right to become the farmer transfer to the player who gets exactly 16. In the event of a tie, priority goes to (a) the farmer, (b) the hand containing ♥6, (c) the hand with fewer cards, (d) the tied player next from farmer's left.

PUNTO BANCO See Baccarat.

QUINZE (FIFTEEN) A two-player Pontoon equivalent, the object being to reach 15 but not bust. Ace counts 1. A stake is agreed and one card dealt to each. Non-dealer may stand or draw cards until he either stands or busts. Dealer does likewise. The player with the better total wins the stake, which, in the event of a tie (including two busts), is doubled and carried forward. The deal alternates.

RED DOG (SLIPPERY SAM) The banker puts up a pool and deals three, four or five cards (whichever is decided upon at the start of the game) to each player except himself, face down and one at a time. The first punter looks at his cards and bets that at least one of them will be of the same suit as the top card of the undealt pack and higher in rank (Ace high, Two low). He must bet at least a previously agreed minimum, but not more than is in the bank. Banker then faces the top card. If the punter can beat it he shows only the card that does so, and draws from the bank the amount of his stake. If not, he loses his stake to the bank and throws his cards in, still face down. His cards and the faced top-card are discarded down. The next player then looks at his cards and the game continues in the same way. (There are more point-less versions in which players bet before looking at their cards.)

SEVEN AND A HALF Italian Pontoon equivalent played with 40 cards lacking Eights, Nines and Tens. Numerals count face value, courts $\frac{1}{2}$ each, ◆K represents any card its holder wishes, and the object is to get as close as possible to $7\frac{1}{2}$ without exceeding it. Each punter antes and receives a card face down. After looking at it he may either stick or call for more cards, dealt face up, until he either sticks or busts. Banker then does likewise. If he busts he pays those with less than 8 the amount of their stake, doubled to the player who has a two-card $7\frac{1}{2}$ count. If not, he collects from anyone with a bust hand or lower count than himself, and pays anyone with a better count. In the event of a tie there is no transaction. A two-card $7\frac{1}{2}$ beats one with more than two and entitles its holder to take over the bank, unless the banker also had a two-card $7\frac{1}{2}$.

Stops Family

The basic idea of these simple but pleasing family games, some of them ideal for children, is that a sequence of cards is built up in a row on the table. Instead of taking turns, whoever has the next card in the sequence plays it. Some cards are undealt, however, and therefore stop the sequence from following its proper course. Hence the name 'Stops' for the whole group.

Stops games have an interesting history, having undergone much change in status. Originally they were serious gambling games of the French aristocracy, one of them, Hoc, being much favoured by Cardinal Mazarin, who succeeded Richelieu of *The Three Musketeers* fame. It was afterwards known as Hoc de Mazarin. Later, they became genteel family games, played for penny stakes, as suggested by references in both Sheridan and Dickens to the popularity of Pope Joan with the rural clergy. Their subsequent decline may have been caused by the popularity of Rummy, which occupies a similar position of domestic favour. But they are far from dead and nowadays keep re-emerging, in various forms, as pub games, providing the researcher with a promising field of study.

This chapter omits 'compendium' games, in which the sequence-play forms but a portion of the whole, such as Pochen and Hoc itself.

Newmarket ◎

3–8 players
1 pack (52)

A wholesome family game, Newmarket is the English equivalent of Michigan. It is a simplified descendant of Pope Joan.

CARDS 52, running in sequence A23456789TJQK.

PRELIMINARIES A layout is needed, consisting of ♠A ♥K ♣Q ♦J of a spare pack, and arranged in a square on the table. Players must be equipped with counters or equivalent.

STAKING Before the deal, each player distributes four counters, or a multiple of four if previously agreed, over the cards of the layout, placing as many as he likes on each card.

DEAL Cards are dealt round one by one amongst the players, together with a spare hand of unfaced or dead cards. It does not matter that some may hold one more card than others.

PLAY The player at dealer's left starts by playing face up to the table the lowest card he has of whichever suit he pleases, announcing what it is as he does so. Whoever has the next higher card of the same suit – for example, ♠4 if the first was ♠3 – then plays and announces it, and so on. This continues until a stop is reached, i.e., a card which no one can follow. All Kings are stops because they are the highest in their suits, and any other card will be a stop if the next in sequence is lying in the dead hand. When this happens the person who played the stop starts a new sequence by playing the lowest card he has of any suit.

COLLECTING Anyone who legally plays a card corresponding to one in the layout immediately wins all the chips staked on it.

ENDING The game ends as soon as one player plays his last card. Everybody else pays him one chip for every card remaining in his own hand.

UNCLAIMED STAKES Any stakes left unclaimed on a layout card are carried forward to the next deal. At some stage in the proceedings – whether at the end of each deal or when everybody has dealt once or at the end of the evening – they may be disposed of by dealing all the cards around face up, one at a time before each player. Whoever is dealt a card corresponding to one in the layout takes all the stakes on it. The longer it is left, the richer it becomes.

RELATED GAMES

COMET (COMMIT) An early, possibly ancestral relative of Pope Joan, played with a pack stripped of ♦8 and as many other Eights and Sevens as required to give everyone the same number of cards. A single pool is formed, which goes to the first player to go out. Cards are played in ascending suit-sequence. The ♦9, known as the *comet*, must be played either when the game is blocked or when its holder, having played regularly, cannot continue the sequence himself. The player on his left may follow it with ♦T or the card in sequence with the one before it, this privilege passing round, if he cannot, until somebody can. Whoever plays the comet wins 2 chips from each opponent, and each King played wins one. First out wins the pool, plus 2 from each opponent and an extra one for each King unplayed. This game seems to have been first played, or at least named, upon appearance of Halley's comet in 1758. The modern form of the game is Pink Nines (below).

MICHIGAN (BOODLE, STOPS) In the American version Aces rank topmost in their suits and therefore replace Kings as stops. The layout, staking and objectives are the same as in Newmarket. Before play the dealer may exchange his hand for the dead hand if he wishes, sight unseen, or may auction this privilege to the highest bidder. Other cards or card combinations may be invented to increase the layout, such as J–Q of the same suit, stakes on it going to anyone who plays them both.

PINK NINES A pub game in line of descent from Comet. Everyone stakes an equal amount. Deal four cards to a dead hand and distribute the rest evenly, any surplus also being dead. Player left of dealer starts by laying out as many cards as he can in ascending sequence but regardless of suit. When he is stuck the next in turn takes over and continues the sequence. Both ♥9 and ♦9 – the 'pink Nines' – are wild and may be played as any card. When no one can go the first who was blocked starts a new sequence. Ace is high and acts as a stop, a new sequence being started by the same player. First out wins the pool.

POPE JOAN This once highly popular family was played with an elaborate piece of stake-and-layout equipment, examples of which are still to be seen in museums. It is played with a 51-card pack lacking ♦8, thus making it difficult to play the card known as Pope Joan, i.e., ♦9 (alternatively known as the Curse of Scotland). The eight divisions of the board or home-made layout are marked as follows:

Pope = ♦9
Matrimony = K–Q of trumps
Intrigue = Q–J of trumps
Ace, King, Queen, Jack, Game

The dealer starts by dressing the board, distributing 15 counters among the eight divisions of the layout thus: 6 to Pope, 2 to Matrimony, 2 to Intrigue, and the others one each. He deals all the cards around as at Newmarket, including a dead hand. The last card of all is turned to establish a trump suit and, if it is Pope, Ace, King, Queen or Jack, he wins the stake from the appropriate division. Play proceeds as at Newmarket, the stakes on Matrimony and Intrigue being taken only when a player is able to play both the cards concerned. Hence anyone fortunate enough to hold and play J–Q–K–A of trumps collects from six of the eight pools. Whoever goes out by playing his last card wins the contents of the division marked Game. Everybody else pays him one counter for each card remaining in his own hand, except that a player who is left with ♦9 in hand is exempt from this penalty. Unclaimed stakes are carried forward.

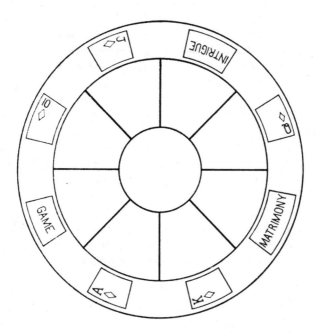

17. POPE JOAN Elaborate Pope Joan boards with labelled compartments for holding stakes were popular during the nineteenth century, and some are preserved in museums. All games of the Stops family require such layouts, which may be simply made by sticking old cards on sheets of paper – or, more elaborately but attractively, by sticking card cut-outs in the compartments of small cake-baking tins.

SPINADO A simplified variant of Pope Joan, see above. A 47-card pack is used, lacking ♦8 and all the deuces, and the layout is marked as follows: Matrimony, denoting ♦K–♦Q; Intrigue, denoting ♦Q–♦J; and Game, being a pool for the player who goes out first. Dealer bestows 12 counters upon Matrimony, and 6 each on the other two, and each player pays 3 to Game. The deal and play are as at New-market, Aces counting low and therefore acting as stops, there being no deuces. The ♦A is known as Spinado, or Spin for short. It gives its holder the power of turning any one of his cards into a stop, which he does by playing a card in the normal way and then immediately covering it with ♦A, announcing 'And Spin!' The others then pay him three counters each and he starts a new sequence. Anyone playing a King immediately receives a counter from each opponent, or two if it is ♦K. The contents of Matrimony or Intrigue go only to a player able to play both cards concerned, and the player of all three wins both pools in addition to the ♦K payment. First out wins the contents of the Game division, and is thereby exempted from contributing to it on the next deal, unless he happens to be dealer. He also receives from each opponent one counter for each card left in hand, and if the holder of Spin has not played it, he pays double.

TWO-HAND COMET uses two packs, less the Aces, each 48-card pack containing all the cards of one colour, i.e., eight of each rank, but with one red and one black Nine interchanged. Only one pack is used at a time. Deal 18 each and leave the other 12 out of play. Non-dealer plays any card face up and each in turn adds one or more cards, either of the same rank or of the next above it, regardless of suit. When one cannot go the other starts a new sequence. The Nine of the wrong colour is called the comet and may be played instead of a proper card, entitling its player to start a new sequence immediately. First out wins, scoring the total value of cards in his opponent's hand (courts count 10 each); or, if both are blocked, the one with the lower count scores the difference between both. His score is doubled if his opponent holds the comet unplayed, or if he himself wins by playing the comet; furthermore, if he wins by playing the comet as a Nine, his score is quadrupled. A simplified form of the game can be played with a single pack, replacing one of the Nines by a Joker.

YELLOW DWARF In this old European game, apparently ancestral to Pope Joan, the layout cards were ♥K ♠Q ♣J ♦T and ♦7 – the latter being the Yellow Dwarf in person – and cards were played in sequence regardless of suit.

Fan Tan ◎
3–8 players, 6–7 best
1 pack (52)

A two-dimensional game of Stops, very suitable for children, but not without elements of skill. It may also be found under the name Card Dominoes, Parliament, or Spoof Sevens (especially in pubs), and is not to be confused with Chinese Fan Tan, a non-card game formerly of ill repute.

CARDS 52, running A23456789TJQK.

PRELIMINARIES Counters are used, and each starts by paying an agreed sum into the pool. Use small cards or a large table.

DEAL Deal all the cards around, one at a time. It does not matter if some players have one more than others.

OBJECT To play one's last card before anyone else.

PLAY The player at dealer's left starts by playing any Seven face up to the table. If he cannot, he pays one to the pool and the turn passes. With a Seven in position, the next in turn must pay one of the following cards: the Six of the same suit to the left of the Seven, or the Eight of the same suit to its right, or any other Seven below it. Thereafter, each in turn must play either a Seven, or the next higher or lower card of a suit-sequence, in such a way as to build up four rows of 13 cards, each of the same suit and reading from Ace at the extreme left to King at the extreme right.

PENALTIES Anyone unable to play at his turn contributes one counter to the pool. Anyone who fails to play, although able to do so, pays 3 to each opponent, plus 5 to the holders of the Six and Eight of a suit if he holds the Seven of it and fails to play. But this does not mean that he is obliged to play a Seven if he has one but prefers to play something else. Indeed, holding up Sevens is part of the strategy.

GOING OUT The first player to go out wins the contents of the pool and one counter from each opponent for each card left in hand.

VARIANT In a version called Five or Nine, the first person able to play may start with a Five or a Nine, and whichever he chooses must be adhered to as the foundation rank for each row for the rest of that hand.

Switch (Eights) ◎
2–8 players, fewer better
1 pack (52)

This member of the Stops family, playable in partnerships and giving some scope for skill, is usually given under the name Swedish Rummy, which is nonsensical, or Eights, which is nondescript. Another name is Rockaway; as a pub game it is known as Switch.

CARDS 52, or 104 (two packs) if six or more play.

DEAL Five each, or seven if only two are playing. Place the remainder face down to form a stock and turn up the top card beside it as the starter. If the starter is an Ace, bury it in the stock and turn up the next card.

OBJECT To rid one's hand of cards.

PLAY Starting at dealer's left, each in turn plays a card from his hand face up to the table to form a pile or row based on the starter. Each card played must match the previous card by either rank or suit unless it is an Ace. Aces are wild. A player unable to match may play any Ace instead, announcing which suit he requires the next player to follow. Any player unable or unwilling to follow must draw cards from the top of the stock, adding them to his hand until he eventually plays one.

ENDING The game ends as soon as one player plays his last card, or when a block is reached and no one can play. The player with no cards left collects from each opponent a payment equivalent to the total face value of cards remaining in his hand, counting Ace 50, courts 10 each, others face value. If the game blocks, the player with the lowest pip-count on cards remaining scores from each opponent the difference between their two hands. In the four-hand partnership game both partners must go out to end the game.

VARIANTS Under the name Eights or Swedish Rummy it is the Eights which are the wild cards. In the final reckoning they count 50 each, and Aces 1 point only. In Hollywood Eights each Eight counts 20 and Ace 15, and the simultaneous-game scoring system of Gin Rummy is used, a game consisting of 100 points.

Patience Games

Although Patience in English is Solitaire in American, it would be convenient to use the former to indicate a game in which the object is to put shuffled cards back into order and to reserve the latter for any one-player card game. From this viewpoint Russian Bank is a patience, though for two players, while the solitaire version of Poker Squares is not, though for one.

Patience games are known from the late eighteenth century and appear to be of German provenance, though many of the best are French by name and terminology. They reached England in the 1820s but only became popular later, through royal patronage at the hands of Victoria's German husband. Tradition associates them particularly with Napoleon, several Patiences incorporating his name in their title, but the tradition seems to be founded upon a misunderstanding of the French word *solitaire* used in reference to his practising hands of Whist alone.

As there are more than enough Patiences to fill a book of this size, no more can be attempted here than to present a few of the best known as an introduction to the subject. There is a general but mistaken belief that Patiences are a form of occupational therapy for village idiots. In fact, many are an exercise in concentration and logical thought, while those that call for less skill are justified by the beauty of their patterns.

Technical terms are not listed in the glossary; they may be better understood from the following context. In most Patiences cards run in sequence from Ace (low) to King (high). Sometimes a sequence is permitted to *turn the corner* from King to Ace, or vice versa in a descending sequence, but this cannot be assumed unless the rules specifically permit it. The object is normally to produce complete 13-card sequences in the same suit, though sometimes suits are ignored and sequences may be of mixed suits. The first card of such a pile, often an Ace, is called the *foundation* upon which the gradual *building* of the pile takes place. Sometimes the Aces or other specified foundation cards are withdrawn from the pack and put in position to start the game, and sometimes the rules state that foundation cards are only laid as and when they turn up in the deal. Except that the latter procedure makes the game longer, there is no essential difference between the two, and any game may be started in either way *ad lib*.

The shuffled pack is called the *stock* (more properly, the *talon*). To get from the randomness of the shuffled pack to the order of the finished suit-sequences is a big jump and requires the assistance of an intermediate stage of partial ordering. This takes place within an arrangement of cards on the table called the *tableau*. In some games all the cards are dealt to the tableau so that all are visible before play begins, producing completely open games. In some, a number of cards are dealt to a tableau to start with and others are then turned from the stock and added to it as they appear. If they cannot legally be entered into the tableau, or on to the appropriate foundation pile, they are discarded face up to a waste pile, the top card of which remains available for transfer to the table if circumstances change in its favour. In some games the waste pile is turned over and becomes the new stock when the old one is exhausted. Most games will always come out eventually if the pile is turned often enough in this way, so custom has come to decree for each game how many such turns are permitted.

Within the tableau, cards are usually arranged in overlapping *rows* (if the longer edge of each card is covered) or *columns* (if the shorter). The purpose of overlapping is to enable covered cards to be identified by their corners even though they are temporarily blocked by those above. The *exposed* card of such a row or column is the one which is uncovered, it being the only one of its row or column available.

An *available* card is one that may be picked up and moved somewhere else, preferably to its appropriate foundation pile to continue the sequence. Available cards, which also include those turned from stock and the top of the waste pile if any, may be placed on top of exposed cards in the tableau, but only in accordance with rules of order specified for the game. For example, if the object is to build cards on foundations in ascending sequence and in the same suit (e.g., ♠A-♠2-♠3 etc.), then cards may be built on the tableau in descending sequence and alternating colour (red Three on black Four, black Two on red Three, etc.), thus enabling them to be picked up again in the right order for transfer to foundation piles when the opportunity arises.

Sometimes the tableau consists of, or includes, cards forming a *reserve*. These are always available for transfer to foundations, but their distinguishing feature is that they do not normally overlap and no building is carried out on them.

Not all Patiences *come out*. That is, certain arrangements of cards created by the shuffle make it impossible for the final order to be achieved, at least within the stated number of deals. Failure, therefore, is not necessarily a sign of bad play. On the other hand, many a Patience may be lost through bad play that would have come out with better. The name of the game is therefore singularly appropriate.

It is advisable to play with special Patience cards as these are smaller than standard playing cards and thus more suited to those games that call for large and elaborate tableaux.

Beleaguered Castle
One pack (52)

Arrange four Aces in a column to form the foundations. On each side of each Ace deal six cards face up in an overlapping row, forming the tableau. The object is to build each Ace up in suit sequence to the King. At each move transfer the exposed card of a row to a foundation pile if it fits, or to the exposed end of another row. Rows in the tableau are built downwards regardless of suit – e.g., place any Six on any Seven, any Five on any Six, etc. An empty row may be filled with any available card. Even with best play it will not always come out.

Belle Lucie (Fan)
One pack (52)

Deal the first 51 cards face up in 17 fans, each fan consisting of three overlapping cards. Traditionally, these small fans are arranged in the form of a larger one, and the odd card is dealt face up to form its handle at the bottom centre. The object is to extract the four Aces as they become available, place them in a separate row of foundations, and build each up in suit and sequence to the King. At each turn transfer an exposed card to a foundation pile if it fits, or to the exposed card of another fan (the odd 52nd card counting as such for this purpose). Fans are built downwards in suit, e.g., ♥6 on ♥7, ♥5 on ♥6, etc. An empty fan may not be re-formed. This rule makes the game very hard to get out.

Canfield

The same name applies to different games on the two sides of the Atlantic. English Canfield is Klondike in America; American Canfield is Demon in Britain. See alternative names.

Clock

Two packs (104)

Several species of clock inhabit the realm of Patience. This one takes a lot of space. Start by arranging the following dozen cards in a circle, proceeding clockwise from the top, their long axes radiating outwards: ◆5 ♠6 ♥7 ♣8 ◆9 ♠T ♥J ♣Q ◆K ♠2 ♥3 ♣4. From the shuffled cards remaining, deal twelve columns of three overlapping cards each, each column extending outwards from, but not touching, the first twelve. The exposed card of each column should be on the outside to allow room for building. Each of the first twelve

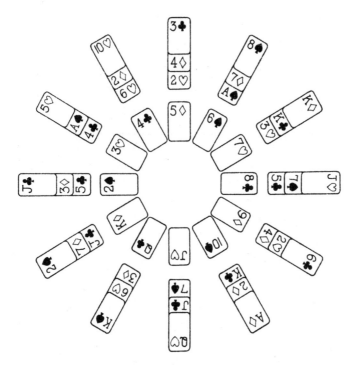

18. CLOCK PATIENCE Initial layout. In this instance, the outermost ♥Q may be played upon the ♥J immediately above it (at six o'clock). Or the other ♥J may be placed upon ♥Q, and ♥T transferred to it in turn.

cards is a foundation and is to be built up in suit and ascending sequence until it reaches the number corresponding to its position on the clock face. For example, ♦5 at the top is to be built up in diamonds to the Queen, which counts as 12 (o'clock), ♠6 up in spades to the Ace, ♥7 up in hearts to the Two (turning the corner at Q–K–A–2), and so on. The end product is the complete representation of a clock face.

The exposed card of a column may always be transferred to a foundation if it fits. For the rest of play, take the remaining cards and turn them up one at a time. Each one may be played straight to a foundaion if it fits, or to the exposed end of a column of three or more cards. Columns are built outward in suit and descending sequence (♥6 on ♥7, etc.), but when a column is reduced to fewer than three cards it is temporarily dead and may not be added to. A card may be played from one column to another if it fits. A turned card that fits nowhere is placed face up on a waste pile. The top card of the waste pile is available for transfer to columns or foundations as appropriate, but the waste pile is never turned for re-use as a new stock.

When the game blocks, or whenever you wish, revive the dead columns of two or fewer cards by dealing from the stock as many more cards as are needed to bring them up to three, starting at the one o'clock position or nearest thereafter, proceeding in a clockwise direction, and filling each up before moving on to the next.

With care, the game usually comes out.

Demon (Canfield)
1 pack (52)

Deal 13 cards face down, square them up and turn them face up so that only the top card is visible. These form the reserve. Deal the next four cards face up in a (non-overlapping) row extending to the right of the reserve, forming the tableau. Deal the next card face up above the first of these to form the first of four foundations. As each other card of the same rank as this becomes available, place it in line with the first to complete the foundations. The object is to build each foundation up in suit and sequence until it contains 13 cards (turning the corner at –K–A–2– if necessary).

Turn cards from the stock in batches of three, and transfer them, without disturbing their order, to a single face-up waste pile. Only the top card of the waste pile is available, but the other cards turned may be examined. Make all moves possible before turning the next batch. A card may be transferred to a foundation from the top of the reserve, the top of the waste pile, or from the tableau if uncovered. Cards may be built on the tableau in descending sequence and alternating colour (red Six on black Seven, black Five on red Six etc.). A whole column may be cleared out by building on top of another, provided that the join follows this rule. As soon as a tableau column is emptied it must be filled with the top card of the reserve, or, if none are left, from the waste pile, in which case the space need not be filled immediately.

When the stock is exhausted turn the waste pile to form a new one. The game rarely comes out.

Klondike (Canfield)
1 pack (52)

Deal seven cards face down in a row. Turn up the extreme left-hand card and deal six more cards face down along the rest of the row. Turn up the first of these six and deal five more face down along the rest of the row. Continue in this way until you have seven piles of cards increasing in number from one to seven from left to right, with only the top card of each pile exposed. These start the tableau. As each Ace becomes available transfer it to a row above the tableau to start a foundation. Build each foundation up in suit and sequence to the King.

After making any opening moves that may be possible, turn cards one at a time from the stock, playing each one to a foundation or to a tableau column if it fits, or face up to a single waste pile if not. The top card of the waste pile is always available, but the pile is not turned for re-use when the stock runs out. On the tableau, build columns of overlapping cards on each exposed card in descending sequence and alternating colour (red Six on black Seven etc.). The exposed card of a column may be transferred to a foundation if it fits, or to another column. A whole column may be transferred to another if the join follows the descending/ alternating rule. When a column is cleared to reveal the top of a face down pile, turn the top card face up. When a pile has been cleared to leave a space it may be filled only with an available King or a whole sequence of descending/alternating cards built on a King.

The game rarely comes out.

Miss Milligan
2 packs (104)

Deal eight cards face up in a row. These form the bases of what will eventually become columns of overlapping cards in the tableau. If an Ace appears transfer it to an eventual row of eight foundations above the eight columns. As each Ace become available move it into this row. The object is to build all eight Aces up in suit and sequence to their Kings. An exposed card in the tableau may be transferred to a foundation if it fits, or to the exposed end of another column in the tableau. Tableau columns are built in descending sequence and alternating colour (red Six on black Seven etc.). Any length of such sequence ending in an exposed card may be transferred as a whole to another column provided that the join follows the rule. A space in the tableau may be filled only with a King. When no further play is possible, deal eight more cards to the tableau, one to the exposed end of each column. When the stock is exhausted, the exposed card of any column, together with any sequence following properly above it, may be taken and placed to one side as a temporary reserve, all cards in it being simultaneously available for play to foundations or tableau. When this reserve is empty, another may be formed and played in the same way. When no cards from the reserve are playable the game is lost. It does not come out very often.

Salic Law
2 packs (104)

This long-standing favourite comes out quite often and finishes with a pretty effect. Remove a King and place it at the head of an imaginary column on the left. Deal cards face up upon the King and towards you to form a column of overlapping cards, keeping a look-out for Queens and Aces. Whenever an Ace appears, place it above the first King to start an eventual row of eight Aces. Whenever a Queen appears, place her above the first Ace to form an eventual row of eight Queens. Whenever a King appears, place him to the right of the previous King and start a new overlapping column. The eight Aces are foundations: the object is to build each up in suit and ascending sequence to the Jack. Whenever, during the deal, you turn a card that fits a foundation, you may (and are generally advised to) so play it. When all cards have been dealt, play consists in transferring the exposed card of any column to a foundation pile that it fits. Cards are not built upon each other in the tableau, but when a King becomes exposed it is permissible to transfer the end-card of a column to it as a temporary reserve. The game ends with a row of uncovered Kings, surmounted by a row of Jacks, surmounted by a row of Queens.

Spider
2 packs (104)

Several different Patiences are called Spider. This one comes out quite often, and follows an unusual procedure in that there are no foundation piles and all building is done within the tableau. Deal ten cards face down in a row, and repeat four times until you have ten piles of five cards each. On each of the first four piles deal a sixth card face up, then turn up the top card of the other six piles. This disposes of the first 54 cards and play now begins, the object of which is to build eight complete suit-sequences of cards from Ace to King within the tableau and reject them from play one at a time as and when they occur.

An exposed card in the tableau may be built upon another, forming an overlapping column in descending sequence regardless of suit (e.g., any Six on any Seven, etc.). Whenever a face-down card is exposed it is turned face up. A whole sequence of cards may be moved to another column if the join follows the descending sequence rule. When a complete pile is emptied it may be restarted with any available card. A King may not be played on an Ace but may only be used (together with any descending sequence it heads) to fill a space. When no further play is possible, deal ten more cards from the stock, one to the exposed end of each column, first filling up any spaces that may have been made. Whenever a complete 13-card suit-sequence has been formed remove it from the tableau. The game succeeds if eight such sequences are formed.

Sultan

2 packs (104)

Sultan is an attractive favourite that comes out often. Remove ♥A and all eight Kings and arrange them in a 3 × 3 square with the Ace in the centre of the top row and ♥K beneath it in the middle of the square. Parallel to each side of the square deal a column of four cards face up to form the tableau. None of these first 17 cards are overlapping. Leaving the ♥K uncovered throughout play, the object is to build every other King up in suit and sequence to the Queen (proceeding K–A–2– etc.), and the Ace also up in suit and sequence to the Queen. Thus eight foundations are formed. The surrounding cards form the reserve.

Turn cards one at a time from the stock, playing each one to a foundation if possible or face up to a single waste pile if not. A card may also be played to the foundation from the top of the waste pile or from the reserve. A space in the reserve is immediately filled from the top of the stock or the waste pile. When the stock is exhausted turn the waste pile down to start a new one. The game succeeds if it comes out after turning the waste pile not more than twice. The end product depicts, according to tradition, a sultan surrounded by his *seraglio*, and the reserve is usually referred to as the *divan*.

Windmill
2 packs (104)

This Patience is another rather mechanical pictorial which comes out less frequently. Take any Ace and place it face upwards in the middle. Deal two cards face up in a row to its right and two to its left, then two in a column above it and another two below. The Ace may thus be pictured as the centre of the sails of the windmill. If any of the exposed cards is a King place it between two sails so as to project diagonally from the corner of the central Ace, but without overlapping. Three more Kings, as they become available, are placed in the other diagonally corresponding positions regardless of suit. Whenever a space occurs in a sail fill it immediately with the top card of the stock or waste pile. The object is to build upon the central Ace four complete 13-card sequences from Ace to King, regardless of suit, producing a pile of 52 cards topped by the fourth and last King. At the same time, each of the four King foundations is to be built in descending sequence, regardless of suit, to produce a pile of 13 cards topped by an Ace.

Turn cards one at a time from the stock and place each on a foundation if it fits, or face up on a waste pile if not. A properly sequential card may be played to a foundation from the sails or the top of the waste pile. The top card of a King foundation may be transferred to the Ace foundation and vice versa, if required, but a King itself cannot be moved and only one card may be taken from a foundation at a time. The game is won if it comes out without having to turn the waste pile for use as a new stock.

Odds-and-end-games

This chapter is a mixed bag of unrelated games that do not adequately fit the previous headings but are too enjoyable to omit.

Calypso is a modern four-player cross between Whist and Rummy, easy to learn and well worth the effort of shuffling four packs together.

Catch-the-Ten is a traditional round game (for any number), also known as Scotch Whist.

Gops is a fast and infuriating two-player pastime which keeps changing every time you think you have found the perfect strategy.

Le Truc is a two- or four-player gambling game that is so hilarious as to be worth playing for peanuts.

Pip-Pip is another traditional round game said to be good for parties.

Poker Squares can be played solitaire or by a hall full of bingo addicts.

Quinto is a delightfully original partnership game which starts as Whist and finishes as something completely different.

Rolling Stone is a round game that can go on for ever.

Russian Bank, or Crapette, is a two-player Patience.

Spite and Malice is a modern relative of Russian Bank, whose title speaks for itself.

Zetema is a recently revived Victorian craze devised for the entertainment of two, three or four players – a cross between Poker, Patience and Bézique.

Calypso ⠿

4 players
4 packs (208)

This unusual partnership game, invented by R. B. Willis of Trinidad and introduced to Britain in 1953, is an exact cross between Whist and Rummy. It combines the best of both and is easy to learn once the unusual idea of 'personal trumps' is understood.

CARDS Four 52-card packs shuffled together. They need not be of identical back design or colour but must be all the same size.

PARTNERSHIPS Partners sit opposite each other. Each player is associated with a particular suit as follows: North ♠, East ♦, South ♥, West ♣, so spades and hearts are partners against clubs and diamonds. These are known as the players' personal trump suits.

OBJECT A game consists of four deals, in each of which 13 tricks are played. Tricks are of little value in themselves, as each side's chief objective is to capture cards which will enable them to build up calypsos. A calypso is a complete suit of 13 cards, consisting of 23456789TJQKA with no duplicater. Each player's object is to build up a calypso in his own personal trump suit. Having completed one he may starts another, and at the end of the fourth deal that side wins which has made the most calypsos. When a trick is taken its winner extracts from it any card or cards he needs for his own calypso, and may give his partner any that he may need for his.

DEAL A game consists of four deals and the turn to deal passes to the left. Deal 13 cards each (remembering to count) and place the remainder face down to one side, where they remain out of play until the next deal. Dealer's left-hand opponent leads to the first trick. It is always obligatory to follow suit if possible, and if two cards of equal rank fall to the same trick the first beats the second.

TRUMP LEAD If the leader to a trick leads a personal trump and everybody is able to follow suit, the leader wins the trick regardless of the ranks of the cards played. But if another cannot follow he may seek to win the trick by playing a higher-ranking card from his personal trump suit, or else he may discard from another suit and so lose the trick. In short, if a personal trump is led the trick is won by the highest-ranking personal trump played to it, bearing in mind that another may only play a personal trump if he cannot follow suit to the card led.

NON-TRUMP LEAD If the card led does not belong to its player's personal trump suit, and everybody follows suit, the trick is won by the highest card played, or the first played of two identical cards. As before, however, a player unable to follow suit may seek to win the trick by playing a card of his personal trump suit, or else he may discard from another suit and lose the trick. In short, if a non-personal trump is led the trick is won by the highest card of the suit led or by the highest personal trump if any are played.

WON TRICKS The winner of a trick, before leading to the next, extracts from it any card or cards needed to build his own or his partner's calypso and turns the rest face down to a waste pile. Each partnership keeps a common waste pile, which may not be examined until the end of the whole game. Cards in it are not accessible for building calypsos but will score to the credit of their winners.

CALYPSOS Each player builds his calypso on the table before him, arranging the cards in an overlapping row and in proper sequence from Two low to Ace high. Only one calypso per player may be in progress at any one time, and it may not contain duplicated cards. If, therefore, a won trick contains the duplicate of a card already present in the partly-built calypso, it cannot be used but must be discarded. There is one exception to this rule. When a calypso is complete its owner stacks the cards face up in a pile with the Ace on top and is entitled to start another. If the trick he won enabled him to complete a calypso in the same turn, any duplicate cards contained in the trick may be kept in order to start the next. The same applies when passing over cards required by one's partner.

SCORE At the end of the fourth deal each partnership scores 10 points for every card in its waste pile, and each partner adds to that score 500 for his first completed calypso, 750 for his second, 1000 for a third or fourth, and 20 for each card in an incomplete calypso on the table before him.

NOTES ON PLAY

It must be understood that, if another player leads your personal trump suit, you can only win by playing the highest card of it. By definition you cannot trump it – you can only follow suit. Beginners are apt to lead personal trumps too soon, and too often, for the thrill of winning tricks effortlessly. This is self-defeating, as opponents will throw duplicate cards whenever they can and so make it impossible to build calypsos. Duplicates that fall early are lost for ever.

Catch-the-ten ◎

2–8 players
1 short pack (36)

A jolly but not unintelligent game, Catch-the-ten is also known as Scotch Whist, though it is neither one nor the other.

CARDS Normally 36, ranking from high to low AKQJT9876. If five or seven play, remove one of the Sixes; if eight, add all Fives.

DEAL Deal all the cards around one at a time, four players receiving 9, five 7, six 6, seven or eight 5 each. If two play, deal each player three separate hands of six cards each; if three, deal two separate hands of six each. Each hand is played separately, the next not being looked at until the previous one has been played out. The last card is always turned up to establish a trump suit.

OBJECT The object is to win tricks, and especially to win the top five trumps, each of which has a point-scoring value. In trumps only, the Jack, worth 11, is the highest card of its suit. It therefore beats the Ace which counts 4, King 3, Queen 2, and Ten, which is worth 10 to the player winning it in a trick (whence the name of the game).

PLAY Eldest hand leads and normal rules of trick-taking apply. Follow suit if possible; otherwise trump or renounce *ad lib.* The trick is captured by the highest card of the suit led or the highest trump if any are played, and the winner of one trick leads to the next.

SCORE At the end of play, each player counts the value of trumps won in tricks – the Jack, of course, counting to the player who was dealt it – and adds 1 point for every card captured in excess of the number originally dealt. (Example: if four play, a player who won three tricks would score 12 won less 9 dealt = 3 points.)

VARIANT In so-called French Whist the ♦T counts 10 to whoever wins it, whether trumps or not.

NOTE ON PLAY The element of luck is reduced by playing with a longer pack and not promoting the Jack of trumps, so that it may be captured by the Ace, King or Queen.

Gops 8

2 players
1 short pack (39)

Gops is a curious game of pure bluff.

CARDS Use three complete suits from a standard pack, normally rejecting hearts.

PREPARATION One player takes all the clubs and the other all the spades. The thirteen diamonds are thoroughly shuffled and placed face down in a pile.

OBJECT To win the greatest value of diamonds. The Ace of diamonds is worth 1, each numeral its face value, Jack 11, Queen 12 and King 13, making 91 in all.

PLAY Turn the top diamond face up. Each player then secretly bids for it by taking a card from his hand and laying it face down on the table. When both are ready, the black cards are turned up and the player showing the higher-ranking card wins the diamond (Ace low, King high). He places the diamond to one side, where it counts to his credit, and turns the next one face up. The two black cards are discarded, and the second diamond is now contested in the same way from the remaining twelve cards. This continues until all the diamonds have been won. If, at any point, both players bid with the same rank, the two bid cards are rejected and the diamond is left untaken. The next diamond is then turned up and the winner of the next bid captures them both. Subsequent ties are dealt with in the same way. If the last card is tied neither wins it, nor any others with which it may be combined in ties.

Le Truc 　

2 or 4 players
1 short pack (32)

The Provençal game of Le Truc is here taken as representative of a small and curious family which includes the Argentine game of El Truco, the Breton game of Aluette, and the old English game of Put, or Putt. It can best be characterized as an hilarious gambling game for two or four, and playable as well for paper clips as for real money – unlike Poker, which, in its emphasis on bluffing, it otherwise resembles.

PLAYERS The game for two is described below; that for four follows as a variant.

CARDS 32, ranking from high to low: 78AKQJT9. Note that the Seven is the highest rank, Eight the second highest, Nine the lowest. (To add to the fun, and for reasons we needn't enter into, the Eight is actually referred to as the 'Six'. Here we will call it the Eight.) All four suits are equal, and the suit of any card played has no bearing on the outcome.

DEAL Three each, in ones.

GENERAL IDEA A deal is theoretically won by the player who takes two or three tricks. The value of a deal – i.e., the amount scored by the winner – is basically 1 point. At each turn to play, however, a player may offer to double the value of the deal. If refused, he wins the deal without further play and scores the (undoubled) value; if accepted, play proceeds. Consequently, a deal may actually be worth 1, 2, 4, 8 or more. A round is won by the first player to reach 12 points in this way, and the rubber by the first player to win two rounds.

CALLING FOR CARDS Non-dealer may either start play or call for cards – i.e., request that the hands be thrown in and new cards dealt to both players. If cards are called, dealer may either refuse, in which case non-dealer must start play, or accept, in which case both hands are thrown face down to one side and three more cards are dealt each. Again, non-dealer may start or call for cards; this procedure can go on for as long as there remain enough cards in the pack for it to do so. If the pack runs out without play, the deal reverts to the other player, who shuffles the pack before dealing.

TRICKS The trick-winning system must be understood before play begins. The game is played at no trump and with no requirement to follow suit, a trick being won simply by the higher-ranking of the two cards played. The winner of a trick leads to the next. If the two cards are of equal rank the trick goes to whichever player was the first to win a trick; but if neither player has yet won one, the trick is said to be *spoiled* and is put to one side in abeyance. The leader to a spoiled trick leads to the next, and the spoiled trick goes to the winner of the second trick – or, if this too is spoiled, both go to the winner of the third. Only if all three are spoiled is the result a draw. It follows that the winner of the first trick has a great advantage, as the second automatically goes to him if it is spoiled. Play ends as soon as one player has won two tricks.

PLAY Throughout the game, when either player is about to play his card to a trick – whether leading or following – he may offer to double the value being played for. In order to keep track of the values it is desirable to specify the amount concerned. Thus the leader to the first trick may say 'Two if I play?' and the dealer, having accepted that double, may himself say 'Four if I play?' before following to the trick. Neither player is obliged to double if he would rather not increase the existing value. When a player offers to double he must wait for his opponent's response. If his opponent says 'No' the cards are thrown in and the player who offered to double wins for the existing amount. If his opponent accepts, the card is played and the value doubled. At any point in the game either player may concede to the other without further play.

As 12 points constitute a round, a player is not allowed to double if the amount he thereby stands to gain would cause him to exceed 12. Instead, he announces 'My remainder', which is simply a claim to the number of points he needs to reach 12 if he should win the deal. In this event his opponent may either refuse (in which case play ends and the claimant merely wins the existing value), or counter by claiming '*My* remainder', in which case the winner of the deal wins the whole round.

(Example: Abel has seven points, Baker two, and the value of the game has so far been doubled to four, which will give Abel eleven if he wins the deal. Abel may not double to eight, as this would put him over the limit of 12. Instead, he says 'My remainder' which is merely a claim to the five he needs to win the round. Now Baker, having accepted Abel's offer, may himself claim 'My remainder' before playing a card to the trick. This means that if his claim is accepted and

he wins, he will get the ten points he needs to make game.
Notice that Baker himself could not have initiated the
'remainder' claim, since he was in a position to double to
eight without busting. It is only because Abel remaindered
that Baker was enabled to do so in return.)

THROWING IN Any cards left unplayed at the end of the
deal are returned to the pack without being shown; at least,
neither player need feel legally or morally obliged to reveal
any card or cards he did not play.

NOTES ON PLAY

Le Truc is clearly a game of bluff, which means that success
depends neither upon analytical skill, nor upon the luck of
the deal, but upon one's powers of deception and psycho-
logical interpretation. As such, it hardly lends itself to advice
on play. The chief requirement is to be alert to your opponent's mannerisms and style of play and to avoid having any
of your own.

Opportunities for bluff occur at every turn of the game.
Non-dealer may play on bad cards, or elect to call even on
good ones in the hope of being refused. Dealer may accept
or refuse the call for cards on equally ambiguous principles.
You may offer to double even when you know you cannot
win on cards alone, in the hope of frightening your opponent
into a concession. Or, having strong cards, you may refrain
from doubling from fear of forcing an early concession
when, by your silence, your opponent may be misled into
doubling to your own advantage. Nothing is more galling
than to be dealt three Sevens, offer to double your opening
lead, and have it refused for a single point. Indeed, three
Sevens is a virtually useless hand to non-dealer, as it provides
practically no opportunity for bluffing – unless the odd point
is needed for game he might as well call for cards.

If trailing badly you need never give away more than one
point, for you can either play it out for one or drop as soon
as your opponent doubles. Or suppose he tries to take advantage of his advanced score by offering his remainder. With

bad cards you can refuse and just lose the point. With good ones you are entitled to offer your own remainder, in which case your backward score ceases to be a weakness. Yet it is no use consistently playing for one point, and then suddenly play in earnest upon being dealt good cards, as you will certainly give yourself away thereby and probably gain only one by concession.

Remember that you can bluff right up to the last minute. Suppose you match the lead of an Ace with an Ace and a Seven with a Seven, so spoiling two tricks. Holding another Ace you accept your opponent's double, whereupon he plays an Eight as his third lead. It is obvious that you cannot win... Or is it? Of course you can, if you promptly offer to double before playing your last card in the hope that your opponent will refuse it.

Various methods of bluffing are illustrated in the following example concocted by Michael Dummett in *Games & Puzzles* (September 1972). Dealt 7, 8, 9 to dealer's 7, 8, K, you would lose the deal, probably for four points, by straight-forward play. By devious play, however, you would start by calling for cards, which is bluff the first, since the ones you have are well above average and you do not know the opposition. Your call refused, you lead the Eight and accept your opponent's double, whereupon he takes it with a Seven. He doubles to four, which again you accept, and he leads an Eight. Before capturing with the Seven you offer to double, and he accepts the second bluff. Now, holding the lowest ranking card, you offer your remainder. Considering himself thoroughly double-bluffed, your opponent refuses, and you have thereby treble-bluffed him into losing the deal for eight points.

It is extraordinary what variety can be got into the play of three tricks.

FOUR-HAND LE TRUC

This game will be found most successful if you have already played the two-hand version. Partners face each other and play in clockwise rotation as at Whist. Deal three each in ones; the opening lead is made by eldest hand. Before play, however, the player at dealer's right may call for cards and dealer may accept or refuse. This business proceeds as at two-handed Le Truc, but only between these two players – their partners have no say in the matter and cannot receive fresh cards. Three tricks are then played, eldest hand leading to the first, and, as at two-hand Le Truc, a trick is spoiled if both sides play an equally high top card, and belongs to the side taking the first unspoiled trick. The leader to a spoiled trick leads to the next.

The dealer acts as the captain of his partnership, and the player on his right as the captain of the other. Only the captains may propose, accept or surrender to a doubling of the game value, and a captain may only propose once per trick, immediately before his side play their *first* card to it. Each captain, moreover, may instruct his partner what to play, in as general terms as he wishes – e.g., 'Play low,' 'Play a Seven if you can,' etc. The subordinate player, for his part, may use conventional gestures to signal to his captain what high cards he possesses. Such gestures include winking, nodding, shrugging, and so on, the general idea being to carry them out, as far as possible, without letting the opponents see.

Pip-Pip ◎
3–7
2 packs (104)

Pip-Pip has been described as 'one of the liveliest (and noisiest) of party games' – which may be true, but should not be held against it.

CARDS Two full packs shuffled together, 104 in all.

DEAL Establish a trump suit by cutting the pack, then deal seven each and place the remainder face down to form a stock.

OBJECT To score points for (a) changing the trump suit and (b) capturing, in tricks, cards with point-values as follows:

Deuces	11 each	Queens	4 each
Aces	10 each	Jacks	3 each
Kings	5 each		

For trick-taking purposes the lowest card is Three and the highest is the deuce of each suit, which outranks the Ace as shown in the list above.

PLAY Eldest leads and others must follow suit if possible; if not, either trump or discard from another suit. The trick is captured by the highest card of the suit led or the highest trump if any are played. Of two identical cards, the second beats the first. The winner of a trick draws the top card of the stock and adds it to his hand, those following him do likewise, and the winner then leads to the next trick. No more cards are drawn when there are not enough cards left in stock to go round, and play continues until no one has any left. Undrawn cards from stock are turned face up.

CHANGING THE TRUMP Immediately before a card is led to any trick, any player who holds a King and Queen of the same suit (other than trumps) may entrump that suit by calling 'Pip-pip' and laying them on the table, where they remain part of his hand. For this he scores a bonus of 50 points. If two players pip-pip before the same trick, both score 50 points and the suit is changed to that of the player who called second. One player may pip-pip twice in the same suit, but only if he produces the other King and Queen: neither of those used the first time may be used again.

SCORE Each player adds his score for pipping and the total value of counting-cards he has won in tricks.

Note: joking apart, this game is similar to Tyzicha (p. 215), and there is no reason why those already used to the card-point system appropriate to that and other games should not play Pip-Pip with top cards Ace 11, Ten 10, King 4, Queen 3, Jack 2 and deuce lowest in its suit.

Poker Squares ◎

1 or more players
1 pack per player

A game of considerable skill, Poker Squares is playable competitively or as a solitaire. A poker square is an array of 25 cards in five rows and five columns. Each row and each column – ten lines in all – is assessed as a Poker hand (see p. 448) and given a score appropriate to its rarity. The value of the square is the total value of the ten hands displayed. The point of the game is that cards are turned up one at a time from a shuffled pack and each has to be put in place before the next is known – once down, it cannot be moved. When played solo, the player 'wins' if he gets above a certain average target. In the competitive version the player with the highest valued square wins.

CARDS One full pack (52) each. One player, the caller, shuffles his pack thoroughly. The others arrange theirs in suit and rank order so as to be able to locate any card rapidly. Each needs enough room to build a square.

PLAY The caller plays a game of Poker Solitaire, turning up the first 25 cards of his pack one by one, and placing each in such a way as to build up a 5 × 5 square. As he turns a card he announces it by rank and suit and each other player extracts that card from his pack and also uses it to build up a square. Once a card has been placed it may not be moved in positional relation to any other.

SCORE When the squares have been built each row and column is scored according to either of the schedules below. The English schedule, which is more accurate, is based on the relative difficulty of making the various hands in this game; the American is based on the frequency with which they are likely to occur in a game of Poker.

Poker hand	English	American
Royal flush	30	100
Straight flush	30	75
Four of a kind	16	50
Straight	12	15
Full house	10	25
Three of a kind	6	10
Flush	5	20
Two pair	3	5
One pair	1	2

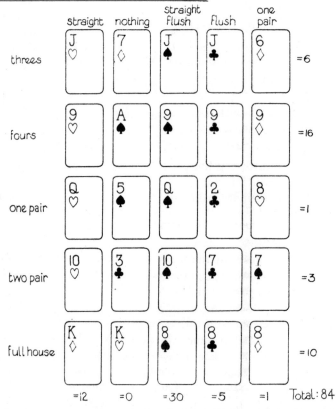

19. POKER SQUARES or Poker Patience if played solitaire. This particular result is worth 84 by the English system of scoring, or 204 by the American.

When played solitaire, consider a 'win' as 70 or more by the English system, 200 by the American. Even more accurately, discover (with hindsight) what was the best possible score that *could* have been made and express your result as a percentage of it. Then keep trying to beat your percentage record.

Quinto ⚇

4 players
1 pack (53)

Invented by Professor Hoffman in about 1900, this delightful partnership game with novel trick-taking features should appeal to anyone looking for something different but not too complicated.

CARDS A 52-card pack plus Joker, 53 in all. Cards rank 23456789TJQKA.

DEAL Deal the top five cards face down to form a blind or *cachette*, which is not to be examined until the end of play, and the remainder around the table one at a time until each player has 12.

OBJECT Twelve tricks are played for a score of 5 points each, and the winners of the last trick also win the *cachette* for another 5. During play, points are also scored for capturing *quints* contained in tricks. The Joker is a quint, known as Quint Royal, and so are the Fives of each suit, and two cards of the same suit with a combined face value of five, i.e., A–4 or 3–2 of the same suit falling to the same trick. The value of a quint is determined entirely by its suit, as follows:

Quint royal = 25
Quint in ♥ = 20   Quint in ♣ = 10
Quint in ♦ = 15   Quint in ♠ = 5

The game is played up to 250 points, taking several deals.

TRUMPS For trick-taking purposes there is no single trump suit but all suits have a relative degree of superiority, the highest being ♥, then ♦, then ♣, with ♠ lowest. A player unable to follow suit to the card led may play from any other suit, and if he plays from a higher suit it beats the card led. Thus all 52 cards have a single order of superiority, ♥A being highest of all and ♠2 lowest. The Joker has no trick-taking power and may be thrown to a trick at any time.

DOUBLING Before play, each in turn has one opportunity to double the value of tricks to 10 points, and an opponent may then redouble to 20. This increases the relative value of tricks to quints, as the latter are not affected by doubling.

PLAY Eldest hand leads. Each subsequent player must follow suit to card led if possible, except that he may play the Joker at any time. If unable to follow, he may play any card. The trick is won by the highest card played to it, and if it contains a quint or quints the appropriate value is immediately credited to the side that wins it. Trick-points are not counted until the end of the hand, but if the capture of a quint brings that side's cumulative total to 250 or more, the game ends without further play and no tricks are counted for that deal at all.

END-GAME The deal normally ends when the last trick has been taken. Whichever side wins it also takes the cachette as if it were a 13th won trick and scores for any quint or quints it may contain. If neither side has yet reached 250, both now count 5 points for each trick they have won, or 10 or 20 if doubled or redoubled. If this still does not give either side 250 the deal passes to the left. In the rare event of a tied game, deal again and stop when the first quint is captured. The side first to win two games wins the rubber for an additional 100 points.

NOTES ON PLAY

The holder of the Joker will seek to drop it as soon as he is certain that his partner is winning, or can win the trick, for which reason the leader to the first trick, if he lacks the Joker, should start with an Ace in case his partner has it. The official rules do not cover the lead of the Joker, which is not desirable but may be forced. It may therefore be agreed that the lead of the Joker does not call for any particular suit and that its trick is won by the highest card played. Since the cachette is valuable, especially in a doubled game, it is desirable to hold back the unbeatable ♥A in order to win the last trick. The management of quints is interesting. If 'trumping' with a higher suit, do so with a Five, unless likely to be overtrumped. Try to throw the Four to a trick won by your partner with the Ace, or the Two or Three if he is winning and either opponent has played the Three or Two.

Rolling Stone ◎

2–6 players
1 short pack (32)

Rolling stone is a simple and unusual game which, if played with computer-like precision, can end in complete deadlock. It is also known as Enflé or Schwellen, names which imply swelling and bursting.

CARDS Two to four players use a 32-card pack, ranking from high to low AKQJT987. If five play, add the Sixes and Fives; if six, add the Fours and Threes.

DEAL Eight each, in batches of 3–2–3.

OBJECT To get rid of all one's cards.

PLAY Eldest leads, others must follow suit. If everyone follows suit the cards are thrown to one side out of play and the player of the highest card leads to the next round. If anybody is unable to follow suit he must pick up all the cards so far played and add them to his hand, leading any card he likes to the next round. As soon as one player plays his last card the game ends, even if the next in turn would have been able to play his last as well.

PAYOFF The winner takes the pool, if any, and in any case collects 1 point or chip from each opponent for each card left in hand.

Russian Bank ⚇

2 players
1 or 2 packs (52 each)

Little known in Britain but widely played elsewhere, Russian Bank – also called Crapette or Robuse – is a sort of competitive Patience for two players. The full game requires two packs, but a one-pack adaptation follows the main description.

CARDS Each player starts with a complete 52-card pack which must be different in back design or colour from his opponent's.

LAYOUT Each player shuffles his opponent's pack, retrieves his own, and deals himself a pile of 13 cards face down and to his right. This forms his stock pile, and he turns the top card face up. Next, he deals four cards face up in a row before him, not overlapping one another. Finally, he places the remaining 35 cards face down in a pile on the left of these cards to form his *hand*. There must be sufficient space on the table between both players' rows of cards to accommodate two more rows parallel to them, though no card yet occupies that space. Each player's four face up cards may be referred to as *houses*, and when other cards are built upon them each pile is a house. If all the cards of a house are cleared out, the space it leaves is an *empty house* and may subsequently be occupied by cards according to the rules of play.

OBJECT To be the first to clear out all the cards from one's hand and stock.

FOUNDATIONS As each of the eight Aces becomes available during play it is placed in the space between the two rows of houses, to form the foundation of a pile of cards which is to be built up in suit and ascending sequence to the King, thus: A23456789TJQK. Although each foundation pile must be of one suit it does not matter if the cards of the two different packs get mixed up.

OPENING PLAY The player with the lower-ranking top card of stock begins (or, if equal, with the lowest-ranking house card). He must, if he can, transfer to the middle of the table any Ace turned up as a house card, or lying on the top of his own stock, and upon this build any Two, Three, etc. of the same suit that may also be visible. Whenever he plays the top card of his stock he turns the one beneath it face up. Having done so or not, as the case may be, he next turns up the top card of his hand and makes any more moves that may then be possible. From here on the following general rules apply.

PLAY At each turn a player may make as many moves as he can and wishes, but must stop when he has no legal continuation or when his opponent stops him for having committed an error in play. Whenever he can transfer an available card to a foundation pile, or his stock card to a house, he must do so immediately. Thereafter, he turns up cards from his hand one by one, pausing to play each to the table if possible and make any subsequent plays before turning up the next. As soon as he turns from his hand a card which is unplayable he lays it face up on the table before him to form a waste pile, and this ends his turn – even if he then notices a possible move on the table that he has neglected to make.

LEGAL MOVES A move consists in transferring an available card from one place to another. An available card is (a) the top card of one's own hand, (b) the top card of one's own stock, (c) the top card of any of the eight houses. It may be moved to (1) a foundation pile, (2) any house, (3) the top of the opponent's stock or waste pile, in accordance with the following rules.

1. *To foundations.* Foundations must be built up in suit and ascending sequence, e.g., ♠A ♠2 ♠3, etc. If an available card can be played to a foundation it must be so played immediately.

2. *To houses.* Houses are built in alternate colour and descending sequence, e.g., black Ten on red Jack, red Nine on black Ten, black Eight on red Nine, etc. Nothing may be built on an Ace, which must immediately be transferred to a foundation. An empty house may be filled with any available card.

3. *To adverse stock or waste.* An available card may be transferred face up to the top of the opponent's stock or waste pile if it is of the same suit and consecutive rank, e.g., upon ♠J may be built either ♠T or ♠Q.

ORDER AND STOPPING Certain moves must be made in a certain order, and if a player contravenes such a rule his opponent may stop him from playing further. The following rules must be observed:

1. If a card can be played to a foundation, it must be played at once.

2. If there is a choice of cards playable to a foundation, priority must always go to cards playable from the stock.

3. If there is an empty house it must be filled from the stock before a card is turned from the hand. Only when the stock is exhausted may an empty house be filled from the hand.

If a player contravenes a rule of play his opponent may say 'Stop', demonstrate the error, and take over the play. A wrongly moved card must be put back and a wrongly turned card in stock or hand turned down again.

ENDING When the last card of a player's hand has been played he turns his waste pile face down to form a new hand. When he has played out all the cards from hand, waste and stock, he wins and the game ends.

SCORE 30 for game, plus 1 point for each card left in opponent's hand and waste piles, and 2 for each card in his stock.

ONE-PACK RUSSIAN BANK

Deal 26 cards each in batches of two and three and place them in a pile (the hand) to the left. The object is to get rid of all one's cards by playing them to the layout or loading them on to one's opponent. There is no foundation building. The first player deals four cards face up to form a row of houses and plays as far as he can, after which his opponent does likewise. Thereafter each in turn turns cards from the hand and plays as far as he can, ceasing only when he turns an unplayable card, which he discards face up to his waste pile. Cards are built on houses or loaded on to the opponent's waste pile in suit and sequence. The sequence may ascend or descend and may turn the corner, e.g., Q–K–A–2, etc. or 3–2–A–K, etc., but, once started, may not change direction. An empty house may be used for shunting or reversing a sequence but must be filled from the hand before a turn ends. A card may not be played from a house to a waste pile nor from a waste pile anywhere. When a player empties his hand he turns the waste pile upside down to replace it. There is no 'stopping' for errors. The first to play out all his cards wins.

Spite and Malice ⚇

2 players
2 packs (108)

A modern competitive Patience, this game is in line of descent from Russian Bank. It may take up to an hour and a half to play, and makes a good after-dinner game, giving one a pleasant feeling of being busy and clever without overtaxing the constitution. Observation, judgement and experience pay off.

CARDS 108, consisting of two packs of different back design or colour. They are kept separate at the outset, but become mixed during the play, and should therefore be of the same card dimensions. One of these packs consists of the normal 52 cards. The other is a 56-card pack incorporating four Jokers. It is slightly disconcerting but does not really matter if two of these Jokers come from the other pack and are therefore distinguishable from the back. Alternatively, since many packs now include three Jokers, it does not really matter if only three are used instead of four.

DEAL Thorough shuffling is essential throughout. The 56-card pack is the common pack, being used by both players. Shuffle it, deal five cards each face down, and place the remainder face down to form a stock. Shuffle the 52-card pack and deal 26 cards face down to each player. Without looking at their faces each places his 26-card 'private' pack face down on the table to his right (or left if left-handed) and then turns the top card face up. Whoever turns the higher-ranking card plays first. If they are equal, shuffle the private packs and turn up the top card again. The five cards dealt form the playing hand and are held accordingly.

OBJECT To be the first to play out all the cards of one's private pack, at which point play ceases and the winner scores 1 point for every card remaining in his opponent's pack.

RANK OF CARDS Cards rank A23456789TJQK. Only ranks count; suits are irrelevant. Jokers are wild, acting as any desired rank upon being played.

GENERAL PROCEDURE Each plays in turn, and a turn may involve the playing of one or several cards. The player in turn must, if an Ace is showing as the topmost card of his private pack, play it face up to the centre of the table. If his topmost card is a Two, and there is an Ace showing on the table, he must play the Two on top of the Ace. Thus an Ace played to the table acts as the base of a pile of cards which is gradually to be built up (regardless of suit) in numerical sequence as far as the King. If a Three or higher card is at the top of the player's pile he is not obliged to build it to a centre pile if he chooses not to: the obligation so to build is restricted to Aces and Twos. There is no restriction on the number of centre piles that may be in progress at any one time: it is always legal to start a new one by playing an Ace.

If the player in turn holds an Ace amongst his five cards he may play it to the table if he wishes, but is not obliged to. Similarly, he may play from the hand a Two to a centre Ace, a Three to a centre Two, and so on for as long as he can and wishes. Whenever the top card of his private pack can be played to the top of a centre pile he may immediately play it there. This is the *only* way in which cards may be played off the private pack.

When the player in turn is unable or unwilling to play to a centre pile (and it usually takes several turns before either player is able to make a start), he may – but is not obliged to – make one discard before ending his turn. This he lays face up on the table before him in accordance with the rules of discarding detailed below. Having discarded, he may not make any other plays. He completes his turn by drawing from the stock as many more cards as he needs to restore his holding to five. If, however, he played all five cards from his hand he continues his turn after replacing them.

The following rules amplify this general procedure.

BUILDING A card properly in sequence may be built to a centre pile from the top of the private pack, from the hand, or from the top of one of the player's own discard piles. An Ace or a Two on the top of the private pack must be played to a centre pile, if possible, and a Two on top of a discard pile *must* be built upon a centre Ace if there is one. Higher ranks are not forced in this way. No card may be played to a King on top of a completed centre pile.

DISCARD PILES Each player may have up to four discard piles in progress at any one time. The single discard optionally made at the end of a turn may be used to start a new discard pile if there are not yet four in progress, or may be added to the top of an existing pile. In this case it must be either of the same rank as the card it is played to, or one rank lower – i.e., upon a Jack may be played another Jack or a Ten, and so on. A Two may be discarded on a Three or a Two, but an Ace may not be discarded at all – it may only be retained or played to the centre. If the top of a discard pile is a Two, and there is an uncovered Ace in the centre, the owner of the pile must cover the Ace (though not necessarily from the discard pile if he can do so from the hand or his private pack). It is not permissible to transfer a card from one discard pile to another, or to play to or from an opponent's pile.

JOKERS The holder of a Joker may use it to represent any rank he wishes when playing it to a centre pile or one of his discard piles. In the latter case he need not state which of the possible ranks he intends it to be until he comes to play another on top of it. (For example, if he has played two successive Jokers upon a Ten he may call them both Tens and add another Ten, or add a Seven and thereby call them a Nine and an Eight, or similarly add a Nine or an Eight to them.) Jokers may be added to discarded Twos without restriction but need not be played as such to centre Aces. Upon transferring a Joker from a discard pile to a centre pile, the player need not use it as the rank it was representing on the discard pile, but may play it without restriction to any centre pile or use it as an Ace to start a new one. It is not permissible to retrieve a Joker in exchange for a natural card of the rank it represents, and Jokers are not to be removed from centre piles.

REPLENISHING THE STOCK Whenever the number of cards remaining in the stock is less than twelve, play is immediately suspended while it is replenished. This is done by taking all centre piles that have been built up to the King, and shuffling them in with the remainder of the stock. It does not matter that cards from the other pack are included with them. It is vital to shuffle the new stock thoroughly before replacing it and continuing the play. If no centre piles have yet been completed, and the stock is eventually exhausted, then all the centre piles as far as they go are gathered up, shuffled together (very thoroughly) and laid down as a new stock.

FREEZING When a player is unable to play anything his hand is said to be *frozen*, and his opponent may then continue playing in a succession of turns until the frozen player announces that he can do something. If both hands are frozen, neither player being able to make a legal move, then all the cards on the table and in the players' hands (other than the private packs) are gathered up, shuffled together and laid aside as a stock, from which five new cards are drawn, and play begins again as if entirely from scratch.

REFUSING The only moves in the game which are compulsory are the play of an Ace from one's private pile to the centre, and the play of a Two from the private pile or a discard pile to a free Ace in the centre. All other moves are optional, neither player being obliged to play from his private pile, or to a centre pile or a discard pile, if he finds it in his interest not to. If, however, both hands are frozen, whether or not voluntarily, the next in turn must, if he can, play an Ace or a Two and his opponent must, if possible, do likewise. This rule does not, however, force the play of a Joker, since the holder may declare it to be something other than an Ace or a Two.

SCORE The game ends as soon as one player plays off the last card of his private pack, and he scores 1 point for every card left unplayed from his opponent's pack. (It is easy to devise more interesting scoring systems.)

NOTES ON PLAY

The most important quality in a player is that of observation, combined with a modicum of counting. Both are required to enable you to spot a sequence of moves that will enable you to play off your top private card. Having done so, face the next card before making any more plays, as the next card may itself be playable. A matter of equal importance is to observe the top card of your opponent's pack, and to avoid playing in such a way as to give him a successful sequence of moves to play it off. The ideal way of doing this is to play on a centre pile to a point above the rank he is trying to play off.

Proper management of discard piles is a matter of importance. The base card of a discard pile should be a higher rather than a lower rank, and it is desirable to build down in sequence without too many duplicates of a rank, though it does not matter if the base card has many duplicates. The more cards there are in a discard pile the more desirable it becomes to avoid duplicating the uppermost rank.

The need for thorough shuffling, when completed centre piles are mixed in with the stock, cannot be overemphasized, as the game can be bitterly spoiled by the continual draw of consecutive ranks from stock.

Zetema

2–6 players
2 packs (65)

Zetema seems to have been introduced in about 1870 as a rival to the then fad game Bézique, which it resembles in spirit, with an added dash of Poker and Patience to please all tastes. It was marketed by J. Hunt & Sons in a package comprising a special pack, booklet of rules and markers. The rules presented below, at least as regards scoring, are those improved by Sid Sackson in his book *A Gamut of Games*. It is a pleasant and sociable game and makes a change from playing for tricks. It works particularly well with three players, while four or six may play in partnerships or not as they please.

CARDS 65, consisting of a standard 52-card pack with the addition of one entire suit from a second pack, which must be indistinguishable from the first in back design and colour.

DEAL Shuffle thoroughly and deal six cards each. Place the remainder face down to form a stock pile.

OBJECT One card at a time is discarded from the hand and drawn from the stock, as at Rummy, and the object is to score for combinations of cards acquired in hand. Discards are arranged in groups of the same rank, called *tricks*, and a second object is to win a trick whenever possible by playing the fifth card to it.

PLAY Each player in turn plays a card face up to the table and draws a replacement from stock. Cards played to the table are arranged in separate groups of the same rank. When a player adds the fifth and last card to such a group he gathers it up and discards it face down to a common waste pile, scoring its value as follows:

Kings or Queens	50
Jacks	20
Aces or Fives	15
Other ranks	5

At his turn to play, and before discarding from the hand, a player may declare and score for holding any one of the following combinations, and must then discard from that combination. The combinations and scores are:

Sequence. Six cards in numerical sequence, not all of the same suit. Ace counts high or low so cards rank A23456789T JQKA. Score 20.

Flush. Six cards of the same suit, but not of the doubled suit, as it is too easy to get. Score 30.

Flush sequence. Six cards of the same suit and in proper sequence. This is valid in the doubled suit. Score 50.

Assembly. Five cards of the same rank. This is difficult to get, and scores vary according to the rank collected, as follows:

Kings or Queens	130
Jacks	120
Aces or Fives	110
Any other rank	100

Marriage. A marriage is the combination of K–Q of the same suit. An imperial marriage is the *second* marriage in the doubled suit. A marriage may be declared in either or both of two ways: first, by holding and showing the two cards in hand, or second, by holding one of them and marrying it off to a partner that has already been discarded and is lying open on the appropriate discard pile. One or more marriages may be declared simultaneously, and it is worth saving them up for this purpose because scores increase as more are declared at a time. The basic score for marriages is as follows: one marriage 10, two 30, three 60, four 100. If one of the marriages is the imperial there is a bonus of 10, and if two of them are in the doubled suit, the bonus is 20. Declaring all five at once scores 150.

Having declared and scored one or more marriages the player takes all the cards concerned and discards them to the common waste pile – which explains why King and Queen tricks are rarely completed on the table. He then draws from stock as many cards as he needs to restore his hand to six, and ends his turn.

END-GAME When the last card of the stock has been drawn, play continues as before except that hands gradually diminish, from six to no cards, and not necessarily at the same rate. Tricks are completed, taken and scored as usual until the table has been cleared of cards and no one has any left.

GAME SCORE As many deals are played as are needed to reach the game score target, which is 300 if two or three play, 200 if four or six play. As soon as the target is reached, play ceases.

Select Bibliography

This is neither a complete list of books consulted nor necessarily a list of recommended works. Rather, it is an acknowledgement to those which have provided unique information used, or reflected, in the foregoing pages. Those marked (*) are British editions of American texts. The date is that of the edition consulted, not necessarily the first or latest.

ALDENHAM (Lord), *The Game of Ombre*, London, 1902.
ANDERSON, DOUGLAS, *All About Cribbage*, Folkestone, 1974.*
ANTON, FRIEDRICH, *Encyclopaedie der Spiele*, Leipzig, 1884.
BERKELEY (pseud.), *Bézique and Cribbage*, London, 1901.
BOHN, HENRY G., *Handbook of Games*, London, 1850.
CAVENDISH (pseud.), *Bézique*, London, 18.
— *Ecarté*, London, 1878.
— *Piquet*, London, 1889.
— *Whist*, London, 1895.
COHEN, BEN, *Solo Whist*, London, 1960.
COTTON, CHARLES, *The Compleat Gamester*, London, 1674, 1972.
CULBERTSON, ELY, *Culbertson on Canasta*, London, 1950.*
CRAWLEY (Captain), *Whist, Loo and Cribbage*, London, 1876.
DAWSON, L. H., *Hoyle's Games, London*, 1953.
FOSTER, R. F., *Foster on Five Hundred*, London, 1909.*
— *Foster's Whist Manual*, London, 1890.*
— *Handbook to the Card Games*, London, undated, prob. 1897.*
FOURNIER (eds.), *Juegos de Naipes Españoles*, Vitoria, 1975.
FOX, G. C. H., *Modern Bidding Systems in Bridge*, London, 1973.
GERVER, FRANS, *Le Guide Marabout de tous les jeux de Cartes*, Verviers, 1966.
GIBSON, WALTER B., *Hoyle's Modern Encyclopedia of Card Games*, London, 1974.*
GRUPP, CLAUS D., *Kartenspiele*, Leinfelden, 1973.
HARBIN, ROBERT, *Waddingtons Family Card Games*, London, 1972.

HERVEY, GEORGE F., *The Hamlyn Illustrated Book of Card Games*, London, 1974.

— *A Handbook of Card Games*, London, 1963.

HOFFMAN (Professor) (pseud.), *Hoyle's Games Modernized*, London, 1906.

HOYLE (pseud.), *Card Games Complete*, Bath, 1824.

KONSTAM, KENNETH, *How to Play Calypso*, London, 1954.

MCLEOD, JOHN, & DUMMETT, MICHAEL, 'Rules of Games' (series), *Journal of the Playing Card Society*, from 1974.

MOREHEAD, ALBERT H. & MOTT-SMITH, GEOFFREY (ed. Phillips), *Culbertson's Card Games Complete*, London, 1954.*

— *Complete Book of Patience*, London, 1973.*

— *Hoyle's Rules of Games*, New York, 1963.

— *Hoyle Up-to-Date*, London, 1952.*

OSTROW, ALBERT A., *The Complete Card Player*, London, 1949.*

PHILLIPS, HUBERT, *Contract Whist*, London, 1935.

— *The Pan Book of Card Games*, London, 1960.

SACKSON, SID, *A Gamut of Games*, London, 1974.*

SCARNE, JOHN, *Scarne on Cards*, London, 1974.*

TAYLOR, ARTHUR, *Pub Games*, St Albans, 1976.

WERGIN, JOSEPH PETRUS, *Wergin on Skat and Sheepshead*, McFarland, Wisconsin, 1975.

Technical Terms

Only those terms are listed which appear generally throughout the book. Terms applying to specific games are explained in the appropriate chapter. In particular, see p. 19 for basic vocabulary, p. 290 for Rummy games, and p. 423 for Patience games.

ANTE A fixed amount staked by the dealer, or by every player, before cards are dealt.

AUCTION Procedure by which players bid for the right to specify certain conditions of the game (such as the trump suit) in return for an undertaking to achieve a higher valued objective than anyone else.

BID Offer to achieve a higher valued objective than anyone else in return for the right to specify certain conditions of play, such as the trump suit.

COMBINATION A set of matching cards for which a score or payment may be due by the rules of the particular game.

CONTRACT An irrevocable undertaking to achieve a certain objective after bidding higher than anyone else and specifying conditions of play.

COURT (CARD) A King, Queen or Jack (originally *coat* card). In American it is called *face-card*.

DECLARE Various meanings according to context, but generally either (a) to announce the conditions of the game or the objective to be achieved, or (b) to show and score for a scoring combination of cards.

DISCARD To reject an unwanted card from the hand. Often used in the sense of RENOUNCE (see below).

ELDEST The player sitting immediately next the dealer (on his left if the game is played clockwise round the table, his right otherwise), who normally has the privilege of bidding or playing first. In two-player games the non-dealer is elder.

EXCHANGE To discard unwanted cards and replace them with fresh ones. In some games the discard is made before replacements are seen; in others, replacements are taken first and may form part of the discard.

FLUSH Cards of the same suit.

FOLLOW (SUIT) Whoever plays first (e.g., to a trick) is said to lead, the others to follow. To play a card of the same suit as the leader is to follow suit.

FOREHAND Same as ELDEST.

GAME Several related meanings. (a) Complete period of play at the end of which all scores are settled – may be anything from one deal to a whole session. (b) The target score which, when reached by at least one player, terminates the period of play and settlement, e.g., a game may be described as '500 up' – i.e., played up to a score of 500. (c) The stated objective and conditions of play for one particular deal – e.g. 'game in diamonds' means diamonds are trumps. (d) In Bridge, the number of points still needed to win a game by a side that may already have a part-score. (e) In contradiction of (a), above, several 'games' may constitute a larger self-contained period of play – see RUBBER below.

GUARD(ED) In trick-play a card in the hand is guarded by at least as many lower cards (guards) as there are cards above it lacking from the hand, e.g., if one's highest spade is the Queen it must be guarded by two lower cards to throw to leads of ♠A and ♠K in order to promote the Queen to top position.

HAND (a) The cards held in a player's hand. (b) A player (as in 'eldest hand'). (c) Period of play between the point at which all cards have been dealt and the point at which all have been played, none remaining in the hand.

HEAD In tricks, to play a higher-ranking card of the suit led than any that have so far been played to the trick. In some games it is obligatory to head the trick if possible.

HONOURS Certain cards for which the rules of the game may prescribe a score or payment to their holder.

LEAD To play the first card of a deal or to a trick.

LONG Describes the holding of more than the average number of cards of a given suit, 'average' being the total number of that suit divided by the number of players.

MELD A winning or scoring set of cards that match one another by rank and/or suit (see p. 289). To show or declare such a set.

MISÈRE An undertaking to lose every trick.

NUMERALS Cards other than court cards. (There is no general English term, but the American is *spot cards*.)

OPPONENT Sometimes has also the specialized meaning of one who is playing against a solo player or declarer. Thus the opponents of the soloist are not necessarily opponents of one another.

OUVERT A game played *ouvert* is one in which the principal player's hand of cards is exposed to the view of his opponents.

OVERCALL To make a higher bid than the preceding bidder.

OVERTRICK A trick in excess of the number required to win.

PASS To refrain from bidding.

PIP (–VALUE) Literally, a pip is a suit symbol printed on a card. The pip-value of a card is its value when captured, for example in a trick. The term avoids confusion with 'points' in the scoring sense.

PLAIN SUIT One that is not trumps.

RENEGE Sometimes used in the senses of ruff or revoke or renounce, but perhaps best used in the sense of failing to follow suit in games or circumstances in which there is no legal requirement to do so.

RENOUNCE Loosely, to fail to follow suit; strictly, to play a card other than a trump when unable to follow suit.

REVOKE To fail to follow suit, even though able and required to do so, for which a penalty may be exacted.

ROUND Circumstance in which everybody around the table has had one, or an equal number, of opportunities to bid, play, receive cards etc. Also, for example, 'third round of trumps' means 'third occasion on which a trump has been led to a trick'.

RUBBER Equivalent to a match or tournament, the winner of a rubber being the first to win a certain number of games.

RUFF A trump. To play a trump to a non-trump lead.

SEQUENCE A set of cards in numerical or ranking sequence, such as A–2–3 or T–J–Q–K–A. In some games a sequence only counts if the constituent cards are also of the same suit.

SINGLETON The holding of only one card in a given suit.

SOLO(IST) A solo game is one in which one player (not usually called the soloist, though it seems the best word) undertakes to achieve his stated objective, without a partner, by playing against the combined efforts of everyone else to beat him.

STOCK The undealt portion of the pack if not all cards are dealt.

VOID The holding of no cards in a given suit.

WIDOW A hand of cards dealt face down to the table (also called the *blind, skat, talon* or *kitty*), usually for the benefit of the highest bidder, who may exchange cards with them.

WILD CARD One that may represent any card its holder wishes.

Index of Games

Games in *italics* are mentioned only in passing